Study Guide
Fourth Edition

Macroeconomics

A Contemporary Introduction

William A. McEachern
Professor of Economics
University of Connecticut

Prepared by
John E. Lunn
Department of Economics
Hope College
Holland, Michigan

SOUTH-WESTERN College Publishing
An International Thomson Publishing Company

Publishing Team Director: Jack C. Calhoun
Acquisitions Editors: Jack C. Calhoun/John Alessi
Developmental Editor: Kurt Gerdenich
Coordinating Editor: Megan Johnson
Production House: Justified Left—A Publishing Alliance
Cover Design: Joseph M. Devine
Cover Illustrator: Copyright © Alan Cober/SIS
Team Assistants: Cory Broadfoot/Kristen Meere

HB83DD1

ISBN: 0-538-85522-3
3 4 5 6 7 GP 2 1 0 9 8 7 6
Printed in the United States of America

I(T)P
International Thomson Publishing
South-Western College Publishing is an ITP Company. The ITP trademark is used under license.

PREFACE

The purpose of this *Study Guide* is to provide a review of the materials in the textbook, exercises for you to practice using the analytical tools presented in the text, and an opportunity for you to check your understanding of the material. Each chapter in the *Study Guide* contains an introduction; an outline of the text chapter; a discussion of the chapter's topics; some extensions or examples of materials in the text in a section entitled "Lagniappe" (which is a French term used in Louisiana—it means "a little extra," something added for good measure); a list of key terms; review questions; and answers to all the questions.

You should always read the text before using the *Study Guide*. The discussion section presented in the *Study Guide* is not a substitute for the textbook. In fact, you will be unable to answer some of the questions in the *Study Guide* if you have not read the text. Work through the questions and answers carefully, making sure that you understand why the correct answers are correct. Note, too, that the answers to the discussion questions are suggestive rather than full and complete.

Thanks to my wife Sheryl and my children—Robert, David, and Shelley—for putting up with my grumbling when I had trouble coming up with just one more multiple-choice question.

John E. Lunn

CONTENTS

CHAPTER 1

The Art and Science of Economic Analysis

I. INTRODUCTION

This chapter presents an overview of economics and tells how economic analysis is performed. In particular, it introduces the concept of the economic problem and an important type of economic analysis: marginal analysis. There is also an appendix that discusses how graphs are used. Other tools of economic analysis are presented in the next chapter.

II. OUTLINE

1. The Economic Problem. Because resources are scarce and human wants are unlimited, people cannot have everything they want. Economics is the study of how individuals choose to use their scarce resources in an attempt to satisfy their unlimited wants.

1.1 Resources
- a. Land (includes all natural resources). Payments to land are called *rent*.
- b. Labor (physical and mental effort). Payments to labor are called *wages*.
- c. Capital. Payments to capital are called *interest*.
  - (1) Physical capital (manufactured items used in the production of goods)
  - (2) Human capital (knowledge and skills people acquire to enhance their ability to produce)
- d. Entrepreneurial ability (the talent of a person who tries to discover and exploit profitable activities). Payments for entrepreneurial ability are called *profit*.

1.2 Goods and Services
- a. Goods and services are produced to satisfy human wants.
- b. Goods are tangible; services are intangible.
- c. Both goods and services require scarce resources and are therefore themselves scarce.
- d. Without scarcity there would be no economic problem.

1.3 Economic Actors
- a. There are four types of actors in the economy: households, firms, governments, and the rest of the world.
- b. Markets are the means by which buyers and sellers carry out exchanges.

1.4 Microeconomics and Macroeconomics
- a. Microeconomics is the study of how individual economic agents make decisions and how the choices of various decision makers are coordinated.
- b. Macroeconomics is the study of the economy as a whole.

2. The Art of Economic Analysis

2.1 Rational Self-Interest

a. Economists assume that individuals act in their own best interests.

b. Economists also assume that individuals are rational, which means that people try to make the best choices possible under the circumstances.

2.2 Economic Analysis Is Marginal Analysis

a. Marginal means "incremental" or "decremental."

b. An individual changes his or her behavior whenever the expected marginal benefit from doing so is greater than the expected marginal cost.

2.3 *CASE STUDY:* Marginal Analysis in the Computer Industry

2.4 Choice Requires Time and Information

3. The Science of Economic Analysis

3.1 The Role of Theory

a. A theory, or model, is a simplification of reality that focuses on only the most important features of a relationship.

b. Theory is needed to determine which facts are relevant to an analysis of a relationship.

c. Theory is also used to make predictions about the real world.

3.2 The Scientific Method

a. Step One: Identify and define the relevant variables. (A variable is a quantity that can take on different possible values.)

b. Step Two: State the assumptions that specify the conditions under which the theory is to apply.

(1) *Ceteris paribus*: other things are held constant

(2) Behavioral assumption: a notion concerning individual behavior that is taken to be true; for example, rational self-interest

c. Step Three: Formulate hypotheses about relations among the key variables.

d. Step Four: Test the theory.

3.3 Economists Tell Stories

3.4 *CASE STUDY:* A Yen for Vending Machines

3.5 Predicting Average Behavior

a. Economic theories do not permit an economist to predict the behavior of individuals because any individual may behave in unpredictable ways.

b. The random behaviors of individuals tend to cancel each other, so the average behavior of a large group can be predicted.

3.6 Normative Versus Positive Analysis

a. A positive statement is one that can be verified by referring to the facts.

b. A normative statement is a statement representing someone's opinion or values; it cannot be proved or disproved.

3.7 Some Pitfalls of Faulty Economic Analysis

a. Fallacy That Association Is Causation. It is a mistake in analysis to think that one event caused another simply because the first event preceded the second.

b. Fallacy of Composition. It is erroneous to believe that what is true for the individual is true for the group.

c. Mistake of Ignoring the Secondary Effects. Economic analysis should not ignore secondary effects, which develop slowly over time as people react to events.

3.8 If Economists Are So Smart, Why Aren't They Rich? The economics profession thrives because its models usually do a better job of explaining the real world than do alternative approaches.

4. Appendix: Understanding Graphs. Graphs are a way of compressing information.

4.1 Drawing Graphs. Graphs can express three types of relations between two variables:

a. Positive (direct) relation: as one variable increases, the other variable increases.

b. Negative (inverse) relation: as one variable increases, the other variable decreases.

c. Independent relation: as one variable increases, the other remains constant; the variables are unrelated.

4.2 The Slopes of Straight Lines. Slope is the change in the vertical distance between two points divided by the corresponding change in the horizontal distance between the points.

4.3 The Slope Depends on How Units Are Measured

a. The mathematical value of the slope depends on the units of measurement on the graph; e.g., the slope of a line relating price and output will be different if output is measured in feet than if it is measured in yards.

b. The slope measures the marginal effects, so it is important in economic analysis.

4.4 The Slopes of Curved Lines

a. Slope of a curved line varies at every point.

b. Slope of a curved line at a point is found by measuring the slope of a straight line tangent to the curve at the point.

4.5 Curve Shifts. A curve can shift when a variable not measured on the horizontal or vertical axis changes.

4.6 Of Mice and Fleas: The 45-Degree Ray from the Origin. Every point on the 45-degree line is of equal distance from both axes.

III. DISCUSSION

The Economic Problem

Two facts of life create the economic problem: scarce resources and unlimited human wants. Resources are combined to produce *goods* and *services*. Since resources are scarce, not all goods and services that people desire can be produced; that is, goods and services are also scarce. Consequently, individuals must make choices. Even though we cannot have everything we want, we can have some of the things we want.

Households, firms, governments, and the rest of the world are the four economic actors in the economy. Households act both as consumers who demand the goods and services produced and as resource owners who supply resources to firms and government. Everybody owns at least one productive resource: his or her own labor. Firms supply goods and services to consumers by hiring resources to produce them. The government provides some goods and services, such as national defense, that tend not to be produced by private firms. The government also makes and enforces rules to be followed by other economic actors. The rest of the world includes foreign households, firms, and governments.

Buyers and sellers come together to carry out exchange in *markets*. Some markets—farmers' markets, for example—are physical places with specific geographic locations. Other markets are less concrete and consist of communications by individuals thousands of miles apart. For example, people can order books from a book club through the mail.

Economics is broken down into two parts: *microeconomics* and *macroeconomics*. Microeconomics concerns the economic behavior of individual decision makers, such as the consumer, the worker, and the manager of a firm. Macroeconomics examines the economic system as a whole and tries to explain unemployment, inflation, and economic growth.

The Art of Economic Analysis

Economists assume that people are motivated by self-interest. This means that they not only act selfishly, but that they also make choices that will make them better off, as they themselves define "better off." Religious or political zealots who risk their lives for a cause presumably do so because they believe they will be better off for doing so. Self-interest, by itself, does not allow us to make predictions or to explain human behavior adequately. However, when the assumption of rationality is added, we can begin to analyze and explain human behavior. By "rational" we mean consistent and reasonable. If we assume that people behave consistently, then we can predict how they will change their behavior when they face different economic environments.

It is very rare for people to have to make all-or-nothing decisions. Instead, decisions usually involve choices between the status quo and something else. One chooses among having apple pie for dessert, cake for dessert, or no dessert at all. A decision is made on the basis of a comparison of the extra (*marginal*) benefits and the extra (marginal) costs of the contemplated change. When marginal benefits exceed marginal costs, the individual makes the change.

Rational choice takes time and information. A choice can be a poor one if a decision maker lacks good information. The collection and assimilation of information take time and use up resources. Rational individuals collect information from a variety of sources as long as the expected marginal benefit of doing so exceeds the expected marginal cost.

The Science of Economic Analysis

An economy as large, diverse, and interrelated as the U.S. economy is too complex for any individual to understand. There is so much economic data that people cannot understand the reason for every transaction. A *theory* is used to reduce the complexity of an economic system to manageable limits. Consequently, a theory does not contain all relevant details and facts. A theory attempts to simplify economic reality by capturing the essential features of economic relations.

Economic analysis follows the scientific method, which can be broken down into four steps. First, the relevant *variables* must be identified and defined. Second, the assumptions that specify the conditions under which the theory applies must be identified. In economics, it is common to employ the assumption of *ceteris paribus*, which means "other things held constant." For example, when we say that a higher price for a good causes fewer units of the good to be sold, we hold income and tastes, among other things, constant. Third, hypotheses about the relations among variables are stated. These generally take the form of if-then statements. Fourth, the hypotheses are tested.

Economists distinguish between positive economic statements and normative economic statements. *Positive economic statements* are associated with economic theory and involve facts or predictions that are testable. *Normative economic statements* involve value judgments and opinions. The statement "Tariffs on imported steel will increase employment in the U.S. steel industry" is an example of a positive statement. "Higher tariffs should be placed on imported steel" is an example of a normative statement.

Some Pitfalls of Economic Thinking

It is easy to fall into several traps that lead to incorrect economic thinking. The *association-causation fallacy* is common. It is especially easy to fall into this trap when one event precedes another in time. It can even be the case that the second event caused the first event. For example, if one observed that many people at the race track were betting on a particular horse and then observed that that particular horse won the race, it would be erroneous to conclude that the horse won because many people bet on it. Rather, people expected the horse to win so they bet on the horse. Another common error is the *fallacy of composition*, which is the mistaken belief that what is true for the individual is also true for the group. One person can see a football game better by standing up, but if everyone stands nobody has a better view. Mistakes are also made when people ignore the *secondary effects* of an economic activity or policy.

Appendix: Understanding Graphs

If this is your first course in economics, read the appendix to this chapter in the textbook carefully. Economists often use *graphs* to represent relations. Graphs generally reflect a relation between two variables, such as price and quantity, money supply and interest rates, or wages and hours worked. An *independent variable* is one that has a causal effect on another variable. The other variable is called the *dependent variable* because its value depends on the value of the first variable.

A question that is often of interest in economics is whether one variable has a *positive*, or *direct*, effect on another variable or an *inverse*, or *negative*, effect. Exhibit 1 shows a line that represents a consumption function. The independent variable is income and the dependent variable is consumption expenditures. The graph represents the assumption that as a family's income increases, its consumption spending also increases. Hence, there is a direct, or positive, relation between a family's income and the amount the family spends.

Exhibit 1

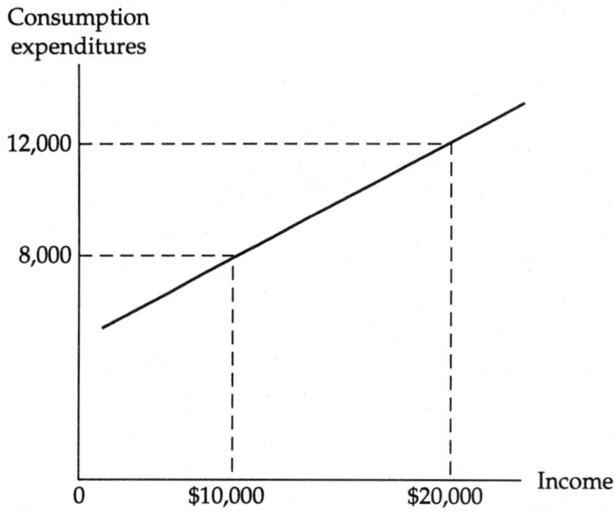

A negative, or inverse, relation is illustrated in Exhibit 2. Here the independent variable is hours of practice and the dependent variable is one's golf score. The more one practices, the lower the golf score will be.

Exhibit 2

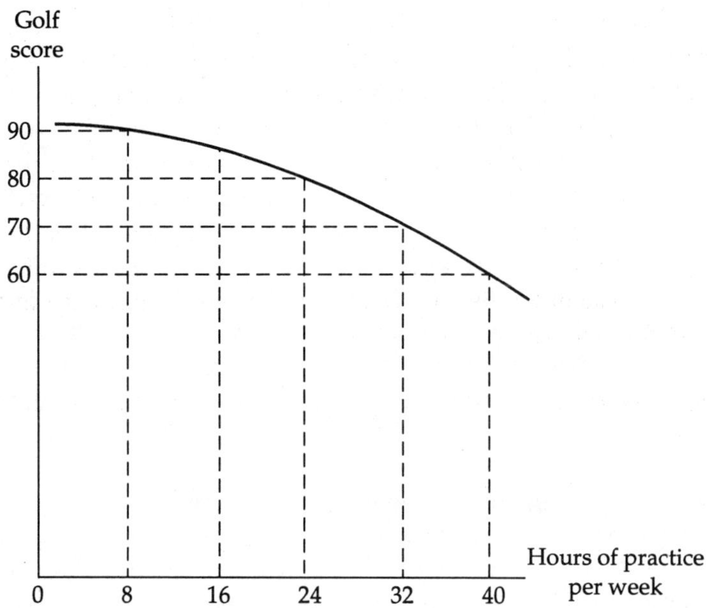

The *slope* of a line is the amount the vertical variable changes for a given increase in the horizontal variable. The slope of an upward-sloping line is positive; the slope of a downward-sloping line is negative. The slope of a straight line is constant, but the slope of a curved line changes at every point. To find the slope of a curved line at a point, draw a straight line *tangent* to the point. The slope of this line is the slope of the curved line at that point. Make sure that you understand the graphs that are used in the appendix in the textbook.

IV. LAGNIAPPE

The Consumption Function

The theory of the consumption function can be used to illustrate the scientific method as it is applied in economics. John Maynard Keynes developed the theory of the consumption function during the Great Depression. He identified two key variables—consumption spending and income—and hypothesized that people spend some percentage of any increase in income on goods and save the rest. Hence, consumption is a function of income. After World War II, many economists forecast a recession on the basis of the consumption function theory. They argued that incomes would fall after the war; this would lead to reduced consumption spending, which would reduce the incomes of even more people. However, the recession did not materialize. This caused some economists to reexamine the consumption function. Milton Friedman altered the theory by pointing out that people do not respond to temporary fluctuations in their incomes by altering consumption spending greatly. Instead, they make consumption spending decisions on the basis of their expected long-term average, or permanent, income. Once the theory was modified to include longer-term considerations, it was used more successfully in making predictions.

Question to Think About: Does the percentage of income spent on consumption goods vary with age?

Heroic Self-Interest

As stated before, the assumption of self-interest does not imply that people always behave in a selfish manner. Each person defines his or her own self-interest in a different way. Most of us probably would not consider actions that are likely to lead to our death as being in our self-interest. Yet it is possible for people to believe that. The ancient Greeks wrote of heroes who valued fame more than life and who were willing to die to gain this fame. In the story of the Trojan War, the gods had foretold that the first Greek who landed on Trojan soil would die. A young man named Protesilaos jumped ashore first so that his name would go down in history. The greatest Greek hero, Achilles, faced the option of going to Troy, where he would gain great fame and die, or staying at home, where he would live a long life and remain unknown. He chose to go to Troy. Evidently, he perceived it to be in his self-interest to gain fame rather than to die an unknown.

Question to Think About: Do you think all ancient Greeks would have made the same decision that Achilles made?

V. KEY TERMS

Scarce resources
Economics
Land
Labor
Capital
Human capital
Entrepreneurial ability
Rent
Wages
Interest
Profit
Good
Service
Scarce
Market
Product market
Resource market
Microeconomics
Macroeconomics
Rational self-interest
Marginal
Economic theory, or economic model
Variable
Other-things-constant assumption
Behavioral assumption
Hypothesis
Positive economic statement
Normative economic statement
Association-causation fallacy
Fallacy of composition
Secondary effects
Origin
Horizontal axis
Vertical axis
Graph
Time-series graph
Functional relation
Dependent variable
Independent variable
Positive, or direct, relation
Negative, or inverse, relation
Slope
Tangent
Intercept
Ray

VI. QUESTIONS

A. Completion

1. __________________ is the study of how individuals use their __________________ resources to satisfy their __________________ wants.

2. The ultimate raw material associated with labor is __________________.

3. There are two kinds of capital, __________________ capital and __________________ capital.

4. __________________ includes management and organizational skills, combined with a willingness to take risks.

5. The entrepreneur is the __________________ claimant.

6. An automobile is a __________________; an airplane ride is a __________________.

7. Exchange is carried out in __________________.

8. A key behavioral assumption concerning human economic behavior is that of __________________.

9. Economic choice usually involves a comparison of ________________ benefits and costs.

10. A ________________ is a simplification of economic reality that tries to capture the most important elements of the relation under consideration.

11. A ________________ is a quantity that can take on different possible values.

12. ________________ are conditional statements of the if-then variety.

13. A ________________ economic statement represents an opinion.

14. Unintended consequences that develop slowly over time as people respond to circumstances are called ________________ effects.

15. The relation between income and consumption is ________________ because increases in income lead to increases in consumption.

B. *True/False*

______ 1. The economic problem results from the fact that resources are scarce but human wants tend to be limitless.

______ 2. A student's knowledge of computer programming is an example of human capital.

______ 3. Profit goes to the owners of capital.

______ 4. All goods are scarce but not all services are scarce.

______ 5. Product markets refer to specific geographic locations.

______ 6. Microeconomics is the study of the economy as a whole.

______ 7. People who give to charity cannot be motivated by rational self-interest.

______ 8. A decision to go to one college instead of another is an example of a marginal decision.

______ 9. Time is a scarce resource.

______ 10. Rational self-interest directs people to make any choice for which the total benefits exceed the total costs.

______ 11. Good theories contain as many details as possible.

______ 12. Assumptions are used to simplify theories by eliminating areas that are not expected to have important effects on the analysis.

______ 13. A theory is not good if it cannot predict accurately all the time.

______ 14. A positive statement is one that can be verified by reference to facts.

______ 15. If one event follows another, then the first event necessarily caused the second event.

______ 16. Policymakers generally pay close attention to both the primary and the secondary effects of policies.

______ *17. Two variables are independent if increases in one leave the second unchanged.

______ *18. The slope of a vertical line is zero.

C. *Multiple Choice*

1. Which of the following is an example of a scarce resource?
   a. coal
   b. water
   c. unskilled labor
   d. time
   e. all of the above

2. Crude oil is considered which kind of resource?
   a. land
   b. labor
   c. physical capital
   d. human capital
   e. none of the above

3. Since goods are scarce,
   a. we always have to pay money for the goods we get.
   b. we never can get what we want.
   c. everybody wants some of each good that exists.
   d. we must choose among them.
   e. a and d

4. Services differ from goods in that services
   a. do not always use scarce resources.
   b. do not always satisfy wants.
   c. often do not have a price.
   d. are intangible.
   e. are provided by the government.

5. Markets include
   a. shopping malls.
   b. arrangements by which buyers and sellers communicate their intentions.
   c. union hiring halls.
   d. all of the above
   e. a and b only

---

*Throughout this study guide, asterisks next to question numbers indiate that the material is discussed in an appendix.

6. Which of the following decisions is not consistent with rational self-interest?
   a. giving money to charity
   b. choosing to work for the Peace Corps instead of for a large corporation
   c. buying a car without knowing everything about it
   d. becoming a bullfighter
   e. All are consistent with rational self-interest.

7. Economic choices are made by comparing
   a. total benefits and total costs.
   b. marginal benefits and marginal costs.
   c. average benefits and average costs.
   d. the behavior of rational people with that of irrational people.
   e. any of the above except d.

8. People are rational if they
   a. have perfect information about the future.
   b. know and understand philosophy.
   c. are selfish.
   d. make the best choices they can given their circumstances.
   e. none of the above

9. If consumers must collect information to make rational decisions, then they should collect additional information as long as
   a. it helps them make good decisions.
   b. they learn something from the additional information.
   c. the marginal cost of the information is less than the expected marginal benefit from the information.
   d. there is anything they do not know about the good.
   e. all of the above

10. A good theory is one that
    a. best replicates reality.
    b. uses the fewest assumptions.
    c. predicts more accurately than other theories.
    d. cannot be proven wrong.
    e. all of the above

11. The validity of a theory is determined by
    a. testing the reasonableness of its assumptions.
    b. testing its predictions with evidence.
    c. making sure its variables are well defined.
    d. none of the above.
    e. all of the above.

12. *Ceteris paribus* means
    a. economic man.
    b. other things constant.
    c. the fallacy of composition.
    d. secondary effects.
    e. positive economics.

13. A positive statement is one that
    a. can be supported or rejected with reference to the facts.
    b. states how things ought to be.
    c. is true.
    d. cannot be refuted.
    e. all economists agree on.

14. Which of the following is an example of a normative statement?
    a. The rate of inflation is lower today than it was ten years ago.
    b. High interest rates cause lower economic growth.
    c. Since price controls cause shortages, the government should not use price controls to combat inflation.
    d. Per capita income is higher in the Soviet Union than in the United States.
    e. Tariffs result in higher prices to consumers.

15. Suppose that some individual decision makers in Los Angeles decide that removing the pollution control equipment on their cars will not have a noticeable effect on pollution in the area. Several months later pollution levels are higher than ever. The decision makers have fallen into
    a. ignoring the secondary effects.
    b. the fallacy that association is causation.
    c. the fallacy of composition.
    d. irrational self-interest.
    e. none of the above.

16. It has been found that minimum wage laws increase unemployment among teenagers. This is an example of
    a. ignoring the secondary effects.
    b. the fallacy that association is causation.
    c. the fallacy of composition.
    d. irrational self-interest.
    e. none of the above.

Exhibit 3

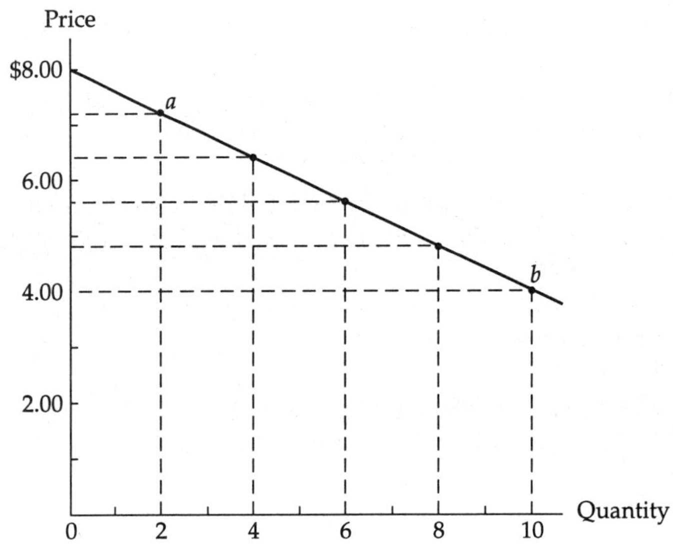

*17. In Exhibit 3, the relationship between price and quantity depicted by line *ab* is
  a. positive, with slope 0.4.
  b. positive, with slope –0.4.
  c. inverse, with slope –2.5.
  d. inverse, with slope –0.4.
  e. positive, with slope 2.5.

*18. The value of a dependent variable is determined by
  a. the value of the independent variable.
  b. the values of other dependent variables.
  c. the assumptions of the model.
  d. the reliability of the theory.
  e. b and d.

*19. A straight line is tangent to a curve at point *A*. If the slope of the straight line is +3, the slope of the curve at *A*
  a. is between 0 and +3.
  b. is equal to +3.
  c. is equal to –3.
  d. is more than +3.
  e. The slope cannot be determined without more information.

*20. If consumption is on the vertical axis and income is on the horizontal axis, a 45-degree line represents
  a. the expected relation between income and consumption.
  b. the marginal benefit from another dollar of income.
  c. the marginal cost of another dollar of income.
  d. the best combination of income and consumption for a rational consumer.
  e. the combination of points where consumption equals income.

D. *Discussion Questions*

1. Explain how scarcity and choice are related.

2. How are human capital and entrepreneurial ability different from labor?

3. The text says that a study of economic aggregates must begin with an understanding of individual choice. Why is this so?

4. Explain the concept of rational decision making. Can decisions a student makes about what to take to college be said to involve rational decision making? Explain.

5. "People don't really act rationally. If they did, there would never be any mistakes." Evaluate this statement.

6. The number of people volunteering to serve in the Peace Corps increased greatly during the late 1960s. Can you offer an explanation for this?

7. Sales of automobiles increased in December 1986 and fell in January 1987. The deductibility of sales taxes ended on December 31, 1986. Did the change in the tax laws affect sales of autos in December and January? Explain.

8. The text says that a company's decision to build a plant in Taiwan can be an example of a marginal decision. Explain how such a large investment can be described as marginal.

9. People usually spend more time deciding which car to buy than they do choosing a brand of toothpaste. Can you offer an explanation for this observation?

10. Economic theory says that a rise in the price of a good will cause people to buy less of it. If the price of meat increases and John Doe buys more meat, has the theory been refuted? Explain.

11. How are economic theory and positive statements related?

12. Discuss the four steps of the scientific method.

13. How do predictions and forecasts differ?

14. If association is not the same as causation, then how can we determine when one variable affects another?

*15. Use the following information to answer the question below:

x	=	0	2	4	6	8	10	12	14	16	18	20
y	=	0	1	2	3	4	5	6	7	8	9	10

Exhibit 4

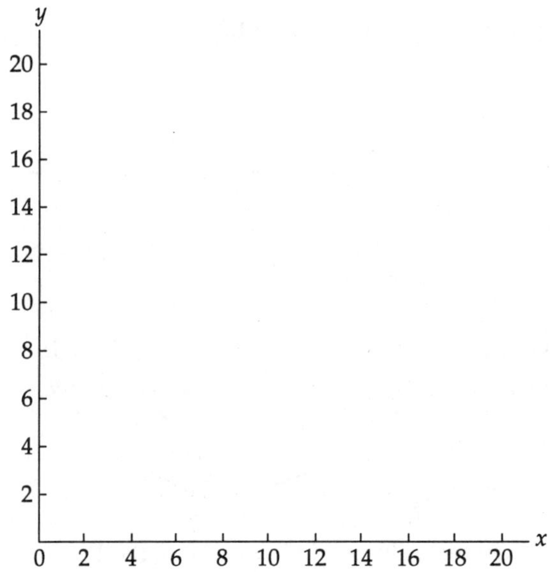

a. Graph the relation between x and y on Exhibit 4.
b. Is this a positive or a negative relation? How do you know?
c. What is the slope of the line?

*16. You are given the following information regarding the price of eggs and the quantity purchased.

Price:	$1.00	0.90	0.80	0.70	0.60	0.50	0.40
Quantity (dozens):	1	2	3	4	5	6	7

Exhibit 5

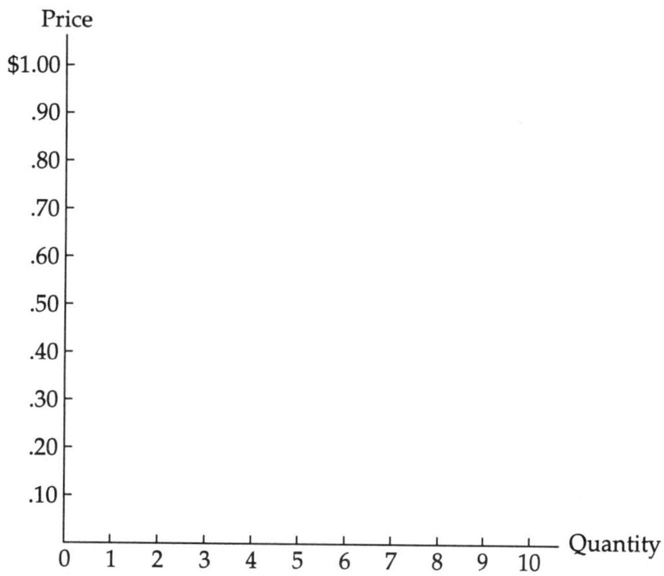

a. Graph the relation between price and quantity purchased on Exhibit 5.
b. What is the slope of the line?

*17. In Exhibit 6, what is the slope of the curve at point *a*? point *b*? point *c*? point *d*?

Exhibit 6

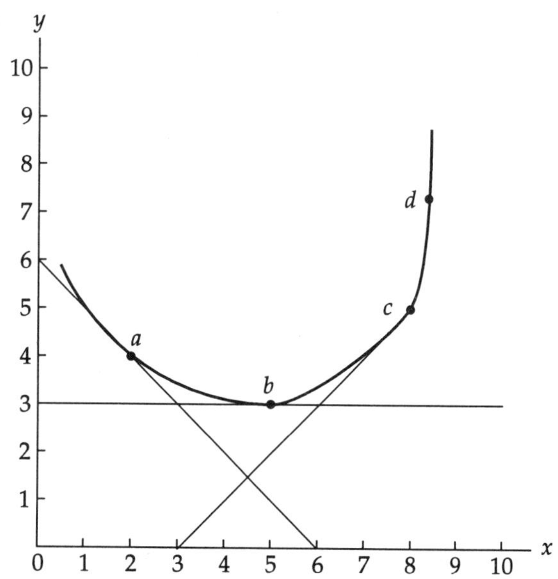

*18. a. Draw a curve whose slope increases with distance from the origin.
b. Draw a curve illustrating a direct relation whose slope decreases as the distance from the origin increases.
c. Draw a curve illustrating an inverse relation whose slope increases as the distance from the origin increases.
d. Draw a curve illustrating an inverse relation whose slope decreases as the distance from the origin increases.

VII. ANSWERS

A. *Completion*

1. Economics; scarce; unlimited
2. time
3. human; physical
4. Entrepreneurial ability
5. residual
6. good; service
7. markets
8. rational self-interest
9. marginal
10. theory (model)
11. variable
12. Predictions
13. normative
14. secondary
15. direct (positive)

B. *True/False*

1. True
2. True
3. False
4. False
5. False
6. False
7. False
8. True
9. True
10. False. Decisions are based on marginal benefits and marginal costs.
11. False
12. True
13. False. A theory is good not because it predicts accurately all the time but because it predicts better than other theories.
14. True
15. False
16. False
17. True
18. False

C. *Multiple Choice*

1. e
2. a
3. d
4. d
5. d
6. e
7. b
8. d
9. c
10. c
11. b
12. b
13. a
14. c
15. c
16. a
17. d
18. a
19. b
20. e

D. *Discussion Questions*

1. Scarcity implies that we cannot have everything that we want. Our resources are limited, so we must choose which of the many possible goods and services we will have. This applies to society as well as to any individual.

2. Human capital differs from labor in that human capital involves knowledge that people acquire to increase their *ability* to produce, whereas labor refers to the human time spent in production. Entrepreneurial ability is the special talent of bringing other resources together to produce goods in new and more profitable ways.

3. All choices are made by individuals. Consequently, to understand how the choices of many individuals affect the economy, it helps to know how the individual choices were made and how they interact to determine the aggregate performance.

4. Rational decision making involves comparing the status quo with the marginal benefits and marginal costs of alternative situations. The rational individual chooses so as to make himself or herself as well off as possible, given the constraints the individual faces. A college student cannot take everything to the dorm, so the student must choose which items to take. The things that are most likely to be used at college will go; those that are less likely to be used will not go. The larger the dorm room and the larger the vehicle taking the things, the more the student will take to college.

5. People do not know all possible effects of every decision. Therefore, people sometimes make mistakes. If individuals had better information, they would choose differently.

6. One explanation is that the military was drafting eligible young men in the late 1960s to fight in the Vietnam War. The Peace Corps was an alternative to the military, so many chose to join the Peace Corps.

7. Yes. People who were considering the purchase of a new car were spurred to act before the end of December to avoid the tax penalty. On the margin, it was more attractive to buy a new car in December 1986 than in January 1987.

8. A new plant increases the productive capacity of a firm. If the firm wants to increase capacity, it must either build a new plant or expand an existing plant. The decision is a marginal decision since it involves a change from the status quo rather than an all-or-nothing decision.

9. People make decisions on the basis of expected marginal benefits and expected marginal costs. Since the marginal costs of buying a new car are greater than those of buying a new tube of toothpaste, we expect people to inquire more about the expected benefits of the automobile.

10. No. Theory applies to people on average, not to specific individuals. There are many possible factors that could explain John Doe's behavior—he may have just quit being a vegetarian, he may have inherited a lot of money, or he may be getting ready to have a big dinner party.

11. The predictions of economic theory are positive statements, since they are capable of being tested and either upheld or refuted. Theory does not involve opinion or value judgments.

12. The first step is to identify and define the key economic variables. The second step is to state the assumptions, including behavioral assumptions, that specify the conditions under which the theory is to apply. Basically, this involves identifying the variables or conditions that would cause the theory not to predict as well as expected. The third step is to develop testable hypotheses about the relations among the variables. The last step is to test the theory.

13. Predictions are based on the implications of a theory and generally take the form of if-then statements. There is no expectation that the prediction will occur if the conditions are not met. A forecast is an educated guess that a certain event will actually occur.

14. One of the roles of theory is to identify likely causal relations. However, there will be occasions when we cannot ascertain causality.

15. a.

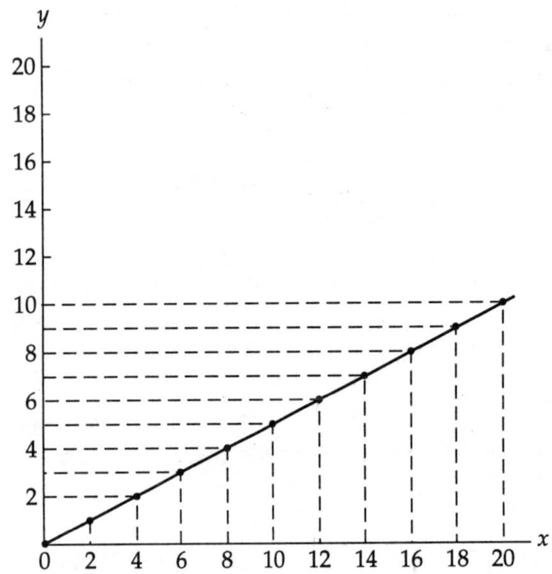

b. The relation is positive because when x goes up, y goes up.
c. 0.5

16. a.

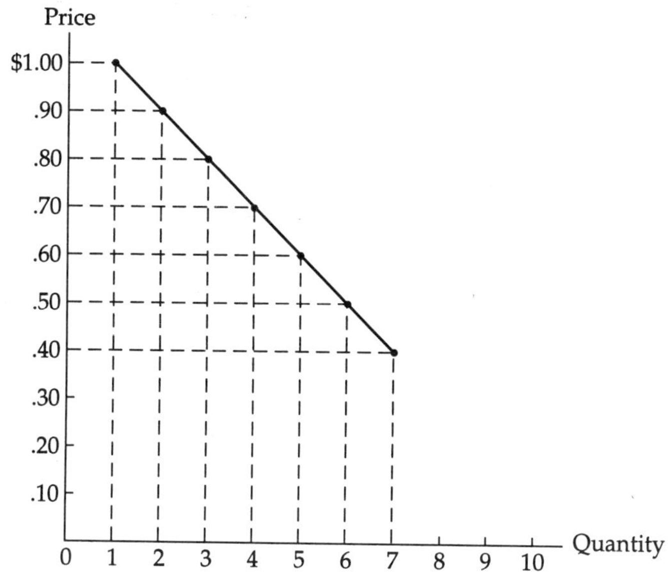

b. −.1

17. Slope at point *a*: −1; at point *b*: 0; at point *c*: 1; at point *d*: infinite

18.

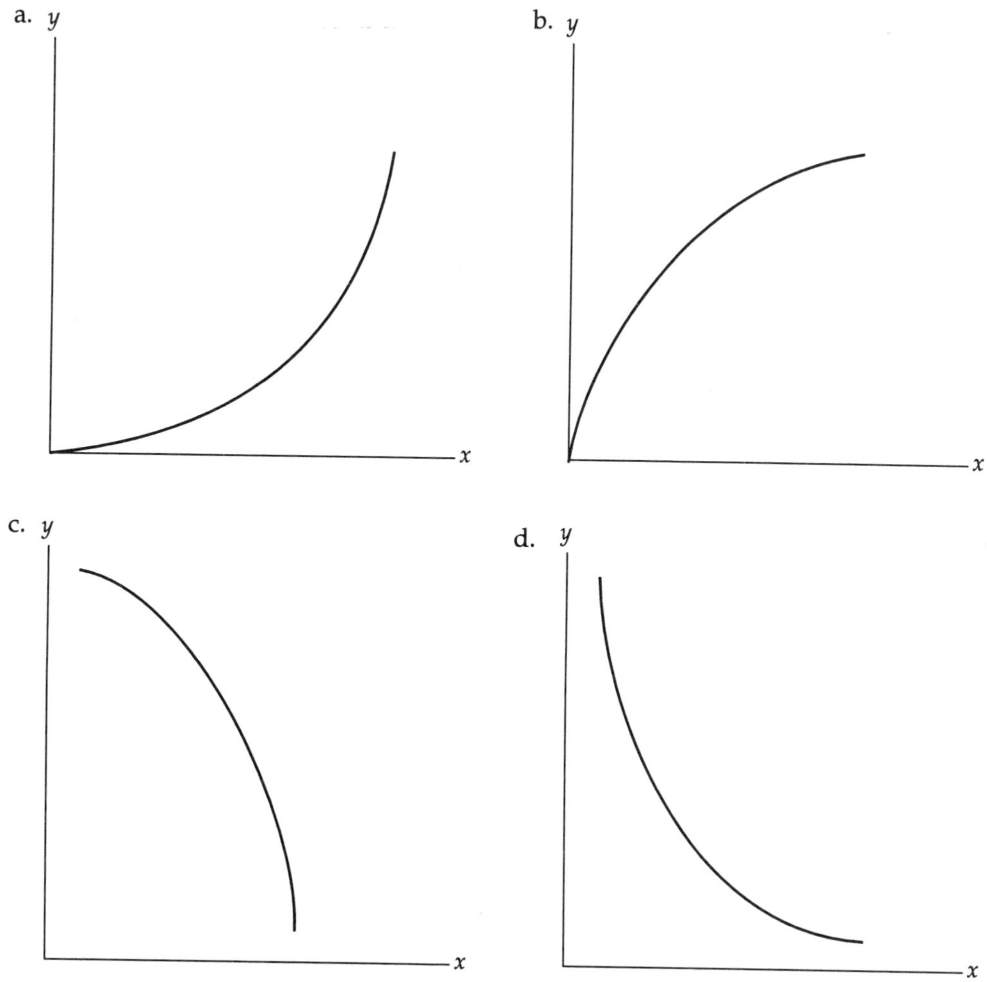

CHAPTER 2

Some Tools of Economic Analysis

I. INTRODUCTION

The previous chapter introduced the concept of scarcity. We saw that people must make choices because of scarcity. This chapter explores the idea of choice in more detail. The cost of a choice and the tools economists use to analyze cost are discussed. The chapter also examines some of the choices that any society must make.

II. OUTLINE

1. Choice and Opportunity Cost

   1.1 Opportunity Cost
   - a. The opportunity cost of a choice is the benefit expected from the best alternative that is forgone.
   - b. We do what we do because we have nothing better to do. If we had something better to do, we would do it.

   1.2 *CASE STUDY:* The Opportunity Cost of College

   1.3 Opportunity Cost Is Subjective
   - a. Each individual must calculate the expected value of the best alternative for himself or herself.
   - b. Calculating opportunity cost requires time and information.
   - c. Time is the ultimate constraint.
   - d. Opportunity cost may vary with circumstance.

   1.4 Sunk Cost and Choice
   - a. A sunk cost is a cost that cannot be recovered no matter what you do.
   - b. Sunk costs should be ignored in making economic decisions.

2. Specialization, Comparative Advantage, and Exchange

   2.1 The Law of Comparative Advantage. Combined output can increase when the individual with the lowest opportunity cost for producing a particular good specializes in producing that good.

   2.2 Absolute and Comparative Advantage
   - a. A person has an absolute advantage when he or she can perform tasks with fewer resources than another person.
   - b. A person has a comparative advantage when he or she can produce a given product at a lower opportunity cost than someone else.

c. Each person should specialize in the task for which he or she has a comparative advantage.
d. The law of comparative advantage applies to firms, regions, and nations as well as to individuals.

2.3 Specialization and Exchange
a. *Barter* is a system in which products are exchanged directly for other products.
b. Money is a medium of exchange because everyone is willing to accept it in exchange for goods and services. Money makes it easier to exchange goods and services.
c. Because of comparative advantage and specialization, people do not produce most of the things they want and must enter into exchange to acquire them.

2.4 Division of Labor and Gains from Specialization
a. Greater specialization can be achieved through division of labor: the separating of production into various tasks and the assigning of individuals to these separate tasks.
b. Division of labor is productive for several reasons:
(1) Tasks can be assigned according to preferences and abilities.
(2) As people perform the same tasks over and over, they become better at them.
(3) There is no time lost in moving from one task to another.
(4) Specialization of labor allows for the introduction of more sophisticated techniques.

2.5 *Case Study:* Evidence of Specialization

3. The Economy's Production Possibilities

3.1 Efficiency and the Production Possibilities Frontier
a. The production possibilities frontier (PPF) describes the possible combinations of two goods that can be produced when resources are used fully and efficiently.
b. Resources are used efficiently when they cannot be combined differently in any way that would increase the production of one good without decreasing the production of the other good.

3.2 Inefficient and Unattainable Production
a. Points outside the PPF represent combinations of the two goods that cannot be attained, given society's resources and technology.
b. Points inside the PPF represent combinations of the two goods that are produced inefficiently.

3.3 Shape of the Production Possibilities Frontier
a. The PPF slopes down because, when resources are used fully and efficiently, more of one good can be produced only by producing less of the other good.
b. The PPF is bowed out when not all resources are equally productive in producing both goods.
c. The law of increasing opportunity cost applies to production of both goods: as additional units of one good are produced, more and more of the other good must be sacrificed.

3.4 What Shifts the Production Possibilities Frontier?
a. Over time the PPF may shift out or in.
b. Shifts in the PPF will occur as a result of

(1) changes in resource availability.
(2) increases in the capital stock.
(3) effects of technological change.

3.5 What We Can Learn from the PPF

a. The PPF demonstrates efficiency since it describes the efficient combinations of output that are possible.
b. The PPF demonstrates scarcity since there is a limit to what can be produced.
c. The downward slope of the PPF indicates opportunity cost.
d. The bowed shape of the PPF indicates the law of increasing opportunity cost.
e. The PPF illustrates the need to make choices.
f. Outward shifts in the PPF reflect economic growth.

3.6 Three Questions Each Economic System Must Answer

a. What goods and services will be produced?
b. How will goods and services be produced?
c. For whom will goods and services be produced?
d. These questions are interrelated, since what will be produced is often determined by the economic and social systems of the people for whom the goods are made.

4. Economic Systems

4.1 Pure Capitalism

a. Pure capitalism is an economic system characterized by private ownership of resources.
b. Coordination of economic activity is accomplished by price signals in free markets.
c. Markets direct decisions concerning the three economic questions.
d. *Laissez faire* means letting people do as they choose without government intervention.

4.2 Command Economy

a. Command economy is an economic system characterized by public ownership of resources.
b. Coordination is accomplished by central planning.

4.3 Mixed and Transitional Economies

a. No society is a pure capitalist or a pure command economy.
b. All societies mix elements of capitalism and the command economy, although the composition of the mix differs considerably.

4.5 Economies Based on Custom or Religion

III. DISCUSSION

Choice and Opportunity Cost

Everybody faces the problem of scarcity—even the very rich. Time is scarce for everyone, and any activity we engage in has an *opportunity cost* associated with it. Opportunity costs are subjective. For one student the opportunity cost of taking an economics course may be the course on Homer not taken, whereas the opportunity cost for another student may be the hours missed from work. Since the opportunity cost of any activity is the value of the best alternative choice that is forgone, and different people have different alternative choices, opportunity costs differ for different people.

The concept of opportunity cost does not mean that the choice actually made will always be the best choice. After taking economics, a student may think that she made a mistake and should have taken Homer. Often, we do not know the true value of the forsaken alternative, so occasionally we make mistakes.

Calculating opportunity costs requires time and information. The time we spend collecting information could be spent doing other things; we do not always spend enough time collecting information and we make mistakes. Opportunity costs may also vary with circumstances. The opportunity cost of studying on a rainy day is less for most people than the opportunity cost of the same activity on a beautiful Saturday afternoon.

Specialization, Comparative Advantage, and Exchange

Dividing production in accordance with the *law of comparative advantage* leads to increased production. Since all people (or firms, regions, or countries) are not equally efficient in producing all goods and services, total output is greater when each individual specializes in producing the goods or services that she or he can produce relatively more efficiently.

The law of comparative advantage applies not only to people but also to all productive resources. Suppose a farmer has two acres of land. One acre can produce 1,000 bushels of wheat, or 800 bushels of corn, or some combination of both. The second acre can produce either 600 bushels of wheat or 200 bushels of corn. Although the first acre has an *absolute advantage* in producing both crops, it has a comparative advantage in producing corn. The opportunity cost of a bushel of corn on the first acre is 1.25 bushels of wheat. For the second acre, the opportunity cost of a bushel of corn is 3 bushels of wheat. The opportunity cost of corn is less for the first acre. What about wheat? The opportunity cost of a bushel of wheat on the first acre is 0.8 bushel of corn, and the opportunity cost for the second acre is 0.33 bushel of corn. The opportunity cost of wheat is less for the second acre than for the first, so the second acre of land has a comparative advantage in producing wheat.

In order to take advantage of comparative advantage, resources must specialize. *Specialization* implies that people do not produce most of the goods and services that they wish to consume. Instead, most people specialize, exchanging a single product or service for money and then exchanging money for the goods and services that they want to consume. This specialization is generally a part of the *division of labor*. Further, most people do not produce a single product by themselves. Instead, they perform a specialized task that helps produce a good or service. In some small commuter airlines, for example, the pilot may also sell tickets, but larger airlines divide tasks and assign different individuals to perform them. As a result, the total output can be larger than it would be without division of labor.

The Economy's Production Possibilities

The *production possibilities frontier* (PPF) describes the possible combinations of two goods that can be produced with maximum efficiency. Exhibit 1 presents a PPF for an economy that produces wheat and sweaters. The curve slopes down, which indicates that the only way to get more wheat is to produce fewer sweaters. At any point on the PPF, more of one good can be produced only by producing less of the other. This is what is meant by producing the goods efficiently. The PPF is also bowed out, which reflects the *law of increasing opportunity cost*. At point *a* only sweaters are produced. If we want to produce 1,000 bushels of wheat, we see that we must give up fewer than 500 sweaters. To produce another 1,000 bushels of wheat, more than 500 sweaters must be sacrificed. Beginning at point *d*, 4,500 sweaters and 8,000 bushels of wheat, the production of sweaters must be curtailed by 2,000 units to increase wheat production by another 1,000 bushels. Between points *e* and *f*, an additional 2,500 sweaters must be sacrificed to produce yet another 1,000 bushels of wheat. In moving from point *a* to point *f*, each 1,000-bushel increase in wheat production requires sacrificing increasing numbers of sweaters. That is, the opportunity cost of wheat increases as more and more wheat is produced.

Exhibit 1

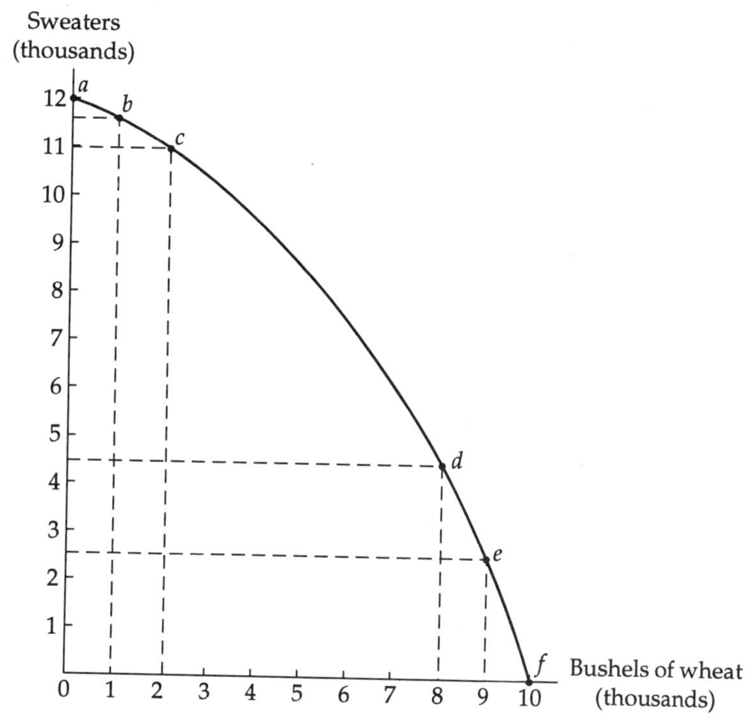

A production possibilities frontier is constructed for a given amount of resources and a given level of technology. If either the number of resources or the technology changes, the PPF shifts. The more capital a country produces in a year, the farther out the PPF shifts in future years. You should review Exhibit 2 in the text to make sure you understand these shifts.

Any society must answer three basic economic questions: What goods and services will be produced and in what quantities? How will the goods be produced? For whom will the goods be produced? Not all societies answer the three basic questions in the same manner. The two extreme types of arrangement are capitalism and the command economy. Under *capitalism*, all productive resources are privately owned. One's income depends on the resources one owns and the prices the resources command. The more income one has, the more "votes" one has in determining the type of goods that will be produced. Markets are used to coordinate the plans of the individual members of society, and changes in prices signal individuals to alter their behavior in certain predictable ways.

A *command economy* operates very differently from a capitalist economy. In a command economy, all productive resources are owned publicly, i.e., by the government. Decisions concerning what to produce and in what quantities are made by government officials. The economy is organized so that decisions are made at the top and carried out by the people lower in the pyramid.

No society on earth today has either a pure capitalist economy or a pure command economy. Instead, all societies use a mixture of government involvement and individual decision making. In some countries, such as the United States, most exchanges are carried out through markets and most productive resources are owned by individuals. In other countries, such as the People's Republic of China, most productive resources are owned by the government and many economic decisions are made by central planners. However, there is extensive government intervention in the economy of the United States and many examples of private ownership in the People's Republic of China.

IV. LAGNIAPPE

Advantages of the Division of Labor

Adam Smith, who is credited with recognizing the advantages of the division of labor, wrote:

> The great increase of the quantity of work which, in consequence of the division of labor, the same number of people are capable of performing, is owing to three different circumstances; first to the increase of dexterity in every particular workman; secondly, to the saving of the time which is commonly lost in passing from one species of work to another; and lastly, to the invention of a great number of machines which facilitate and abridge labor, and enable one man to do the work of many. [Adam Smith, *The Wealth of Nations* (Chicago: The University of Chicago Press, 1976), p. 11. Originally published in 1776.]

Question to Think About: How do these three advantages of the division of labor coincide with the four reasons given in the text?

Ricardo and Comparative Advantage

David Ricardo (1772–1823) was the first to identify comparative advantage as the source of trade. As an example, he used the production of wine and cloth in England and Portugal. If England required 100 men per year to produce cloth and 120 men per year to produce wine, and it took only 90 men per year to produce the same amount of cloth in Portugal and 80 men per year to produce the same amount of wine, then Portugal had an absolute advantage in both. However, as Ricardo pointed out:

> It would therefore be advantageous for her (Portugal) to export wine in exchange for cloth. This exchange might even take place notwithstanding that the commodity imported by Portugal could be produced there with less labor than in England. Though she could make the cloth with the labor of 90 men, she would import it from a country where it required the labor of 100 men to produce it, because it would be advantageous to her rather to employ her capital in the production of wine, for which she would obtain more cloth from England, than she could produce by diverting a portion of her capital from the cultivation of vines to the manufacture of cloth. [David Ricardo, *The Principles of Political Economy and Taxation* (London: A. M. Dent & Sons, 1973), p. 82. Originally published in 1821.]

Question to Think About: What is the opportunity cost of wine in Portugal? in England? What is the opportunity cost of cloth in England? in Portugal?

V. KEY TERMS

Opportunity cost
Sunk cost
Law of comparative advantage
Absolute advantage
Comparative advantage
Barter
Division of labor
Specialization of labor
Production possibilities frontier (PPF)
Efficiency
Law of increasing opportunity cost
Economic system
Pure capitalism
Command economy
Mixed economy

VI. QUESTIONS

A. *Completion*

1. The ____________________ of any action is the expected benefit of the best alternative not chosen.

2. A cost that cannot be recovered no matter what you do is a ____________________ cost.

3. ____________________ is the ability to produce something with fewer resources than other producers.

4. ____________________ is the ability to produce something at a lower opportunity cost than other producers.

5. The ____________________ leads to greater output because it results in greater specialization of labor.

6. ____________________ is a system of exchange in which products are traded directly for other products.

7. Something that everyone is willing to accept in return for all goods and services is called a ____________________.

8. A society is producing on its ____________________ if it uses its resources fully and efficiently.

9. A bowed-out production possibilities frontier indicates that the cost of producing either good ____________________ as greater amounts of the good are produced.

10. Production is ____________________ if there is no way to rearrange resources that will allow more of one good to be produced without causing less of any other good to be produced.

11. Any economic system must decide what goods will be produced, for whom they will be produced, and ____________________.

12. Most societies are a mixture of ________________ and ________________.

13. The idea that people should be allowed to do as they choose without government interference is called ________________.

14. In a command economy, resources are directed through ________________.

B. *True/False*

______ 1. The opportunity cost of an activity is the expected benefit from the best alternative that is forsaken.

______ 2. The price of something is usually the best measure of the opportunity cost of the activity.

______ 3. The opportunity cost of a given activity is usually the same for all people.

______ 4. Opportunity cost measures the cost of the alternative given up less the expected benefit from the opportunity chosen.

______ 5. Opportunity costs vary with circumstances.

______ 6. Opportunity costs tend to be constant over time.

______ 7. Comparative advantage is caused by absolute advantage.

______ 8. The law of comparative advantage calls for specializing in the task in which one has a comparative advantage.

______ 9. One function of money is to make it easier for exchange to take place.

______ 10. Barter decreases as an economy becomes more specialized.

______ 11. The division of labor allows the introduction of specialized machinery that makes workers more productive.

______ 12. A production possibilities frontier shifts out when society moves from inefficient to efficient production.

______ 13. A production possibilities frontier illustrates opportunity cost by sloping downward.

______ 14. The law of increasing opportunity cost generates a production possibilities frontier that bows outward.

______ 15. The PPF would not be bowed outward if the resources in an economy were all perfectly adaptable for the production of both goods.

______ 16. We would expect a society's PPF to shift out over time.

______ 17. If existing capital wears out faster than new capital is produced, the PPF will shift in over time.

______ 18. The answer to the question of how goods are to be distributed helps shape the incentives people have to produce.

______ 19. Under capitalism, market prices guide resources to their highest valued use.

______ 20. In a command economy, central planners decide how a good will be produced.

C. *Multiple Choice*

1. The opportunity cost of a vanilla ice cream cone is
   a. a chocolate ice cream cone.
   b. a piece of apple pie.
   c. a hamburger.
   d. a gallon of gasoline.
   e. All of the above are possible.

2. Which of the following is a true statement about opportunity costs?
   a. The opportunity cost of an activity includes the expected benefit of the most attractive alternative passed up.
   b. Opportunity cost implies that people are always pleased with the decisions they make.
   c. Opportunity cost is an objective notion.
   d. When making choices, people exhaustively calculate costs and benefits for all possible alternatives.
   e. All of the above are true.

3. For a toy store, the opportunity cost of closing for a day is likely to be greatest
   a. on any given Wednesday.
   b. on any given day in February.
   c. on the second Saturday of December.
   d. on the third Friday in June.
   e. on the Fourth of July.

4. Opportunity costs are subjective because
   a. they depend on circumstances, which may vary.
   b. the best alternative may differ for different people.
   c. they do not reflect money costs.
   d. all of the above
   e. a and b only

5. Sunk costs should be ignored in making economic choices because
   a. they are usually trivial.
   b. they are marginal costs so they are not as relevant as total costs.
   c. they are not affected by the choice.
   d. they are not monetary costs.
   e. none of the above. They should not be ignored.

6. Fred and Samantha cook and clean. They have identical opportunity costs for cooking, but Samantha has an absolute advantage in cooking. We know, then, that
   a. Fred has an absolute advantage in cleaning.
   b. Fred has a comparative advantage in cleaning.
   c. Samantha has an absolute advantage in cleaning.
   d. Samantha has a comparative advantage in cleaning.
   e. None of the above. More information is needed.

7. A man has two sons, Robbie and David. Robbie can mow the lawn in 1 hour and wash the car in 50 minutes. David can mow the lawn in 40 minutes and wash the car in 30 minutes. Which statement below is true?
   a. David has an absolute advantage in both chores and a comparative advantage in mowing the lawn.
   b. David has an absolute advantage in both chores and a comparative advantage in washing cars.
   c. Robbie has an absolute advantage in both chores and a comparative advantage in mowing the lawn.
   d. Robbie has an absolute advantage in both chores and a comparative advantage in washing cars.
   e. Robbie has an absolute advantage in washing cars and David has an absolute advantage in mowing the lawn.

8. In the preceding example,
   a. Robbie should wash the car and David should mow the lawn.
   b. David should both mow the lawn and wash the car.
   c. David should wash the car and Robbie should mow the lawn.
   d. Robbie and David should share both jobs.
   e. We cannot tell who should do what chore without more information.

9. Specialization of labor implies that
   a. people must engage in exchange to acquire the goods they want.
   b. barter is an efficient way to carry out exchange.
   c. money is not a necessary part of the economy.
   d. the economy must be characterized by absolute advantage.
   e. output falls if labor is divided into too many specialized tasks.

10. Which of the following is a source of the increased productivity due to specialization of labor?
   a. People are assigned various tasks to perform so they will not get bored.
   b. Employees can be assigned tasks on the basis of the manager's preference and prejudices.
   c. People become better at a job the more they perform it.
   d. Workers can replace expensive machines in production.
   e. all of the above

11. If the opportunity cost in the United States of 1 unit of wheat is 4 units of cloth, then
   a. the opportunity cost of wheat in England is more than 4 units of cloth.
   b. the opportunity cost of wheat in England is less than 4 units of cloth.
   c. the opportunity cost of 1 unit of cloth in the United States is 1/4 unit of wheat.
   d. the United States has a comparative advantage in producing cloth.
   e. both a and d

12. If the United States has an absolute advantage in producing wheat and England has an absolute advantage in producing cloth, then
    a. neither country has a comparative advantage in either good.
    b. the United States has a comparative advantage in wheat and England has a comparative advantage in cloth.
    c. the United States should specialize in wheat and England should specialize in cloth.
    d. b and c
    e. none of the above. More information is needed.

13. Disadvantages of increased specialization include
    a. reduced standards of living.
    b. reduced contact with other people.
    c. increased job dissatisfaction.
    d. increased reliance on money.
    e. all of the above.

Exhibit 2

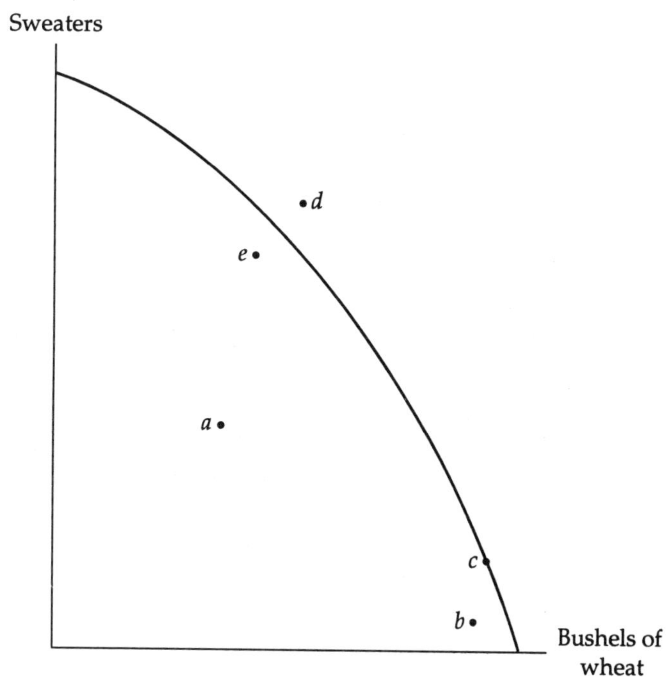

14. Which point in Exhibit 2 indicates where production is efficient?
    a. point *a*
    b. point *b*
    c. point *c*
    d. point *d*
    e. point *e*

15. Which point in Exhibit 2 cannot be attained?
    a. point *a*
    b. point *b*
    c. point *c*
    d. point *d*
    e. All points except *c* are unattainable.

Exhibit 3

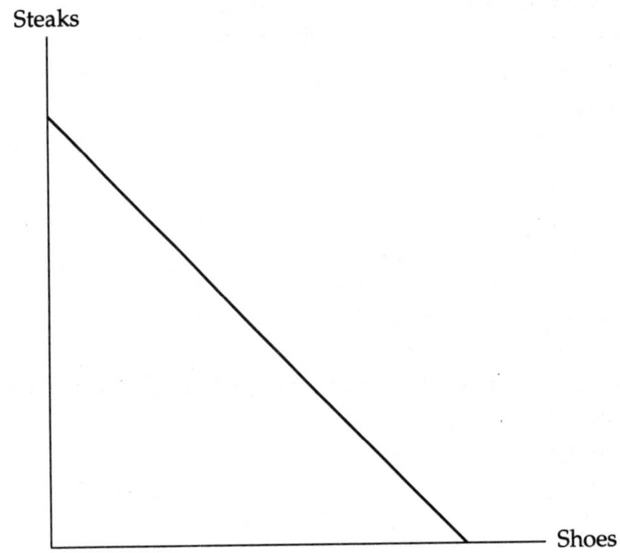

16. The production possibilities frontier in Exhibit 3 indicates
    a. the law of increasing opportunity cost.
    b. that the opportunity cost of producing shoes is constant.
    c. that production is not efficient.
    d. decreasing opportunity costs.
    e. none of the above.

17. Which of the following can cause the PPF to shift out?
    a. an increase in vacation time
    b. an increase in immigration
    c. a decrease in the retirement age
    d. migration of unskilled workers to other countries
    e. none of the above

18. In a capitalist economy, productive resources are owned by
    a. the government.
    b. the people collectively.
    c. individuals.
    d. the rich.
    e. the army.

19. Which of the economic questions does not have to be solved in a primitive economy?
    a. What will be produced?
    b. How will goods be produced?
    c. For whom will goods be produced?
    d. both b and c
    e. They must all be solved.

20. In which country does the government own some resources?
    a. the United States
    b. France
    c. Cuba
    d. Canada
    e. all of the above

D. *Discussion Questions*

1. How are opportunity cost and scarcity related?

2. The textbook says that we always do what we do because we have nothing better to do. Explain what this means.

3. Why are the opportunity costs of law school greater than the opportunity costs of undergraduate school?

4. The textbook says, "Time is the ultimate constraint." Explain why this is so.

5. If people always choose the alternative that provides the highest expected benefit, how can mistakes ever be made?

Use the information in Exhibit 4 about production of cloth and wheat in the United States and England to answer questions 6 and 7.

Exhibit 4

Output Produced per Day by One Worker

	England	*United States*
Wheat	3	10
Cloth	1	2

6. a. What is the opportunity cost of wheat in England? in the United States?
   b. Which country has a comparative advantage in the production of wheat? Which has a comparative advantage in the production of cloth?
   c. If the two countries trade, which will specialize in wheat and which in cloth? Which will export wheat and which will export cloth?

7. a. Which country has an absolute advantage in wheat and which in cloth?
   b. Why is trade based on comparative advantage rather than on absolute advantage?

8. What does money have to do with specialization and comparative advantage?

9. Explain how the division of labor increases productivity.

10. Under what conditions is it possible to increase production of one good without decreasing production of another good?

11. Suppose there are two resources used in an economy: labor and capital. Capital is relatively more useful in producing wheat, whereas labor is relatively more useful in producing cloth. Suppose the supply of capital falls by 10 percent and the supply of labor increases by 10 percent. How will the production possibilities frontier for wheat and cloth change?

12. What can we learn from the production possibilities frontier?

13. Suppose 10 percent of a country's capital stock wears out every year. What will happen to the PPF in future years if the country produces new capital each year equal to 20 percent of its capital stock at the beginning of the year? if it produces new capital equal to 5 percent of its beginning capital?

14. What are the three questions that all societies must answer and why must they be answered?

15. How are the three questions answered differently in a capitalist system and a command economy?

VII. ANSWERS

A. *Completion*

1. opportunity cost
2. sunk
3. Absolute advantage
4. Comparative advantage
5. division of labor
6. Barter
7. medium of exchange
8. production possibilities frontier
9. increases
10. efficient
11. how goods will be produced
12. capitalism; a command economy
13. laissez faire
14. central planning

B. *True/False*

1. True
2. False. Calculations of opportunity cost must also include the time spent away from the most valued alternative.
3. False
4. False
5. True
6. False
7. False
8. True
9. True
10. True
11. True
12. False
13. True
14. True
15. True
16. True
17. True
18. True
19. True
20. True

C. *Multiple Choice*

1.	e	6.	c	11.	c	16.	b
2.	a	7.	b	12.	d	17.	b
3.	c	8.	c	13.	c	18.	c
4.	e	9.	a	14.	c	19.	e
5.	c	10.	c	15.	d	20.	e

D. *Discussion Questions*

1. Scarcity implies that we must make choices since we cannot have everything that we want. Every choice involves an opportunity cost, so opportunity costs result from scarcity.

2. At any time we have many choices available to us. The alternative that we choose is the most preferred alternative. Consequently, there is no choice better than the one we choose—we have nothing better to do. If we had something better to do, we would do it.

3. Both law students and undergraduate students forgo earning a living while they are in school. The opportunity costs of law school are greater than those of undergraduate school, however, because undergraduate students are forgoing the relatively small salaries earned by workers with only high school diplomas, whereas law students are forgoing the salaries earned by college graduates.

4. Time is the ultimate constraint because consumption of goods and services takes time. One may have three cars but can only drive one at a time. A person can only do one thing at a time, so choices always have to be made.

5. People do not always have perfect information concerning alternatives. Information is scarce, and it takes time to collect accurate and complete information. Consequently, people sometimes make decisions that they later regret. At the time the decision is made, the person assumes it is a good decision, but events often do not turn out as expected; information can turn up later to prove a decision wrong.

6. a. Opportunity cost of wheat in England is 1/3 unit of cloth; in the United States it is 1/5 unit of cloth.
   b. The United States has a comparative advantage in the production of wheat, since the opportunity cost of producing wheat is lower in the United States. England has a comparative advantage in the production of cloth because the opportunity cost of producing cloth in England is 3 units of wheat compared to a cost of 5 units of wheat in the United States.
   c. The United States will specialize in wheat and England will specialize in cloth. The United States will export wheat and England will export cloth.

7. a. The United States has an absolute advantage in both wheat and cloth, since more of each good is produced by a worker in the United States.
   b. The cost of a good is measured not in terms of the hours of work required to produce it but rather in terms of opportunity cost, i.e., the amount of another good that must be given up to consume the first good. Basing trade on comparative advantage allows a country or producer with the lowest opportunity cost to specialize in producing a good.

8. Specialization results from comparative advantage. When people specialize, they tend to produce few of the things they consume and to consume few of the things they produce. They must rely on exchanging the goods they produce for the goods they want to consume. This would be difficult to do with a barter system, so money helps make exchange easier.

9. The division of labor allows people to work in their area of comparative advantage. By performing tasks over and over, people become better at performing them. There is also no time lost in workers' going from one task to another. Finally, the division of labor allows for the introduction of specialized machinery, which makes labor more productive.

10. We can produce more of one good without sacrificing production of another good when we are inside the PPF. If we can do so, we are either not using all available resources or not using them efficiently.

11. In the graph below, *AB* is the original PPF. The decrease in capital causes the production of wheat to fall more than the production of cloth, since capital is more efficient in producing wheat. The increase in labor causes the production of cloth to increase more than the production of wheat. The net effect is an increase in the production of cloth and a decrease in the production of wheat. *CD* is the new PPF.

Exhibit 5

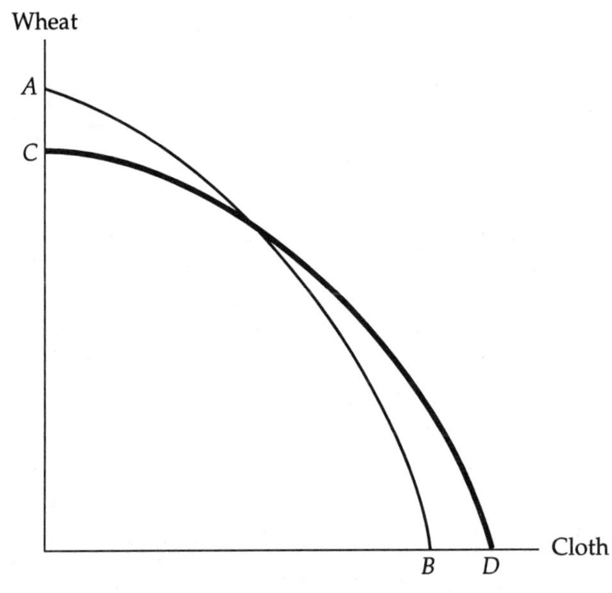

12. By showing the limits to productivity, the PPF illustrates the concept of scarcity and the need to make choices. It illustrates the concept of opportunity cost with its downward slope, and it illustrates increasing opportunity cost with its bowed-out shape. Finally, it illustrates the concept of efficiency, since there is at least one point on the PPF that is preferable to any point inside the PPF, and the concept of economic growth, since the entire PPF can shift away from the origin.

13. Annual production of new capital equal to 20 percent of the capital stock at the beginning of the year will cause the capital stock to increase by 10 percent in the future, since only 10 percent of the capital is consumed each year. The PPF will shift out the next year, indicating economic growth. A 5-percent yearly production of capital will cause the total capital stock

to decrease by 5 percent in the future, since 10 percent of the capital stock is consumed each year. The PPF will shift in toward the origin.

14. Each society must decide what will be produced and in what quantities. People want goods and services, but they cannot have all they want because of scarcity. Hence, some criteria must be established to decide which goods will be produced. Different resource combinations can be used to produce a given good, so once a society decides what will be produced, it must also decide how goods will be produced. Finally, since everybody wants more than is available, society must decide who will get the goods that have been produced.

15. In a capitalist economy, individuals own the resources and decide how they will be used. Seeking the best places for their resources, they make their decisions on the basis of prices and changes in prices. Consumers decide what will be produced by demonstrating their willingness to pay for the goods. Entrepreneurs decide how the goods will be produced by making decisions designed to keep costs low. Goods are distributed based on incomes and the prices of the goods. The whole process is coordinated by people's responses to price changes. In a command economy, central planners decide what will be produced and how it will be produced. They also decide who gets what products. (The Marxist ideal is expressed by the axiom "From each according to his ability, to each according to his need.")

CHAPTER 3

The Market System

I. INTRODUCTION

The workhorses of economic analysis are the concepts of supply and demand. These tools are introduced in this chapter, although both tools will be developed much further in later chapters. Because the material in this chapter is a foundation for much of the course, be certain that you understand it and that you can use the tools developed here.

II. OUTLINE

1. Demand. Demand reflects the quantity of a good that people are both willing and able to buy at various prices, other things constant.

   1.1 The Law of Demand

   a. The law of demand states that the quantity demanded of a good is inversely related to its price.

   b. Demand differs from wants and needs.

   c. The substitution effect of a price increase will be to encourage consumers to switch to other goods that are relatively cheaper.

   d. A change in price also generates an income effect, since the price change affects the buying power of consumer income, or real income.

   1.2 The Demand Schedule and Demand Curve

   a. A demand schedule indicates the quantity of a commodity that consumers wish to buy at each possible price for a given period of time.

   (1) Demand is a rate per period of time.

   (2) Prices of other goods are held constant.

   (3) A demand schedule looks at the effects of a relative price change.

   b. A demand curve provides a graphical representation of the information in a demand schedule.

   c. *Demand* refers to the entire demand schedule or demand curve.

   d. *Quantity demanded* refers to an individual point on the demand curve.

   e. A change in demand occurs when the entire demand schedule or demand curve shifts.

   f. A change in quantity demanded occurs when the price of a good changes and one moves along the demand curve.

   g. The market demand curve is found by horizontally summing the individual demand curves of all consumers in a market.

2. Changes in Demand

   2.1 Changes in Consumer Income

a. A change in income causes the entire demand curve to shift, i.e., causes a change in demand.
b. If the demand for a good increases as income increases, then the good is a normal good.
c. If the demand for a good decreases as income increases, then the good is an inferior good.

2.2 Changes in the Prices of Related Goods
a. Two goods are substitutes if they are alternative ways of satisfying a particular want.
b. Two goods are complements if they are used in combination to satisfy a particular want.
c. If an increase in the price of one good causes the demand for a second good to increase, the two goods are substitutes.
d. If an increase in the price of one good causes the demand for a second good to decrease, the two goods are complements.

2.3 Changes in Consumer Expectations
a. If consumers expect the price of a good to increase in the future, demand for the good will increase today.
b. If consumers expect an increase in future income, demand for goods will increase today.

2.4 Changes in the Number or Composition of Consumers. The more people there are in the market, the greater the market demand.

2.5 Changes in Consumer Tastes
a. Tastes are assumed to be relatively stable over time.
b. A change in demand cannot be attributed to a change in tastes before other possible reasons for the change are carefully considered.

3. Supply. The law of supply states that the quantity of product supplied in a given time period is usually directly related to its price, other things constant.

3.1 The Supply Schedule and Supply Curve
a. A higher price makes producers more willing to offer more for sale because they are rewarded more for doing so.
b. A higher price enables producers to produce more because it allows them to cover the higher marginal costs that result as quantity produced increases, according to the law of increasing opportunity costs.
c. The market supply curve is found by horizontally summing the individual supply curves of all suppliers in a market.

4. Changes in Supply

4.1 Changes in Technology. A technological advance is reflected by a shift to the right in the market supply curve.

4.2 Changes in the Prices of Relevant Resources. Lower resource costs lead to an increase in supply.

4.3 Changes in the Prices of Alternative Goods. An increase in the price of an alternative good raises the opportunity cost of producing other goods that use the same resources.

4.4 Changes in Producer Expectations. If producers expect the price of a good to rise in the future, current supply could increase or decrease, depending on the type of good.

4.5 Changes in the Number of Producers
   a. An increase in the number of producers increases the market supply.
   b. A change in supply is a shift of the entire supply curve; a change in the quantity supplied is a movement along a supply curve when the price of a good changes.

5. Demand and Supply Create a Market

5.1 Markets
   a. Markets coordinate the independent decisions of buyers and sellers.
   b. The transaction costs of an exchange are the costs of the time and the information required to complete the transaction.
   c. Markets reduce the transaction costs of exchange.
   d. Coordination takes place through markets by the operation of the "invisible hand" described by Adam Smith.

5.2 Specialized Markets. The degree of specialization is limited by the extent of the market.

5.3 Market Equilibrium
   a. The equilibrium price is the price at which quantity demanded equals quantity supplied.
   b. An excess quantity supplied, or surplus, exists when the quantity supplied exceeds the quantity demanded at prices above equilibrium.
   c. An excess quantity demanded, or shortage, exists when the quantity demanded exceeds the quantity supplied at prices below equilibrium.

5.4 Markets Allocate Resources.
   a. An equilibrium is achieved through the independent actions of thousands of buyers and sellers in the economy.
   b. Markets allocate a resource to its highest valued use.

6. Changes in Equilibrium Price and Quantity

6.1 Impact of Changes in Demand. Any change in demand, holding supply constant, will change equilibrium price and quantity in the same direction as the changes in demand.

6.2 Impact of Changes in Supply. A shift in the supply curve, holding demand constant, changes equilibrium quantity in the same direction but changes equilibrium price in the opposite direction.

6.3 Simultaneous Changes in Demand and Supply
   a. When both curves shift simultaneously, the outcome depends on the nature of the shifts.
   b. If supply and demand both increase, the equilibrium quantity increases, but the effect on the equilibrium price depends on the size of the shift in demand relative to the size of the shift in supply. If both supply and demand decrease, the equilibrium quantity falls.
   c. If supply and demand shift in opposite directions, the equilibrium price rises with an increase in demand and falls with a decrease in demand. However, the effect on the equilibrium quantity depends on the size of the shift in demand relative to the size of the shift in supply.

6.4 *Case Study:* The Market for Professional Basketball

7. Disequilibrium Prices

7.1 Price Floors. Price floors, or minimum prices set by the government, tend to create surpluses.

7.2 Price Ceilings. Price ceilings, or minimum prices set by the government, tend to create shortages.

7.3 *Case Study:* Toys Are Serious Business

III. DISCUSSION

Demand

Demand is a relation that indicates the quantity of a commodity that consumers wish to buy at all possible prices during a given time period, other things constant. The *law of demand* states that the relationship between price and quantity demanded is an inverse relationship, i.e., that fewer units are demanded at higher prices than at lower prices. Demand reflects consumers' willingness and ability to buy the commodity.

The inverse relationship between price and quantity demanded refers to the real, or relative, price of the commodity. If the price of shoes increases 10 percent but all other prices also increase by 10 percent, then the relative price of shoes has not changed and quantity demanded will not change.

A change in the price of a commodity has two effects on quantity demanded. The first is the *substitution effect*. If the price of one good increases while all other prices remain constant, then the good becomes more costly relative to other goods. Many consumers will respond by substituting a cheaper good for the now more expensive good, so the quantity demanded of the original good decreases. An increase in the price of one good encourages consumers to switch to other goods. The second effect—the *income effect*—affects consumers' ability to buy a good. If you have been buying ten hamburgers a week at $1.00 per hamburger and the price increases to $1.25, then the $10 that used to buy ten hamburgers can now buy only eight hamburgers. The higher price reduces your *real income*, or purchasing power, which has the tendency to induce you to purchase fewer units of the good.

The inverse relationship between price and quantity demanded can be shown by a demand schedule for any specific commodity. Exhibit 1 illustrates the quantities of gasoline demanded at various prices. Exhibit 2 provides the same information in the form of a *demand curve*. More units are demanded at lower prices, reflecting the law of demand. Several things are held constant: the prices of other goods and the incomes, expectations, and tastes of the consumers. A movement along the demand curve represents a *change in quantity demanded*. The market demand is found by adding up the demands of all consumers in the market.

Exhibit 1

The Demand Schedule for Gasoline

	Price per Gallon	*Quantity Demanded (millions of gallons per week)*
a	$1.25	8
b	1.00	10
c	.90	12
d	.80	14
e	.70	16
f	.60	20
g	.50	25

Exhibit 2

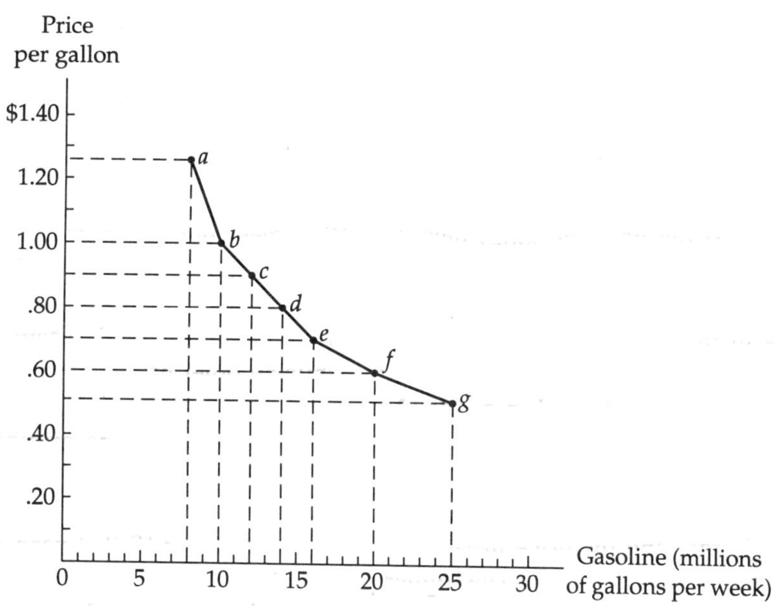

Changes in Demand

In the demand schedule and the demand curve in Exhibits 1 and 2, only the price of gasoline varied. However, demand can be affected by factors other than the price of the good being considered, such as consumer income, the prices of substitutes and complements, consumers' expectations, the number of consumers in the market, and consumer tastes. If any one of these factors changes, the entire demand schedule changes. That is, the demand curve shifts. When this occurs, there is a *change in demand*. (Be sure you understand how a change in demand differs from a change in quantity demanded.)

An increase in income increases demand for most products. Increasing demand means that the quantity demanded at every price increases. Exhibit 3 provides an example. When consumer income averages $20,000 a year, the demand schedule for gasoline is identical to that in Exhibit 1; this demand schedule is shown in the second column of Exhibit 3. When average income increases to $30,000 a year, the demand schedule changes. At each price, consumers demand a greater quantity of gasoline when income is greater. Exhibit 4 shows this change in demand by a shift in the demand curve from *D* to *D*′.

Exhibit 3

The Demand for Gasoline

		Quantity Demanded (millions of gallons per week)	
	Price per Gallon	*When Average Income is $20,000*	*When Average Income is $30,000*
a	$1.25	8	10
b	1.00	10	12
c	.90	12	14
d	.80	14	16
e	.70	16	18
f	.60	20	22
g	.50	25	27

Exhibit 4

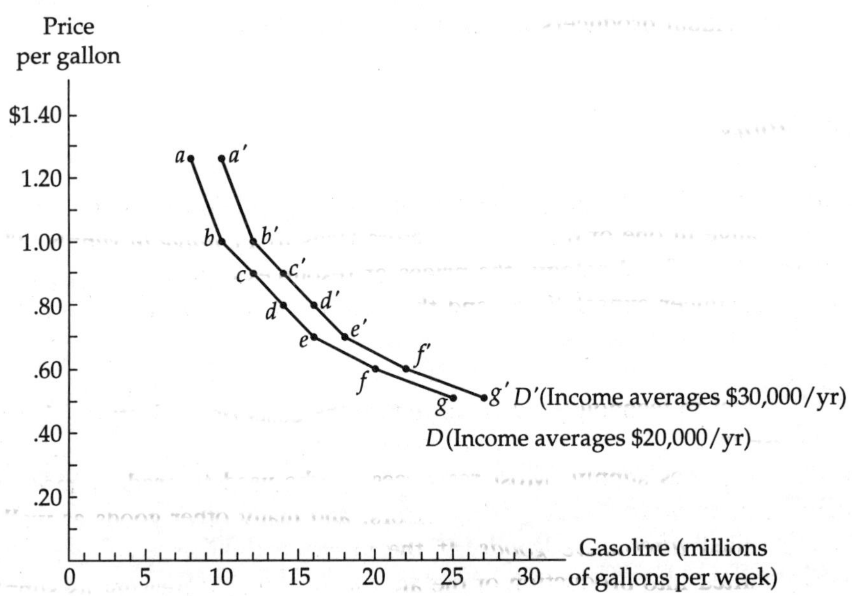

An increase in income may lead to a decrease in demand for some goods. Such goods are called *inferior goods*. People want fewer units of inferior goods when they have more income. Examples of such goods (at least for some consumers) are margarine, hamburger, bus travel, and inexpensive brands of many goods. People substitute a better product for the inferior good when they have more income. A good whose demand increases as income increases is called a *normal good*.

Any change in one of the other factors that affect demand (other than the price of the good itself) will cause a shift in the entire demand curve similar to the one shown in Exhibit 4. A change in the price of a substitute or complement will cause a change in demand. If an increase in the price of one good leads to an increase in demand for another good, the two goods are *substitutes*. If an increase in the price of one good leads to a decrease in demand for another good, the two goods are *complements*. If the goods are unrelated, a change in the price of one will have no effect on demand for the other.

Changes in consumer expectations about the future price of a good or future income can cause a shift in the current demand for the good. If price or income is expected to be higher in the future, current demand will increase. An increase in the number of consumers in the market will also cause an increase in market demand. A change in the composition of the population changes market demand. For example, demands change as population ages. Finally, a change in consumer tastes can cause a shift in demand. Again, make sure you understand the difference between a change in the quantity demanded and a change in demand. A change in quantity demanded is caused by a change in the price of the good itself; a change in demand is caused by a change in one of the other factors of demand.

Supply

The analysis of *supply* is similar in many respects to the analysis of demand. The law of supply states that the quantity of product supplied in a given time period is usually directly related to its price. An increase in quantity supplied is a result of producers' greater willingness and ability to supply more units at higher prices. Keep in mind the difference between demand and supply. The law of demand says there is an inverse relationship between price and quantity demanded, and the law of supply says there is a direct relationship between price and quantity supplied.

Determination of the market supply is analogous to determination of market demand: all the supply schedules of the individual producers in a market are added up.

Changes in Supply

A change in the price of a good causes a *change in the quantity supplied*. However, other factors affect supply. A change in one of these other factors leads to a *change in supply*. The factors that affect supply include the state of technology, the prices of resources used to produce the good, the prices of alternative goods, producer expectations, and the number of producers. The last two have effects very similar to those discussed for demand.

An improvement in technology tends to reduce the costs of production; cheaper production costs generate an increase in supply. Similarly, a decrease in the price of a resource used to produce the good reduces costs and increases supply. Most resources can be used to produce more than one good. For example, steel is used in autos, trucks, refrigerators, and many other goods as well as in construction. These goods are called *alternative goods*. If the price of an alternative good increases, additional resources will be shifted into production of the alternative good, increasing its supply.

Putting It All Together: Supply, Demand, and Equilibrium

Suppliers and demanders are brought together by markets. The *transaction costs* of exchange (the cost of time and information) are reduced by markets. A market is in *equilibrium* when the quantity demanded by consumers equals the quantity supplied by producers at a given price. Exhibits 5 and 6 illustrate a supply and demand schedule and supply and demand curves, respectively. The market is in equilibrium at a price of 80 cents per gallon because the quantity demanded equals the quantity supplied at that price. Any other price will generate either a shortage or a surplus. For example, if the price of a gallon of gasoline is $1.00, quantity demanded is 10 million gallons but quantity supplied is 20 million gallons, yielding a surplus of 10 million gallons. Any time the price is greater than the equilibrium price there will be a *surplus*. If the price is 60 cents per gallon, quantity demanded is 20 million gallons and quantity supplied is 10 million gallons; there is a shortage of 10 million gallons. Any time the price is below the equilibrium price there will be a *shortage*.

Exhibit 5

Market Supply and Demand for Gasoline

Price per Gallon	*Quantity Demanded (millions of gallons per week)*	*Quantity Supplied (millions of gallons per week)*
$1.25	8	28
1.00	10	20
.90	12	16
.80	14	14
.70	16	12
.60	20	10
.50	25	6

Exhibit 6

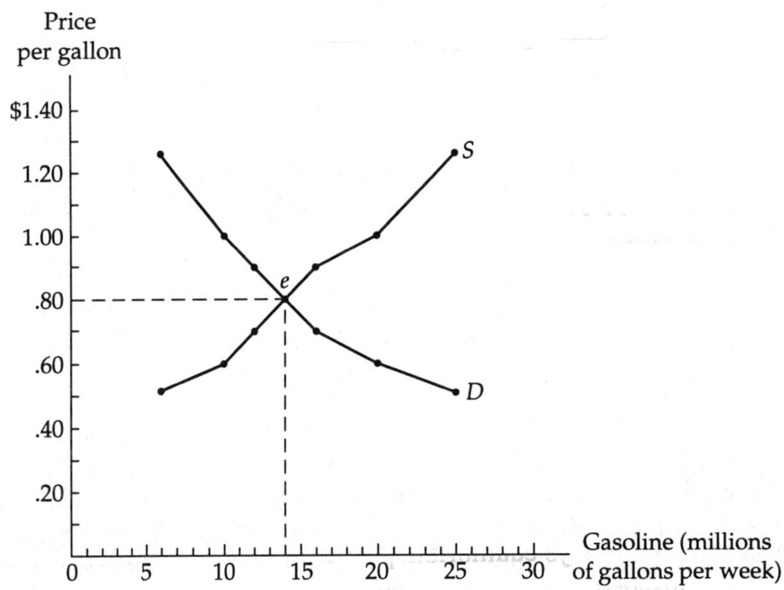

Changes in Equilibrium Price and Quantity

A market is in *equilibrium* when no economic agent in the market has any reason to alter his or her behavior. This is the case at the equilibrium price. That is, there is no reason for price to change unless either the supply or the demand changes. An increase in demand causes the demand curve to shift out, which generates a higher price and induces suppliers to increase the quantity supplied. What can cause demand to shift? Demand shifts when income, the price of a substitute or complement, consumer expectations, population, or consumer tastes change.

Exhibit 7 shows the effects of an increase in demand for gasoline. The demand curve shifts out to D', which causes the price to increase to 90 cents per gallon. The higher price encourages producers to increase the quantity supplied from 14 million gallons per week to 16 million gallons per week. That is, the new equilibrium price is 90 cents per gallon, and the new equilibrium quantity is 16 million gallons per week.

Exhibit 7

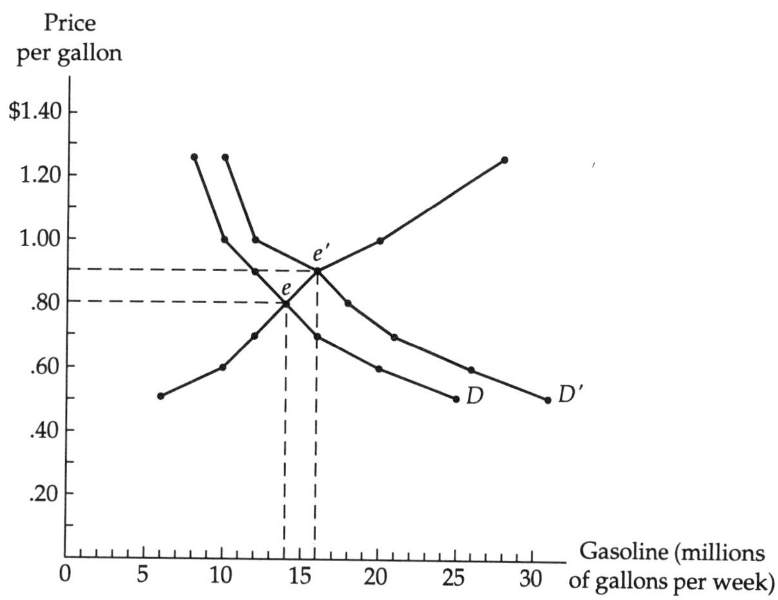

A change in supply has similar effects. An increase in supply shifts the *supply curve* down and out. Because of the increased supply, the price falls, which encourages consumers to buy more gasoline, i.e., quantity demanded increases.

It is possible for several factors to change at the same time; this generates shifts in both the demand curve and the supply curve. Review Exhibits 8 and 9 in the text to make sure that you understand the impact of simultaneous shifts in supply and demand.

Disequilibrium Prices

Actual prices are not always equilibrium prices. A market is in *disequilibrium* when the price does not equate quantity demanded and quantity supplied. In free markets, such disequilibria usually do not prevail for long periods of time. However, when the disequilibrium is due to the government's imposing either price ceilings or price floors, the disequilibrium can persist. When the government mandates a price floor above the equilibrium price, the result is a surplus. When the government mandates a price ceiling below the equilibrium price, the result is a shortage.

IV. LAGNIAPPE

The Market for Calculators

In the 1960s, engineering students did calculations using slide rules. Today slide rules have been replaced by hand-held calculators. When such calculators first appeared on the market, their prices were fairly high (a minimum of $400) and their capabilities were fairly limited. During the 1970s, technological change increased the capabilities of calculators and reduced their production costs. Demand increased as calculators were designed to perform more functions, and quantity demanded increased as prices fell. Both supply and demand have increased, but the increase in supply has been much larger than the increase in demand.

Question to Think About: How do we know that the change in the supply of calculators has been much greater than the change in demand?

Stock Market Activity

The stock market has changed considerably in the last fifteen years. A typical sales volume for the New York Stock Exchange fifteen years ago ranged from 60 million to 85 million shares per day. Today it is not uncommon for 150 million shares to be traded in one day. What happened? The Securities and Exchange Commission changed its rules: high commission rates were no longer permitted. Consequently, rates fell and volume increased. Also, technological changes have enabled the New York Stock Exchange to handle larger volumes.

Question to Think About: Are there any other factors that may have caused the demand for stocks to increase in the last fifteen years?

V. KEY TERMS

Demand
Law of demand
Relative price
Substitution effect
Real income
Income effect
Demand curve
Market demand
Normal good
Inferior good
Substitutes
Complements
Change in demand
Change in quantity demanded
Supply
Law of supply
Supply curve
Relevant resources
Market supply
Alternative goods
Change in quantity supplied
Change in supply
Transaction costs
Surplus
Shortage
Equilibrium
Disequilibrium
Price floor
Price ceiling

VI. QUESTIONS

A. Completion

1. Demand is a relation indicating the quantity of a commodity that consumers are ________________ and ________________ to purchase at various prices during a given time period, other things constant.

2. A price increase has two effects. The ________________ effect means that a consumer switches to a relatively less expensive good; the ________________ effect means that the consumer's purchasing power changes.

3. Bread is a ________________ good if demand for it increases when income increases.

4. Two goods are ________________ if an increase in the price of one causes the demand for the other to increase.

5. Consider a demand schedule. A change in the price of the good leads to a change in ________________; a change in a relevant factor other than the price of the good leads to a change in ________________.

6. Supply is a relationship between price and ________________ during a given time period, other things constant.

7. An increase in price causes a(n) ________________ in quantity supplied.

8. ________________ are goods that are produced using the same resources.

9. A change in technology causes a change in ________________.

10. The costs of time and information required for exchange are called ________________

11. If quantity demanded equals quantity supplied at a specific price, the market is in ________________.

12. Government-imposed price floors tend to produce a ________________.

13. A shortage exists when, for a given price, quantity demanded exceeds ________________

14. Price ceilings tend to produce ________________.

B. True/False

______ 1. Demand is the rate of desired and attainable purchase at each possible price, other things constant.

______ 2. A demand schedule indicates what an individual desires.

T ______ 3. Prices of all other goods are held constant for a given demand schedule.

______ 4. An increase in the price of one good, other things constant, encourages consumers to switch to other goods.

______ 5. A price increase results in a decrease in a consumer's real income.

______ 6. The demand curve for a normal good slopes down, but the demand curve for an inferior good slopes up.

______ 7. Movements along a demand curve represent changes in quantity demanded.

______ 8. A change in income causes a change in quantity demanded.

______ 9. Generally, economists assume that tastes change frequently and are the causes of changes in demand.

______ 10. An increase in the price of a good provides an incentive to suppliers to switch resources from other goods and use them in producing more of the good with the higher price.

______ 11. The market supply curve represents the sum of individual supply curves.

______ 12. An increase in the price of a required resource shifts the supply curve of the good produced with it to the right.

______ 13. Technological change causes an increase in quantity supplied.

______ 14. Markets reduce the transaction costs of exchange.

______ 15. If price is above the equilibrium price, there is an excess quantity supplied.

______ 16. An increase in demand lowers the equilibrium price.

______ 17. An increase in the price of a required resource will cause a change in quantity demanded of the good produced with it.

______ 18. Disequilibrium can never exist if markets are allowed to operate without government intervention.

______ 19. A price ceiling often leads to an excess quantity demanded.

C. *Multiple Choice*

1. Demand reflects the quantity that consumers
   a. want at alternative prices.
   b. need at alternative prices.
   c. are willing and able to buy at alternative prices.
   d. can buy at alternative prices.
   e. none of the above

2. Which of the following is not held constant in defining the demand schedule?
   a. income
   b. prices of related goods
   c. tastes
   d. price of the good in question
   e. number of consumers

3. The substitution effect of a change in the price of good X is to
   a. increase the demand for good X if its price falls.
   b. decrease the demand for good X if its price rises.
   c. increase the quantity demanded of good X if its price rises.
   d. encourage consumers to substitute more of good X for other goods if X's price falls.
   e. encourage consumers to substitute other goods for good X if X's price falls.

4. A price change
   a. affects the consumer's ability to buy the good.
   b. affects the consumer's willingness to buy the good.
   c. changes the tastes of consumers.
   d. all of the above
   e. a and b

5. The income effect of a price change will be greatest for which of the following goods?
   a. house
   b. automobile
   c. dinner at a restaurant
   d. gasoline
   e. The question cannot be answered without more information.

6. A movement along a demand curve can be caused by a change in
   a. income.
   b. the price of a substitute or complement.
   c. expectations about future prices.
   d. the price of the good in question.
   e. quantity supplied.

7. A change in quantity demanded is caused by a change in
   a. technology.
   b. income.
   c. the price of a related good.
   d. consumer tastes.
   e. quantity supplied.

8. Which of the following will cause an increase in the demand for an inferior good?
   a. an increase in income
   b. an increase in the price of a complement
   c. a drop in preferences for the good
   d. an increase in the number of consumers
   e. all of the above

9. Supply indicates the quantity that producers
   a. are willing to offer for sale at a given price.
   b. can supply for a profit at a given price.
   c. will offer for sale if technical change takes place.
   d. all of the above
   e. a and b only

10. Price and quantity supplied are usually directly related because
   a. higher prices mean that producers are rewarded more for production.
   b. the law of increasing opportunity cost applies.
   c. there is more prestige associated with producing a high-priced good.
   d. changes in technology lead to higher prices.
   e. a and b

11. Which of the following does not change supply?
   a. a change in price of the good in question
   b. a change in technology
   c. a change in producer expectations
   d. a change in the number of producers
   e. all of the above

12. A movement along a supply curve is caused by
   a. a change in the number of consumers.
   b. a change in the number of producers.
   c. technological change.
   d. a change in supply.
   e. a change in quantity demanded.

13. If the price of an alternative good falls, but the price of good X remains the same,
   a. quantity supplied of good X will increase.
   b. quantity supplied of good X will decrease.
   c. quantity demanded of good X will decrease.
   d. supply of good X will decrease.
   e. supply of good X will increase.

14. The larger the market,
   a. the greater the transaction costs.
   b. the greater the degree of specialization.
   c. the less specialization there is.
   d. the lower the price.
   e. the more likely it is that producers will be large.

Exhibit 8

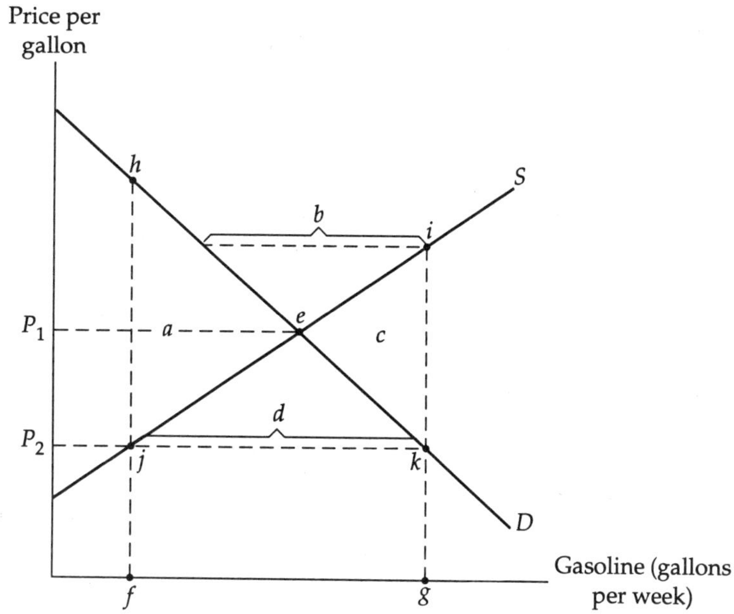

15. In Exhibit 8, equilibrium, shortage, and surplus are indicated by
    a. *e*, *d*, and *b*, respectively.
    b. *e*, *b*, and *d*, respectively.
    c. *e*, *a*, and *c*, respectively.
    d. *a*, *b*, and *d*, respectively.
    e. *c*, *d*, and *e*, respectively.

16. In Exhibit 8, if price is set by the government at P_2, the result is
    a. a surplus represented by *gf*.
    b. a surplus represented by *gi*.
    c. a shortage represented by *gf*.
    d. a shortage represented by *jh*.
    e. a shortage represented by *ke*.

17. An excess quantity demanded tends to
    a. put downward pressure on price.
    b. put upward pressure on price.
    c. cause demand to increase.
    d. cause supply to increase.
    e. b and d

18. A shift in the supply curve with demand held constant will
    a. cause equilibrium quantity to change in the same direction and equilibrium price to change in the opposite direction.
    b. cause equilibrium quantity to change in the opposite direction and equilibrium price to change in the same direction.
    c. cause both equilibrium quantity and equilibrium price to change in the same direction.
    d. cause both equilibrium quantity and equilibrium price to change in the opposite direction.
    e. cause changes that cannot be predicted without more information.

D. *Discussion Questions*

1. Explain why there is an inverse relationship between quantity demanded and price.

2. Explain the difference between a change in demand and a change in quantity demanded.

3. The correct answer to multiple choice question 7 is *a*. Why?

4. Explain the substitution effect and the income effect of a price change.

5. What would be the effect on the current price of coffee in this country if a period of unseasonably cold weather in Brazil destroyed a large portion of the coffee trees there?

6. Why are economists reluctant to attribute a change in demand to a change in taste?

7. Explain why there is usually a direct relationship between quantity supplied and price.

8. What is the effect on the supply of corn of an increase in the price of wheat?

9. A change in quantity demanded is caused by a change in price, and a change in quantity supplied is caused by a change in price. What causes the price to change?

10. In Exhibit 9, what are the results if the government sets the price of gasoline at $1.00 per gallon? What are the results if the price is set at 50 cents a gallon? How can these results be handled by the government?

Exhibit 9

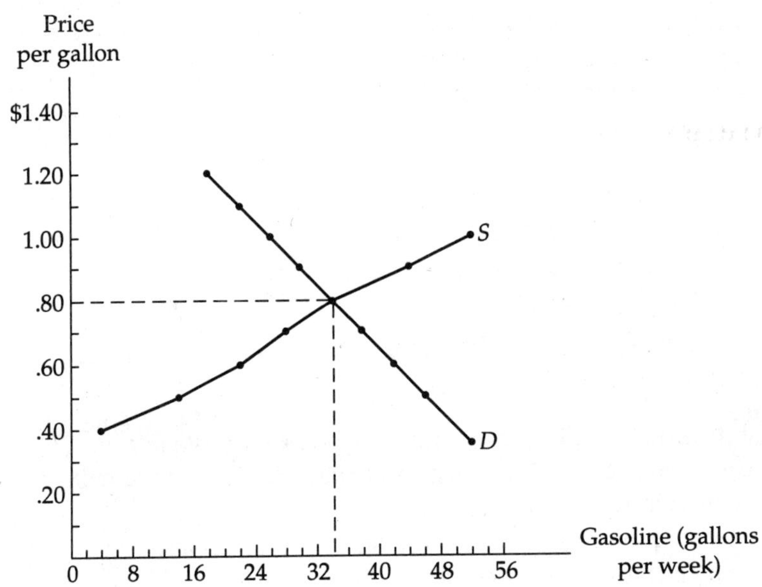

11. What are the effects on a market if demand increases and supply decreases?

12. Tickets for popular sporting events are often scalped at prices considerably above the prices printed on them. Using the concepts of supply and demand, explain why this happens. Why do those who produce the sporting events set such "low" prices for tickets when they know scalpers get much more?

13. In the mid-1970s no one had a personal computer at home. Today many people do. Using demand and supply curves, show the market for personal computers in the mid-1970s and today. Explain the difference between then and now.

14. Explain why disequilibrium can occur even in markets that are allowed to operate freely.

15. Offer a brief explanation for each of the following empirical observations:
    a. Americans began importing large quantities of Japanese autos in the 1970s.
    b. The price of medical care has increased substantially in recent years.
    c. A smaller proportion of the population smokes today than did so 20 years ago.
    d. Cable TV channels that show movies for a monthly fee have been losing viewers for the last couple of years.
    e. The number of people using the services of airlines has increased substantially over the last 15 years.

VII. ANSWERS

A. Completion

1. willing; able
2. substitution; income
3. normal
4. substitutes
5. quantity demanded; demand
6. quantity supplied
7. increase
8. Alternative goods
9. supply
10. transaction costs
11. equilibrium
12. surplus
13. quantity supplied
14. shortages

B. True/False

1. True
2. False. A demand schedule indicates willingness and ability to buy.
3. True
4. True
5. True
6. False
7. True
8. False
9. False
10. True
11. True
12. False
13. False
14. True
15. True
16. False
17. True. Supply of the good falls, raising the price and thus reducing the quantity demanded.
18. False
19. True

C. *Multiple Choice*

1. c
2. d
3. d
4. e
5. a
6. d
7. a
8. d
9. a
10. e
11. a
12. a
13. e
14. b
15. a
16. c
17. b
18. a

D. *Discussion Questions*

1. There is an inverse relationship between quantity demanded and price because people are willing and able to buy more at a lower price, other things constant. People are willing to buy more because of the substitution effect—they can substitute more of the lower priced good for the higher priced good. People also are able to buy more at a lower price because of the income effect—their real incomes have increased.

2. A change in quantity demanded occurs when there is a change in the price of the good. A change in demand occurs when there is a change in any factor that affects demand other than price. Changes in income, tastes, the prices of substitutes or complements, expectations about price and income in the future, and the number or composition of consumers in the market can all cause a change in demand. In these cases, the quantity demanded at each price changes, causing a change in the entire demand schedule, which shows up as a shift of the demand curve. A change in quantity demanded is a movement along the demand curve.

3. A change in quantity demanded is caused by a change in price. The change in price must be caused by a change in supply. Technology (answer *a*) is the only choice that causes supply to change.

4. When the price of one good goes up while the prices of all other goods remain constant, the good becomes relatively more costly. Consequently, some people consume less of the more costly good and more of other goods. This is the substitution effect. A price change also affects one's real income—that is, it causes an income effect. If real income increases, the consumer will want to buy more normal goods and fewer inferior goods; if real income decreases, the opposite will occur.

5. Unseasonably cold weather in Brazil would cause the current price of coffee in this country to rise because consumers would expect a shortage of coffee and thus a higher price in the future; this expectation would increase demand today. Further, suppliers would expect a higher price in the future; this expectation would induce them to remove some coffee from the market today and keep it to sell in the future. Hence, demand would increase and supply would decrease, so price would have to increase.

6. Tastes cannot be directly observed or measured. Hence, one can always attribute a change in demand to a change in taste and never be proven wrong. Because it is not observable, taste is not a good explanation of behavior. Since price and income changes can be observed, they are more useful as explanations of consumer behavior.

7. Producers are more willing and able to supply units at higher prices. They are more willing because the reward they earn by producing the product increases as price increases. They are also more able because higher prices allow them to pay the opportunity costs of resources used to produce the good. The law of increasing opportunity costs tells us that as production expands, opportunity costs increase. A higher price is required to cover these increased costs.

8. An increase in the price of wheat encourages producers to increase production of wheat, which takes resources. Some of these resources are likely to come from corn production, so the supply of corn will decrease.

9. A change in demand causes a change in price, which then causes a change in quantity supplied. A change in supply causes a change in price, which then causes a change in quantity demanded. So, price changes whenever a factor other than price causes either demand or supply to change.

10. If the price is set at $1.00 per gallon, there is an excess quantity supplied; 52 gallons are supplied but only 26 gallons are demanded. Someone must purchase the extra 26 gallons (presumably the government). When the price is 50 cents per gallon, there is an excess quantity demanded, since 46 gallons are demanded but only 14 gallons are supplied. Some way must be found to ration these 14 gallons of gasoline among those who want it.

11. The price increases. The quantity purchased either increases or decreases, depending on whether the demand change or the supply change is greater.

12. Refer to the following exhibit. There are 60,000 tickets available, a number corresponding to the capacity of the stadium. $80 is the price that would clear the market, but the producers of the sporting event charge only $40. Hence, there is an excess demand for the tickets. Some who get the tickets would rather make a profit by selling them for the market-clearing price, $80, than go to the game, so they scalp their tickets. The people who set the price may set it low because they do not know what price is best or because it tends to be the best price on average.

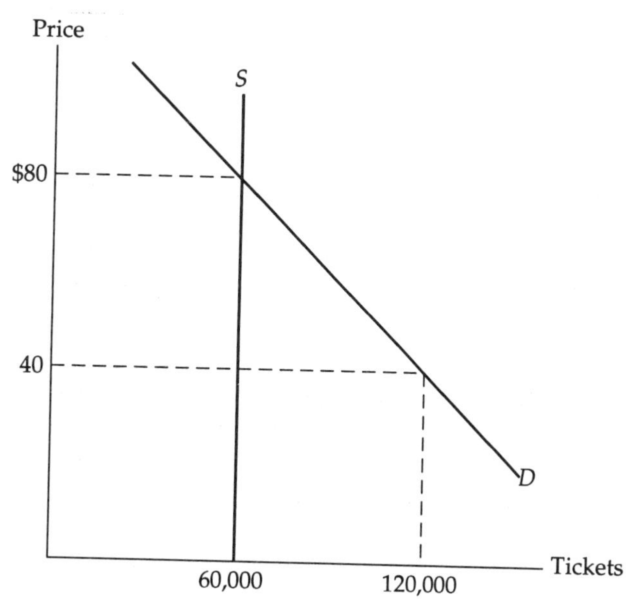

13. The following exhibit illustrates the answer to this question. Demand in the 1970s is indicated by *D*; supply is indicated by *S*. The supply curve intersects the vertical axis above the point where the demand curve intersects the vertical axis. This indicates that in the 1970s the cost of producing personal computers was too high, given the demand. Because of technological changes, the supply curve has shifted out to *S´*. The demand curve has also shifted out, to *D´*, indicating increased demand. Demand has increased in part because of the increase in the availability of complementary goods such as computer games and software to make the personal computer useful in homes. The equilibrium price, $2,000, and quantity, 100,000, are indicated by point *e*.

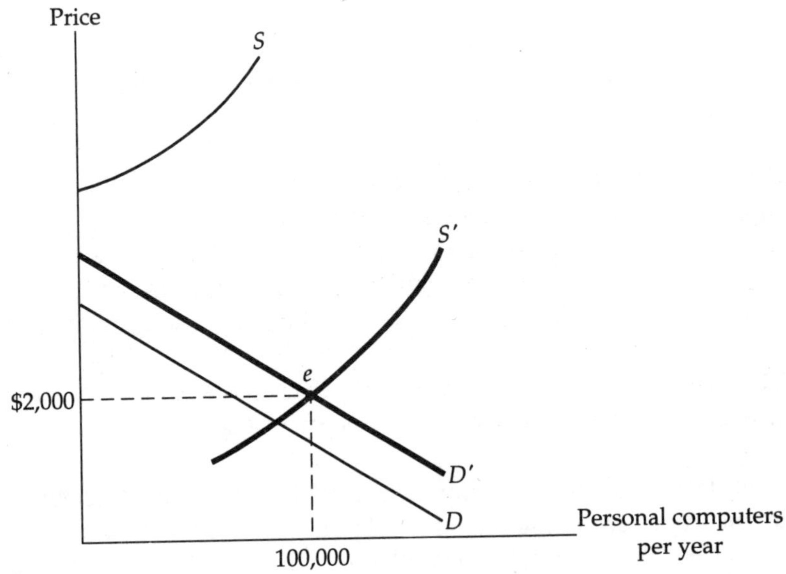

14. Disequilibrium exists whenever quantity demanded does not equal quantity supplied at the market price. If demand increases, there is an excess quantity demanded, which puts upward pressure on price. When price moves to the new equilibrium price, equilibrium is restored.

15. a. The price of gasoline rose significantly in the 1970s, decreasing the demand for cars that use a lot of gasoline. Since Japanese cars were more fuel efficient than American cars, imports of Japanese autos increased.
    b. Increased insurance coverage through Medicare and Medicaid programs has increased demand for medical care, raising the price. Second, technical changes have made medical treatment better, which also has caused greater expenditures on medical care.
    c. To explain the change in smoking habits, we can only argue that tastes are changing, since the relative price of cigarettes has not changed very much, and increases in income do not change smoking habits very much. The increased awareness of the link between smoking and cancer has contributed to a change in tastes.
    d. The price of a substitute good has decreased—that is, the availability of video recorders and inexpensive movie rental outlets have decreased the demand for movie channels.
    e. With the deregulation of the airline industry, the price of air travel fell; this encouraged people to travel more by air. That is, there has been an increase in quantity demanded.

CHAPTER 4

The Economic Actors: Households, Firms, Governments, and the Rest of the World

I. INTRODUCTION

This chapter introduces the economic agents whose behavior we will analyze in the coming chapters. Of these, households are the most important because the demand for goods and services originates with households, and the resources used to produce goods and services are owned by households. Firms, governments, and the rest of the world are in some sense fictional characters—for example, there is no individual known as "Government" who makes decisions. Rather, people make decisions.

II. OUTLINE

1. The Household. The decisions of households are major factors in determining what is produced.

   1.1 The Evolution of the Household
      a. In earlier times, most households were farm families who were relatively self-reliant.
      b. Industrialization and urbanization altered the role of families in production.
      c. Since World War II, women, especially married women, have entered the labor force in significant numbers.
      d. Many two-income households demand more goods and services in product markets because they produce fewer goods and services at home.

   1.2 Households Maximize Utility
      a. Households are viewed as rational decision makers.
      b. Utility maximization is based on each household's subjective goals.

   1.3 Households as Resource Suppliers
      a. All resources are owned by households.
      b. Households can use resources to produce goods and services within the home.
      c. Households can supply their resources to firms or to governments.
      d. Labor is the most valuable resource owned by most households.

   1.4 Households as Demanders of Goods and Services
      a. Households can allocate money in three ways:
         (1) To personal consumption expenditures
         (2) To savings
         (3) To taxes
      b. Personal consumption is broken down into three categories:
         (1) Durable goods
         (2) Nondurable goods
         (3) Services

2. The Firm

2.1 Transaction Costs and Evolution of the Firm

a. Most production takes place outside the home because of the benefits of specialization and comparative advantage and because transaction costs make it too costly to use markets for every transaction.
b. During the Cottage Industry era, entrepreneurs arranged for production of goods and services and sold them to consumers. Production took place in the home.
c. During the Industrial Revolution, technological developments led to the organization of work in factories.
d. Firms are economic units formed by entrepreneurs to produce goods and services.
e. Firms seek to maximize profits.

2.2 Why Do Firms Specialize?

a. As firms become larger, the costs of internal coordination of all steps of a process begin to exceed the benefits; firms maintain efficiency by specializing in certain aspects of production and purchasing other inputs from other specialists.
b. Different entrepreneurs have different abilities.

2.3 Why Does Household Production Still Exist?

a. Households produce at home when the opportunity cost of home production is less than the opportunity cost of using the market.
b. Some household production requires few specialized resources.
c. People can avoid taxes by relying on household production instead of on market purchases.
d. Household production reduces transaction costs in some cases.
e. Technological advances have made household production more efficient in some cases.

2.4 *Case Study:* The Electronic Cottage

2.5 Kinds of Firms

a. A *sole proprietorship* is a single-owner firm.
   (1) Advantages
      (a) Owner in complete control
      (b) Easy to organize
   (2) Disadvantages
      (a) Unlimited liability
      (b) Difficult to raise money for construction and expansion
      (c) Business generally ends at death of owner.
b. A *partnership* is two or more individuals working together in return for a share of the profit or loss.
   (1) Advantages
      (a) Relatively easy to form
      (b) Easier to raise startup funds
   (2) Disadvantages
      (a) Decision making is more difficult.
      (b) Each partner is liable for the debts of the partnership.
      (c) Death or departure of one partner necessitates reorganization.

c. A *corporation* is a legal entity recognized by the state and treated as if it were an individual.
   (1) Advantages
      (a) Easy to amass large sums of financing
      (b) Liability for the firm's losses limited to the value of an owner's stock
   (2) Disadvantages
      (a) Individual stockholder has little control over the firm's decisions.
      (b) Corporate profits passed on to stockholders are taxed twice.
   (3) The *S corporation* is a hybrid type of corporation.
      (a) The S corporation provides limited liability.
      (b) Corporate profits are taxed only once.
      (c) A firm must have no more than 35 stockholders to qualify as an S corporation.

2.6 Nonprofit Institutions

3. The Government

3.1 The Role of Government
   a. Government establishes and enforces the rules of the game: government protects private property and enforces contracts.
   b. Antitrust laws attempt to promote competition by preventing collusion.
   c. Government regulates natural monopolies.
   d. Government produces public goods.
   e. Government deals with problems associated with externalities.
   f. Government attempts to promote a more equal distribution of income.
   g. Government attempts to promote full employment, price stability, and economic growth.

3.2 Government's Structure and Objectives
   a. The United States has a federal system of government.
   b. It is difficult to define the objectives of the government. One useful theory is that elected officials are vote maximizers.
   c. Market exchange is based on voluntary exchange; public political choices may be enforced by the policing power of the government.
   d. Prices in the political system are not necessarily linked to costs.

3.3 Size and Growth of U.S. Government
   a. Government spending as a percentage of gross national product has increased from 10 percent in 1929 to 34 percent in 1995.
   b. The major source of growth has been federal outlays, particularly for Social Security and other transfer programs.

3.4 Sources of Government Revenue. Most of the government's revenue comes from income, sales, and property taxes.

3.5 Tax Principles and Tax Incidence
   a. Some think taxes should be based on the principle of ability to pay.
   b. Others think taxes should be based on the principle of benefits received.

c. Tax incidence indicates who actually bears the burden of the tax.
d. Important tax terms
    (1) *Marginal tax rate*: how much of each additional dollar of income must be paid in taxes
    (2) *Proportional taxes*: taxes for which the percentage of income paid is constant as income increases
    (3) *Progressive taxes*: taxes for which the percentage of income paid increases as income increases
    (4) *Regressive taxes*: taxes for which the percentage of income paid decreases as income increases

4. The Rest of the World. The rest of the world consists of the households, firms, and governments of other countries. Some countries have formed economic alliances.

4.1 International Trade
a. International trade occurs because the opportunity cost of producing specific goods differs across countries.
b. The volume of U.S. trade with the rest of the world has increased dramatically since 1970.
c. The merchandise trade balance equals the value of commodities exported minus the value of commodities imported.
d. A nation's balance of payments is the record of transactions between its residents and the residents of the rest of the world.

4.2 Exchange Rates
a. *Foreign exchange* is the currency of another country that is used to carry out international transactions.
b. The exchange rate measures the price of one currency in terms of another.

4.3 Trade Restrictions
a. Trade restrictions include
    (1) Tariffs, or taxes on imports and exports
    (2) Quotas, or legal limits on the quantity of a commodity that can be imported or exported
    (3) Other restrictions
b. Restrictions tend to benefit domestic producers and to harm consumers.

4.4 *Case Study:* The World of Automobiles

III. DISCUSSION

The Household

Households are the most important economic agents because they are the ultimate demanders of goods and services and ultimate suppliers of all resources. Households make decisions about what goods and services to buy and what resources to sell so as to maximize *utility*. Utility is a subjective concept; activities that provide utility to one household may not be desirable to another.

Households receive income when they sell their resources to either firms or governments. The most important resource owned by most households is the labor services of family members. Labor earnings account for the majority of personal income in the United States. Most of the income received is spent on personal consumption of both durable and nondurable goods and services. The rest of the income is either saved or spent on taxes.

The Firm

A hundred years ago most households produced most of what they consumed. Today, households purchase most of the goods and services they consume from firms. Increased specialization, fueled by technological change and increased industrialization, explains much of the change in household production and consumption. Firms developed to capture many of the gains from increased specialization. The transaction costs associated with households' attempting to contract with all the individual resource owners needed to produce even simple products are too great. Entrepreneurs handle these contracts so that exchange can occur between households and firms.

Production still takes place within the home if the task requires very few specialized resources and is easy for households to perform. Generally, households will perform tasks whenever the opportunity cost of home production is less than the opportunity cost of purchasing the good or service in the marketplace.

Firms tend to specialize in certain tasks rather than produce everything. Entrepreneurs also specialize; an entrepreneur who is good at producing automobiles may not be good at finding oil. Firm size also tends to be limited because of the costs associated with coordinating the activities of more and more people. (Make sure you are familiar with the types of firms and their relative strengths and weaknesses.)

The Government

Not all goods are produced by households and firms. Voluntary exchange does not always produce all goods that society desires and does not always produce goods in an optimal manner. The government exists to handle situations that the market economy cannot handle adequately. One function of government is to promote an environment in which voluntary exchange can take place. That is, the government defines and enforces property rights so that theft and failure to fulfill contracts are limited.

The government also tries to limit the effects of *monopoly* in the economy. Some goods are produced in ways that make it most efficient for a single firm to supply the entire market. The government regulates such *natural monopolies* so that firms do not charge higher prices than necessary. Firms sometimes get together to try to raise prices above the competitive level; the government enacts antitrust laws designed to limit this behavior.

Another important role for the government is to provide public goods. A *public good* is a good that is available to everyone once it is produced. Private firms usually will not produce public goods in the quantities that society wishes or needs because people who have not paid for use of public goods can still consume them. The government, however, can produce public goods and force people to pay for them through taxes. One example of a public good is national defense.

The government also intervenes in the economy to correct the problems associated with *externalities*, which are unpriced by-products of consumption or production. Reckless behavior (brought on by consumption of too much beer) and pollution (caused by industrial production) are examples of negative externalities; increased voting rates (a by-product of consumption of education) and less need for public landfills (a by-product of producing cardboard with recycled paper) are examples of positive externalities.

Finally, government also tries to promote equal distribution of income, full employment, price stability, and economic growth. A progressive tax system combined with *transfer payments* to the poor is used to promote the first goal; *fiscal* and *monetary policy* are used to promote the latter three goals.

The Rest of the World

People in the United States often trade with people in other countries. The rest of the world consists of all the other countries in the world. International trade occurs because the opportunity costs of producing specific goods differ across countries. A country exports goods for which its opportunity costs are relatively low. Even though international trade creates economic gains, most countries impose some sort of trade restrictions. These restrictions tend to benefit domestic producers at the expense of domestic consumers.

Trade with other countries involves using other currencies. If an American buys a sweater from an English firm, the sweater manufacturer expects to be paid in British pounds. *Foreign exchange*, the currency of other countries needed to carry out international transactions, can be bought and sold in foreign exchange markets. The *exchange rate* measures the price of one currency in terms of another. The *balance of payments* is the record of transactions between residents of one country and residents of the rest of the world.

IV. LAGNIAPPE

More on Households

We can see more clearly the role of households as suppliers of resources and buyers of goods by looking at the Jones family. Mr. Jones owns his own hardware store. Mrs. Jones works as an accountant for a corporation in the area. The family owns stock in the company where Mrs. Jones works, and they own government bonds. The family is also renting out a house they own.

Mr. Jones's income is classified as proprietor's income. Mrs. Jones earns a salary. The dividends they receive from their stock are another form of income, as is the interest from the government bonds. Finally, they receive rental income from the tenants who live in the house they own.

The Jones family earns money from the sale of the resources mentioned here. The family also purchases goods and services. Purchases of goods and services provide revenues for firms. The Jones's taxes provide revenue to the government, which helps pay the salaries of government workers. Their savings also are used by others: government bonds help finance government activity and the stock helps finance investments of the firm.

Question to Think About: How does government borrowing fit into the flow of expenditures and receipts discussed here?

Quasi-Public Goods

National defense is a public good because it is impossible to prevent nonpayers from receiving the benefits of the good once it is produced. Some goods do not have all the characteristics of a public good but are close enough so that the government generally provides them. For example, nonpayers can be excluded from receiving fire or police protection. But the high cost of determining whether someone who has just been mugged has paid for police protection makes it more efficient for government to provide police protection for all. Similarly, fire protection is provided for all even though it is possible not to serve nonpayers.

Question to Think About: On what other grounds besides those mentioned here might government-sponsored fire protection be extended to all citizens?

V. KEY TERMS

Utility
Transfer payments
Personal consumption
Firms
Sole proprietorship
Partnership
Corporation
Limited liability
S corporation
Market failure
Monopoly
Natural monopoly
Public good
Externality
Fiscal policy
Monetary policy
Tax incidence
Proportional taxes
Progressive taxes
Regressive taxes
Rest of the world
Merchandise trade balance
Balance of payments
Foreign exchange
Exchange rate
Tariff
Quota

VI. QUESTIONS

A. *Completion*

1. Households are assumed to maximize their levels of satisfaction, or ________________.

2. Some households receive ________________ from the government.

3. Most personal income goes to ________________.

4. ________________ are people who work for themselves.

5. The gains made possible by one firm's coordinating resources are limited because those running the firm have ________________.

6. The most common form of business is a ________________.

7. Stockholders are protected in the case of bankruptcy by the idea of ________________.

8. If a good is available to all once it is produced, it is a ________________ good.

9. ________________ externalities convey unpriced benefits.

10. The government's regulation of the money supply is called ________________.

11. ________________ policy involves the government's taxing and spending powers.

12. Under ________________, the percentage of income paid in taxes decreases as income increases.

13. Legal limits on the quantities of particular goods that can be imported are called ________________.

14. The ________________ measures the price of one currency in terms of another.

15. The merchandise trade balance is one component of a country's ________________.

16. Households demand goods and services in the ________________ and supply resources in the ________________.

B. *True/False*

______ 1. The decisions made by households about consuming goods and services determine what is produced.

______ 2. Utility maximization is based on an objective standard.

______ 3. All resources are owned ultimately by households.

______ 4. Rents and dividends make up about one-quarter of all personal income.

______ 5. For most households, personal consumption expenditures use the largest share of personal income.

______ 6. Farm families tend to be more self-sufficient than urban families.

______ 7. Firms exist because of transaction costs.

______ 8. Households with the highest opportunity cost of time tend to hire others to perform household tasks rather than to engage in household production.

______ 9. Partnerships offer limited liability.

______ 10. The bulk of all business sales are made by corporations.

______ 11. Market transactions generally reflect private benefits and costs as well as external benefits and costs.

______ 12. A natural monopoly exists when one firm controls all of a natural resource.

______ 13. Coercion is often a part of government involvement in the economy.

______ 14. In recent years, local and state governments have been growing faster than the federal government.

______ 15. Sales taxes provide the bulk of revenues to most states.

______ 16. The gasoline tax is based on the principle of benefits received.

______ 17. The marginal tax rate indicates how much of each additional dollar earned is paid in taxes.

______ 18. Trade restrictions are imposed to benefit domestic consumers.

______ 19. An increase in the dollar price of the yen is associated with a decrease in the yen price of the dollar.

______ 20. It is impossible to run a deficit in all accounts in the balance of payments.

______ 21. Demand and supply apply to product markets but not to resource markets.

C. *Multiple Choice*

1. Utility is
   a. a statement about who consumes a good or service.
   b. a measure of the usefulness of a good.
   c. the satisfaction received from consuming a good or service.
   d. the satisfaction received from making a decision.
   e. none of the above.

2. Which of the following could be produced either by individual households or by firms?
   a. lawn care
   b. cleaning services
   c. cooking
   d. child care
   e. all of the above

3. The majority of personal income in the United States comes from
   a. labor earnings.
   b. ownership of land.
   c. ownership of capital.
   d. profits and dividends.
   e. the sum of b, c, and d.

4. The service sector has been growing rapidly in recent years because
   a. households are producing fewer of these services themselves.
   b. the opportunity cost of time for many households has increased.
   c. more married women are in the labor force.
   d. all of the above
   e. none of the above

5. Economists who have studied labor markets attribute the increase since World War II in the number of women who work outside the home to
   a. the high cost of living, which requires a family to have two incomes to maintain its standard of living.
   b. increasing demand for labor, which has raised wages and expanded job opportunities.
   c. inclusion of women under the Civil Rights Act.
   d. declines in the number of women who have children and delays in getting married.
   e. increasing college attendance by women relative to men.

6. Production by firms can be explained by
   a. increased specialization.
   b. increased specialization and comparative advantage.
   c. increased specialization and positive transaction costs.
   d. tax incentives.
   e. b and d.

7. Which of the following is most likely to be purchased from a firm rather than produced by the household?
   a. termite control
   b. child care
   c. washing the car
   d. painting the house
   e. putting in storm windows

8. Firms tend to specialize because
   a. entrepreneurs tend to have different abilities.
   b. the costs of coordinating and monitoring increase as the firm gets larger.
   c. the market does a poor job of coordinating economic activity.
   d. a and b
   e. b and c

9. Corporations account for the majority of sales in the economy because
   a. the corporation is the easiest form of business to begin.
   b. there are tax advantages for corporations that are not available to sole proprietorships or partnerships.
   c. corporations can more easily raise large sums for financing projects.
   d. owners have the greatest control over the decision making of the firm.
   e. a, b, and c

10. A natural monopoly evolves when
    a. there is only one firm in the industry.
    b. it is cheaper for one firm than for two or more firms to serve the market.
    c. the government establishes one firm as the only firm in a market.
    d. public goods are produced.
    e. firms successfully collude.

11. According to one theory of government behavior, elected officials attempt to maximize which of the following?
    a. utility
    b. votes
    c. the size of their administrative agencies
    d. profits
    e. tax revenues

12. Since World War II, federal government revenues have increasingly come from
    a. excise taxes.
    b. personal income taxes.
    c. corporate income taxes.
    d. payroll taxes.
    e. tariffs.

13. Which of the following sources of government revenue is based on the individual's ability to pay?
    a. the gasoline tax
    b. the toll on a government-owned bridge
    c. the progressive income tax
    d. the admission charge to a federal park
    e. all of the above

14. In the absence of trade restrictions, exchange among countries
    a. is due to cultural differences.
    b. follows the law of comparative advantage.
    c. tends to harm consumers in less developed countries.
    d. benefits only those who are engaged in international trade.
    e. has declined in importance in the last twenty years.

15. The exchange rate of a foreign currency will tend to increase if
    a. demand for that country's goods increases.
    b. the value of the dollar also increases.
    c. the supply of the foreign currency in foreign exchange markets increases.
    d. people in that country increase their import buying.
    e. all of the above

16. If a firm receives $100 million from selling its products, which portion of the $100 million must it give to resource owners?
    a. the portion that is interest
    b. the portion that is profit
    c. the portion that is the return on capital
    d. b and c
    e. The firm must give up the entire $100 million to resource owners.

17. If consumers buy $10 million worth of dolls from toy companies, the firms
    a. pay resource owners all of the $10 million except the amount that is profit.
    b. pay resource owners all of the $10 million except the amount that goes to stockholders.
    c. pay workers and suppliers of materials part of the $10 million. Profits, interest, and rent do not go to resource owners.
    d. pay the entire $10 million to resource owners.
    e. none of the above

D. *Discussion Questions*

1. Firms often own resources—for example, many oil firms own oil wells. How, then, can the text say that all resources are owned by households?

2. Why is the household considered the most important actor in the economy?

3. Discuss the factors that have changed the household in the last hundred years. What effects have these changes had on the economy?

4. The text says that the rise of two-worker families reduces the advantages of specialized resources within the family. Explain.

5. Over the years, food prices at grocery stores have increased faster than the prices received by farmers. Can you offer a (partial) explanation for this?

6. Discuss the factors that determine whether tasks are performed by members of a household or by firms.

7. What are the weaknesses and strengths of the various forms of business? Why do corporations tend to be so much larger than sole proprietorships or partnerships?

8. Why does the government, rather than private firms, provide the judicial system?

9. What is a public good? Why does the government tend to produce public goods?

10. Why is it so difficult to determine the objectives of the government?

11. How does market exchange differ from exchange in political markets?

12. Discuss the two principles of taxation. Why are not all taxes collected on the basis of benefits received?

13. Why would a country impose trade restrictions if free trade is beneficial to the country?

14. What would be the effect of an increased demand in the United States for German goods?

15. During the 1980s, the amount of imports Americans purchased was greater than the amount of exports they sold. How was the deficit financed?

VII. ANSWERS

A. *Completion*

1. utility
2. transfer payments
3. personal consumption expenditures
4. Proprietors
5. bounded rationality
6. sole proprietorship
7. limited liability
8. public
9. Positive
10. monetary policy
11. Fiscal
12. regressive taxation
13. quotas
14. exchange rate
15. balance of payments
16. product market; resource market

B. *True/False*

1. True
2. False
3. True
4. False
5. True
6. True
7. True
8. True
9. False
10. True
11. False
12. False
13. True
14. False
15. True
16. True
17. True
18. False
19. True
20. True
21. False

C. *Multiple Choice*

1. c
2. e
3. a
4. d
5. b
6. c
7. a
8. d
9. c
10. b
11. b
12. d
13. c
14. b
15. a
16. e
17. d

D. *Discussion Questions*

1. Firms are owned by individual stockholders, so ultimately all resources are owned by households.

2. Households are the ultimate demanders of goods and services, and they determine what will be produced by what they are willing and able to purchase. Households also ultimately supply all resources used in production.

3. Technological change increased farm productivity, and the Industrial Revolution created opportunities for employment off the farm. As people left farms and moved to cities, family size decreased and families undertook less home production of many goods and services. The increased demand for goods and services by households has been met by firms. The demand for such services increased as married women entered the labor force in larger numbers.

4. The higher opportunity cost of time for women who work outside the home implies that they will substitute market-produced goods for home-produced goods on many occasions. The reduced reliance on household production reduces the advantages of specialization in the home.

5. The increase in two-income families reduced the amount of "cooking from scratch" performed by households. Instead, families purchase foods that take less time to prepare. Such foods are already processed, at least to some degree, and this extra preparation by producers increases the price.

6. In general, a task will be performed by a household if the opportunity cost of home production is less than the opportunity cost of purchasing the good or service from a firm. The opportunity cost of home production depends on how specialized the required resources are and on the opportunity cost of time for the members of the family. A household may also perform certain tasks in order to have more control over the final products or to avoid taxes. In general, as the family income increases, more services will be bought rather than produced by members of the household.

7. Both sole proprietorships and partnerships are fairly easy to establish. The major weakness of each is the limited ability to raise financial capital for starting the company or increasing productive capacity. Owners and partners are also more exposed to risk in the case of lawsuits, and the death or departure of an owner can necessitate closing or reorganizing the firm. Corporations are more difficult to establish, but they provide limited liability and a much greater ability to raise financial capital (so they tend to be larger than other types of firms). However, corporate profits are often taxed twice, which is not true of the profits of sole proprietorships or partnerships.

8. Judicial services are not public goods, since it would be possible to exclude nonpayers from the system. However, society deems it inappropriate to rely on private firms to provide judicial services and charge people to use the system because that would put the poor at a disadvantage. A well-run judicial system provides external benefits to society, so providing judicial services is seen as a legitimate role for government.

9. Public goods are goods that nonpayers cannot be prevented from using once the goods are produced. Private firms are not likely to produce public goods because they cannot be assured of payment. The government provides such goods and requires people to pay for them by means of taxes.

10. Government is not a single entity—it includes the federal government, state governments, and local governments. Further, there are many agencies in the various branches of government. The legislative branch may have different objectives than the executive branch, and the agency heads may have different objectives yet. In addition, citizens disagree about what the objectives of the government should be.

11. Market exchange is voluntary and involves market prices. Exchange in political markets involves votes rather than dollars and often involves coercion, as in the case of the payment of taxes.

12. The two principles of taxation are the principle of ability to pay and the principle of benefits received. Proponents of the former argue that taxes should be based on one's ability to pay, i.e., the rich should pay more than the poor. Proponents of the latter argue that taxes should be related to benefits received from the government. According to this principle, schools should be supported by parents rather than by all taxpayers. Not all taxes can be collected on the basis of benefits received, however, since the actual benefits received are often very difficult to measure. In some cases, people would have an incentive to lie about the benefits they received if it meant a lower tax bill. This would especially be true in the case of public goods. Further, any programs designed to help the poor could not be financed on a benefits received principle—in such cases the people who receive the benefits are too poor to pay the taxes.

13. Countries impose trade restrictions because domestic producers that face competition from cheaper imports lobby for protection.

14. The German goods must be bought with German marks, so the demand for marks would increase. The increased demand for marks would cause the exchange rate to increase. More dollars would be needed to buy a given number of marks, so the dollar prices of the German good would increase.

15. The deficit was financed by borrowing from foreigners.

CHAPTER 5

Introduction to Macroeconomics

I. INTRODUCTION

This chapter presents an overview of the field of macroeconomics. Macroeconomics is the study of the economy as a whole. Topics covered in this chapter include inflation, depression, unemployment, monetary policy, full employment, and stagflation.

II. OUTLINE

1. The National Economy. Macroeconomics is concerned with the overall performance of the economy. The *gross product* is the market value of final goods and services produced in a particular geographic region during a specific period of time.

   1.1 What's Special about the National Economy?
      a. There are great differences between the economies of different countries, so each must be treated as a separate entity.
      b. The focus of macroeconomics is the performance of the national and world economies.

   1.2 Similarities Between the Human Body and the Economy
      a. Money is the medium of exchange that facilitates the exchange of goods and services.
      b. Flows and stocks:
         (1) A flow variable measures an amount per unit of time.
         (2) A stock variable measures an amount at a particular point in time.
      c. Role of expectations. Expectations are often an important determinant of the performance of the economy and are often self-fulfilling.
      d. Differences of opinion. Economists may offer conflicting diagnoses of the problems of the economy and disagree on possible cures.

   1.3 Testing New Theories. It is very difficult to test new macroeconomic theories because there is no laboratory in which controlled experiments can be performed.

   1.4 Knowledge and Performance
      a. As long as the economy runs smoothly, we do not need to know how it operates.
      b. When the economy performs poorly, we need to know how it operates in order to repair it.
      c. Poor theories lead to poor decisions by policymakers.

2. Economic Fluctuations and Growth. The rise and fall of economic activity relative to the long-term growth trend of the economy are called *economic fluctuations*.

2.1 Economic Fluctuation Analysis
   a. A *recession* is any decline in the nation's total production lasting six months or more.
   b. A *depression* is a severe recession lasting more than a year.
   c. The economy generally has periods of expansion and periods of contraction, with total output increasing over the long run.

2.2 *Case Study:* The Global Economy

2.3 Leading Economic Indicators. Certain activities called *leading economic indicators* tend to foreshadow turning points in the business cycle.

3. Aggregate Demand and Aggregate Supply

3.1 Aggregate Output and the Price Level
   a. *Aggregate demand* is the relationship between the price level (an average of all prices in the economy) and total demand for goods and services produced in the economy, other things constant.
   b. *Aggregate output* is the total quantity of all goods and services produced in an economy during a given time period.
   c. The *price level* is a composite measuring the prices on average of all goods.
   d. *Gross domestic product* (GDP), which is the market value of all goods and services in the United States in a year, is the most common measure of aggregate output.
   e. The price level can be measured by the consumer price index or the implicit price deflator.

3.2 Aggregate Demand Curve
   a. The *aggregate demand curve* shows the relation between the price level and aggregate output demanded.
   b. As the price level falls, the aggregate quantity demanded increases.
      (1) People are able to buy more when the price level declines because their real wealth increases.
      (2) A drop in the U.S. price level means that U.S. goods are less expensive relative to foreign goods, so people buy more U.S. goods.

3.3 Aggregate Supply Curve
   a. *Aggregate supply* is the relationship between the price level and aggregate output supplied in the economy, other things constant.
   b. The shape of the aggregate supply curve is a much-debated topic.

3.4 Equilibrium. The intersection of the aggregate demand and aggregate supply curves yields the equilibrium price level and aggregate output. Higher levels of aggregate output reflect higher levels of employment.

4. A Short History of the U.S. Economy

4.1 The Great Depression and Before
   a. The economy was characterized by cycles of boom and depression.
   b. The Great Depression of the 1930s was the worst of these depressions.
   c. The cause of the Great Depression was a dramatic shift in aggregate demand due in part to grim expectations and the collapse of the banking system.

4.2 The Age of Keynes: Between the Great Depression and the Early 1970s
   a. John Maynard Keynes argued that the economy might stay in a depression indefinitely.
   b. Keynes's recommendations focused on how to increase aggregate demand through fiscal policy and are called *demand-side policies.*
   c. The Employment Act of 1946 set a federal policy of maintaining "maximum employment, production, and purchasing power."

4.3 The Great Stagflation
   a. Keynesian policies did not work so well in the 1970s, when inflation was associated with economic stagnation.
   b. The problems in the 1970s tended to be associated with declining aggregate supply.

4.4 Experience Since 1980
   a. Supply-side economics emphasizes the importance of aggregate supply and economic incentives.
   b. During the 1980s output increased, unemployment declined, inflation fell and remained low, and the federal deficit increased.

4.5 The Twin Deficits

CASE STUDY: Half Century of Price Levels and Real GDP

III. DISCUSSION

The National Economy

An important measure of the performance of the national economy is the *gross domestic product:* the market value of final goods and services currently produced in the country. We focus on the national economy because there are few differences within a country with respect to economic activity; however, there are considerable differences between countries.

Money is a medium that circulates throughout the economy and facilitates the exchange of goods and services. At any given time there are a certain number of dollars in the economy. This amount of dollars is referred to as the money *stock*. But the average dollar is spent more than once in a year, so we can also speak of money as a *flow* variable. The distinction between stocks and flows is an important one in economics, and you should pay special attention whenever the distinction is made in the text.

Macroeconomics seems difficult to grasp at times. In part this difficulty is due to the key role of expectations. The expectations of economic agents are often self-fulfilling, which sometimes frustrates the efforts of policymakers to stabilize the economy. Another difficulty for students is that macroeconomists often seem to disagree on the problems facing the economy and on the solutions to the problems. Unfortunately, macroeconomic theories are difficult to test because controlled laboratory experiments are not feasible.

Economic Fluctuations and Growth

All industrial market economies experience fluctuating periods of expansion and contraction. Over the long run, economic output tends to increase, but it does not do so without fluctuations. Expansions tend to last longer than contractions, and the overall trend in the United States has been an increase in the standard of living. There are some similarities between various contractions and between various expansions, so economists have tried to look for signals that indicate when a turning point is coming. This process is still rather undeveloped.

Aggregate Demand and Aggregate Supply

The total demand for goods and services at various price levels, other things constant, is known as *aggregate demand.* The aggregate quantity demanded increases as the price level falls. The behavior of the aggregate demand curve is similar to that of a demand curve for a particular commodity, and the reason is similar. At a lower price level people are willing and able to buy more, so the quantity demanded of all goods and services increases. The aggregate quantity supplied at various price levels, other things constant, is known as *aggregate supply*. The shape of the *aggregate supply curve* is a source of debate among economists and will be discussed further in a later chapter. An upward-sloping curve indicates a positive relation between the price level and the quantity of aggregate output supplied. The equilibrium of the economy as a whole is determined by the intersection of the aggregate demand and the aggregate supply curves.

A Short History of the U.S. Economy

Before World War II, the economy was characterized by numerous fluctuations, and the government did not actively intervene to stabilize the economy except in a few rare circumstances. The worst *depression* occurred during the 1930s. In response to this economic event, John Maynard Keynes developed a theory that argued that depressions are not necessarily self-correcting and that if left to itself the economy might remain in a depression for a long period of time. To help restore economic expansion, he argued, the federal government should engage in deficit spending.

Between the end of the Great Depression and the inflation associated with the Vietnam War, Keynesian policies seemed to work well. However, when the aggregate supply shocks of the 1970s led to stagflation, Keynesian policies fell into disrepute. To stimulate aggregate supply, the Reagan administration attempted to increase incentives to work and invest by cutting income taxes. One result was large federal deficits through the 1980s.

IV. LAGNIAPPE

Economic Fluctuations

Economists have long tried to understand economic fluctuations and predict turning points in them. There is still a long way to go. Theories have ranged from associating sunspot activity with economic fluctuations to hypothesizing that activities of entrepreneurs start upswings that ultimately end in recession.

Students may wonder if these economic fluctuations are regular. Since the economy is highly integrated, events that affect one industry often cause repercussions in many other industries. For example, the automobile industry is an important force in the economy. When auto sales are high, so are sales of steel, tires, rubber, and all other inputs used in auto production. Further, the communities where automobile plants are located do well, and people have a lot of money to spend, which benefits other businesses. When auto sales are down, however, the opposite happens, and a downturn in the auto industry causes a downturn in many other industries and communities. A cycle can develop because autos are durable goods. In difficult times people can postpone purchases of new cars. Eventually old cars wear out, however, and people buy new cars. This generates an upswing in auto sales and production.

Question to Think About: What are the repercussions of swings in housing activity?

Expectations After World War II

Economists and business people who believed that the end of World War II would cause a depression similar to the one that preceded the war were proven wrong. During the war, consumer durable goods either were not produced at all or were produced in very small amounts so that the materials that would otherwise go into them could be used to produce military equipment instead. As a result, by the end of the war the durable goods held by households were old and often in disrepair. After the war, the large demand for such products generated many jobs and the depression did not occur. Owners of businesses who believed a downturn was coming tended to be very cautious, failed to expand productive capacity, and were unprepared for the large demand for goods. Firms that expected a business upturn invested heavily and were prepared to meet the large demand. Such firms prospered and expanded in the immediate postwar years.

Question to Think About: Think of firms that expanded during the postwar years and some that did not. How are these firms doing today?

V. KEY TERMS

Gross product
Money
Stock
Flow
Mercantilism
Economic fluctuation
Depression
Recession
Expansion
Leading economic indicators
Aggregate demand
Aggregate output
Price level
Aggregate demand curve
Aggregate supply
Aggregate supply curve
Federal budget deficit
Demand-side economics
Employment Act of 1946
Inflation rate
Stagflation
Supply-side economics

VI. QUESTIONS

A. *Completion*

1. The __________________ is the market value of final goods and services produced in a geographic region in a certain period of time.

2. The focus of __________________ is the performance of the national and world economy.

3. A __________________ variable represents an amount of something at a particular point in time.

4. In economics, __________________ can often be self-fulfilling.

5. __________________ is a policy that restricts international trade so that a country can export more than it imports.

6. A ____________________ is a decline in the nation's total output lasting at least six months.

7. Activities that tend to predict turning points in economic fluctuations are called ____________________ indicators.

8. Aggregate ____________________ consists of all final goods and services produced in the economy.

9. The ____________________ reflects the average prices of goods and services produced in the economy.

10. The most common measure of aggregate output is the ____________________.

11. The aggregate ____________________ curve slopes down.

12. The prevailing view before the Great Depression was that the economy was basically ____________________.

13. The Keynesian approach to promoting full employment focuses on ways to increase aggregate ____________________ and is often called ____________________-side economics.

14. ____________________ is a combination of economic contraction and inflation.

15. Advocates of ____________________-side economics emphasize the importance of economic incentives.

B. *True/False*

______ 1. Macroeconomists tend to agree on how the economy works but disagree on what should be done when the economy performs poorly.

______ 2. Each country answers the three economic questions in different ways.

______ 3. Gross domestic product is a flow variable.

______ 4. The expectations of economic agents are often self-fulfilling.

______ 5. Economic fluctuations tend to affect just a few important sectors of the economy.

______ 6. Over the long run, the total output of the economy tends to increase.

______ 7. A recession is an increase in the unemployment rate.

______ 8. The average expansion and the average contraction in the United States since the end of World War II have been about the same length.

______ 9. Turning points in the economy are identified after the fact.

______ 10. A change in the price level is a change in relative prices.

______ 11. The GDP deflator tracks price changes of all items in the gross domestic product.

______ 12. One reason the aggregate demand curve slopes down is that as the domestic price level falls, people buy more foreign goods.

______ 13. An increase in the supply of resources causes the economy to move along the aggregate supply curve.

______ 14. Higher levels of aggregate output are associated with higher levels of employment.

______ 15. Prior to the Great Depression most economists believed that recessions were natural and self-correcting.

______ 16. John Maynard Keynes argued that the economy was not always self-correcting.

______ 17. The Council of Economic Advisers was established in 1932 by President Roosevelt.

______ 18. An important part of demand-side economics is the idea that public policy should focus on the incentives people have to produce goods and services.

______ 19. Stagflation is a combination of an economic contraction and inflation.

______ 20. The goal of supply-side economics is to increase aggregate output while reducing the price level.

C. *Multiple Choice*

1. Which of the following would not be included in the gross domestic product?
   a. a meal at a restaurant
   b. an afternoon spent mowing your lawn
   c. tuition at a private college
   d. purchase of an airline ticket
   e. a trip to the car wash

2. Which of the following is a flow variable?
   a. the total deposits in all checking accounts today
   b. the total shares of all stocks outstanding
   c. a family's weekly income
   d. the number of people in the labor force
   e. the national debt

3. The first term is a flow and the second a stock in all but which one of the following pairs?
   a. income; wealth
   b. annual income tax collections; national debt
   c. a business's receipts; a business's capital stock
   d. a family's weekly spending; the amount in the family's checking account
   e. gross domestic product; the national spending in a year

4. It is difficult to test macroeconomic theories because
   a. economic theories are not testable.
   b. economic variables are impossible to measure.
   c. there is not enough agreement about which theories to test.
   d. the theories cannot be tested in laboratories or controlled settings.
   e. all of the above

5. An expansion
   a. begins when the economy moves above its long-term growth trend.
   b. is the period between a trough and the subsequent peak.
   c. is usually followed by a recession of the same length.
   d. is the period six months before and six months after a peak.
   e. b and c only

6. Compared to those before World War II, recessions since the war have been
   a. shorter.
   b. less severe.
   c. more severe.
   d. more frequent.
   e. both a and b.

7. Which of the following is a leading economic indicator?
   a. gross domestic product
   b. unemployment
   c. the stock market
   d. the NBER
   e. all of the above

8. A change in the price level is a change in
   a. the price of domestic goods relative to imported goods.
   b. the average price of all goods and services produced in the economy.
   c. the price of goods relative to services.
   d. all of the above.
   e. a and b only.

9. An increase in the cost of living
   a. increases aggregate demand.
   b. decreases aggregate supply.
   c. decreases the quantity demanded of aggregate output.
   d. decreases aggregate demand.
   e. increases the quantity demanded of aggregate output.

10. There is an inverse relationship between the price level and the quantity of output demanded, other things constant, because
    a. a reduction in the price level means that consumers can buy more goods and services with their savings.
    b. a reduction in the price level makes domestic goods relatively cheaper than foreign goods and causes an increase in consumption of domestic goods and services.
    c. a reduction in the price level decreases everyone's real wealth so people save less and buy more.
    d. the substitution effect of a lower price level is always greater than the income effect.
    e. a and b

11. The quantity of aggregate output producers supply
    a. rises when the price level rises faster than the cost of production.
    b. is independent of the price level.
    c. rises when wages increase.
    d. decreases when the price level increases.
    e. none of the above

12. Greater output is associated with
    a. higher levels of employment.
    b. reduced unemployment.
    c. a higher price level.
    d. all of the above.
    e. a and b only.

13. If there is a decrease in aggregate demand, the price level will tend to
    a. increase.
    b. remain unchanged.
    c. decrease.
    d. be unpredictable without more information.
    e. decrease in real terms.

14. The Great Depression can be viewed as a
    a. shift to the left of the aggregate supply curve.
    b. shift to the right of the aggregate supply curve.
    c. shift to the left of the aggregate demand curve.
    d. shift to the right of the aggregate demand curve.
    e. shift to the left of aggregate demand and a shift to the right of aggregate supply.

15. Prior to the Great Depression, government policy regarding economic fluctuations was
    a. to let the economy correct itself.
    b. to raise taxes in a depression and cut taxes in a recession.
    c. to follow demand-side economic policies.
    d. to follow supply-side economic policies.
    e. to increase government spending during a recession.

16. According to Keynes, aggregate demand is inherently unstable because
    a. the government is not able to fine-tune the economy.
    b. the investment decisions of business people are often destabilizing.
    c. taxes reduce the incentives people have to work and invest.
    d. the money supply is hard to control.
    e. all of the above

17. An expansionary fiscal policy calls for
    a. a balanced federal budget.
    b. a federal budget deficit.
    c. a federal budget surplus.
    d. an increase in the money supply.
    e. none of the above.

18. The Keynesian approach to macroeconomics is to focus on
    a. increasing aggregate supply.
    b. increasing aggregate demand.
    c. keeping inflation relatively low.
    d. laissez faire.
    e. none of the above.

19. Under the Employment Act of 1946, the federal government is responsible for encouraging
    a. full employment.
    b. maximum production.
    c. maximum purchasing power.
    d. maximum price levels.
    e. a, b, and c.

20. The purpose of the tax cuts in the 1980s was to
    a. increase the incentives for resource owners to supply their resources to productive activity.
    b. decrease the federal deficit.
    c. increase aggregate demand.
    d. decrease aggregate demand.
    e. control the money supply.

D. *Discussion Questions*

1. How is the U.S. national economy different from those of other nations?

2. Distinguish between a stock variable and a flow variable.

3. What role do expectations play in the economy?

4. Why is it difficult to test macroeconomic theories?

5. What are the characteristics of a recession?

6. Why is war associated with economic expansions?

7. How is an aggregate demand curve like a demand curve for a good? How is it different?

8. Explain why the aggregate demand curve slopes down.

9. Suppose the economy is initially in equilibrium. What are the effects on the economy of an increase in labor productivity?

10. What differences are there between the way economists after Keynes and economists prior to Keynes viewed the economy?

11. How has the government's role in the economy today changed from what it was prior to World War II? What caused the change?

12. What is stagflation? What policy did the government implement in the 1980s in an attempt to combat stagflation?

13. How does demand-side economics differ from supply-side economics?

14. Why has real GDP per capita increased in the United States from 1940 to 1995?

VII. ANSWERS

A. *Completion*

1. gross product
2. macroeconomics
3. stock
4. expectations
5. Mercantilism
6. recession
7. leading economic
8. output
9. price level
10. gross domestic product
11. demand
12. self-correcting
13. demand; demand
14. Stagflation
15. supply

B. *True/False*

1. False
2. True
3. True
4. True
5. False
6. True
7. False
8. False. Expansions have been longer than contractions, on average.
9. True
10. False
11. True
12. False. People buy fewer foreign goods.
13. False. The aggregate supply curve shifts.
14. True
15. True
16. True
17. False
18. False
19. True
20. True

C. *Multiple Choice*

1. b
2. c
3. e
4. d
5. b
6. e
7. c
8. e
9. c
10. e
11. a
12. d
13. c
14. c
15. a
16. b
17. b
18. b
19. e
20. a

D. *Discussion Questions*

1. The U.S. national economy differs from those of other nations because the United States has a unique mix of economic resources, a unique cultural and political climate, its own monetary and banking system, and because it answers the three economic questions in its own ways.

2. A stock variable represents an amount of something at a particular time. Examples would include the stock of money in the economy on January 1, the number of cars licensed in the United States today, and the wealth of a family. A flow variable represents an amount per unit of time. Examples would include the number of cars produced in a week, the hours worked in a month, and the income of a family for a year.

3. Expectations often can be self-fulfilling. When consumers and business people are optimistic, jobs are plentiful and provide income for consumers that enables them to buy the goods that are produced. If everyone is pessimistic, then people are fearful to spend money or make investments.

4. There is no lab in which experiments can be performed. Comparisons across nations are tricky because each national economy is a unique blend of economic, cultural, and political conditions. The chance discovery is not very likely.

5. A recession is a decline in a nation's total output lasting at least six months. It is characterized by declining output and increasing unemployment.

6. Wars are characterized by increases in output of goods used by the military, such as planes and tanks; this means that economic activity increases in wartime.

7. The shape of the aggregate demand curve is like the shape of a demand curve for a good in that both slope down. Both also deal with a quantity and a price. However, the quantity for aggregate demand is the total quantity of goods and services produced. The price on a demand curve is a relative price, whereas the price on the aggregate demand curve is an average price for all goods.

8. The quantity of aggregate demand depends in part on household wealth; a reduction in the price level increases the amount of goods and services that can be purchased with a given amount of dollars. Another reason the aggregate demand curve slopes down is that a fall in the price level reduces the price of domestic goods relative to foreign goods; Americans then increase their purchases of U.S. goods and services.

9. Increased labor productivity means increased aggregate supply, represented by a shift to the right of the aggregate supply curve. The increase in aggregate output causes the price level to fall.

10. Prior to Keynes economists believed the economy was basically self-correcting. This meant that they believed a recession would not persist and that counter forces would take effect that would bring the economy out of the recession. After Keynes, most economists believed that the economy could stay in recession for a long time and that the self-correcting tendencies of the economy acted too slowly or were too weak to be relied on.

11. The government takes a much more active role today in trying to stabilize the economy. The Employment Act of 1946 gave the responsibility for full employment and economic growth to the federal government. The Great Depression of the 1930s caused people to reconsider the laissez-faire attitude that prevailed prior to the war.

12. Stagflation is a combination of inflation and high unemployment. In the 1980s the government used tax cuts to try to encourage an increase in aggregate supply to combat stagflation.

13. Demand-side economics seeks to increase output by stimulating aggregate demand; supply-side economics attempts to stimulate aggregate supply. Hence, the former focuses on increasing government spending or stimulating business investments, and the latter focuses on tax cuts to increase the incentives for productive activity.

14. Real GDP per capita has increased because of increases in human capital and physical capital.

CHAPTER 6

Productivity and Growth

I. INTRODUCTION

Economic growth is essential if the standard of living of the population as a whole is to increase. Economists can identify factors that contribute to economic growth. It is much more difficult, however, to manipulate the determinants of growth in any systematic way. In this chapter we examine the sources of growth and recent trends in productivity.

II. OUTLINE

1. U.S. Productivity

1.1 What is Productivity?

a. Productivity refers to how efficiently resources are employed.
b. *Productivity* is defined as the ratio of a specific measure of output to a specific measure of input.

1.2 Labor Productivity

a. *Labor productivity* is the total output divided by total employment.
b. Increases in capital lead to increases in labor productivity.

1.3 The Per-Worker Production Function

a. The *per-worker production function* shows the relation between capital per worker and output per worker.
b. An increase in the amount of capital per worker leads to an increase in the amount of output per worker.
c. Output per worker increases at a decreasing rate because of the law of diminishing marginal returns.
d. An increase in capital causes a movement along the per-worker production function; a change in the quality of capital causes the function to shift.

1.4 Long-Term Productivity Growth

a. U.S. labor productivity grew at an average annual rate of 2.1 percent from 1870 to 1995.
b. Over long time periods, small differences in productivity growth rates generate large differences in the economy's ability to produce.

1.5 The Recent Slowdown in Productivity Growth. There has been a decline in the rate of growth of U.S. labor productivity in the last two decades.

2. Why the Slowdown in Labor Productivity Growth?

2.1 Rate of Capital Formation. A slowdown in the growth rate of capital per worker may have contributed to the slowdown in labor productivity growth.

2.2 Changes in the Labor Force

a. Younger workers tend to be less productive than more experienced workers. The decline in the average age of the labor force as more members of postwar generations entered the labor force could be a cause of the labor productivity slowdown.

b. Student achievement, as measured by standardized test scores, declined from 1967 to 1980.

2.3 Changing Composition of Output. The changing composition of output has also been blamed, since service industries tend to be less capital intensive than manufacturing industries.

2.4 Increased Role of Government. The growth in government regulation, which diverts resources from capital investment into expenditures to comply with the government regulations, has been cited as a cause of the slowdown in productivity growth.

2.5 Huge Budget Deficits. Although some analysts assert that federal deficits lead to massive borrowing, which "crowds out" private investment and thus limits investment in human capital, the link between federal deficits and labor productivity growth remains unclear.

3. Research and Development

3.1 Basic and Applied Research

a. *Basic research* is the search for knowledge without concern for the commercial possibilities of the knowledge.

b. *Applied research* is the application of scientific discoveries to the development of particular products.

c. A technological breakthrough usually becomes embodied in new capital.

3.2 Expenditures for Research and Development. U.S. R&D expenditures as a percent of GDP is high compared to other countries.

3.3 Patents and Productivity

a. Patents granted to U.S. corporations and individuals fell during the 1970s.

b. The U.S. federal government has tried to stimulate research activity by providing special tax incentives.

3.4 *Case Study:* Computers and Productivity

4. Other Issues of Technology and Growth

4.1 Industrial Policy

a. *Industrial policy* refers to the idea that the government should encourage certain technologies and industries to gain an advantage over foreign competition.

b. The government support comes in the form of subsidies, tax breaks, and regulations.

4.2 *Case Study:* Picking Technological Winners

4.3 Does Technological Change Lead to Unemployment?
   a. Since technological change often reduces the number of workers needed to produce a given amount of output, some think it causes unemployment.
   b. Empirical evidence suggests that unemployment rates are lower in countries that have experienced a great deal of technological change.

4.4 Output Per Capita
   a. The slowdown in economic growth experienced by the United States after 1973 also occurred in other developed countries.
   b. The U.S. decline was less than that in many other countries.

4.5 Do Economies Converge?
   a. The *convergence theory* argues that economies around the world will grow more alike over time.
   b. Differences in the quality of human capital across countries may prevent convergence.

III. DISCUSSION

U.S. Productivity

Productivity, which is a measure of how efficiently resources are used, is the ratio of a specific measure of output to a specific measure of input. *Labor productivity*, the most commonly used measure of productivity, is the ratio of GDP to total employment. The growth rate in labor productivity is used to measure changes in the economy's productive capability over time.

Labor productivity depends critically on the quantity and quality of capital for labor to use. This capital includes both physical and human capital. The *per-worker production function* depicts the relation between the amount of capital per worker and the output per worker in the economy. The more capital per worker, the more output per worker. The per-worker production function reflects the law of diminishing marginal returns, which implies that as capital per worker increases, the amount of the additional output produced gets smaller. An improvement in the quality of capital due to technological change causes the entire production function to change.

In the last two decades the growth rate of U.S. labor productivity has declined relative to its long-term trend. It is very difficult to determine the causes of this phenomenon, but there are probably several contributing factors. An important determinant of labor productivity is the amount of capital labor has to work with. If the rate of capital formation declines, it is likely that labor productivity will decline. There has been a slight decline in the U.S. capital–labor ratio, but it is unlikely that this decline is large enough to explain fully the decline in U.S. labor productivity growth.

The quality of labor is another important determinant of labor productivity. Younger, inexperienced workers tend to be less productive than their older counterparts. Beginning in the mid-1960s, the composition of the U.S. labor force shifted toward younger workers as members of the postwar generations entered the labor force. There has also been a decline in standardized test scores, which suggests that new entrants into the labor force are less qualified than new entrants in prior years.

The composition of U.S. output has changed as well, having moved toward service industries and away from manufacturing industries. Because service industries tend to be less capital intensive, labor productivity growth would tend to decline as an economy became more service oriented. Another source of the decline in U.S. labor productivity growth may be the increased role of government in economic life. Government regulations have forced many firms to make capital expenditures on such items as pollution control equipment; this has reduced the spending on capital goods that increases output. The government regulations may have improved the quality of life despite any reduction in productivity growth, however. Some argue that the budget deficits of the federal government also have contributed to the slowdown in productivity. Further, investment in public capital has declined.

Research and Development and Other Issues of Technology and Growth

Technological change is perhaps the most important source of productivity growth and economic growth. Most improvements in technology are the result of scientific research. *Basic research* is the search for knowledge without regard for the commercial applicability of the knowledge. *Applied research* is the attempt to find commercial applications for scientific knowledge. Often, technological change is embodied in new capital investment. Technological change frees resources for new uses. In particular, labor is often freed as a result of technological change.

Research and development spending of firms is one measure of efforts to improve the economy's productivity through technological change. Research and development expenditures in the United States fell during the 1970s; this suggests to many economists that the decline in productivity was due to the decline in research activity.

Given the importance of research and development, it is not surprising that the federal government often tries to stimulate research. Some argue the government should develop an industrial policy, which is a policy of using taxes, subsidies, or regulations to nurture the technologies and industries that are most likely to be important in the future. Others argue that the government is not likely to be good at picking winners and that the policy will become another example of pork-barrel politics.

Another concern of some is that technological change may lead to unemployment. We all know of jobs that have been phased out as a result of the introduction of labor-saving capital. However, the jobs created in the industry that makes the capital may balance out those lost elsewhere. Further, empirical evidence suggests that overall unemployment is lower in countries that are technologically progressive than in countries that utilize less technology.

For several decades following World War II, the United States was the undisputed world leader in terms of production and technology. Since then, the U.S. dominance has disappeared. During 1948–1973, the U.S. annual growth rate in real GDP was about half that of other industrialized countries such as Germany and Japan. Part of the reason for this was because the other countries started at lower levels of productivity after the war due to wartime destruction. In the 1980s the growth rates of real GDP per capita were more similar among industrialized countries. To some, this suggests that over time economies around the world have a tendency to converge. That is, growth in the rich countries will be slower than in the poorer countries until they become more alike. The examples of Germany and Japan after the war and of Korea in more recent years offer evidence to support this theory. But many poor countries show no signs of such growth. Differences in human capital across countries may account for the failure of countries to converge.

IV. LAGNIAPPE

Living and Dying by Industrial Policy

Japan used industrial policy for many years, and many attribute Japan's rise since World War II to this policy. Japan's Ministry of International Trade and Industry (MITI) has helped identify and support many industries and technologies that became important. Many argue that MITI has been crucial in Japan's success in areas such as electronics and computers. But not all of MITI's plans have succeeded. In the early 1980s MITI pushed Japanese firms to invest in producing memory (RAM) chips for computers. The U.S. Commerce Department also urged U.S. firms to focus attention on RAM chips. The Japanese firms did as MITI suggested, but most U.S. firms did not take the advice. Instead, U.S. firms focused on integrated circuits. Over the last eight to ten years, the integrated circuit market has been more lucrative than the RAM market. Consequently, the U.S. semiconductor industry strengthened relative to the Japanese industry, largely as a result of American success in integrated circuits.

Question to Think About: Would you have more confidence in the judgment of someone who invests his or her own funds or someone who invests taxpayers' money?

Productivity Growth and Different Types of Research and Development

Research and development activity is not homogeneous. Some R&D is directed toward basic research and some toward applied research. Another distinction can be made between research directed toward the development of new products and research directed toward improving production processes. It is likely, as Albert Link found, that R&D expenditures allocated to process innovations had a greater impact on productivity than R&D expenditures allocated to product innovations. (See Albert N. Link, "A Disaggregated Analysis of Industrial R&D," in *The Transfer and Utilization of Technical Knowledge*. Edited by Devendra Sahal. Lexington, MA: D. C. Heath, 1982.)

Question to Think About: Would the development of a new computer system be considered a product innovation or a process innovation?

V. KEY TERMS

Productivity
Labor productivity
Per-worker production function
Capital deepening
Public capital

Basic research
Applied research
Industrial policy
Convergence

VI. QUESTIONS

A. Completion

1. Total output divided by total input of a specific kind of resource indicates the __________________ of that resource.

2. The resource most responsible for increasing labor productivity is __________________.

3. The relation between the amount of capital per worker and the amount of labor per worker is known as the per-worker ________________.

4. Output per worker increases at a ________________ rate as capital per worker increases.

5. Over time, improvements in a country's standard of living result from more capital per worker and better ________________ per worker.

6. Increases in capital intensity is called capital ________________.

7. Some economists believe that changes in the ________________ of the labor force have contributed to the decline in U.S. productivity growth.

8. There are more opportunities for technological change when producing goods than when producing ________________.

9. Declining investment in ________________ or infrastructure may serve as a drag on productivity growth.

10. According to Simon Kuznets, 90 percent of the increase in economic growth in developed market economies is attributable to improvements in the ________________ of inputs.

11. ________________ research seeks answers to specific questions or seeks to develop particular products.

12. Technological change impacts the economy by becoming ________________ in capital.

13. The variations in R&D spending in the United States in the last twenty years are mostly due to changes in the share of R&D financed by ________________.

14. The objective of ________________ policy is to secure a leading role for American industry in the future.

15. The ________________ theory argues that economies around the world grow more alike over time.

B. *True/False*

______ 1. Labor productivity is measured by the ratio of GDP to total employment.

______ 2. As workers accumulate more human capital, their productivity increases.

______ 3. Because the per-worker production function is characterized by diminishing marginal returns, a 10-percent increase in capital and a 10-percent increase in labor will lead to less than a 10-percent increase in output.

______ 4. The level of technology is held constant along a per-worker production function.

______ 5. Technological change is pictured by a movement along a per-worker production function.

______ 6. The growth in U.S. productivity was negative during much of the 1970s.

______ 7. Because younger workers tend to be more productive than older workers, one explanation for the decline in U.S. labor productivity growth is the increasing age of the work force.

______ 8. If productivity is inversely related to the quality of the air, then the slowdown in labor productivity does not imply a declining quality of life.

______ 9. Capital formation is a major contributor to economic growth.

______ 10. Technological change can free resources for new uses.

______ 11. Basic research is the search for knowledge without regard to how the knowledge will be used.

______ 12. About 50 percent of applied research is embodied in capital.

______ 13. Research suggests that a dollar's worth of federally funded R&D contributes less to economic growth than a dollar's worth of company-supported R&D.

______ 14. Most federal funding of R&D in the United States goes to support military research.

______ 15. The drop in economic growth in the United States in the 1970s was larger than that in any of the other industrialized countries.

______ 16. Proponents of industrial policy usually believe the market is the best allocator of scarce resources.

______ 17. An increase in productivity would probably encourage greater unemployment.

______ 18. According to the convergence theory, the rich get richer and the poor get poorer.

C. *Multiple Choice*

1. When an economy's labor productivity increases,
   a. the standard of living always rises.
   b. the standard of living rises if employment growth exceeds population growth.
   c. the standard of living rises if population growth exceeds employment growth.
   d. the standard of living rises if population growth equals employment growth.
   e. the standard of living falls.

2. Productivity is difficult to measure because
   a. it is difficult to account for changes in environmental quality.
   b. some activities are not counted in GDP.
   c. government output is difficult to measure.
   d. all of the above
   e. a and b

3. With regard to the per-worker production function, diminishing marginal returns applies to
   a. labor.
   b. capital.
   c. labor per unit of capital.
   d. output.
   e. output per unit of labor.

4. If GDP per capita is $20,000 and 40 percent of the population is employed, then labor productivity is
   a. $8,000.
   b. $40,000.
   c. $50,000.
   d. $100,000.
   e. The question cannot be answered without more information.

5. All of the following have been suggested as causes of the slowdown in U.S. productivity growth except
   a. deregulation of many industries.
   b. reduced capital formation.
   c. changing composition of the labor force.
   d. reduced spending on R&D.
   e. changing composition of output.

6. A change in the composition of the labor force would contribute to a slowdown in productivity growth if
   a. the proportion of new workers was constant over time.
   b. the share of employment accounted for by new workers increased.
   c. the share of employment in service industries decreased.
   d. higher energy prices caused the substitution of capital for labor.
   e. none of the above

7. Labor productivity can be increased most easily in which sector of the economy?
   a. government
   b. retailing
   c. education
   d. manufacturing
   e. all of the above

8. Research and development expenditures financed by the U.S. federal government
   a. tend to be used for military research.
   b. tend to replace company-financed expenditures dollar for dollar.
   c. tend to increase economic growth more than an equal amount of company-financed expenditures.
   d. rose significantly as a percent of sales during the 1970s.
   e. a and b

9. Which of the following is likely to increase potential output?
   a. increasing the minimum wage
   b. eliminating job discrimination
   c. raising welfare payments
   d. raising unemployment benefits
   e. strengthening labor unions' control over entry into occupations

10. Which of the following is true regarding research and development?
    a. Technological breakthroughs are the direct result of success in basic research.
    b. Basic research has a larger immediate payoff than applied research.
    c. Basic research is likely to have a higher rate of return to society as a whole than applied research.
    d. Basic research is more likely to be embodied in capital than applied research.
    e. a, b, and c only

11. Both research and development spending and the number of patents awarded by the U.S. Patent Office declined in the 1970s. In more recent years there has been an increase in the total number of patents but
    a. most of the increase has been in patents granted to foreign corporations.
    b. research and development spending has continued to decline.
    c. research and development spending has increased at a faster rate than patenting has increased.
    d. the value of the patents has declined.
    e. none of the above

12. Industrial policy is a policy that
    a. encourages industrial development rather than agricultural development.
    b. the United States has followed since the end of World War II.
    c. encourages the development and growth of industries that the government thinks will be important industries in the future.
    d. b and c only
    e. none of the above

13. Industrial policy has been advocated by
    a. Ronald Reagan.
    b. George Bush.
    c. Bill Clinton.
    d. Gene Grossman.
    e. all of the above

14. Which of the following is a problem with industrial policy, according to its critics?
    a. The beneficiaries may share their expertise with foreign companies.
    b. The support from the government may be allocated on the basis of political influence rather than economic criteria.
    c. Government bureaucrats are less likely to know where to allocate funds than people in the business world.
    d. all of the above
    e. none of the above

15. Technological change
    a. can lead to structural unemployment in some industries.
    b. can lead to increases in production and employment by making products more affordable.
    c. has caused the natural rate of unemployment to increase 50 percent over the last forty years.
    d. causes a larger reduction in employment in the long run than in the short run.
    e. a and b only

16. During the 1980s the growth rate in GDP per capita exceeded the growth rate in output per labor hour because
    a. employment grew faster than population.
    b. population grew faster than employment.
    c. the rate of technological change fell to close to zero.
    d. the quality of high school graduates increased substantially.
    e. none of the above

17. The convergence theory states that
    a. economies around the world are getting less similar all the time.
    b. economies around the world are getting more alike all the time.
    c. the rich countries are getting more alike all the time.
    d. the gap between rich and poor within the United States is narrowing.
    e. the short-run growth rate converges on the long-run growth rate more rapidly in rich countries than in poor countries.

18. Which of the following is more likely to make the convergence theory correct?
    a. It is easier to copy new technology than to develop it.
    b. Technology is portable.
    c. The human capital needed to take advantage of new technology is very portable.
    d. all of the above
    e. a and b only

D. *Discussion Questions*

1. What is productivity and how is it measured?

2. What factors determine the productivity of labor?

3. Explain how the law of diminishing marginal returns is related to the per-worker production function.

4. Distinguish between a movement along the per-worker production curve and a shift of the curve.

5. Suppose in 1980 one worker could produce 100 VCRs. How many VCRs can the worker produce in 1990 if the growth in labor productivity is 2 percent per year? 2.5 percent per year? 3 percent per year? What do these figures suggest about long-term growth?

6. What factors have been suggested as causes of the slowdown in U.S. labor productivity growth in the 1970s? Explain how each of these factors could contribute to the slowdown.

7. What role does technological change play in determining productivity growth?

8. Would you expect business firms to spend a greater proportion of their R&D expenditures on basic research or on applied research? Why?

9. What factors led to the slowdown in economic growth in the 1970s experienced by industrialized nations other than the United States?

10. How have the federal budget deficits affected productivity growth?

11. Why do economists believe that U.S. federally financed R&D has less impact on economic growth than company-financed expenditures?

12. What is meant by industrial policy?

13. Discuss the strengths and weaknesses of an industrial policy.

14. Does technological change lead to unemployment?

VII. ANSWERS

A. Completion

1. productivity
2. capital
3. production function
4. diminishing (decreasing)
5. capital
6. deepening
7. composition
8. services
9. public services
10. quality
11. Applied
12. embodied
13. the federal government
14. industrial
15. convergence

B. True/False

1. True
2. True
3. False
4. True
5. False
6. False
7. False
8. True
9. True
10. True
11. True
12. False
13. True
14. True
15. False
16. False
17. False
18. False

C. Multiple Choice

1. b
2. d
3. b
4. c
5. a
6. b
7. d
8. a
9. b
10. e
11. a
12. c
13. c
14. d
15. e
16. a
17. b
18. e

D. *Discussion Questions*

1. Productivity measures how effectively resources are employed. It is defined as the ratio of a specific measure of output to a specific measure of a particular input. Generally, total output divided by total input yields a measure of productivity.

2. The most important factor that determines the productivity of labor is the capital with which labor works. The more capital and the higher the quality of the capital, the more productive labor will be. This includes both physical capital (such as machines and tools) and human capital (such as formal education, formal training programs, and on-the-job training).

3. The per-worker production function relates the capital per worker to the output per worker. An increase in capital per worker means that capital is varying while labor is held constant. That is, capital is treated as a variable input and labor as a fixed input. The law of diminishing marginal returns applies to capital in this situation, so the additional output from additional units of capital (holding labor constant) will eventually diminish. Graphically, the curve relating capital per worker and output per worker is bowed.

4. An increase in the quantity of capital causes a movement along the per-worker production curve, since capital per worker is along the horizontal axis. An increase in the quality of capital arising from technological change causes the entire curve to shift.

5. One worker would produce 121.9 VCRs in 1990 at a growth rate of 2 percent per year, 128 at a growth rate of 2.5 percent, and 134.4 at a growth rate of 3 percent. The compounding of growth rates leads to large changes in labor productivity over even a short time period. (If the time period were 100 years, growth in labor productivity of 2 percent would yield 724.5 VCRs per worker in 2090; growth of 2.5 percent would yield 1,181.4 VCRs per worker in 2090.)

6. Six factors have been cited as sources of the slowdown in U.S. productivity growth. (1) The rate of capital formation fell. There is a direct relationship between the capital-labor ratio and labor productivity, so a decline in capital formation would lead to a decline in productivity growth. (2) The composition of the U.S. labor force changed. New workers are less productive than more experienced workers. Since the mid-1960s, the proportion of new workers in the work force has increased, so the labor force is likely to be less productive. (3) The quality of entrants into the labor force is declining. (4) The composition of output changed. Capital is more important in manufacturing than in service industries, so there is less opportunity for labor productivity increases in the service industries. (5) Increased government regulation caused firms to spend resources complying with regulations instead of using those resources for capital formation. (6) Reduced spending on research and development has caused technological change to be less rapid.

7. Technological change encourages productivity growth because it permits the same output to be produced with fewer resources. Often the resource that is freed is labor. Consequently, less labor is used to produce the same output, so labor productivity increases.

8. Business firms are likely to spend more resources on applied research because the payoff with applied research is more certain and faster than it is with basic research.

9. Since all industrialized nations experienced a slowdown in the 1970s, it seems reasonable that the causes of the U.S. slowdown were not unique to the United States. In particular, all

developed nations were affected by one likely determinant of the slowdown: higher energy prices. Similarly, Japan and the European developed nations experienced the kinds of changes in the composition of the labor force that affected the United States.

10. No one knows for sure. Government investment in public capital could actually increase productivity.

11. A large share of U.S. federally funded research has military objectives, which often have little or no effect on productivity in the rest of the economy.

12. Industrial policy refers to the government's picking certain industries and/or technologies as important for the future growth of the economy and supporting them with subsidies or tax breaks.

13. The idea of industrial policy relies on two phenomena. First, some technologies or industries have effects that spill over into other areas of the economy so that development of these industries will create benefits in a much larger section of the economy. Since firms in the key industries will not reap all the benefits from development of the industry, they will under invest in research and in capital formation. The government can encourage more investment in both by subsidizing the industry. Second, the market often fails to allocate capital efficiently, so the government needs to help correct the situation.

    Opponents of industrial policy argue that those who run the businesses are more likely to know better where to allocate capital than government bureaucrats. The subsidies of the government are likely to be directed more by political than by economic considerations.

14. Technological change does cause some people to become unemployed: technological change means that more can be produced by fewer workers. However, employment increases in the industry producing the capital that embodies the technological change. Further, the technological change may lower costs sufficiently to stimulate sales and production so that unemployment does not develop. The increased productivity of labor increases the income of labor, which increases spending and production in other sectors of the economy. Consequently, technological change will tend to increase employment in the economy as a whole, especially over time.

CHAPTER 7

Unemployment and Inflation

I. INTRODUCTION

Inflation and unemployment are two of the most important problems with which policymakers have to grapple. Policymakers face a major dilemma in that policies designed to cure one of the problems often exacerbate the other. The causes of each phenomenon and their relationships are addressed in later chapters. In this chapter the two phenomena are described and defined.

II. OUTLINE

1. Unemployment. Unemployment has been linked to illness and crime. The real social costs of unemployment are the lost potential output and the economic and psychological damage to the unemployed and their families.

    1.1 Measuring Unemployment
    - a. The adult population includes all persons sixteen years or older, except those in prisons or mental institutions.
    - b. The labor force consists of those in the adult population who are either working or looking for work.
    - c. People are counted as unemployed if they have looked for work at least once in the previous four weeks.
    - d. The unemployment rate equals the number of unemployed divided by the number in the labor force.
    - e. Not all people who are not working are considered unemployed.
        - (1) Full-time students
        - (2) Retired people
        - (3) Full-time homemakers
        - (4) Discouraged workers: those who no longer seek employment because they have given up
    - f. The *labor force participation rate* is the number of people in the labor force divided by the adult population.
    - g. The *civilian unemployment rate* is the number unemployed divided by the civilian labor force; i.e., it excludes military personnel from the labor force.

    1.2 Changes over Time in Unemployment Statistics
    - a. The adult population changes slowly over time.
    - b. The labor force participation rate can change more quickly than the adult population and has been increasing in the United States over the last forty years.
    - c. The unemployment rate is more volatile than the labor force participation rate. There has been an upward trend in the U.S. unemployment rate since 1950.

1.3 Unemployment in Various Groups
   a. Unemployment rates tend to be higher for teenagers and blacks.
   b. Unemployment rates of all groups tend to increase during recessions.

1.4 Duration of Unemployment
   a. The duration of unemployment is not the same for all the unemployed.
   b. Higher unemployment rates usually reflect both a larger number of unemployed and a greater average duration of unemployment.

1.5 Unemployment Differences across the Country. Some areas of the United States have much higher unemployment rates than others.

1.6 *Case Study:* Poor King Coal

1.7 Types of Unemployment
   a. A change in the unemployment rate can occur because of a change in the labor force or a change in the number of unemployed.
   b. Four types of unemployment:
      (1) Frictional unemployment
         (a) Frictional unemployment arises from the difficulty of matching labor suppliers and labor demanders.
         (b) Frictional unemployment exists because information concerning job vacancies and job candidates is costly to acquire and digest.
      (2) Structural unemployment
         (a) Structural unemployment exists when the skills possessed by job seekers do not match the skills demanded by employers or when job seekers do not live in regions where the jobs are.
         (b) Structural unemployment arises from shifts in the demand and supply of goods due to changes in consumer tastes, technological change, or trade factors.
      (3) Seasonal unemployment
         (a) Seasonal unemployment is unemployment that follows seasonal patterns.
         (b) Seasonal unemployment mirrors weather or holiday demand patterns; e.g., ski resorts close in the summer.
      (4) Cyclical unemployment
         (a) Cyclical unemployment reflects the decline in aggregate output that occurs during recessions.
         (b) Cyclical unemployment is caused by declines in aggregate demand.

1.8 The Meaning of Full Employment
   a. Full employment does not mean zero unemployment.
   b. There will always be some frictional, seasonal, and structural unemployment.
   c. Unemployment associated with frictional, structural, and seasonal factors has risen in the last thirty years.
   d. One of the reasons for the increased trend in unemployment is the changing composition of the labor force.

1.9 Unemployment Insurance
   a. Upon losing their jobs, those who qualify can receive government unemployment benefits for up to six months, provided they are actively seeking employment.

b. Those who are unemployed because they quit their jobs or were fired for just cause, who are just entering the labor force, or who are reentering the labor force do not qualify for unemployment benefits.
c. The amount and availability of unemployment benefits can affect workers' incentives to find new employment and thus the level and average duration of unemployment.

1.10 International Comparisons of Unemployment
a. Not all countries calculate unemployment in the same way.
b. Cultural factors also affect the unemployment rates of other countries.

1.11 Problems with Official Unemployment Figures
a. Unemployment data ignore the problem of underemployment; people are counted as employed even when they work only part time or are vastly overqualified for their jobs.
b. Since discouraged workers are not included, unemployment figures tend on net to understate the true rate of unemployment.

2. Inflation. *Inflation* is a sustained and continuous increase in the average level of prices. *Hyperinflation* is extremely high inflation. *Deflation* is a sustained and continuous decrease in the average level of prices.

2.1 *CASE STUDY:* Hyperinflation in Brazil

2.2 Two Sources of Inflation
a. *Demand-pull inflation* is inflation arising from increases in aggregate demand.
b. *Cost-push inflation* is inflation arising from a decrease in aggregate supply.

2.3 A Historical Look at Inflation and the Price Level
a. For much of U.S. history, the periods of inflation and the periods of deflation about evened out.
b. Since the end of World War II, inflation has been more persistent, and the price level has risen steadily.

2.4 Anticipated Versus Unanticipated Inflation
a. Anticipated inflation poses fewer problems for the economy than unanticipated inflation.
b. Unanticipated increases in inflation tend to hurt those who lend money at fixed interest rates and those on fixed incomes.

2.5 The Transaction Costs of Variable Inflation
a. Stable prices mean that people can be confident about the purchasing power of a dollar.
b. Inflation uncertainty increases the difficulty of making business decisions; this raises the cost of producing goods and lowers productivity.
c. Inflation diverts time and effort from productive concerns to finding ways to hedge against inflation.

2.6 Adapting to Relative Price Changes
a. Not all prices change at the same rate with inflation, so relative prices change.
b. Inflation makes it more difficult to determine relative price changes, which are important for efficiently allocating resources.

2.7 International Comparisons of Inflation. Comparisons of inflation rates across countries must be made carefully because the quality of inflation statistics varies across countries.

2.8 Inflation and Interest Rates

a. The *interest rate* is the amount of money earned for supplying the use of one dollar for one year.

b. The *nominal rate of interest* measures interest in terms of actual dollars paid.

c. The *real rate of interest* equals the nominal rate minus the inflation rate.

d. Lenders and borrowers must base decisions on the expected real rate of interest—the nominal rate minus expected inflation.

2.9 Why Is Inflation So Unpopular?

a. Inflation means higher expenditures but also higher incomes; however, many people do not recognize the link between prices and incomes.

b. Inflation affects everyone, whereas unemployment affects only a portion of the population.

c. Most tax laws do not distinguish between nominal and real income, so inflation affects taxes unfairly.

III. DISCUSSION

Unemployment

The *unemployment rate* is the figure used to measure the extent of unemployment in the economy. To calculate the unemployment rate, it is necessary first to calculate the number of people in the labor force. The *labor force* is composed of those noninstitutionalized adults (at least sixteen years of age) who are working or who are looking for work. Hence, full-time students, full-time homemakers, retired people, young teenagers, and any who choose to be idle are not included in the labor force. To be classified as unemployed, one must be actively seeking employment; that is, one must have looked for work at least once in the previous four weeks. The *unemployment rate* represents the percentage of the labor force that is unemployed; it is the number of people who are looking for work divided by the number in the labor force. Another figure often used is the *civilian unemployment rate*, which is found by dividing the number of unemployed by the civilian labor force; the civilian labor force excludes military personnel.

There are several problems with the government's method of measuring the unemployment rate. First, it tends to understate the true extent of unemployment because *discouraged workers* are not included among the unemployed. Discouraged workers are those who have become so discouraged and frustrated in their search for work that they have quit looking for work. Since they no longer seek work actively, they are considered neither part of the labor force nor among the unemployed. Second, the unemployment rate does not take into consideration the underemployed: those who want to work full time but can only find part-time jobs or those who are overqualified for their jobs. On the other hand, the unemployment rate includes people who are not very serious in their search for work and who would actually prefer to remain idle. Finally, the unemployment rate does not tell how long people have been unemployed.

The unemployment rate is the measure most commonly used to examine employment trends in the economy. However, another important measure is the *labor force participation rate*, which is the percentage of the adult population that is in the labor force. The labor force participation rate increases when a larger proportion of the adult population wants to work. It is possible for the total number of employed to increase at the same time that the unemployment rate increases if the labor force participation rate is also increasing.

The unemployment rate tends to rise during recessions and fall during expansions. Since 1950 there has been an upward trend in the U.S. unemployment rate. This trend has been brought about at least in part from the rapid increase in the labor force, as large numbers of women have entered the labor force and those in the post-World War II generation have become members of the adult population. During this time period both the number of employed people and the number of unemployed people increased.

Unemployment rates can also be calculated for various groups in the labor force. The overall unemployment rate may cover up some important differences among groups. For example, unemployment among teenagers usually is significantly greater than among adults, and unemployment among blacks generally is greater than among whites. Rates of the groups usually vary together.

People can be unemployed for many reasons. The majority of unemployed persons in the United States in 1989 were unemployed voluntarily (they had quit their jobs) or were just entering the labor force. If such people are unemployed for only a short period of time, the economy is functioning well. Of course, others are unemployed involuntarily, and unemployment causes more problems in these cases. The seriousness of unemployment is often related to the reason for unemployment. *Frictional unemployment* exists because it takes time for a person seeking work and an employer with a job opening to match up. The potential worker must find out about the job opening and determine whether the job is one that he or she would like and if the pay is satisfactory. The employer wants to know something about the background of the prospective jobholder: is the person reliable, does the person have the needed skills, does the person have a reputation for being a troublemaker, and so forth. Collecting the necessary information takes time, and there will be some unemployment while all parties take the time to collect and assimilate information.

A second kind of unemployment is *structural unemployment*; it reflects the fact that the economy is not static, but constantly changing. As a result of changes in tastes or income, consumers alter their buying patterns. Further, costs of production change as a result of technological change in some industries or changes in the prices of inputs that are important to some industries. The result of all these changes is that production of some goods expands and production of other goods contracts. As production of a good contracts, some people are laid off and become unemployed. If their skills are valuable in other industries in the region where they live, they usually can find new jobs relatively quickly. But if their skills are not wanted by the growing industries, they may be unemployed for a much longer period of time. In some cases, a person may have to be retrained and relocated in order to find a new job, or the person may be forced to accept a job at a wage that is significantly lower than his or her previous wage.

Seasonal unemployment is very straightforward. Some occupations depend a great deal on the weather; demand for labor is great when the weather is right but much smaller when the weather is inappropriate. Construction and agriculture are obvious examples. Other jobs are tied to specific times of the year. Extra hiring by department stores during the Christmas season, in hotels and restaurants in New Orleans during Mardi Gras, or in Louisville during Kentucky Derby week creates seasonal employment. The government adjusts unemployment rates to account for seasonal variations.

The final type of unemployment is called *cyclical unemployment* because it is related to fluctuations in the economy. During a recession, aggregate output falls and unemployment increases; during an expansion, aggregate output increases and unemployment decreases.

Although four types of unemployment have been defined, it is not always easy to determine which type is operating at any given time or what type of unemployment a specific individual is experiencing.

The stated goal of public policy is to promote full employment. Full employment does not mean zero unemployment, however, for that is an impossible goal in a dynamic economy. It is neither possible nor desirable to eliminate all frictional, seasonal, or structural unemployment. Government policy tends to focus on cyclical unemployment, although attempts have been made to alleviate the effects of structural unemployment by offering relocation and training programs to workers.

To reduce the cost of unemployment to the unemployed, the U.S. government operates an unemployment insurance system financed by a tax on employers. To qualify for unemployment benefits, one must have lost his or her job for certain reasons and must be actively seeking employment. New entrants and re-entrants into the labor force are not covered by government unemployment insurance; neither are those who quit their jobs or were fired for just cause. Unemployment benefits reduce the cost of unemployment; some believe that the more attractive the unemployment benefits, the longer recipients will remain unemployed, contributing to an increase in frictional unemployment.

Inflation

Inflation is a sustained and continuous rise in the average level of prices; *deflation* is a sustained and continuous decline in the average level of prices. If inflation is due to an increase in aggregate demand, it is called *demand-pull inflation*; if it is due to a decrease in aggregate supply, it is called *cost-push inflation*. Throughout most of U.S. history, the periods of inflation and deflation about evened out. However, since the end of World War II, inflation has been more persistent, and the price level has increased an average of 4.3 percent per year.

When there is inflation, prices of all goods and services increase, on average, including the prices paid to owners of resources. This means that everyone's expenditures rise, but everyone's income rises too. If all prices increase by the same rate, then everyone's real income and expenditures are unchanged. But prices seldom go up at the same rate under inflation—some go up by more than the average rate of price increase, some go up by less, and some remain unchanged or even decrease. If a family's income remains unchanged while its expenditures increase, the family is worse off.

Economists distinguish between anticipated and unanticipated inflation. If people can correctly anticipate the inflation rate, then they can take inflation into account when entering into contracts. However, inflation cannot be anticipated correctly all of the time. When inflation is unanticipated, economic agents make decisions on the basis of poor information and thus make poor decisions. Those who are on fixed incomes or who have lent money at a fixed interest rate that is too low to compensate for inflation are hurt by unexpectedly high inflation; those who have borrowed money benefit.

In the real world, inflation does not cause all prices to rise exactly the same amount at exactly the same time. Instead, the price of wheat may increase by 5 percent one month, the price of autos may increase by 8 percent the next month, the price of gasoline may increase by 3 percent the next month, and so forth. Consequently, it is difficult to know whether a specific change in price is due to a change in demand or supply (and is thus a relative price change) or to inflation. Such uncertainty makes it difficult for economic decision makers to make correct decisions. The transaction costs of drawing up contracts increase, and individuals spend time and resources trying to find ways to hedge against the effects of inflation. Business executives spend time analyzing financial problems instead of production or distribution problems. These real costs associated with inflation cause a decline in productivity and a lower growth rate for the economy.

Unanticipated inflation can cause particular problems in credit markets. Families who bought homes in the early 1960s found that inflation caused the nominal value of their homes and their incomes to increase while their mortgage payments remained fixed. Such families were better off, but the institutions that lent money to the home buyers were harmed. Eventually, financial institutions established variable mortgage rates to protect themselves against inflation. When inflation is anticipated, *nominal interest rates* merely adjust to reflect the expected inflation. The *real interest rate* equals the nominal interest rate less the inflation rate.

IV. LAGNIAPPE

"Farewell! Othello's occupation's gone."
Othello, Act III, Scene 3, Line 357

The words above, from Shakespeare's *Othello*, are the poignant words of a man who no longer has his work to occupy him. Like many others who have had to give up their occupations, Othello has a difficult time coping with the change.

What can be done when demand shifts or technological change causes some occupations to become obsolete? Society cannot lock into a set of job skills and a type of technology forever. Blacksmiths disappeared when the auto was invented, but a demand for auto mechanics was created. Railroad employment falls as airline and trucking employment increases.

Question to Think About: How is the specialization of labor related to structural unemployment?

Inflation Versus a Price Increase

Inflation, the sustained and continuous increase in the average level of prices, must be distinguished from an increase in the price of a single good, no matter how important that good is in the economy. The increase in oil prices in the 1970s caused much disruption in the U.S. economy and caused many other prices to increase. However, an oil price increase may not have the sustained effect of causing prices to rise each year. Hence, a price increase is not the same thing as inflation. Further, if oil prices increase, the prices of some other goods must fall, *ceteris paribus*. Hence, we have relative price changes but not inflation.

Question to Think About: How much of the inflation in the 1970s was related to higher oil prices?

V. KEY TERMS

Adult population
Labor force
Unemployment rate
Discouraged worker
Labor force participation rate
Civilian unemployment rate
Frictional unemployment
Structural unemployment
Seasonal unemployment
Cyclical unemployment
Full employment
Unemployment insurance
Underemployment
Inflation
Hyperinflation
Deflation
Demand-pull inflation
Cost-push inflation
Disinflation
Unanticipated inflation
Anticipated inflation
Interest rate
Nominal rate of interest
Real rate of interest

VI. QUESTIONS

A. *Completion*

1. The ________________ consists of those in the noninstitutional adult population who are working or are looking for work.

2. A ________________ worker is one who has given up looking for employment.

3. The ________________ unemployment rate does not include military personnel.

4. A person entering the labor force for the first time contributes to ________________ unemployment.

5. ________________ unemployment refers to jobs lost because of shifts in buying patterns when consumer tastes change.

6. A recession leads to an increase in ________________ unemployment.

7. ________________ refers to jobs in which people are underutilized or working at tasks below their level of skill.

8. A country experiences ________________ when there is a sustained and continuous decrease in the average level of prices.

9. Inflation that is due to an increase in aggregate demand is called ________________ inflation; inflation that is due to a decrease in aggregate supply is called ________________ inflation.

10. A change in the inflation rate that fools people is known as ________________ inflation.

11. If all prices do not increase by the same percentage, then there are changes in ________________ prices as well as in average prices.

12. ________________ occurs when the inflation rate declines.

13. An increase in ________________ inflation will cause nominal interest rates to increase.

14. The ________________ interest rate is the rate earned after adjustment for inflation.

15. Because of inflation, a nominal capital ________________ may actually be a loss in real terms.

B. *True/False*

______ 1. The unemployment rate is the number of unemployed people divided by the number of people in the adult population.

______ 2. Discouraged workers are included in the unemployment rate.

______ 3. The labor force participation rate can change more quickly than the adult population.

______ 4. In the United States there has been an upward trend in both the unemployment rate and the labor force participation rate since 1950.

______ 5. Usually a rise in the unemployment rate results from both larger numbers of people being unemployed and a greater average duration of unemployment.

______ 6. The civilian unemployment rate is higher than the overall unemployment rate.

______ 7. Frictional unemployment may help increase the economy's level of efficiency.

______ 8. Full employment means that everyone who wants a job has one.

______ 9. The unemployment rate that corresponds to full employment is constant over time.

______ 10. Unemployed people who receive unemployment benefits tend to search for employment less actively than those who do not receive unemployment benefits.

______ 11. The price level falls both in times of deflation and in times of disinflation.

______ 12. An increase in the price of oil represents inflation.

______ 13. Before World War II, inflation was more common than deflation.

______ 14. Inflation raises incomes as well as expenditures.

______ 15. Anticipated inflation poses fewer problems for the economy than unanticipated inflation.

______ 16. Inflation tends to increase the difficulty of making economic decisions.

______ 17. Since centrally planned economies are more controlled, their inflation figures are more reliable than those of market economies.

______ 18. With inflation, the nominal rate of interest is greater than the real rate of interest.

______ 19. An unexpected increase in the inflation rate causes the real rate of interest to decline, at least for a while.

______ 20. An important difference between inflation and unemployment is that inflation tends to affect everyone whereas unemployment affects only a fraction of the population.

C. *Multiple Choice*

1. If a large number of people take early retirement, which of the following will decrease?
   a. the noninstitutionalized adult population
   b. the labor force
   c. the number of unemployed
   d. the number of discouraged workers
   e. the unemployment rate

2. The unemployment rate declines when
   a. an unemployed person goes to prison.
   b. a high school student goes straight to college.
   c. a person leaves the Navy and goes to work for an engineering firm.
   d. a fourteen-year-old gets a job mowing lawns.
   e. a person moves from a part-time job to a full-time job.

3. The unemployment rate increases when
   a. the number of discouraged workers increases.
   b. the adult population increases.
   c. retired people live longer.
   d. aggregate demand increases.
   e. none of the above

4. Of the U.S. adult population, the biggest group of people not working is
   a. the unemployed.
   b. discouraged workers.
   c. those who do not want to work.
   d. military personnel.
   e. none of the above.

5. Suppose the adult population is 180 million and there are 60 million adults who are not in the labor force. If there are 115 million employed individuals with 5 million in the military, the unemployment rate is ___________ and the labor force participation rate is ___________.
   a. 4.3 percent; 66.7 percent
   b. 4.17 percent; 66.7 percent
   c. 8.3 percent; 75.0 percent
   d. 4.17 percent; 75.0 percent
   e. 4.3 percent; 63.9 percent

6. Which of the following is an accurate characterization of employment over the last forty years in the United States?
   a. The adult population increased slightly, the labor force participation rate increased significantly, and the unemployment rate increased somewhat.
   b. The adult population increased slightly, the labor force participation rate remained unchanged, and the unemployment rate increased significantly.
   c. The labor force participation rate for both men and women increased significantly, and the unemployment rate increased somewhat.
   d. The labor force participation rate fell, and the unemployment rate increased significantly.
   e. none of the above

7. Which group in the United States has the highest unemployment rate?
   a. white males
   b. black males
   c. black teenagers
   d. white teenagers
   e. black females

8. A rise in the unemployment rate is usually due to
   a. an increase in the number of people unemployed.
   b. an increase in the average duration of unemployment.
   c. a decrease in the labor force.
   d. all of the above.
   e. a and b only.

9. Which of the following is an example of structural unemployment?
   a. an auto worker laid off because of increased imports
   b. a woman quitting her job to raise her children
   c. a clerk who had worked for an accounting firm who is laid off April 16
   d. a person quitting a job to look for a higher-paying job
   e. a college professor told she cannot teach summer school this year

10. Which of the following is an example of seasonal unemployment?
   a. an auto worker being laid off because of increased imports
   b. a woman quitting her job to raise her children
   c. a clerk who had worked for an accounting firm being laid off in late April
   d. a person quitting a job for a higher-paying job
   e. a college professor deciding not to teach summer school

11. An increase in unemployment benefits is likely to
   a. cause an increase in the unemployment rate.
   b. cause an increase in the number of unemployed.
   c. cause an increase in the average duration of unemployment.
   d. all of the above
   e. b and c

12. An economy at full employment will still have some
   a. frictional unemployment.
   b. seasonal unemployment.
   c. structural unemployment.
   d. cyclical unemployment.
   e. a, b, and c only

13. For most of U.S. history, inflation has been associated with
   a. recessions.
   b. Democratic administrations.
   c. times of war.
   d. Republican administrations.
   e. periods of high taxation.

14. Inflation will increase when
   a. aggregate demand increases faster than aggregate supply.
   b. aggregate supply increases faster than aggregate demand.
   c. aggregate supply falls.
   d. aggregate demand falls.
   e. both a and c

15. Which of the following is likely to benefit from unanticipated higher inflation?
   a. a savings and loan institution
   b. a homeowner with a fixed-rate mortgage
   c. a retired person
   d. a holder of government bonds
   e. all of the above

16. A major problem with inflation is
   a. that it raises people's expenditures without raising their incomes.
   b. that it makes it harder to determine changes in relative prices.
   c. that it raises the real interest rate.
   d. that it makes all homeowners worse off.
   e. the rising unemployment rate in the early stage of an inflationary period.

17. The term that describes a decline in the inflation rate from 8 percent to 3 percent is
   a. disinflation.
   b. deflation.
   c. reinflation.
   d. recessionary inflation.
   e. none of the above

18. An increase in the expected inflation rate increases
   a. the real rate of interest.
   b. the nominal rate of interest.
   c. both the real and the nominal rates of interest.
   d. neither of the above, unless the increase in inflation is anticipated.
   e. the real rate of interest only if the inflation is unanticipated.

19. Inflation causes the economy's overall productivity to decrease because
   a. inflation makes everyone poorer.
   b. inflation hurts more people than it helps.
   c. inflation raises real interest rates.
   d. people spend more time and resources coping with the uncertainty created by the inflation.
   e. c and d

20. The inflation rate is 5 percent and you make a capital gain of $50 on a $1,000 investment. The tax rate is 30 percent. What is your real after-tax gain?
   a. $50
   b. $35
   c. -$15
   d. -$35
   e. The question cannot be answered without more information.

D. *Discussion Questions*

1. Use the information in Exhibit 1 concerning population and employment to answer the questions.

Exhibit 1

	1987	*1992*
Adult population	182,753,000	191,576,000
Employed persons	112,440,000	117,598,000
Unemployed persons	7,425,000	9,384,000

   a. What was the labor force participation rate in 1987? in 1992?
   b. What was the unemployment rate in 1987? in 1992?

2. Explain how the unemployment rate can increase even if the number of people employed is increasing.

3. How has the labor force participation rate changed over the last forty years?

4. Suppose the unemployment rate is 10 percent and that the average duration of unemployment is ten weeks. Each week one million workers become unemployed and another one million people find jobs.
   a. Suppose an additional 100,000 workers lose their jobs every week. What is the unemployment rate in the first week? What is the unemployment rate in the fifth week? What is the unemployment rate after ten weeks if 1.1 million people are able to find work that week?
   b. Suppose that the average duration of unemployment increases to twelve weeks. What is the new unemployment rate?

5. Describe the four types of unemployment. How do the four types differ in their effects on the economy and on the unemployed?

6. What is the purpose of unemployment insurance? What are the effects of unemployment insurance on unemployment rates?

7. What is meant by full employment? Why might it change over time?

8. What is the difference between demand-pull and cost-push inflation?

9. What is the difference between anticipated and unanticipated inflation? How do they differ in their effects on economic agents? Does inflation have no effects on the economy if it is anticipated? Explain.

10. How are inflation and relative price changes related?

11. What is the difference between disinflation and deflation?

12. Who is harmed by inflation? Who benefits? Explain.

13. During the early stages of unanticipated inflation, frictional unemployment often falls. Can you provide an explanation for this observation?

14. How are inflation rates and interest rates related?

15. Why do people dislike inflation?

VII. ANSWERS

A. *Completion*

1. labor force
2. discouraged
3. civilian
4. frictional
5. Structural
6. cyclical
7. Underemployment
8. deflation
9. demand-pull; cost-push
10. unanticipated
11. relative
12. Disinflation
13. anticipated
14. real
15. gain

B. *True/False*

1. False. The number of unemployed is divided by the number in the labor force.
2. False
3. True
4. True
5. True
6. True
7. True
8. False
9. False
10. True
11. False. The price level still increases in times of disinflation.
12. False. An increase in the price of oil is a relative price change and not an increase in all prices.
13. False
14. True
15. True
16. True
17. False
18. True
19. True
20. True

C. *Multiple Choice*

1. b	6. a	11. d	16. b
2. a	7. c	12. e	17. a
3. e	8. e	13. c	18. b
4. c	9. a	14. e	19. d
5. b	10. c	15. b	20. c

D. *Discussion Questions*

1. a. Labor force participation rate = $\frac{\text{Unemployed + employed}}{\text{Adult population}}$

1987 = 7,425,000 + 112,440,000/182,753,000
= 65.58%

1992 = 9,384,000 + 117,598,000/191,576,000
= 66.28%

b. Unemployment rate = $\frac{\text{Unemployed}}{\text{Labor force}} = \frac{\text{Unemployed}}{\text{Unemployed + employed}}$

1987 = 7,425,000/119,865,000
= 6.2%

1992 = 9,384,000/126,982,000
= 7.4%

2. The unemployment rate is the number of unemployed divided by the labor force. The labor force is made up of the employed and the unemployed. If the labor force increases, both the number of employed and the number of unemployed can be increasing. If the latter increases faster, the unemployment rate can increase even while employment is increasing.

3. The labor force participation rate of women has increased by about 20 percentage points, whereas the participation rate of men has declined somewhat. The overall labor participation rate has increased.

4. a. Since there are 10 million unemployed and the unemployment rate is 10 percent, we know the total labor force is 100 million. When an additional 100,000 workers become unemployed, the unemployment rate increases to 10.1 percent (10,100,000/100,000,000). In the fifth week the total number unemployed is 10,500,000, so the unemployment rate is 10.5 percent. After the tenth week the total number unemployed is 11 million, so the unemployment rate is 11 percent.
   b. The total number unemployed at any one time is now 12 million, so the new unemployment rate is 12 percent.

5. Frictional unemployment is experienced by those who are unemployed because it takes time to find the right match between job seekers and employers with job openings. Structural unemployment is experienced by those who are unemployed because changes in buying patterns or the structure of production causes demand for their skills to fall, or because they do not live in the regions where jobs are available. Seasonal unemployment is experienced by those who are unemployed because their work is affected by the weather or takes place in certain periods of the year. Cyclical unemployment is experienced by those who are unemployed because the economy has entered a recessionary period.

   Frictional unemployment is necessary in a dynamic economy because it allows people to find the best alternatives; the economy becomes more efficient. Structural unemployment can have lasting negative effects, as the unemployed may be able to find work only by retraining or moving, both of which can be costly. Structural unemployment is a natural by-product of a dynamic economy, however. Seasonal unemployment can be anticipated. In addition, people in seasonal jobs (for example, construction work) often receive high wages while they are working, so the effects of seasonal unemployment are not as damaging on the unemployed as those of structural unemployment. Cyclical unemployment can have a great effect on the economy in terms of lost output. The effect on the unemployed depends on the length of the recession and the availability of unemployment benefits.

6. The purpose of unemployment insurance is to make it easier for workers who have lost their jobs to get by until they find new jobs or are recalled to work. One effect of unemployment insurance is to increase the level of unemployment and the average duration of unemployment, since unemployment benefits reduce the cost of unemployment.

7. Full employment refers to the situation when the economy is producing its potential output. There will still be some unemployment because the economy is dynamic—things are constantly changing. Hence, there will be seasonal, frictional, and structural unemployment. The unemployment rate associated with full employment may change over time as a result of institutional and demographic changes.

8. Demand-pull inflation refers to aggregate demand increasing faster than aggregate supply. Cost-push inflation refers to a situation in which aggregate supply is decreasing relative to aggregate demand. Increases in aggregate demand pull up the price level; decreases in aggregate supply cause resource prices to increase, which then pushes up the price level.

9. Inflation is anticipated when economic agents are able to predict the inflation rate correctly; unanticipated inflation occurs when the actual inflation rate is greater than people had predicted. People can take steps to offset the effects of inflation when it is anticipated, so the effects of anticipated inflation are less severe than those of unanticipated inflation. Inflation always has economic effects, however, unless everyone perfectly anticipates it and all prices increase at exactly the same rate at the same time.

10. Inflation makes it more difficult to tell whether an increase in price is due to the good becoming relatively more scarce or due to inflation. Hence, inflation raises the transaction costs of operating in the economy.

11. Deflation refers to a sustained period of falling prices; disinflation refers to a reduction in the inflation rate. That is, with disinflation there is still inflation.

12. Among the people harmed by inflation are those who hold dollars, since the purchasing power of the dollar decreases with inflation. People who have fixed incomes or who have signed contracts to receive payments of a fixed amount are also harmed. Among the people who benefit are those who have signed contracts to pay a fixed amount over time, such as homeowners.

13. People who make up the pool of the frictional unemployed are looking for the right jobs. One important characteristic of any job is the wage. People may be seeking a certain level of real wages, which they anticipate will result from a particular nominal wage, based on their expectations about inflation. Suppose they receive job offers at the desired nominal wages as inflation affects resource prices. With unanticipated inflation, the real wages are lower than people want, but they may not realize this. Hence they accept jobs and are no longer unemployed. But they might continue looking for jobs if they knew what the true inflation rate was.

14. The nominal interest rate is measured in terms of actual dollars paid. The real interest rate is the nominal interest rate minus the inflation rate. So, an increase in the inflation rate causes nominal interest rates to increase. Since contracts often involve fixed interest rates, nominal interest rates will be determined by expected inflation rates. If the actual inflation rate differs from that expected, then real interest rates change until the borrowers and lenders alter their expectations.

15. Inflation affects everyone in some way. People see their expenses increasing and are unhappy, even though they may be receiving pay increases as well. Inflation makes it more difficult to make good economic decisions because it is difficult to distinguish between price changes that are due to inflation and price changes that signal changes in relative prices. People end up spending extra resources on gathering information and finding ways to hedge against the effects of inflation.

CHAPTER 8

Measuring Economic Aggregates

I. INTRODUCTION

In order to diagnose what is right or wrong with the economy, one must be able to measure its health. The national income accounting system does this. This chapter discusses the calculation of the gross domestic product and some other important measures of economic performance. It is important for you to be very familiar with the terms and concepts introduced here.

II. OUTLINE

1. The Product of a Nation. Economic activity is measured as a flow. The national income accounting system summarizes economic activity in the United States.

   1.1 National Income Accounts
   - a. Gross domestic product (GDP) measures the market value of all final goods and services produced by resources located in the United States.
   - b. National income accounts use double-entry bookkeeping.
   - c. There are two ways of measuring GDP: the expenditure approach and the income approach.
   - d. To prevent double counting, GDP figures do not include sales of intermediate products, which are goods purchased for additional processing and resale. Purchases of goods produced in prior years are also excluded from current GDP.

   1.2 GDP Based on the Expenditure Approach
   - a. Consumption, or personal consumption expenditures, refers to purchases of final goods and services by households during the year. It is the largest spending category.
   - b. Investment, or gross private domestic investment, refers to spending during the year on output that is not used for present consumption.
     - (1) Physical capital is the most important category of investment.
     - (2) Investment also includes new residential construction and changes in inventories held by firms.
   - c. Government purchases, or government consumption and gross investment, refer to spending for goods and services by all levels of government. Transfer payments are not included.
   - d. For the U.S. economy, net exports refer to the value of U.S. goods and services purchased by foreigners minus the value of foreign goods and services purchased by Americans.
   - e. The nation's aggregate expenditure, or GDP, is the sum of consumption, investment, government purchases, and net exports.

1.3 Composition of Aggregate Expenditure
   a. Consumption's share of GDP changes little from year to year.
   b. Investment spending is fairly volatile.
   c. Government spending as a percent of GDP has been falling, although this is because transfer payments are not included.
   d. Net exports have been negative in most years since 1959.

1.4 GDP Based on the Income Approach
   a. The income approach computes the aggregate income generated by production.
   b. Aggregate income equals the sum of all income earned by resource suppliers in the economy.
   c. To calculate GDP, we add the income earned, or value added, at each stage of production.
   d. Value added by a firm equals the firm's selling price minus the amount paid to other firms for materials.

2. Limitations of National Income Accounting

2.1 Some Production Is Not Included in GDP
   a. GDP does not include household production because the products are not sold in markets.
   b. GDP does not include transactions for which there are no official records, such as those in the underground economy.
   c. Imputed income from certain activities outside of formal markets, such as a farm family's production of food for its own consumption, is included in GDP.

2.2 Leisure, Quality, and Variety
   a. Leisure is not included in GDP.
   b. GDP does not measure improvements in the quality of products.

2.3 *Case Study:* Tracking a $7 Trillion Economy

2.4 Gross Domestic Product Ignores Depreciation
   a. GDP does not account for depreciation of the capital stock.
   b. Net domestic product equals GNP minus depreciation.

2.5 GDP Does Not Reflect All Costs. For example, costs to the environment are not included.

2.6 GDP Values All Output Equally. GDP measures dollar values of goods and services and does not distinguish among the social values of the goods and services produced.

3. Accounting for Price Changes. GDP is computed in current dollars. The real value of GDP must be used to compare GDP in different years.

3.1 Price Indexes
   a. To compute price levels over time, we need a reference point from which to create index numbers.
   b. The prices of goods in a certain year are selected as a reference point; the year selected is the base year.
   c. Prices in other years are expressed in terms of the base year prices; the price index in the base year is always 100.
   d. A price index allows comparison between any two years.

3.2 Consumer Price Index
   a. The CPI measures change over time in the cost of buying the "market basket" of goods and services purchased by a typical family.
   b. A price index can be calculated for different market baskets.

3.3 Problems with the CPI
   a. The CPI neglects quality improvements.
   b. The CPI neglects buyer responses to changes in relative prices.
   c. The CPI has failed to keep up with the shift consumers have made toward discount outlets.

3.4 GDP Price Index
   a. Real GDP is output in a current year measured in base year prices.
   b. The GDP price index includes the prices of all domestically produced final goods and services.
   c. Nominal GDP divided by real GDP multiplied by 100 generates the GDP price index.

3.5 Moving from Fixed Weights to Chain Weights
   a. Since relative prices change over time, distortions occur when a base year is used to compare with many years.
   b. The BEA moved from a fixed-weighted system to a chain-weighted system in early 1996.
   c. The chain-weighted real GDP index adjusts to price weights more or less continuously.

3.6 *CASE STUDY:* Computer Prices and GDP Estimation

3.7 Real GDP Estimates

4. Appendix A: A Closer Look at the National Income Accounts

4.1 National Income. National income measures income earned by resource suppliers; it equals NNP plus government subsidies minus indirect business taxes.

4.2 Personal Income. Personal income (PI) measures all income received by individuals; it equals national income plus income received but not earned and minus income earned but not received.

4.3 Disposable Income. Disposable income (DI) measures the income available for households to spend; it equals personal income minus personal taxes and other government charges.

4.4 Summary of National Income Accounts. The components of the national income accounts are GDP, NDP, national income, PI, and DI.

4.5 Summary Income Statement of the Economy
   a. National income represents the sum of all earnings from producing domestic product.
   b. There are five components of national income:
      (1) Employee compensation
      (2) Proprietors' income
      (3) Corporate profits
      (4) Net interest
      (5) Rental income of persons
   c. The largest source of personal income is employee compensation.

5. Appendix B: The Chain-Weighted Index. Prices of individual goods are weighted by their quantities to compute the GDP price index.

   5.1 Real GDP Index
      a. Different values are calculated when real GDP is measured in one year's prices instead of another year's prices.
      b. The BEA uses a geometric average of the two quantity indexes.

   5.2 GDP Price Index. The geometric average is also used to calculate the GDP index.

III. DISCUSSION

The Product of a Nation

The federal government collects large quantities of data in order to measure the performance of the economy. The U.S. national income accounts, which have been devised by some of the top economists in the last fifty years, organize the data into a coherent framework. The government uses *gross domestic product* (GDP), which is the market value of all final goods and services produced by resources located in the United States, as its measure of product. GDP excludes income of Americans living in foreign countries and includes the income of foreigners living in the United States.

It is important to know what is and what is not included in gross domestic product. GDP includes *final goods and services* but does not include *intermediate goods and services*. Final goods and services are those that are sold to the ultimate user. Intermediate goods and services are those purchased for additional processing and resale. The classification of a good as a final good or an intermediate good depends on the identity of the buyer and the purpose of the purchase. A carburetor produced by General Motors and installed in one of its cars is an intermediate good; a carburetor sold to an individual who goes home and installs it herself is a final good.

Gross domestic product is a flow variable, so the calculation of GDP is for a particular period of time—generally a year. However, the government also makes quarterly calculations of GDP. GDP measures domestic production, so goods and services produced in the United States but exported to other countries are included; goods and services that are produced elsewhere and imported into the United States are deducted.

There are two ways to measure GDP. The *expenditure approach* measures GDP by adding up the *aggregate expenditure* on all final goods and services. There are four components of aggregate expenditure: *consumption*, *investment*, *government purchases*, and *net exports*. Consumption is the purchase of final goods and services by households; final goods include both durable goods and nondurable goods. Investment includes all spending on output that is not used for present consumption. Included in investment are the purchase of new plants and equipment by firms, changes in firms' *inventories*, and new residential construction. Government purchases include spending for goods and services by all levels of government but do not include transfer payments. This is because transfer payments do not involve the government purchase of goods and services. Net exports are exports minus imports and include expenditures on goods and services.

The second method of measuring GDP is the *income approach*. Income categories include wages, rent, interest, and profit. Production involves the use of inputs to produce the goods and services. Each input is owned by someone, and that person receives a payment for the use of the input. The total value of a good that is produced equals the total of payments made to input owners. Hence, if we measure the value of a good by its sale price, we will get the same figure as if we measure its value as the total of all payments to the owners of inputs used to produce the good.

Double counting is avoided by including only the market value of final goods and services or by calculating the *value added* at each stage of production. Value added is found by taking the selling price of the firm and subtracting the amount paid to other firms for materials. Hence, the value added reflects the amount paid to resource owners at that stage of production. By adding up the value added at each stage of production, we include the contribution of all resource owners to production.

Limitations of National Income Accounting

As we mentioned earlier, it is important to know what is and what is not included in national income accounting. We have already seen that intermediate goods and services are not included, but other important categories are also not included. With some exceptions, GDP includes only products sold in formal markets, so it does not include household production. Child care, food preparation, lawn care, home maintenance, and the like, when produced by the members of a household, are not included in GDP. GDP measurements also exclude transactions in the *underground economy*, although this is not intentional. The government would like to include these transactions and tax the unreported income.

GDP also fails to reflect *depreciation* of capital goods. GDP ignores changes in the availability of leisure, changes in the quality of products, and changes in the availability of new products. It also fails to distinguish among types of goods, treating $100 spent on education the same as $100 spent on theft prevention. Further, it fails to include some important costs, especially costs to the environment from producing and consuming goods and services.

Accounting for Price Changes

Because national income accounts are based on *nominal values* (current dollars), it is difficult to make meaningful comparisons of the accounts over time. The government attempts to adjust for changes in GDP due to inflation so that it can measure changes in real GDP. To compare figures over time, an index number must be calculated as a reference point. Many types of price indexes can be calculated, but the government tends to use two: the *consumer price index* and the *GDP price index.*

The consumer price index identifies a "market basket" of goods and services consumed by a typical family in the base period. The cost of buying this basket of goods each year is determined, and changes in the cost reflect changes in the cost of living.

There are several problems with the CPI. First, it fails to account for changes in quality over time. Second, the prices of all goods do not go up by the same amount every year. Hence, even in inflationary times, relative prices are changing too. Consequently, buyers respond to relative price changes by altering the amount of the goods they purchase. The CPI presumes that the same quantities of each good are purchased each year and fails to consider buyer responses to changes in relative prices. Third, it neglects changes in consumer behavior such as the shift toward discount outlets.

Appendix A: A Closer Look at the National Income Accounts

The GDP price index keeps track of price changes for all production in the economy. The *GDP price index* is nominal GDP divided by real GDP. The real GDP is measured as a weighted sum of different goods and services produced in the economy. The important question is: What weights should be used? Recently, the BEA moved from a fixed-weighted system to a chain-weighted system. The weights change from year to year. The index of real GDP for 1995 is based on a geometric average of the prices for 1994 and 1995.

The appendix takes a closer look at some of the national income accounts. Exhibit 1 shows how disposable income is derived from GDP.

Exhibit 1

National Income Accounting 1992 (billions of dollars)

Consumer expenditures	$4,108.7	
Investment	781.6	
Net exports	-36.0	
Government purchases	1,103.1	
Gross domestic product		$5,957.4
Less: Depreciation	-684.2	
Net domestic product		5,273.2
Plus: Subsidies	-3.4	
Less: Indirect business taxes	-571.4	
National income		4,698.4
Plus: Government transfers	849.3	
Private business transfers	24.8	
Interest and dividend income	804.2	
Less: Corporate profits	-374.1	
Social insurance taxes	-407.3	
Other	-554.4	
Personal income		5,040.9
Less: Personal taxes and nontax payments	-628.8	
Disposable income		$4,412.1

Appendix B: The Chain-Weighted Index

To compute the real GDP index, quantities of individual goods and services are weighted by their prices, while the GDP price index weights prices by their quantities. Instead of using year 1 or year 2 prices, a geometric average is used.

IV. LAGNIAPPE

GDP, Home Production, and Cross-Country Comparisons

Gross domestic product does not include household production, which can be an important source of production. This is especially true in less developed countries where formal markets are not well developed. Thus, home production as a percentage of total production in a country will be greater in less developed countries than in industrialized countries. When we compare the GDP of an industrialized country with that of a less developed country, the gap between the countries as measured by GDP is greater than it would be if we measured all production. Similarly, per capita income figures in less developed countries tend to understate the actual standard of living because they ignore home production.

Question to Think About: How could home production be measured in GDP figures?

Price Indexes and Quality

Price indexes tend to overstate the actual inflation rate because they ignore quality changes. Quality differences over time are often very significant. For example, in the early 1960s most television sets were black and white rather than color. Further, they used tubes that often burned out and had to be replaced. Today we have color TVs that are based on much more reliable technology. The quality of the color on television sets has also improved. Early color TVs required adjustments by professionals if they were moved from one location to another. Similar quality improvements have been made in shirts (we now have wash-and-wear shirts instead of shirts that need ironing), refrigerators, ovens, automobiles, and most other products. In addition, there are new products that did not exist in the 1960s: personal computers, video games, microwave ovens, and hand calculators, to name a few.

Question to Think About: Are there any products in existence today that did not exist in 1980?

V. KEY TERMS

Gross domestic product (GDP)
Expenditure approach
Income approach
Final goods and services
Intermediate goods and services
Consumption
Investment
Physical capital
Inventories
Government purchases
Net exports
Aggregate expenditure
Aggregate income
Value added
Underground economy
Depreciation
Current dollar value
Nominal value
Real GDP
Base year
Consumer price index (CPI)
GDP price index
Net domestic product (NDP)
Gross investment
Net investment
Government subsidies
Indirect business taxes
National income (NI)
Personal income (PI)
Disposable income (DI)
Employee compensation
Proprietors' income
Corporate profits
Net interest
Rental income of persons
Geometric average

VI. QUESTIONS

A. *Completion*

1. Only __________________ goods and services are used in calculating gross domestic product.

2. Goods purchased for additional processing are __________________ goods.

3. GDP can be calculated by either the __________________ approach or the __________________ approach.

4. An increase in firm __________________ is counted as an investment in the national income accounts.

5. Disinvestment occurs when there is a net ________________ on inventories during a year.

6. Aggregate __________________ is equal to the sum of consumption spending, investment spending, government purchases, and net exports.

7. The _______________ by a firm is the difference between the value of a product and the cost of intermediate products purchased from other firms.

8. Market transactions that go unreported are part of the __________________ economy.

9. GDP fails to account for the _________________ of existing products and the changes in the __________________ of new products.

10. The difference between gross domestic product and net domestic product is __________________.

11. The manufactured capital stock is depreciated but the _________________ capital stock is not.

12. The __________________ GDP is based on prices that prevail at the time of the transaction.

13. Real GDP is found by deflating __________________ GDP with a __________________.

14. __________________ investment rather than __________________ investment is used in calculating GDP.

15. __________________ income is the amount of income received by suppliers of resources before personal taxes have been paid.

B. *True/False*

______ 1. The national income accounts are based on a double-entry bookkeeping system.

______ 2. In the national income accounts, the total value of output produced must equal the total value of resource payments.

______ 3. All goods and services sold in a year are included in GDP.

______ 4. A sale of a used car in 1991 would be included in GDP in 1991.

______ 5. Consumption refers to purchases of final goods and services by households.

______ 6. Gross private domestic investment consists of spending during the year on current output that is not used in present consumption.

______ 7. Disinvestment occurs when there is a net increase in inventories.

______ 8. Social Security payments are included in the expenditure measure of GDP.

______ 9. Net exports includes the value of U.S. exports minus imports on goods only.

______ 10. Consumption spending as a percent of GDP is volatile over time.

______ 11. Investment spending as a percent of GDP is volatile over time.

______ 12. The value added at each stage of production represents income to resource suppliers at that stage.

______ 13. The market value of a good equals the sum of the value added at each stage of production.

______ 14. National income accounts always look at economic activity after the transaction has occurred.

______ 15. GDP fails to reflect changes in the availability of leisure time.

______ 16. GDP is the same whether people do their own taxes or have accountants do their taxes.

______ 17. The government reduces GDP figures to reflect the costs associated with negative externalities.

______ 18. In calculating the GDP price index, the government includes all final goods and services produced in the economy.

______ 19. The consumer price index holds constant the bundle of commodities consumed over time.

______ 20. The CPI and the GDP price index differ only with respect to the goods and services included.

C. *Multiple Choice*

1. The total value of output is measured by
   a. the amount people pay for the output.
   b. the total amount paid at each stage of production.
   c. disposable income.
   d. GDP plus depreciation.
   e. the value added at the final stage of production.

2. Which of the following is included in GDP?
   a. purchase of a computer by General Motors
   b. sale of a car to IBM
   c. value of homeowner's time when mowing the lawn
   d. sale of U.S. wheat to Russia
   e. all of the above

3. Which of the following is an example of a final good or service?
   a. steel purchased by General Motors
   b. milk purchased by a grocery store
   c. pickles purchased by McDonald's
   d. a truckload of tropical fish purchased by a pet store
   e. a new factory built by IBM

4. The difference between gross domestic product and net domestic product is
   a. investment spending.
   b. net exports.
   c. depreciation.
   d. the former uses the expenditure approach and the latter uses the income approach.
   e. saving.

5. The largest spending category is
   a. personal consumer expenditures.
   b. gross private domestic investment.
   c. government consumption and gross investment.
   d. imports.
   e. a and c are about the same size

6. Invisible is another term for
   a. inventories.
   b. services.
   c. indirect business taxes.
   d. depreciation.
   e. none of the above.

7. Which of the following would not be included in U.S. GDP?
   a. a waiter's cash tips that are not reported to the IRS
   b. cash payment made at a grocery store
   c. purchase of a new house
   d. payment of military salaries
   e. sale of an airline ticket by American Airlines for a flight from London to New York

8. In terms of the national income accounts, which of the following is an example of an investment?
   a. purchase of one hundred shares of IBM stock
   b. building of a new hospital by the government
   c. a farmer's purchase of a used tractor
   d. an increase in inventories during the year
   e. transfer of funds from a checking account to a savings account

9. Which of the following is not included in government purchases?
   a. The Pentagon's purchase of a new jet fighter
   b. The salary of the President
   c. An increase in Social Security benefits
   d. Purchase of office supplies by the Senate
   e. All are included in government purchases.

10. Suppose you pay 80 cents for a gallon of gasoline. Further, suppose the owner of the oil well received 20 cents per gallon, the oil refiner received 65 cents per gallon, and the gasoline wholesaler received 75 cents from the gas station. What is the contribution to GDP from the sale of the gasoline? What is the gasoline station's value added?
    a. $2.40; 80 cents
    b. 80 cents; 80 cents
    c. 80 cents; 5 cents
    d. 80 cents; 75 cents
    e. 75 cents; 75 cents

11. GDP equals
    a. the market value of all final goods and services.
    b. the sum of all the income earned by resource suppliers in the economy.
    c. the sum of the value added at all stages of production.
    d. all of the above.
    e. b plus c.

12. Which of the following would increase GDP?
    a. A man repairs his car himself.
    b. A family sells its house.
    c. Ford buys a spark plug from an auto parts manufacturer rather than making it itself.
    d. A family takes its baby to day care rather than to the baby's grandmother for babysitting.
    e. All of the above increase GDP.

13. The U.S. nominal GDP was $3,777.2 billion in 1984 and $4,038.7 billion in 1985. The increase in GDP was due to
    a. an increase in the value of total production of the United States.
    b. inflation.
    c. an increase in government purchases.
    d. a reduction of import spending.
    e. All of the above are possible explanations.

14. The CPI was 87.2 for 1983 and 91.0 for 1984 (1987 base year). What was the rate of inflation, calculated using the CPI?
    a. 4.3 percent
    b. 3.8 percent
    c. 178.2 percent
    d. 3.4 percent
    e. The question cannot be answered without more information.

15. CPI and the GDP price index differ in that
    a. the CPI takes into consideration quality differences and the GDP price index does not.
    b. the GDP price index compares current prices to prices in a base year and the CPI does not.
    c. the CPI uses prices for a sample of consumption goods and services whereas the GDP price index uses prices of all final domestic production.
    d. the GDP price index holds the weight of each item's price constant over time whereas the CPI allows the weights to vary over time.
    e. c and d

16. GDP tends to grow as an economy becomes less rural and more urban, in part because
    a. people living in cities want more things than people on farms.
    b. people on farms tend to produce more of their own goods and services than people in cities.
    c. net exports tend to be greater in urban economies than in rural economies.
    d. farmers do not engage in investment spending.
    e. all of the above

17. Which of the following is a problem with using GDP as a measure of economic welfare?
    a. GDP excludes environmental costs.
    b. GDP excludes the value of household production.
    c. GDP fails to distinguish among types of commodities.
    d. GDP fails to consider the value of leisure.
    e. all of the above

*18. The largest source of income is
    a. employee compensation.
    b. corporate profits.
    c. proprietors' income.
    d. government transfer payments.
    e. any of the above, depending on the year in question.

*19. Which of the following is an indirect business tax?
    a. sales taxes
    b. excise taxes
    c. corporate income taxes
    d. all of the above
    e. a and b only

*20. The GDP price index is a ______________ index that uses a ______________ or two ______________ indexes.

   a. fixed-weighted; moving average; chain-type
   b. fixed-weighted; geometric average; quantity
   c. chain-type; geometric average; fixed-weighted
   d. chain-type; arithmetic average; fixed-weighted
   e. CPI; geometric average; chain-type

D. *Discussion Questions*

1. Discuss what is and what is not included in calculating GDP.

2. State whether each of the following transactions is a part of GDP and explain why.
   a. Profits made by an IBM plant in England
   b. Profits made by a Honda plant in Ohio

3. How do the expenditure and income approaches to calculating GDP differ? Why do they yield the same number for GDP?

4. How are changes in inventories handled in GDP accounts?

5. Why are welfare payments not included in government spending?

6. What is value added? How is value added related to the market value of the final good?

7. Suppose a firm sells its product for $10 and pays $6 for materials. If the cost of materials increases to $7 but the firm still sells its product for $10, what happens to GDP? What happens to the value added of the firm? Explain.

8. Discuss the limitations of national income accounting.

9. Why does national income accounting ignore changes in leisure time and household production?

10. Fill in the blanks in Exhibit 2 on the following page.

Exhibit 2

Year	*Basket of Goods (Nominal)*	*Basket of Goods (Real)*	*CPI*	*Inflation Rate*
1988	$4,053.6	$4,294.1	94.4	________
1989	4,277.7	________	96.9	________
1990	4,544.5	4,544.5	________	________
1991	________	4,728.5	103.9	________
1992	5,266.8	4,854.2	________	________
1993	________	4,896.6	113.2	________
1994	5,694.9	________	117.8	________
1995	________	4,943.9	________	2.9%

11. Why does the consumer price index exaggerate the inflation rate?

12. Per capita GDP is much higher in the United States than in China. Does this imply that U.S. consumers are that much better off than Chinese consumers? Explain.

*13. Use the following information to answer the questions.

Consumer expenditures	$1,732.6
Depreciation	303.9
Government purchases	530.3
Government transfers	312.6
Indirect business taxes	230.3
Interest and dividend income	324.9
Investment	437.0
Net exports	32.1
Other income not received	200.9
Personal taxes and nontax payments	340.5
Private business transfers	12.1
Social insurance taxes	216.5
Net income from American resources abroad	5.7
Corporate profits	177.2

a. What is GDP?
b. What is NDP?
c. What is national income?
d. What is personal income?
e. What is disposable income?

Use the following information to answer questions 14 and 15.

	Units of Output		*Price per Unit*	
Good/Service	*Year 1*	*Year 2*	*Year 1*	*Year 2*
Gasoline	10,000	12,000	$1.15	$1.00
Movies/Rentals	1,000	1,000	$2.00	$2.00
Steaks	5,000	4,000	$4.00	$6.00

14. What is the change in real output from year 1 to year 2?

*15. What is the rate of inflation using the chain-weighted approach?

VII. ANSWERS

A. *Completion*

1. final
2. intermediate
3. expenditure; income
4. inventories
5. decrease
6. expenditure
7. value added
8. underground
9. quality; availability
10. depreciation
11. natural
12. nominal (or current-dollar)
13. nominal; price index
14. Actual; planned
15. Personal

B. *True/False*

1. True
2. True
3. False. Only currently produced final goods and services are included.
4. False
5. True
6. True
7. False
8. False
9. False. Services are included too.
10. False
11. True
12. True
13. True
14. True
15. True
16. False
17. False
18. True
19. True
20. False

C. *Multiple Choice*

1. a
2. d
3. e
4. c
5. a
6. b
7. a
8. d
9. c
10. c
11. d
12. d
13. e
14. a
15. c
16. b
17. e
18. a
19. e
20. c

D. *Discussion Questions*

1. GDP includes the total market value of all domestically produced final goods and services. It includes exports because they are produced here, but it does not include imports because they are not produced in the United States. It does not include intermediate goods because their value is included in the value of the final goods and services. With some exceptions, GDP does not include the value of production undertaken by households because such production does not involve market transactions. It also does not include transactions that take place in the underground economy, since they are not recorded.

2. a. No, because the plant is not located in the United States.
   b. Yes, because the plant is located in the United States.

3. The expenditure and income approaches differ in that they focus on different portions of the circular flow. The expenditure approach focuses on purchases made by different members of society; the income approach focuses on the income received by different resource owners. The two must be equal because the total expenditure on a good or service must exactly equal the sum of the incomes of all the resource owners who contributed resources to producing the good or service.

4. A net increase in inventories during the year adds to investment spending while a net decrease in inventories is subtracted from investment spending.

5. Government spending involves spending on goods and services. Welfare payments are a transfer payment, and so they are not included.

6. Value added is the difference at each stage of production between what the firm sells its product for and what the firm pays for the materials it purchased to make the product. The market value of the final good must equal the sum of the value added at each stage of production.

7. Since the price of the final good does not change, GDP does not change, but the firm's value added falls from $4 to $3. The higher income of owners of resources associated with the production of the product is exactly offset by the lower income received by resource owners associated with the firm. Value added at an earlier stage of production has increased.

8. National income accounting has several limitations. GDP does not include most household production, which may often be an important source of production. GDP also misses unreported transactions. The national income accounts cannot account for changes over time in the availability of leisure, quality of products, and availability of new products. Further, GDP ignores some costs, such as the costs associated with pollution.

9. Presumably because both would be difficult to put dollar values on. The value a person places on leisure is subjective, and difficult to measure. The value of household production could be included theoretically, but it would also be difficult to do practically. What activities would be included? Feeding the baby, getting dressed, and combing one's hair could all be done by hiring someone, yet these seem like unlikely candidates to include in GDP.

10.

Year	Basket of Goods (Nominal)	Basket of Goods (Real)	CPI	Inflation Rate
1988	$4,053.6	$4,294.1	94.4	______
1989	4,277.7	**4,414.6**	96.9	**2.6%**
1990	4,544.5	4,544.5	**100.0**	**3.2%**
1991	**4,908.2**	4,728.5	103.9	**3.9%**
1992	5,266.8	4,854.2	**108.5**	**4.4%**
1993	**5,542.9**	4,896.6	113.2	**4.3%**
1994	5,694.9	**4,843.4**	117.8	**4.1%**
1995	**5,992.0**	4,943.9	**121.2**	2.9%

11. The CPI holds the weight of each price constant over time. When the price of a good increases relative to all other prices, people may respond by curtailing consumption of the good. Since the CPI operates as though consumption of the good were the same even though the relative price is higher, it overstates the weight of the good and overstates the inflation rate. It also fails to account for the introduction of new products, changes in quality, and changes in quantity of leisure time.

12. China has a more rural economy than the United States, so household production is likely to be much more extensive in China than in the United States. Further, China is a centrally planned economy, so the goods produced do not always reflect consumers' desires, and prices tend to be set by government rather than by the interaction of supply and demand. In short, comparison between the GDPs of the two countries is very difficult to make.

13. a. GDP = $1,732.6 + 530.3 + 32.1 + 437 = $2,732.0
    b. NDP = $2,732.0 - 303.9 = $2,428.1
    c. National income = $2,428.1 + 5.7 - 230.3 = $2,203.5
    d. Personal income = $2,203.5 + 312.6 + 12.1 + 324.9 - 177.2 - 216.5 - 200.9 = 2,258.5
    e. Disposable income = $2,258.5 - 340.5 = $1,918.0

14. Calculate the value of output each year using year 1 prices:

Gasoline:	10,000 x $1.15	=	$11,500	12,000 x $1.15	=	$13,800
Movie Rentals:	1,000 x 2.00	=	2,000	1,000 x 2.00	=	2,000
Steaks:	5,000 x 4.00	=	20,000	4,000 x 4.00	=	16,000
			$33,500			$31,800

Quantity index = 31,800/33,500 x 100 = 94.93 (or a 5.07% reduction in real output).

Calculate the value of output each year using year 2 prices:

Gasoline:	10,000 x $1.00	=	$10,000	12,000 x $1.00	=	$12,000
Movie Rentals:	1,000 x 2.00	=	2,000	1,000 x 2.00	=	2,000
Steaks:	5,000 x 6.00	=	30,000	4,000 x 6.00	=	24,000
			$42,000			$38,000

Quantity index = 38,000/42,000 x 100 = 90.48 (or a 9.52% reduction in real output).

Geometric average - $(94.93 \times 90.48)^{1/2}$ = 92.68, or a 7.32% reduction in real output

15. The GDP price index in year 2 based on year 1 quantities equals:
    $42,000/33,500 x 100 = 125.4

    and the price index on year 2 based on year 2 quantities equals:
    38,000/31,800 = 119.5

    The geometric average is: $(125.4 \times 119.5)^{1/2}$ = 122.4.

    The inflation rate was 22.4%

CHAPTER 9

Consumption and Aggregate Expenditure

I. INTRODUCTION

We have already introduced aggregate demand and aggregate supply curves. Now we begin a closer look at aggregate demand. In particular, this chapter examines two important components of aggregate demand: consumption and investment. Both activities originate in the private sector of the economy. A third component of aggregate demand—net exports—is examined in the appendix. Aggregate supply will be discussed in future chapters.

II. OUTLINE

1. Early Views of the Macroeconomy

    1.1 The Classical View
    a. Adam Smith believed people pursued their own self-interests, but they were led as if by an invisible hand to promote the general good.
    b. Smith and other classical economists were very critical of mercantilism and advocated a laissez-faire policy.
    c. Classical economists believed the economy would naturally tend toward the full-employment level of output.
    d. Depressions and unemployment were believed to be short-run phenomena caused by external shocks to the economy.
    e. It was thought that any disequilibrium would be corrected by natural market forces, particularly the flexibility of wages and prices.

    1.2 Keynes and the Great Depression
    a. The prolonged unemployment during the Great Depression caused economists to reevaluate the classical view.
    b. Keynes argued that prices and wages are not flexible enough to ensure full employment.
    c. At times, business expectations may be so bad that planned saving exceeds planned investment regardless of the interest rate.

2. The Circular Flow of Income and Expenditure. The circular flow illustrates how aggregate expenditure is equal to aggregate income.

    2.1 The Income Half of the Circular Flow
    a. Production generates income for the suppliers of resources to firms.
    b. GDP equals aggregate income.
    c. Because of taxes, not all the aggregate income earned in the economy is available to households.
    d. *Disposable income* is aggregate income plus transfer payments minus taxes.

2.2 The Expenditure Half of the Circular Flow
   a. Disposable income flows to either consumption spending or saving.
   b. Financial markets link savers and borrowers.
   c. The primary borrowers are firms and government.
   d. Investment spending and government purchases are injections into the circular flow.
   e. Exports are an injection into the circular flow, and imports are a leakage from the flow.
   f. Aggregate expenditure equals aggregate income.

2.3 Leakages Equal Injections. Leakages from the circular flow must equal injections into the circular flow.

2.4 Planned Investment Versus Actual Investment. National income accounting reflects actual investment, which includes planned investment plus unplanned changes in inventories.

3. Consumption

3.1 An Initial Look at Income and Consumption
   a. Keynes thought that the most important determinant of how much people consume is their disposable income.
   b. Consumer spending and disposable income tend to move together over time.

3.2 The Consumption Function
   a. People decide how much to consume based on their disposable income, so consumption depends on disposable income.
   b. The consumption function shows the relation between the amount spent on consumption and the level of income in the economy, other things constant.

3.3 Marginal Propensities to Consume and to Save
   a. The *marginal propensity to consume* (MPC) shows how much of an extra dollar received is spent on consumer goods, and it equals the change in consumption divided by the change in income.
   b. The *marginal propensity to save* (MPS) equals the change in saving divided by the change in income.
   c. The sum of the marginal propensity to consume and the marginal propensity to save must equal 1 because disposable income is either spent or saved.

3.4 MPC, MPS, and the Slope of the Consumption and Savings Functions
   a. The marginal propensity to consume equals the slope of the consumption function.
   b. The marginal propensity to save equals the slope of the saving function.

3.5 Nonincome Determinants of Consumption
   a. The greater the level of their net wealth, the more willing households are to consume instead of save.
      (1) Along a given consumption function, household net wealth is held constant.
      (2) A change in net wealth causes the consumption function to shift; a change in income causes a movement along the consumption function.
   b. An increase in the price level reduces consumption (the consumption function shifts down) and increases saving; a decrease in the price level increases consumption and decreases saving.
   c. An increase in the interest rate promotes more saving and shifts the consumption function down; a decrease in the interest rate promotes less saving and shifts the consumption function up.

d. Changes in expectations also shift the consumption function.
   (1) Expectations of higher income levels generate greater consumption prior to the actual change in income.
   (2) Expectations of higher prices in the future also encourage people to increase current consumption spending.

3.6 *CASE STUDY:* The Life-Cycle Hypothesis

4. Investment. Investment consists of spending on construction of factories and equipment, construction of housing, and net increases in inventories. Investment does not consist of purchases of stocks, bonds, land, and so forth.

4.1 The Demand for Investment
   a. Firms buy capital goods when the investment is expected to be more profitable than other possible uses of the funds.
   b. The opportunity cost of funds is the market interest rate.
   c. A firm will invest in capital stock when the expected rate of return exceeds the market rate of interest.
   d. The demand for investment spending is inversely related to the interest rate.

4.2 From Micro to Macro
   a. Just as a particular business's demand curve for investment slopes down, so does the market demand curve for investment.
   b. The lower the interest rate, the greater the quantity of investment demanded, other things equal.

4.3 Planned Investment and the Economy's Level of Income
   a. Investment is assumed to be autonomous; that is, it is assumed to be independent of the level of income.
   b. In making decisions, investors look more at expected future profits than at current income levels.
   c. The investment function, which relates planned investment to the current level of disposable income, is a horizontal line at the current level of investment demand.

4.4 Nonincome Determinants of Investment
   a. The investment function shifts up when interest rates fall and shifts down when interest rates increase.
   b. Business expectations of profit prospects greatly affect the level of investment spending.

4.5 *CASE STUDY:* Variability of Consumption and Investment

5. Government

5.1 Government Purchase Function
   a. The government purchase function relates government purchases to the level of income in the economy.
   b. It is assumed that government purchases are autonomous, or independent of the level of income.

5.2 Net Taxes. *Net taxes* are taxes minus transfer payments, and they are treated as autonomous.

6. Net Exports

6.1 Net Exports and Income

a. When disposable income increases, people spend more on all normal goods, including imports.
b. There is a positive relationship between disposable income and imports.
c. Exports are autonomous, since they depend on the income of foreigners.
d. *Net exports* are exports minus imports, which decline as income increases.
e. The analysis is simplified by assuming net exports are autonomous.

6.2 Nonincome Determinants of Net Exports

a. The net export function shows the relationship between net exports and the level of income, other things constant.
b. Factors held constant include
   (1) U.S. price level
   (2) Price levels in other countries
   (3) Interest rates in the United States and in other countries
   (4) Foreign income levels
   (5) Exchange rates between the dollar and foreign currencies
c. A fall in the value of the dollar causes an increase in net exports, and a rise in the value of the dollar causes a fall in net exports.

7. Appendix: Variable Net Exports

7.1 Net Exports and Income. Net exports are inversely related to U.S. income.

7.2 Shifts in Net Exports. The net export function shifts up if the value of the dollar falls and shifts down if the value of the dollar increases.

III. DISCUSSION

Early Views of the Macroeconomy

The classical economists believed that the economy was basically self-regulating. Firms hire resources and pay the resource owners out of the income generated from selling the output produced using the resources. The value of the output thus equals the income. For classical economists the question was whether the income generated would be used to buy the output that was produced. If it was not, then there would be an excess supply, firms would cut back their hiring of resources, and unemployment would result.

Resource owners either spend their incomes on goods and services or save them. If resource owners saved some of their income, then total spending on society's output would be less than the value of the output. That is, the economy would experience an excess supply along with unemployment. The classical economists pointed out, however, that saving did not sit idle but was generally converted into investment spending. Even when savers and investors are different people, the interest rate adjusts to ensure that planned saving equals planned investment. Hence, the production of output tends to generate the spending necessary to sell the output.

The Great Depression of the 1930s caused many economists to question the classical viewpoint. Keynes argued that business expectations might be so grim that even very low interest rates might not be able to ensure that planned saving always equaled planned investment. If saving can exceed investment, then an excess supply is possible and can lead to unemployment. Keynes further argued that prices and wages were relatively inflexible, so natural market forces would not return the economy to full employment under such conditions.

The Circular Flow of Income and Expenditure

The circular flow model pictures the relationships among households, firms, the government, and the foreign sector, as well as the flow of aggregate expenditure and the flow of aggregate income that make up GDP. Make sure you understand the circular flow, illustrated in Exhibit 1 in the text. *Aggregate income* flows from firms to households, with a *leakage* of taxes and an *injection* of transfer payments. Households spend *disposable income* on consumption and saving. Savings flow into *financial markets*, where governments and firms come to borrow funds for government spending and investment spending. Consumption spending is combined with investment spending, government purchases, and net exports and flows back to firms. Net exports are either a net injection or a net leakage, depending on whether exports or imports are larger. Total leakages from the circular flow must equal total injections into the circular flow.

Since national income accounting uses double-entry bookkeeping, aggregate expenditure must equal aggregate income, and leakages must equal injections. However, double-entry bookkeeping does not imply that the plans of all people are always fulfilled or that the plans of all people mesh perfectly. In particular, GDP figures include *actual investment*, not *planned investment*. Unplanned changes in inventories can make actual investment different from planned investment. Potential differences between planned and actual investment is an important topic that is addressed more fully in a later chapter.

Consumption

Consumption is a positive function of disposable income. The relationship between U.S. disposable income and consumption has been very stable, especially since World War II. The *consumption function* shows the relationship between the amount spent on consumption and the level of income, other things constant. Consumption spending increases as disposable income increases; that is, consumption spending and income are directly related. A graph of a consumption function is an upward-sloping line, as shown in Exhibit 4 in the text. Since Keynes, economists have focused on what happens when disposable income changes. If disposable income increases, some of the additional income will be spent on consumption goods and some will be saved. The proportion of the additional income that is spent on consumption is called the *marginal propensity to consume* (MPC). That is, the marginal propensity to consume is the change in consumption spending divided by the change in income. Further, the change in income is the cause of the change in consumption spending. Similarly, the *marginal propensity to save* (MPS) is the change in saving divided by the change in disposable income.

Be sure that you understand Exhibits 5 and 6 in the text. Columns 1 and 3 in Exhibit 5 show levels of disposable income and consumption; columns 2 and 4 show the changes in disposable income and consumption. The MPC, then, is column 4 divided by column 2. In Exhibit 6, the MPC is measured by the slope of the consumption function, and the MPS is measured by the slope of the saving function. Since the only uses of additional income are consumption and saving, MPC + MPS = 1.

Consumption also depends on things other than income. In particular, consumption depends on net wealth, the price level, consumer expectations, and the interest rate. Net wealth is a stock, whereas income is a flow. That is, *net wealth* is the value of all the assets owned by a household less liabilities and debts owed to others. To increase net wealth, a household must either increase savings or pay off debt. Since an important motive for saving is to increase one's wealth, the greater the wealth, the less the incentive to save and the more the household will spend on consumption. An increase in net wealth causes the consumption function to shift up; a reduction in net wealth causes the consumption function to shift down. Note that in either case the consumption function shifts because of a change in net wealth. A change in income has a different effect: it causes a movement *along* the consumption function.

An increase in the price level makes a household poorer because the purchasing power of the household's savings falls. As a result, the household will reduce consumption and increase saving, which generates a downward shift in the consumption function. A change in expectations will also shift the consumption function. Expectations of higher income in the future tend to encourage more consumption today, as do expectations of higher prices in the future. Finally, a change in the market rate of interest will cause the consumption function to shift. If the interest rate falls, savers are rewarded less and generally respond by saving less and consuming more. Keep in mind that a change in disposable income causes a movement along the consumption function, whereas changes in net wealth, in the price level, in expectations, or in the interest rate cause shifts in the consumption function.

Investment

Investment consists of spending on new factories and equipment, construction of housing, and net increases in inventories. Investment adds to the economy's stock of capital goods and is generally carried out by business firms. Firms engage in investment spending when they believe that the investment will be more profitable than other possible uses of their funds. This will be the case whenever the expected rate of return exceeds the opportunity cost of investing in capital, which is the market rate of interest. The demand for investment funds tends to be a negative function of the interest rate.

Investment spending tends to be related to businesses' expectations about future profits rather than to current income. Hence, investment tends to be independent of income, or *autonomous*. The autonomous investment function can be represented graphically as a horizontal line when disposable income is on the horizontal axis. An increase in the rate of interest will cause the investment function to shift down, and a decrease in the rate of interest will cause the investment function to shift up. A more optimistic business climate causes the investment function to shift up, and a less optimistic business climate causes the investment function to shift down.

Government

Governments purchase goods and services, borrow money, and collect taxes. Government purchases are assumed to be autonomous, that is, independent of the level of income. Net taxes (taxes - transfer payments) are also assumed to be autonomous.

Net Exports

Imports are consumer goods just like any other goods. When disposable income increases, Americans buy more of all goods, so spending on imports increases. Hence, imports are a positive function of disposable income. On the other hand, the level of exports is determined by spending in other countries, so exports are autonomous with respect to U.S. disposable income. Combining imports and exports yields net exports, which are inversely related to disposable income, other things constant. However, usually we will assume net exports are autonomous. Factors held constant along the net export function include domestic and foreign price levels, domestic and foreign interest rates, and the exchange rates between domestic and foreign currencies.

Appendix: Variable Net Exports

Since imports are goods like those produced domestically, Americans buy more imports when their incomes increase. Similarly, foreigners buy more U.S. goods when their incomes increase. Imports of foreigners are U.S. exports, so U.S. exports depend on income levels in other countries rather than on U.S. income. Hence, U.S. exports are not a function of U.S. disposable income; that is, U.S. exports are autonomous. U.S. imports, though, are positively related to U.S. disposable income. Net exports are exports minus imports ($X - M$). Since exports are autonomous and imports are directly related to disposable income, net exports are inversely related to U.S. disposable income.

V. LAGNIAPPE

Saving Versus Hoarding

The link between saving and investment will be broken if savers actually hoard their money. If people do not place their funds in some type of financial intermediary and instead keep their funds at home, it is not possible for the funds to be invested. In such cases there will clearly be an imbalance between saving and investment. As long as people who save also want to receive interest on their funds, however, the link between saving and investment can exist.

Question to Think About: Why would anyone choose to hoard funds rather than place them in a financial intermediary?

Saving, Investing, and the Stock Market

Buying stocks and bonds is not considered investment. The stock market is related to investment activity in an important way, however. Firms often raise investment funds by selling shares of stock. Those who buy the shares are not investing. Instead, they are saving and providing the funds to the firm, which does invest by buying plants or equipment. If a person who buys newly issued shares of stock from a firm later sells the stock in the stock market, the firm receives no additional funds. The transaction involves only individuals, who interact through the stock market. The presence of the stock market does encourage investment activity. Firms would find it more difficult to attract funds if it were not possible to resell shares of stock. Since shareholders can sell their shares if they so desire, they are more willing to buy the initial offering of shares from the firm. The stock market is essentially a market for used shares, but this secondary market reduces firms' costs of raising investment funds.

Question to Think About: How is the bond market similar to the stock market?

V. KEY TERMS

Classical economists
Circular flow of income and expenditure
Expenditure approach
Income approach
Financial markets
Leakages
Injections
Planned investment
Actual investment
Consumption function
Marginal propensity to consume
Marginal propensity to save
Saving function
Net wealth
Investment demand curve
Investment function
Autonomous
Net export function

VI. QUESTIONS

A. *Completion*

1. Classical economists criticized the economic policy of __________________ and favored laissez faire.

2. According to the classical economists, depressions were due to external _______________.

3. Adam Smith thought that people saved only because they wanted to __________________.

4. Keynes believed that business expectations might be so low that planned saving would exceed planned investment even at very low __________________.

5. According to Keynes, prices and wages were relatively __________________.

6. In the flow of income and spending, total __________________ (such as savings and taxes) must equal total __________________ (such as transfer payments, investment, government purchases, and exports).

7. Financial markets channel funds from consumer __________________ to be used for government purchases and __________________ spending by firms.

8. The income available to households to spend or save is called __________________.

9. __________________ investment includes planned investment and unplanned inventory changes.

10. The __________________ shows a positive relationship between consumption spending and the level of income in the economy.

11. The fraction of additional income that is saved is indicated by the __________________.

12. The slope of the consumption function equals the marginal propensity to _______________.

13. ________________ consists of the value of all the assets that a household owns minus any liabilities.

14. The opportunity cost of investing in capital is the ________________.

15. Investment spending is said to be ________________ when it is independent of the level of income.

B. *True/False*

______ 1. Classical economists argued that people consciously pursued the general good.

______ 2. Adam Smith advocated mercantilism even though most classical economists opposed it.

______ 3. Classical economists argued that prices and wages were sufficiently flexible for the economy to be self-correcting.

______ 4. To the classical economist, saving was not a leakage because it converted directly into investment.

______ 5. According to Keynes, there is no reason to think that savers and investors have the same intentions.

______ 6. According to Keynes, prices and wages tend to be relatively inflexible.

______ 7. According to Keynes, business expectations can be so low during a depression that planned saving can exceed planned investment at any rate of interest.

______ 8. Saving represents an injection into the circular flow.

______ 9. The sum of the leakages from the flow of income and spending must equal the sum of the injections into the flow.

______ 10. Government debt is a stock variable whereas the government deficit is a flow variable.

______ 11. The most important determinant of how much people spend on goods and services is their disposable income.

______ 12. Consumption spending can never be greater than disposable income.

______ 13. Since consumption spending increases with disposable income, saving must decrease with disposable income.

______ 14. The entire consumption function shifts when income changes.

______ 15. A decrease in the interest rate will shift the consumption function down.

______ 16. When a person buys shares of stock, he or she is saving and investing at the same time.

______ 17. Investment spending tends to increase as interest rates fall.

______ 18. According to the textbook's simple model, investment spending is a positive function of disposable income.

______ 19. Spending on imports is a negative function of disposable income.

______ *20. An increase in an economy's disposable income causes exports to increase.

C. *Multiple Choice*

1. Classical economists believed that depressions and unemployment
   a. did not really exist.
   b. were essentially short-term phenomena.
   c. required massive government spending to correct.
   d. were due to the inflexibility of wages and prices.
   e. were due to flaws in the economic system.

2. According to classical economists, a depression would be short-lived because
   a. prices and wages would fall until both product and resource markets again achieved equilibrium.
   b. government would act and lead the economy out of the depression.
   c. surplus goods could be sold to foreigners.
   d. the lower incomes during the depression would reduce saving until saving and investment equaled each other.
   e. none of the above

3. In the classical view, planned saving will always equal planned investment spending because
   a. the interest rate will adjust to bring them into equality.
   b. savers and investors are the same people.
   c. saving and investing are two sides of the same coin.
   d. b and c
   e. none of the above

4. Keynes's main quarrel with classical economists was that
   a. business expectations are often more optimistic than the classical economists thought.
   b. prices and wages are too flexible.
   c. he thought investment spending would generally be greater than saving.
   d. tax cuts were needed to encourage more production.
   e. prices and wages were not flexible enough to ensure full employment.

5. Which of the following proverbs expresses Keynes's view of why a depression can persist in the long run?
   a. "It's always darkest before the dawn."
   b. "I won't throw good money after bad."
   c. "A penny saved is a penny earned."
   d. "A fool and his money are soon parted."
   e. "The best things in life are free."

6. Saving is a leakage from the circular flow. Which of the following may be an injection financed by the flow of saving?
   a. investment spending
   b. government purchases of goods and services
   c. government transfer payments
   d. all of the above
   e. a and b

7. Which of the following does not constitute a leakage?
   a. transfer payments
   b. taxes
   c. savings
   d. imports
   e. none of the above

8. According to Keynes, the most important determinant of how much people spend is
   a. their tastes.
   b. tax policy.
   c. the inflation rate.
   d. the interest rate.
   e. how much they have available to spend.

9. The difference between disposable income and consumption is
   a. saving.
   b. taxes.
   c. net income.
   d. investment.
   e. consumption of consumer durables.

10. Disposable income is $2,000, $3,000, and $5,000 over a three-year period, and consumption is $2,000, $2,800, and $4,400 for the same three years. The marginal propensity to consume is
    a. 1.
    b. 0.933.
    c. 0.88.
    d. 0.80.
    e. different for each year.

11. In the previous question, saving in the first year is
    a. zero.
    b. $200.
    c. $600.
    d. $1,000.
    e. unknown. More information is needed.

12. (Refer to the information in question 10.) If consumption in the fourth year is $4,800, what is disposable income that year?
    a. $5,400
    b. $5,500
    c. $5,600
    d. $6,000
    e. The question cannot be answered without more information.

13. Which of the following is not held constant along a given consumption function?
   a. the price level
   b. the market rate of interest
   c. net wealth
   d. income
   e. expectations

14. Which of the following would cause a consumption function to shift up?
   a. a reduction in net wealth
   b. an increase in the price level
   c. a reduction in the interest rate
   d. expectations of lower future income
   e. none of the above

15. Which of the following is an example of an investment?
   a. the manufacture of a lathe
   b. Chrysler's purchase of an American Motors factory
   c. an individual's purchase of one hundred shares of stock in General Motors
   d. IBM's purchase of an existing office park in Houston
   e. all of the above

16. A firm purchases capital goods as long as
   a. the expected rate of return exceeds the market rate of interest.
   b. the firm has funds available to invest.
   c. the firm is making a profit on all of its activities.
   d. the firm can borrow at the market rate of interest.
   e. none of the above

17. According to the textbook's model of investment, which of the following affects the level of investment?
   a. disposable income
   b. the market rate of interest
   c. net wealth
   d. the inflation rate
   e. all of the above

18. To say that investment spending is autonomous means that
   a. investment spending is not determined by the interest rate.
   b. investment spending is not determined by disposable income.
   c. investment spending has no effect on the economy.
   d. no one can determine what variables affect investment spending.
   e. the investment function coincides with the 45-degree line.

*19. Net exports are inversely related to the level of income because
   a. exports are inversely related to the level of income.
   b. imports are positively related to the level of income, exports are inversely related to the level of income, and the effect of exports is greater than the effect of imports.
   c. imports are positively related to the level of income and exports are autonomous.
   d. Americans buy fewer foreign goods and more U.S. goods at higher levels of income.
   e. none of the above; net exports are autonomous.

*20. A rise in the value of a dollar will cause
   a. imports to increase.
   b. exports to decrease.
   c. net exports to decrease.
   d. all of the above.
   e. none of the above.

D. *Discussion Questions*

1. Discuss the differences between the classical view of the economy and Keynes's view of it.

2. Explain how each of the proverbs in multiple choice question 7 relates to Keynes's view of depressions.

3. Why do total leakages and total injections have to be equal?

4. Why does investment spending not equal saving in the circular flow?

5. What is a consumption function? Describe the graph of a consumption function and explain its shape.

6. What is the marginal propensity to consume? to save? How are they related?

7. How is the marginal propensity to consume shown on a graph of the consumption function?

8. Explain how the following affect the consumption function:
   a. A decrease in net wealth
   b. An increase in the price level
   c. An expectation of lower prices in the future

9. Investment is not determined by income. Why not?

10. Why is there a negative relationship between the demand for investment funds and the interest rate?

11. Why does a reduction in the interest rate cause the investment function to shift up?

12. If total spending is consumption plus investment spending, how does an increase in the interest rate affect total spending?

*13. Explain why net exports are inversely related to the level of income.

*14. Explain why a country might reduce the value of its currency relative to the currencies of other countries.

*15. If total spending is $C + I + G + (X - M)$, how does an increase in domestic interest rates affect total spending? How would an increase in interest rates in foreign countries affect U.S. total spending?

VII. ANSWERS

A. *Completion*

1. mercantilism
2. shocks
3. invest
4. interest rates
5. inflexible (or sticky)
6. leakages; injections
7. savings; investments
8. disposable income
9. Actual
10. consumption function
11. marginal propensity to save
12. consume
13. Net wealth
14. market interest rate
15. autonomous

B. *True/False*

1. False
2. False
3. True
4. True
5. True
6. True
7. True
8. False
9. True
10. True
11. True
12. False
13. False
14. False
15. False
16. False
17. True
18. False
19. False
20. False

C. *Multiple Choice*

1. b
2. a
3. a
4. e
5. b
6. d
7. a
8. e
9. a
10. d
11. a
12. b
13. d
14. c
15. a
16. a
17. b
18. b
19. c
20. d

D. *Discussion Questions*

1. Classical economists believed that depressions were caused by things external to the economy, such as war or droughts. Part of their analysis depended on the assumption that prices and wages would be sufficiently flexible to clear all markets. In particular, they assumed that changes in the interest rate would keep planned saving and planned investment in equality. Keynes argued that prices and wages are not flexible downward, so unemployment, rather than lower wages, would be the result of an excess aggregate supply. He also argued that investors and savers have different motives, so planned saving and planned investment may not be equal. The interest rate will not clear the market in times of depression because business people may be so pessimistic about the future that they will refuse to borrow no matter how low the interest rate falls. Consequently, according to Keynes, a depression could persist indefinitely.

2. "It's always darkest before the dawn" implies that, when things are bad, business people expect them to get better and begin to invest, which directly contradicts Keynes's view. Instead, Keynes believed that, as the next proverb implies, when business expectations are extremely low, business people will not "throw good money after bad," even when the interest rate is low. That is, if they believe that the economy will not improve in the foreseeable future, they will refuse to commit funds to increase investment spending. "A penny saved is a penny earned" implies that saving is always beneficial, and "A fool and his money are soon parted" suggests that consumers often make foolish mistakes—neither of which Keynes believed. The final proverb, "The best things in life are free," is irrelevant to Keynes's views on depressions.

3. Total leakages and total injections must be equal because any dollar given up by one member of society must go to another member of society. For example, taxes reduce disposable income but increase government revenues. Whether a dollar is spent by consumers or by the government, it contributes to GDP.

4. There are other injections and leakages besides investment spending and saving. The requirement is that total leakages and total injections be equal, or $S + (T - R) + M = I + G + X$. If saving and investment are not equal, the totals still can be equal because of the offsetting values of the other variables.

5. The consumption function shows the relation between the amount spent on consumption goods and the level of income. The graph of a consumption function is an upward-sloping line because there is a positive relationship between consumption and income. That is, the greater one's income, the greater one's consumption spending, *ceteris paribus*. Disposable income is the major determinant of consumption. Where the consumption function intersects the 45-degree line, consumption and income are equal. To the left of this intersection, consumption exceeds income; to the right, income exceeds consumption.

6. The marginal propensity to consume is an expression of the proportion of additional income that is spent on consumption goods. The marginal propensity to save is an expression of the proportion of additional income that is saved. Households either consume or save, so the marginal propensity to consume and the marginal propensity to save must add up to one.

7. The marginal propensity to consume is shown as the slope of the consumption function.

8. a. A decrease in net wealth causes the consumption function to shift down. People save to increase their net wealth, so a reduction in net wealth tends to encourage people to save more and consume less at every level of income.
   b. An increase in the price level makes the real value of a given amount of money fall, which tends to reduce the value of the savings people have accumulated. Consequently, people increase saving and reduce consumption and the consumption function shifts down.
   c. An expectation of lower prices in the future shifts the consumption function down. People put off spending today to spend more in the future if they expect prices to be lower in the future.

9. The investment decision depends on anticipated profits and opportunities and the market rate of interest rather than on current income.

10. Firms demand investment funds whenever the expected rate of return on an investment exceeds the market rate of interest. The lower the interest rate, the greater the number of

investment projects that are profitable to undertake. Hence, the greater the demand for investment funds.

11. The investment function relates investment spending and disposable income. The investment function is autonomous, which means that disposable income has no effect on investment, and investment spending can be pictured as a horizontal line when disposable income is on the horizontal axis. Hence, the increased investment spending induced by a reduction in the interest rate is shown by an upward shift of the investment function.

12. An increase in the interest rate decreases total spending for two reasons. First, higher interest rates cause the quantity demanded of investment spending to decrease. Second, higher interest rates encourage people to save more and to spend less, reducing total spending.

13. People buy more goods and services when their incomes increase. Since some of the goods and services they buy are made by foreign firms, rising levels of income induce greater import spending. Exports are determined by the income levels of foreigners rather than those of domestic residents. Hence, exports are autonomous. Net exports, which are exports minus imports, are inversely related to the level of income.

14. Countries reduce the value of their currencies relative to foreign currencies in order to increase net exports. When a currency has a lower value relative to foreign currencies, domestic products are cheaper to foreigners and foreign-produced products are more expensive to domestic residents. Hence, exports increase, imports fall, and net exports increase.

15. The answer is the same as for question 12, with the addition that the change in interest rates would also affect net export spending. The increase in interest rates reduces spending, which includes spending on imports. Hence, net exports would increase, offsetting to some extent the effects on consumption spending and investment spending. An increase in interest rates abroad would decrease net exports because foreigners would buy fewer U.S. exports.

CHAPTER 10

Aggregate Expenditure and Demand-Side Equilibrium

I. INTRODUCTION

In this chapter we derive the equilibrium level of aggregate output demanded for the economy. We focus on consumption and investment, although the government sector is included. The text treats net exports as autonomous; the appendix presents the situation when net exports are inversely related to income. The chapter introduces the multiplier, an important concept that you should be sure you understand. Aggregate supply is discussed in the next chapter.

II. OUTLINE

1. Aggregate Expenditure and Income

    1.1 The Components of Aggregate Expenditure
    a. *Real GDP* is GDP measured in terms of real goods and services produced.
    b. The economy will exhibit different levels of planned spending and saving for different levels of real GDP.
    c. There are two uses of disposable income: consumption and saving.
    d. There are three injections of spending into the circular flow: planned investment, government purchases, and net exports.
    e. Investment, government purchases, and net exports are treated as autonomous.
    f. The equilibrium quantity of aggregate demand occurs when planned aggregate expenditure equals real GDP.

    1.2 Quantity of Real GDP Demanded
    a. The income-expenditure model relates real GDP (that is, aggregate income or aggregate output) on the horizontal axis and aggregate expenditure on the vertical axis.
    b. The aggregate expenditure function shows the amount people plan to spend at each level of real GDP, holding the price level constant.
    c. The 45-degree line from the origin identifies all points where aggregate expenditure equals real GDP.
    d. Equilibrium is reached when aggregate expenditure equals aggregate output, which is where the aggregate expenditure function intersects the 45-degree line.

    1.3 When Output and Planned Spending Differ
    a. If planned spending and output are not equal, inventories change so that actual spending and output are equal.
    b. When planned spending is greater than output, there is an unintended drop in inventories and firms respond by increasing output.
    c. When planned spending is less than output, there is an unintended rise in inventories and firms respond by decreasing output.
    d. Equilibrium occurs when planned spending and output (or income) are equal. This occurs where the aggregate expenditure function crosses the 45-degree line.

1.4 Leakages Equal Planned Injections

a. Equilibrium can be found by equating leakages and injections.
b. The leakages from the system are saving and net taxes, and injections are planned investment spending, government purchases, and net exports.
c. For a given price level, there is only one point along the aggregate expenditure function at which planned spending equals real GDP.
d. Actual investment equals planned investment plus any unintended inventory changes.
e. At any level of real GDP, consumption plus actual investment equals real GDP. This will be an equilibrium only if actual investment equals planned investment.
f. In equilibrium, production of aggregate output generates exactly enough income to purchase that output.
g. For a given price level, there is only one quantity of output demanded at which income is equal to planned spending.

2. The Simple Spending Multiplier

2.1 Effects of an Increase in Aggregate Expenditure

a. A change in planned investment spending causes a proportionately larger shift in the equilibrium quantity of real GDP demanded in the same direction.
b. The simple spending multiplier equals the number of times by which the change in real GDP demanded exceeds the change in planned investment spending.

2.2 The Spending Multiplier and the Circular Flow

a. An increase in investment generates higher incomes for some resource owners.
b. Higher incomes generate increased consumption spending, which generates additional income for other resource owners. Saving also rises as income rises.
c. The process stops when the entire change in investment spending drains from the circular flow as saving. Saving increases just enough to finance the increase in investment.
d. If planned investment does not remain at the new, higher level, equilibrium spending will fall back to its initial level.
e. The change in the equilibrium quantity of aggregate output demanded depends on how much the aggregate expenditure shifts and not on which spending component causes the shift.

2.3 Numerical Value of the Spending Multiplier

a. The expansion resulting from an increase in autonomous spending is limited by the leakage of income to saving.
b. The smaller the portion of a change in income that is saved, the more that is spent in each round and the greater the multiplier.
c. The simple multiplier equals the reciprocal of the marginal propensity to save.

2.4 *Case Study:* Hard Times in Connecticut

3. Changes in the Price Level

3.1 A Higher Price Level

a. An increase in the price level makes consumers poorer, so they reduce consumption.
b. A higher price level also reduces investment and net exports.
c. When aggregate spending falls, the equilibrium quantity of aggregate output demanded falls.

3.2 A Lower Price Level

a. A decrease in the price level causes consumption, investment, and net exports to increase.

b. The equilibrium quantity of aggregate output demanded is inversely related to the price level.

c. The aggregate expenditure function shows how, for a given price level, consumption plus planned investment relates to the level of real GDP.

d. The aggregate demand curve shows the quantity of real GDP demanded for various price levels.

3.3 The Multiplier and Shifts in Aggregate Demand

a. An autonomous increase in planned spending shifts the aggregate expenditure function.

b. For a given price level, the increase in planned spending increases the equilibrium quantity of aggregate output by an amount determined by the simple multiplier.

c. The aggregate demand curve also shifts out as a result of the autonomous change in planned spending. At the prevailing price level, the size of the shift in the aggregate demand curve is determined by the simple multiplier.

3.4 *CASE STUDY:* Not Enough Saving

4. Appendix A: Variable Net Exports. Since imports are directly related to disposable income, it is more realistic to treat net exports as inversely related to the level of disposable income. Since net exports and income are inversely related, the addition of net exports reduces the slope of the aggregate expenditure function. The effect of net exports on equilibrium output demanded depends on the level of income where net exports equal zero.

4.1 Net Exports and the Spending Multiplier

a. The marginal propensity to import (MPI) indicates the fraction of each additional dollar of income that is spent on imports.

b. The multiplier equals 1/(MPS + MPI).

c. The multiplier with net exports is lower than the simple domestic multiplier.

4.2 A Change in Autonomous Spending. An autonomous increase in net exports increases equilibrium output demanded; an autonomous decrease in net exports decreases equilibrium output demanded.

5. Appendix B: Algebra of Income and Expenditure

5.1 The Aggregate Expenditure Function

a. The level of consumption when income is zero is called *autonomous consumption*.

b. Increases in consumption that result when income increases are called *induced consumption*.

5.2 A More General Form of Income and Expenditure

a. The consumption function, $C = a + b(Y - NT)$, is composed of autonomous consumption (a) and induced consumption, $b(Y - NT)$, where b is the marginal propensity to consume, Y is real income, and NT is net taxes.

b. The investment function is autonomous and so is constant at the given level of investment, I.

c. Government purchases, G, and autonomous net exports, $X - m$, are also added to the equation.

d. Equilibrium is reached when income equals planned expenditure, or when $Y = C + I + G + X - m = a - bNT + bY + I + G + (X - m)$, which is equivalent to $Y = [1/(1 - b)](a - bNT + I + G + X - m)$.
e. $(a - bNT + I + G + X - m)$ is autonomous spending (spending that occurs when income is zero) and $1/(1 - b)$ is the multiplier.

5.3 Introducing Variable Net Exports
a. Exports are autonomous but imports are not, so net exports are $X - m(Y - NT)$, where m is the marginal propensity to import.
b. Equilibrium is reached when $Y = a + b(Y\text{-}NT) + I + G + X - m(Y - NT)$, or $Y = [1/(1 - b + m)](a - bNT + I + G + X - mNT)$.

III. DISCUSSION

Aggregate Expenditure and Income

The *aggregate expenditure* at each level of income is the total planned spending, or, according to the chapter's model, the sum of consumption, planned investment spending, government purchases, and net exports. Real GDP is equal to the total output of the economy, which is also equal to the aggregate income generated by production. In equilibrium, aggregate expenditure must equal aggregate income.

It is important to note that aggregate income and planned aggregate expenditure are equal only if the economy is in equilibrium, whereas aggregate income and actual total expenditure are equal by definition. For the equilibrium condition to hold, planned consumption expenditures plus planned investment expenditures plus government purchases plus net exports must equal real GDP. When this happens, nobody has an incentive to change his or her actions or plans, and equilibrium is established. Even when we do not have equilibrium, actual total expenditure must equal real GDP because, as the circular flow model indicates, one individual's expenditure is another's income.

Exhibit 1 illustrates these concepts. In every row, actual total expenditure equals real GDP, but only in the sixth row does aggregate expenditure equal real GDP. Therefore, $10 trillion is the equilibrium level of real GDP demanded. At no other level of GDP does aggregate expenditure equal real GDP. For example, consider the second row, where real GDP is $6.0 trillion. Consumption is $4.8 trillion and saving is $0.2 trillion, but planned investment is $0.4 trillion. Planned aggregate expenditure is greater than real GDP. The economy is not producing enough output, so inventories are drawn down, generating an unanticipated inventory adjustment of $0.8 trillion. This yields an actual investment of -$0.4 trillion, not $0.4 trillion; this yields an actual total expenditure level of $6.0 trillion. This is not an equilibrium, since business planned on investing $0.4 trillion but actually disinvested $0.4 trillion. At real GDP of $10.0 trillion, there are no unintended inventory adjustments, so actual investment equals planned investment ($0.4 trillion). Finally, actual total expenditure equals real GDP and also equals (planned) aggregate expenditure. Hence, the equilibrium quantity of real GDP demanded is $10.0 trillion.

Exhibit 1
(trillions of dollars)

Real GDP (Y) (1)	Net Taxes (NT) (2)	Disposable Income Y - NT (3)	Consumption (C) (4)	Savings (S) (5)	Planned Investment I (6)	Gov't Purchases G (7)	Net Exports (X - m) (8)	Manual Aggregate Expenditure (9)	Unintended Inventory Adjustment (10)	Actual Investment (11)	Actual Total Expenditure (12)
$5.0	1.0	4.0	4.0	0	0.4	1.0	0.6	6.0	-0.4	-0.6	5.0
$6.0	1.0	5.0	4.8	0.2	0.4	1.0	0.6	6.2	-0.8	-0.4	6.0
$7.0	1.0	6.0	5.6	0.4	0.4	1.0	0.6	7.6	-0.6	-0.2	7.0
$8.0	1.0	7.0	6.4	0.6	0.4	1.0	0.6	8.4	-0.4	0	8.0
$9.0	1.0	8.0	7.2	0.8	0.4	1.0	0.6	9.2	-0.2	0.2	9.0
$10.0	1.0	9.0	8.0	1.0	0.4	1.0	0.6	10.0	0	0.4	10.0
$11.0	1.0	10.0	8.8	1.2	0.4	1.0	0.6	10.8	0.2	0.6	11.0
$12.0	1.0	11.0	9.6	1.4	0.4	1.0	0.6	11.6	0.4	0.8	12.0

Exhibit 2 presents the information from Exhibit 1 graphically. The 45-degree line shows the points where real GDP equals aggregate expenditure.

Exhibit 2

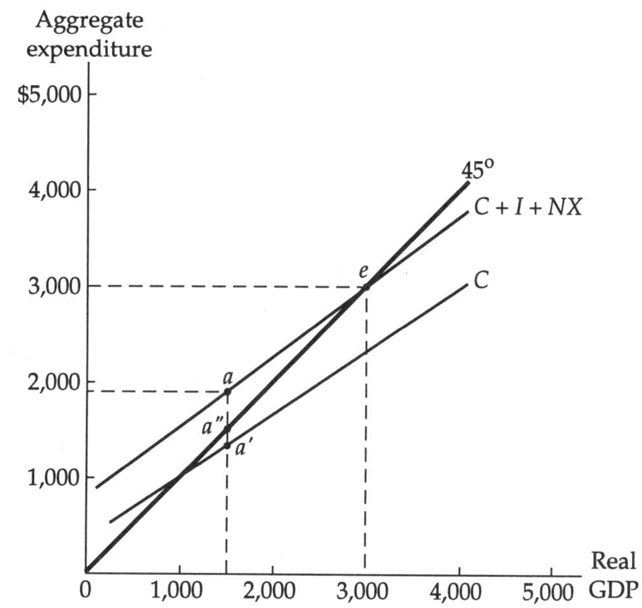

Point *e* is the equilibrium point, where real GDP and aggregate expenditure both equal $10.0 trillion. At real GDP of $5.0 trillion, point *a* indicates planned aggregate expenditure, *a*′ indicates consumption, and *a*″ indicates actual total expenditure. The distance between *a* and *a*″ measures the unintended drop in investment of $0.4 trillion. The plans of consumers and business indicate a desire to purchase the amount at point *a*, but the economy actually spends the amount at point *a*″. As long as business responds to the unexpected decline in inventories by increasing production, the economy will expand and eventually arrive at the equilibrium real GDP demanded of $10.0 trillion (point *e*).

The Simple Spending Multiplier

Suppose we are at equilibrium in Exhibit 2. If businesses decide to change investment spending, then adjustments must be made by all participants in the economy until a new equilibrium is achieved. We can determine what these changes will be as long as we know the MPC. Suppose planned investment increases by \$0.1 trillion, to \$0.5 trillion. At the previous equilibrium level of real GDP demanded of \$10.0 trillion, we have an excess demand for goods, since aggregate expenditure now equals \$10.1 trillion instead of \$10.0 trillion. There is an unintended reduction of inventories of \$0.1 trillion. Those businesses that face excess demand for their output will increase production and hire more productive inputs. The payments to the productive inputs are income, which the input owners spend. That is, income increases by the amount of the extra payments to resource owners, and these individuals increase both consumption spending and saving. By how much do they increase consumption? Since the MPC is 0.8, consumption spending increases by \$80 for every \$100 in extra income.

This is not the end, though. The extra consumption spending provides income to those who produce and sell the extra consumption goods. The higher incomes of these individuals lead them to increase their own consumption spending, increasing income for other people, and another round of increased consumption spending and income occurs. Where does it end? It ends when the extra \$0.1 trillion of investment spending increases income to the point where saving increases by \$0.1 trillion. Since the MPS is 0.2, every extra \$100 of income generates an extra \$20 of saving. For saving to increase by \$0.1 trillion, income must increase by \$0.5 trillion. That is, real GDP must increase from \$10.0 trillion to \$10.5 trillion for saving to increase from \$1.0 trillion to \$1.1 trillion.

Exhibit 3 illustrates these changes. The $C + I + NX$ curve is the same as in Exhibit 2, and point *e* is the original equilibrium. The increase in planned investment spending causes the $C + I + NX$ curve to shift up to $C + I' + NX$. The distance from *e* to *f* is \$100. The extra investment spending is income to others and generates increased consumption spending, as described. The new equilibrium is *e*′, where real GDP and aggregate expenditure are equal at \$3,500.

Exhibit 3

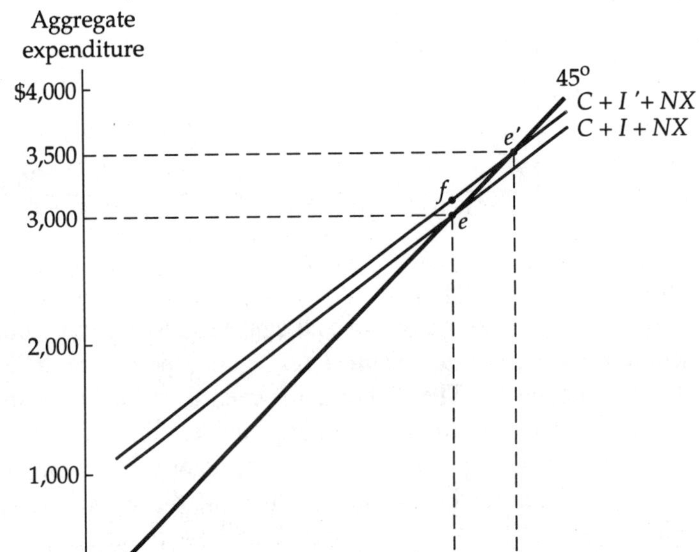

The *multiplier* is a number that indicates the number of times by which the change in the quantity of real GDP demanded exceeds the change in planned investment spending. In the previous case, the multiplier is equal to 5, since real GDP increased by $0.5 trillion after planned investment spending increased by $0.1 trillion. There is a relation between the multiplier and the MPS, as the previous discussion suggests. Since income must increase enough to allow saving to increase by an amount equal to the increase in planned investment, the multiplier equals 1/MPS. In the previous case, the multiplier equals 1/0.2 = 5. Further, MPS = 1 - MPC, so the multiplier also equals 1/(1 - MPC). The multiplier can also be used to calculate the change in real GDP demanded that follows a decrease in planned investment spending or autonomous changes in consumption spending and saving.

Changes in the Price Level

In the last chapter we saw how changes in the price level shift the consumption function: increases in the price level lower the consumption function, and decreases in the price level raise the consumption function. The aggregate demand curve illustrates the relationship between the price level and real GDP demanded. Exhibit 5 in the textbook derives the aggregate demand curve. Changes in the price level cause the consumption function, the investment function, and net exports to shift, which causes the aggregate expenditure function to shift. Hence, there is a different equilibrium level of real GDP demanded for each price level. The aggregate demand curve is found by relating the equilibrium level of real GDP demanded with the appropriate price level. Be sure that you understand how the aggregate demand curve is derived.

Autonomous changes in consumption, investment, government purchases, or net exports induce shifts in the aggregate demand curve. An increase in planned investment spending shifts the aggregate expenditure curve upward, which generates a new, higher real GDP demanded. Since the increase in planned investment does not imply a change in the price level, the higher real GDP demanded is associated with the same price level as before. That is, as a result of the increase in planned investment spending, the aggregate demand curve shifts to the right by an amount equal to the multiplier times the change in planned investment spending.

Appendix A: Variable Net Exports

The text treats net exports as autonomous, but spending on imports actually is directly related to the level of income. When disposable income increases, consumption spending increases, and part of this increased spending is on imports. Since exports are autonomous, an increase in disposable income causes increased imports and decreased net exports. In this model, with net exports inversely related to the level of income, the new aggregate expenditure function is flatter than the domestic function. Further, the multiplier is lower, since imports increase with income and imports are a leakage from the circular flow. The new multiplier equals 1/(MPS + MPM), where MPM equals the marginal propensity to import.

Appendix B: Algebra of Private-Sector Demand

The aggregate expenditure function can be derived algebraically. The consumption function has two components: an autonomous component (that is, consumption that occurs when income equals zero) and an induced component (that is, consumption that depends on the level of income); thus, $C = a + b(Y - NT)$, where a is the autonomous component and b is the marginal propensity to consume. Investment spending is autonomous, so it is constant at level I. Government purchases are also autonomous, so they are constant at level G. When net exports are treated as autonomous, net exports are constant at level $X - M$. Since $Y = C + I + G + (X - M)$, we can substitute the individual functions into this equation and get:

$$Y = a - bNT + bY + I + G + (X - M)$$
$$Y = [1/(1 - b)](a - bNT + I + G + X - M)$$

When exports vary with the level of income, we substitute $m(Y - NT)$ for m, where m is the marginal propensity to import. The equilibrium level of real GDP can be found as above:

$$Y = a + bNT + I + G + X + mNT + (b - m)Y$$

or

$$Y = [1/(1 - b + m)](a + I + G + X + mNT)$$

The term $(a - b\,NT + I + G + X + mNT)$ represents autonomous spending and $1/(1 - b + m)$ is the multiplier.

IV. LAGNIAPPE

On Autonomous and Induced Spending

The relationship between aggregate expenditure and real GDP is not a simple one, but it is extremely important. There are two kinds of spending: autonomous and induced. *Autonomous spending* is any spending that is independent of the level of income. In our model autonomous spending includes investment spending, government purchases, export spending (and sometimes net exports), and a component of consumption spending. In the income-expenditure model the consumption function intercepts the vertical axis above the origin. This means that real GDP equals zero, yet expenditures on consumption are positive. This amount of consumption spending is autonomous spending. (If $C = a + bY$, the autonomous portion is a.)

Induced spending is spending that occurs because of changes in the level of income. When there is a "marginal propensity to ... ," there is induced spending. Changes in income cause changes in spending. When autonomous spending increases, income increases. But the increase in income (real GDP) causes changes in induced spending. So the relationship between spending and income is complex.

Question to Think About: Is saving autonomous or induced?

Multipliers and Public Works

The principles behind the multiplier are at work in many situations. If Honda builds a factory in a community, many jobs are created and spending in the area increases. The effects are more than just the immediate effects of building the plant and hiring people to work in the plant. The higher incomes of the people who work there increase their spending, which causes the incomes of others to increase, thus increasing their spending. The multiplier is at work.

It is also possible for multiplier effects to be exaggerated. Suppose a local sports team threatens to move unless it gets a better deal with respect to renting the local stadium. Newspapers are likely to report that the "economic impact" of the loss of the team would be fairly large. The impact would include the loss of salaries by those who work for the team and at the stadium on game days. It also would include the loss of dollars spent at the game on tickets, merchandise, and concessions. A multiplier is estimated and a total loss to the city is calculated. But this analysis would probably exaggerate the influence of the team on the local economy. Attending a sporting event can be thought of as entertainment. If the team was not in the area, people would do something else: go to a movie, eat dinner at a restaurant, go to the zoo, or any number of other things. If most of the money spent at the game would have been spent in the local area anyway, the economic impact of the team is reduced.

Question to Think About: If many people who attended the games traveled a long distance, would the multiplier associated with the team be higher or lower?

V. KEY TERMS

Income-expenditure model
Aggregate expenditure function
Actual investment
Unintended inventory adjustments
Simple spending multiplier
Marginal propensity to import (MPM)
Autonomous consumption
Induced consumption

VI. QUESTIONS

A. *Completion*

1. GDP measured in terms of goods and services is known as ________________ GDP.

2. Disposable income is real GDP less ________________.

3. Households have two possible uses for disposable income: ________________ and ________________.

4. The diagram that relates aggregate expenditures and aggregate income is called the ________________ model.

5. For a given price level, the total planned spending at each level of income is shown by the ________________.

6. If net exports and government purchases are zero, the difference between the aggregate expenditure function and the consumption function is ________________.

7. An unintended inventory reduction occurs when ________________ investment exceeds ________________ investment.

8. In equilibrium, planned spending exactly equals the amount produced and exactly equals ________________ spending.

9. For a given price level, there is only one quantity of output demanded for which ________________ spending equals income.

10. The __________________ relates an autonomous change in spending to the resulting change in equilibrium real GDP demanded.

11. The larger the marginal propensity to save, the __________________ the multiplier.

12. An increase in planned saving at each level of income causes a decrease in __________________ consumption.

13. A decrease in the price level increases __________________ spending.

14. The aggregate expenditure function and the aggregate demand curve look at __________________ from different perspectives.

*15. When import spending is directly related to income, the multiplier is __________________.

B. *True/False*

______ 1. In the model without government, households either consume their incomes or save part of them.

______ 2. The consumption function relates consumption spending to the price level.

______ 3. The difference between the 45-degree line and the consumption function measures planned investment.

______ 4. When planned spending and output are not equal, there is an unintended change in inventories.

______ 5. Actual investment equals planned investment plus unintended changes in inventories.

______ 6. Unintended changes in inventories are signals to producers to change their rates of production.

______ 7. In the income-expenditure model, planned investment always equals actual investment.

______ 8. Consumption plus actual investment plus government purchases plus net exports always equal real GDP.

______ 9. There are many quantities of output demanded at which income equals planned spending for a given price level.

______ 10. The marginal propensity to consume equals total consumption spending divided by total income.

______ 11. MPC = 1 - MPS.

______ 12. An increase in autonomous investment of $100 will increase equilibrium real GDP demanded by $100.

______ 13. If the multiplier is 3, equilibrium real GDP demanded will fall by $3,000 if planned investment falls by $1,000.

______ 14. The multiplier increases if the MPS increases.

______ 15. A decrease in the price level causes consumption spending to increase but causes net exports to decrease.

______ 16. An increase in the price level increases equilibrium real GDP demanded.

______ 17. The simple multiplier overstates the real-world multiplier.

______ *18. An increase in exports leads to a higher equilibrium real GDP demanded.

______ *19. The marginal propensity to import is usually less than zero.

______ *20. The multiplier is lower when net exports are included than when they are not included.

C. *Multiple Choice*

1. Planned aggregate expenditures include
   a. consumption.
   b. actual investment.
   c. net exports.
   d. all of the above.
   e. a and c only.

2. In the income-expenditure model described in the textbook,
   a. consumption, saving, and investment increase with income.
   b. consumption, saving, and investment spending are autonomous.
   c. saving and investment are autonomous.
   d. saving is autonomous.
   e. consumption and saving increase as income increases.

3. The distance between the 45-degree line and the consumption function at each income level measures
   a. saving.
   b. taxes.
   c. net income.
   d. investment.
   e. consumption on consumer durable goods.

Exhibit 4

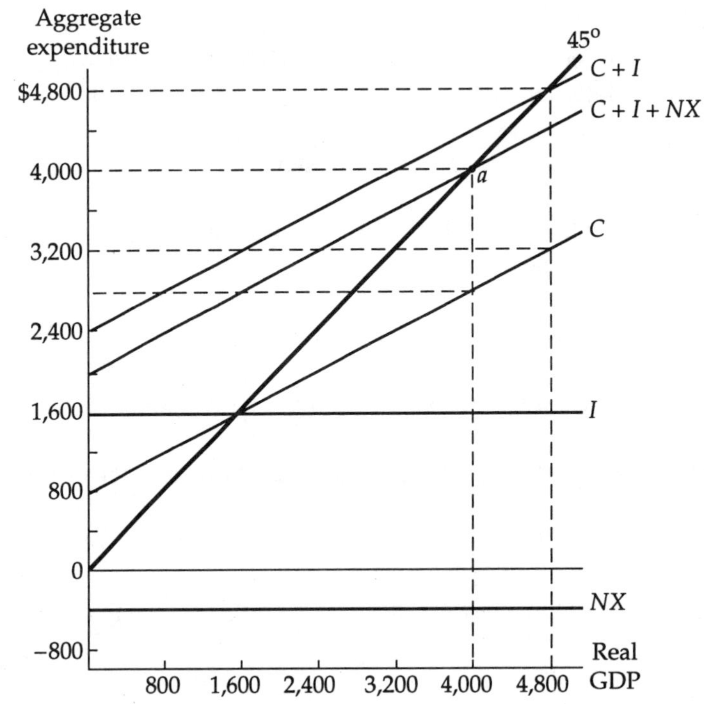

4. In Exhibit 4, the equilibrium level of consumption is
   a. $800.
   b. $1,600.
   c. $2,800.
   d. $4,000.
   e. The answer cannot be determined without more information.

5. In Exhibit 4, saving at the equilibrium level of real GDP equals
   a. $0.
   b. $400.
   c. $800.
   d. $1,000.
   e. $1,200.

6. In Exhibit 4, if the economy is at point *a*,
   a. aggregate expenditure is greater than real GDP.
   b. inventories will tend to grow, forcing producers to decrease their rate of production.
   c. inventories will tend to decrease, forcing producers to increase their rate of production.
   d. real GDP will increase.
   e. actual investment equals planned investment.

7. In Exhibit 4, the marginal propensity to consume is
   a. 0.5.
   b. 0.6.
   c. 0.7.
   d. 0.75.
   e. 0.9.

8. In Exhibit 4, if net exports increased by $400, the new equilibrium level of real GDP would equal
   a. $3,200.
   b. $4,000.
   c. $4,400.
   d. $4,800.
   e. $6,000.

9. In Exhibit 4, the value of the multiplier is
   a. 0.
   b. 1.
   c. 2.
   d. 4.
   e. 5.

10. Actual investment always equals
    a. planned investment.
    b. consumption.
    c. consumption minus saving.
    d. unplanned inventory changes.
    e. none of the above.

11. In an economy in equilibrium,
    a. production of the equilibrium quantity of aggregate output demanded generates enough income to purchase that output.
    b. aggregate expenditure equals real GDP.
    c. planned injection equals leakages.
    d. unintended inventory changes equal zero.
    e. all of the above

12. If the marginal propensity to consume is 0.7 and income falls by $500, saving falls by
    a. $150.
    b. $200.
    c. $350.
    d. $70.
    e. none of the above. Saving will increase.

13. If the MPC is 0.9, the simple multiplier is
    a. 1.
    b. 1.11.
    c. 5.
    d. 9.
    e. 10.

14. Suppose the equilibrium real GDP demanded is $2,500 and the MPC is 0.75. If planned investment falls by $250, equilibrium real GDP demanded will
    a. remain unchanged.
    b. fall by $250.
    c. fall by $1,000.
    d. fall by $750.
    e. The answer cannot be determined without more information.

15. An increase in planned investment increases equilibrium real GDP demanded by an amount larger than the change in planned investment. The increase in income stops when
   a. the increase in real income doubles the increase in investment spending.
   b. the marginal propensity to consume falls to zero.
   c. the inflation rate increases.
   d. the multiplier becomes 1.
   e. saving increases by the same amount as planned investment.

16. An increase in the price level ________ the equilibrium quantity of aggregate output demanded by ________________.
   a. reduces; lowering the aggregate expenditure function
   b. increases; increasing the aggregate expenditure function
   c. reduces; lowering the saving function
   d. reduces; lowering the marginal propensity to consume
   e. increases; reducing the marginal propensity to save

17. The aggregate demand curve slopes down
   a. because the aggregate expenditure function shifts down as the price level falls.
   b. because the aggregate expenditure function shifts up as the price level falls.
   c. because people are willing to save less as the price level falls.
   d. all of the above
   e. b and c

*18. When net exports are variable, a decrease in exports leads to
   a. a reduction in real GDP demanded.
   b. a reduction in imports.
   c. a reduction in consumption spending.
   d. a reduction in aggregate expenditure.
   e. all of the above.

*19. An economy that opens up trade with other countries and has variable exports will experience
   a. a flatter consumption function.
   b. a flatter aggregate expenditure function.
   c. a steeper saving function.
   d. all of the above.
   e. none of the above.

*20. Refer back to Exhibit 4. Suppose the net exports function had a vertical intercept of $400 and equaled –$400 at real GDP of $4,000. The new equilibrium level of real GDP and the new multiplier would be
   a. $4,800 and 3.
   b. $4,000 and 2.
   c. $4,000 and 1.48.
   d. $3,600 and 1.48.
   e. $3,600 and 1.7.

D. Discussion Questions

Use the following table to answer questions 1 through 3.

Exhibit 5

Real GDP	*Consumption*	*Saving*	*Planned Investment*	*Unintended Inventory Adjustment*	*Actual Investment*
$5,000	$4,900	$100	$1,000	______	______
$5,500	$5,250	$250	$1,000	______	______
$6,000	$5,600	$400	$1,000	______	______
$6,500	______	______	$1,000	______	______
$7,000	______	______	$1,000	______	______
$7,500	______	______	$1,000	______	______
$8,000	______	______	$1,000	______	______
$8,500	______	______	$1,000	______	______
$9,000	______	______	$1,000	______	______
$9,500	______	______	$1,000	______	______
$10,000	______	______	$1,000	______	______

1. a. Fill in the blanks in the table.
   b. What is the equilibrium aggregate output demanded? How do you know?
   c. Graph the 45-degree line, the consumption function, and the aggregate expenditure function. Show the equilibrium point on the graph.
   d. Suppose real GDP is initially $10,000. Explain how the equilibrium real GDP demanded is attained.
   e. What is the MPC? the MPS? the multiplier?

2. In Exhibit 5, if net exports are –$300, what is the new equilibrium level of real GDP? What is saving?

3. Suppose the economy represented in Exhibit 5 is in equilibrium, but then planned investment falls to $800. What is the new equilibrium quantity of aggregate output demanded?

4. Suppose the economy represented in Exhibit 5 is in equilibrium; let the government purchases increase from 0 to $500. What is the new equilibrium quantity of aggregate output demanded?

5. What role do unintended inventory changes play when an economy moves to an equilibrium position?

6. How are the marginal propensity to consume, the marginal propensity to save, and the simple multiplier related to each other?

7. What would happen if the marginal propensity to consume were greater than 1?

8. "Savings can be greater or less than investment spending in equilibrium." Do you agree or disagree? Why?

9. If the multiplier is 4 and society wants income to increase by $8 billion, does it matter whether investment increases or net exports increase?

10. A decrease in the price level causes aggregate spending to increase. Why?

11. How is an aggregate demand curve derived? What would cause the aggregate demand curve to shift to the right?

12. What happens to the aggregate demand curve if the MPC falls?

13. Let $C = \$1{,}000 + 0.75(Y - NT)$, $I = \$2{,}000$, and $G = NT = \$1{,}000$.
    a. Find the equilibrium aggregate expenditure.
    b. What is the level of consumption spending at equilibrium? of saving?
    c. What is the value of the multiplier?

*14. Given the information in question 12, suppose a country starts trading and net exports are $1,000. What is the new equilibrium level of real GDP?

*15. In the previous situation, if $M = .25Y$ and autonomous exports are $1,000, what is the new equilibrium level of real GDP?

*16. U.S. exports are the imports of other countries. Suppose the demand function for the rest of the world is $.1Y^*$, where Y^* equals income of all countries except the United States. If the MPM of the rest of the world increases to .2, what happens to the U.S. multiplier? Explain.

VII. ANSWERS

A. *Completion*

1. real
2. net taxes
3. consumption; saving
4. income-expenditure
5. aggregate expenditure function
6. planned investment
7. planned; actual
8. actual
9. planned
10. multiplier
11. smaller
12. autonomous
13. aggregate
14. real GDP
15. smaller

B. *True/False*

1. True
2. False. It relates consumption spending to the level of income for a given price level.
3. False
4. True
5. True
6. True
7. False
8. True
9. False
10. False
11. True
12. False
13. True
14. False
15. False
16. False
17. True
18. True
19. False
20. True

C. *Multiple Choice*

1. e
2. e
3. a
4. c
5. e
6. e
7. a
8. d
9. c
10. e
11. e
12. a
13. e
14. c
15. e
16. a
17. e
18. e
19. b
20. c

D. *Discussion Questions*

1. a.

Real GDP	*Consumption*	*Saving*	*Planned Investment*	*Unintended Inventory Adjustment*	*Actual Investment*
$5,000	$4,900	$100	$1,000	-$900	$100
$5,500	$5,250	$250	$1,000	-$700	$250
$6,000	$5,600	$400	$1,000	-$600	$400
$6,500	$5,950	$550	$1,000	-$450	$550
$7,000	$6,300	$700	$1,000	-$300	$700
$7,500	$6,650	$850	$1,000	-$150	$850
$8,000	$7,000	$1,000	$1,000	$0	$1,000
$8,500	$7,350	$1,150	$1,000	$150	$1,150
$9,000	$7,700	$1,300	$1,000	$300	$1,300
$9,500	$8,050	$1,450	$1,000	$450	$1,450
$10,000	$8,400	$1,600	$1,000	$600	$1,600

b. The equilibrium aggregate output demanded is $8,000. At that level, aggregate expenditure equals $8,000, which is also the real GDP.

c.

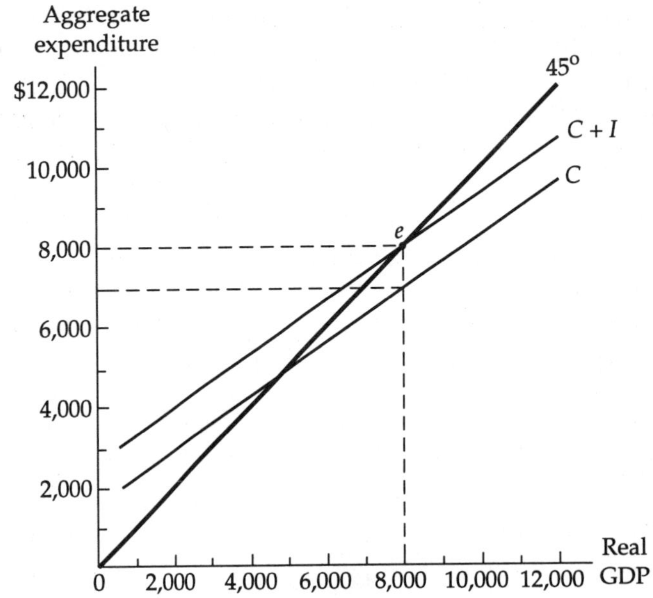

d. At real GDP of $10,000, aggregate expenditure equals $9,400, which is less than real GDP. Therefore, actual output exceeds aggregate expenditure by $600, and firms experience an unintended increase in their inventories. The firms respond by cutting back output, which means that resource owners see their incomes fall. When resource owners receive less, they spend less, which causes output to fall further. This process stops when aggregate expenditure exactly equals real GDP, so there are no unintended inventory adjustments.

e. The MPC is 350/500 = 0.7. The MPS is 150/500 = 0.3. The multiplier is 1/MPS = 1/0.3 = 3.33.

2. $7,000; $700.

3. To find the change in the equilibrium quantity of output demanded, we first multiply the change in planned investment spending by the multiplier: (–$200)(3.33) = –$666.67. This figure is the change in real GDP, so the new equilibrium is $8,000 – 666.67 = $7,333.33. At this real GDP, consumption spending is $6,533.33 and saving (and planned investment) is $800.

4. Multiply the change in government purchases ($500) by the multiplier (3.33). The new real GDP is $8,000 plus $1,665 or $9,665.

5. When the economy is not in equilibrium, planned spending either exceeds or falls short of output. When this happens, business inventories either decrease or increase. The unintended change in inventories is a signal to businesses that their output rate is incorrect. If inventories are falling, then the output rate is too low and output should increase. As businesses increase production, the economy moves closer to equilibrium. When there is no unintended change in inventories, businesses know they are producing the correct quantity, and they will not make any other production changes. At this point the economy is in equilibrium.

6. Since any change in income must be either spent or saved, the marginal propensity to save and the marginal propensity to consume must total 1. The multiplier indicates how a change in autonomous spending leads to a larger change in equilibrium real GDP demanded. It is related to the MPC and the MPS because a change in spending leads to a change in income for resource owners; this induces them to change their levels of both consumption and saving. The extent of the change is given by the MPC and MPS. The change in spending generates another change in income, which induces still more changes in consumption and saving. The process stops when planned saving equals planned investment. Hence, saving must change enough to bring planned saving and planned investment back to equality. The MPS tells us how much saving changes with a change in income, so we can use the MPS to find out how much income must change to generate the correct amount of saving. Income must change by 1/MPS, so the multiplier equals 1/MPS. Further, since MPS + MPC = 1, the multiplier must also equal 1/(1 – MPC).

7. An MPC greater than 1 would indicate that an increase in income leads to a greater increase in consumption spending. Such a situation cannot last for long, since the extra consumption must be financed somehow. The only sources of financing are savings and borrowing. For the economy as a whole, borrowing would have to be from foreigners. An MPC greater than 1 is unstable and cannot persist.

8. Injections equal leakages. In this model, saving and net taxes are leakages, and investment, government purchases and net exports are injections. So, $S + NT = I + G + (X - M)$. Saving equals investment only if government spending plus net exports equal net taxes.

9. No. The multiplier effect will be the same as long as autonomous spending increases, regardless of the source of the autonomous spending.

10. The lower price level increases consumption because people perceive that their wealth has increased. This shifts the consumption function up. The lower price level also makes U.S. goods cheaper relative to foreign goods, so exports will increase, imports decrease, and net exports increase. Finally, the lower price level also causes investment spending to increase. Since all components of aggregate spending increase, aggregate spending also increases.

11. The aggregate expenditure function generates an equilibrium real GDP demanded for a given price level. If the price level changes, people change their consumption and saving because the change in price level changes the real value of their net wealth. The aggregate demand curve is derived by tracing out the equilibrium real GDPs demanded with their respective price levels. The aggregate demand curve will shift to the right if planned investment increases or autonomous consumption increases.

12. A fall in the MPC means that both the consumption function and the aggregate expenditure function are flatter, and both rotate down. Equilibrium real GDP demanded falls as a result, so the real GDP associated with the prevailing price level falls. This is also true for any other price level, so the aggregate demand curve shifts to the left.

13. a. $Y = C + I + G = \$1{,}000 + 0.75(Y - 1000) + \$2{,}000 + \$1{,}000$
   $Y - 0.75Y = \$4{,}000 - 750 = 3{,}250$
   $Y = \$3{,}250/0.25 = \$13{,}000$

   b. $C = \$1{,}000 + 0.75(\$12{,}000 - 1{,}000)$
   $= \$1{,}000 + 0.75(12{,}000)$
   $= \$1{,}000 + \$9{,}000 = \$10{,}000$
   $S = (Y - NT) - C = \$12{,}000 - \$10{,}000 = \$2{,}000$

c. Multiplier = 1/(1 – MPS) = 1/0.25 = 4

14. Autonomous spending is $4,250, so Y = $4,250 x (1/.25) = $17,000.

15. The new multiplier is 1/(MPS + MPI) = 1/(.25 + .25) = 1/.5 = 2. Autonomous expenditures are $4,250, so Y = $4,250 x 2 = $8,500.

16. Nothing. The change in import spending in the rest of the world would show up in the United States as changes in exports, which is a type of autonomous spending because they are independent of U.S. income levels.

CHAPTER 11

Aggregate Supply

I. INTRODUCTION

The previous two chapters introduced the concept of aggregate expenditure and derived an aggregate demand curve. In this chapter we examine the concept of aggregate supply. When aggregate supply and aggregate demand are combined, we can determine the equilibrium level of prices and output in the economy. The following chapters begin to examine how government policy affects the equilibrium level of prices and output.

II. OUTLINE

1. Aggregate Supply in the Short Run. The aggregate supply curve relates the price level to the quantity of aggregate output firms are willing and able to supply, other things constant. The supply of resources in the economy, the state of technology, and the set of formal and informal institutions that undergirds the economy are held constant along an aggregate supply curve.

    1.1 Labor Supply and Aggregate Supply
    a. The higher the nominal wage, other things constant, the greater the quantity of labor supplied.
    b. The *nominal wage* is the wage measured in terms of current dollars.
    c. The *real wage* is the wage measured in terms of goods and services; it equals the nominal wage divided by the price level.
    d. Labor agreements are based on expectations about the future price level and are negotiated in terms of nominal wages.

    1.2 Potential Output and the Natural Rate of Unemployment
    a. The economy's *potential output* is the level of output that exists if the actual price level equals the expected price level.
    b. Potential output is the economy's maximum sustainable output level, given the supply of resources and the state of technology.
    c. Potential output is also called the *natural rate of output*, the *high-employment level of output*, and the *full-employment level of output*.
    d. Not all resources are employed at the potential level of output, since a dynamic economy requires some frictional, structural, and seasonal unemployment to function smoothly.
    e. The *natural rate of unemployment* is the rate of unemployment that occurs when the economy is producing its potential output.
    f. The *short run* is a period in which resource owners and firms have insufficient time to adjust completely to a price level that differs from the expected price level. The prices of many resources are fixed in the short run.
    g. The *long run* is a period in which resource owners and firms have sufficient time to adjust fully to a price level that differs from the expected price level.

1.3 Actual Price Level Higher Than Expected

a. In the short run, when the price level increases, the prices of firms' products increase, on average, while some resource costs remain fixed by contract in the short run. Profits will increase if output expands.

b. When the actual price level exceeds the expected price level on which long-term contracts are based, firms find it profitable to expand production.

c. At such times, the economy's output is greater than its potential output.

d. The economy can produce more than its potential output for only a short period of time, since resources must be used more intensively than is optimal.

1.4 Why Costs Rise When Output Exceeds Potential

a. The increased output creates increased demand for resources, which generates higher prices for the resources.

b. Higher resource prices lead to higher marginal costs of production.

c. Since the costs of some resources are contractually fixed in the short run, the marginal cost of production rises less than the marginal revenue generated from the higher price level.

d. Therefore, profit-maximizing firms increase the quantity supplied.

1.5 The Price Level, Real Wages, and Labor Supply

a. In the short run, workers may increase the quantity of labor supplied even though their real wage falls as the actual price level rises.

b. Workers may do this because

(1) they are fulfilling their contracts.

(2) firms are operating as described by the efficiency wage theory, which argues that firms keep wages above the market-clearing level in order to have an abundant worker pool from which to hire.

1.6 Actual Price Level Lower Than Expected

a. If the price level decreases, production is less profitable, since the product prices fall while some resource prices remain constant in the short run.

b. When nominal wages are fixed by contract, a lower-than-expected price level means that workers' real wages increase.

c. Firms lay off some workers since wage contracts usually do not specify both the wage rate and a guaranteed number of hours worked; actual output falls below potential output.

d. Marginal costs decline as output declines because the prices of some resources fall as firms lay off less productive resources.

1.7 The Short-Run Aggregate Supply Curve

a. There is a positive relationship between the price level and the quantity of aggregate output supplied in the short run.

b. The short-run aggregate supply curve is drawn for a particular contract period, based on a given expected price level.

c. The slope of the short-run aggregate supply curve depends on how quickly marginal production costs rise as aggregate output expands. The more quickly marginal costs rise, the steeper the short-run aggregate supply curve.

2. Equilibrium in the Short Run and Long Run

2.1 Actual Price Level Higher Than Expected

a. The difference between the actual output in the short run and potential output is called the *expansionary gap*. Unemployment is below the natural rate.
b. In the long run, all resource suppliers adjust their contracts in response to the higher actual prices.
c. As resource suppliers negotiate higher resource prices, the short-run aggregate supply curve shifts back to intersect the aggregate demand curve at the potential output.
d. In long-run equilibrium,
   (1) the actual price level equals the expected price level.
   (2) the quantity supplied equals the potential output.
   (3) the quantity supplied equals the quantity demanded.
e. Actual output can exceed potential output in the short run but not in the long run.

2.2 Actual Price Level Lower Than Expected
a. In the short run, actual output falls short of potential output by an amount called the *contractionary gap*. Unemployment exceeds the natural rate.
b. The short-run aggregate supply curve shifts outward when resource owners adjust in the long run to the lower actual price level. Nominal resource payments fall, or at least rise more slowly than output prices.
c. The length of the adjustment process depends on downward flexibility in product and resource prices. The more inflexible the wages and prices, the longer the contractionary gap persists.

2.3 Tracing Potential Output
a. The long-run aggregate supply curve is vertical at the economy's potential output.
b. The potential output is consistent with any price level in the long run; it depends only on the supply of resources and level of technology.

2.4 Evidence on Aggregate Supply
a. Nominal wages do not change as quickly in a downward direction as they do in an upward direction. Therefore, unemployment may remain above the natural rate for prolonged periods.
b. The *efficiency wage theory* argues that firms do not lower wages in times of unemployment because they use a relatively high wage to encourage greater productivity.
c. Nominal wages may also be sticky downward as a result of factors such as long-term wage contracts, minimum wage laws, workers' psychological resistance to wage cuts, and the like.
d. Nominal wages need not decline to close a contractionary gap but must rise more slowly than prices.

2.5 *CASE STUDY:* Output Gaps and Wage Flexibility

3. Changes in Aggregate Supply

3.1 Increases in Aggregate Supply
a. Potential output changes as the quantity and quality of resources change.
b. Technological change can also change the potential output.
c. Long-term improvements in the economy's ability to produce generate shifts to the right in both the short-run aggregate supply curve and the long-run aggregate supply curve.
d. *Beneficial supply shocks* are unexpected events that increase aggregate supply. For a given aggregate demand curve, output rises and the price level falls.

3.2 Decreases in Aggregate Supply
   a. *Adverse supply shocks* are unexpected events that reduce aggregate supply, often only temporarily.
   b. Stagflation can occur when an adverse supply shock reduces output and raises prices.

3.3 *CASE STUDY:* Why Is Unemployment So High in Europe?

4. Appendix: The Market for Resources. Households supply resources to firms that produce goods and services. The willingness and ability of households to supply resources depend on the expected earnings of the resources. The higher the expected earnings, other things constant, the greater the quantity of resources supplied.

4.1 The Market for Labor
   a. Supply of Labor. The supply curve for labor tends to slope upward.
      (1) For a given expected price level, workers believe they can buy more goods and services as the nominal wage increases.
      (2) Individuals are therefore more willing to give up leisure if they receive a higher nominal wage, so the quantity of labor supplied rises.
   b. Demand for Labor
      (1) The demand curve for labor slopes down because of the law of diminishing marginal returns.
      (2) Since the marginal value of labor declines as more labor is employed, other things constant, the wage a firm is willing to pay for each additional unit of labor also declines as more labor is employed.

4.2 Changes in the Expected Price Level
   a. A higher expected price level causes the supply curve for labor to shift to the left.
   b. An increase in the expected price level causes the demand curve for labor to shift to the right.
   c. The new equilibrium will be at the original level of unemployment but at a higher nominal wage.
   d. The expected real wage does not change, so the level of employment does not change.
   e. A lower expected price level generates a lower equilibrium nominal wage.

4.3 Potential GDP
   a. The potential GDP is that associated with the equilibrium level of employment of each resource.
   b. The *potential output* is the amount produced when all resource owners and firms have fully adjusted to the actual price level.
   c. Potential output is determined by real factors such as the quantity and quality of resources available to the economy and the level of technology.

III. DISCUSSION

Aggregate Supply in the Short Run

Workers and other resource owners make decisions concerning how much of their resources to supply for a particular time period on the basis of expected *real wages* or prices. But wages and prices are always stated in dollar terms, i.e., as *nominal wages* and prices. Often nominal resource prices, including wages paid to labor, are set for a given time period by explicit or implicit contracts. If the actual price level differs from the expected price level on which the contracts are based, resource owners will not receive the real return that they expected. If the actual price level is greater than expected, the real wage falls as the nominal wage remains constant; the opposite occurs if the actual price level is less than expected.

Some resource prices adjust more quickly than others. Some workers may agree to twelve-month contracts, others may agree to six-month contracts, and still others may not agree to contracts at all. Similarly, one electric utility may agree to long-term contracts with coal suppliers; others may rely on spot markets. Prices set by contracts tend to be more stable than those set in spot markets. Consequently, when the actual price level exceeds the expected price level, some resource prices adjust quickly while others remain constant for a while. Production costs rise more slowly than product prices, on average, because of the stability of some resource prices.

If a firm's product price increases at the same rate as the average level of prices, expanding output increases the firm's profit because the extra cost of producing an additional unit of output rises more slowly than the extra revenue received from an additional unit of output. Hence, the firm has an incentive to increase production in the short run when the actual price level rises above the expected price level reflected in long-term contracts. When the actual price level falls below the expected price level, costs do not fall as quickly as product prices. Again, the relative stability of some resource prices is the reason costs do not change at the same rate as the price level. Firms respond to the lower profitability by curtailing production and laying off some resources.

We have seen that firms increase output when the price level is higher than had been expected and decrease output when the price level is lower than had been expected. What happens when the actual price level equals the expected price level reflected in long-term contracts? When expectations about prices prove correct, economic agents have no reason to change their actions. If all households and firms find their expectations about prices are correct, then the output decisions of firms and the resource-supply and consumption decisions of households are correct. There are no surprises, and the economic actors will continue doing the same thing until something fundamental changes, such as tastes or technology. Since all resource owners and all firms continue doing what they have been doing, output remains constant until a fundamental change occurs. Hence, the output level in this situation is the natural level of output. This output level is often called the *potential output*, or the full-employment level of output. The unemployment rate that prevails when the potential output is being produced is called the *natural rate of unemployment*.

Because firms expand production when the actual price level exceeds the expected price level, actual output exceeds potential output and the actual rate of unemployment is less than the natural rate of unemployment. Such a situation cannot last for a long time because higher prices mean that some resource owners are earning less in real terms than they expected. These resource owners will try to negotiate higher payments at their next opportunity, which will increase production costs, reduce profits, and encourage firms to reduce output. This process will stop when actual output again equals potential output. Similarly, when the actual price level is less than expected, firms' profitability falls, so they reduce output below potential output and unemployment rises above the natural rate. When they can renegotiate resource prices to reflect the actual state of the economy, then their resource costs will adjust to reflect the lower actual price level, they will again increase production, and aggregate output will equal potential output.

The changes in output that result when actual prices differ from the expected prices reflected in long-term contracts are short-run changes. Once the economic actors learn the true state of the economy and have time to adjust their behavior, output becomes equal to potential output. In the *short run*, there is a positive relationship between the price level and the quantity of aggregate output supplied. At prices greater than expected prices, actual output exceeds potential output; at prices lower than expected prices, actual output falls below potential output. The short-run aggregate supply curve slopes upward and is defined for a given contract period reflecting a given expected price level. If expectations about prices change, the short-run aggregate supply curve shifts.

Equilibrium in the Short Run and Long Run

The short-run aggregate supply curve is relevant only as long as some resource prices remain fixed. As these resource prices respond in the long run to new situations, the short-run aggregate supply curve shifts. As a result, the economy returns to the potential output and the natural rate of unemployment. In Exhibit 1, potential output is $5 trillion and the expected price level is 100.

Exhibit 1

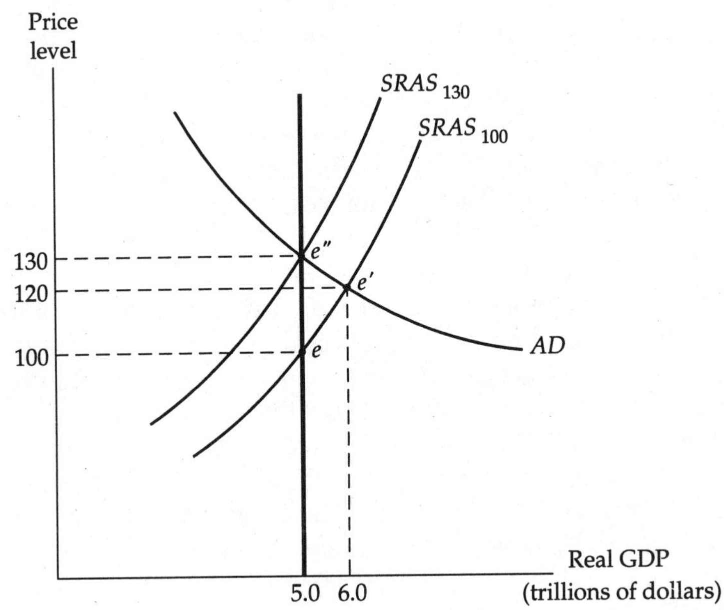

Suppose the short-run aggregate supply curve is $SRAS_{100'}$, which intersects the aggregate demand curve (*AD*) at *e′*. Hence, actual output is $6.0 trillion, and there is an *expansionary gap* of $6.0 – 5.0 = $1.0 trillion. The actual price level is 120, which is greater than the expected price level of 100. The output, $6.0 trillion, cannot be sustained for long because it exceeds the potential output. Nothing fundamental to the economy has changed; instead, output has increased because people's expectations have not been realized. Economic actors negotiate higher resource prices in the long run, firms curtail production, and the short-run aggregate supply curve shifts to the left, to $SRAS_{130}$. New long-term contracts reflect the expected price level of 130. The new long-run equilibrium is at *e″*, with output of $5.0 trillion and an actual price level of 130. A similar adjustment process occurs when the actual price level is lower than expected, only in that case the short-run aggregate supply curve shifts to the right as a result of the pressures created by a *contractionary gap*.

Whenever the economy is in long-run equilibrium—that is, whenever the actual price level equals the expected price level reflected in long-term contracts—the real GDP is equal to the potential output. That is, the long-run aggregate supply curve is vertical at the potential output. This potential GDP is consistent with any price level as long as all resource prices adjust to the actual price level.

Changes in Aggregate Supply

Potential output is determined by real factors in the economy—factors such as the quantity and quality of the resources available to the economy and the state of technology. Potential output will change only when one of these factors changes. An increase in the labor force, the discovery of new sources of raw materials, an increase in education levels of the population, and technological change are events that can cause potential output to increase. Both the long-run and the short-run aggregate supply curves will shift when potential output changes. The short-run aggregate supply curve also can shift without a change in potential output. The short-run aggregate supply curve shifts in response to *supply shocks*—unexpected events that affect the supply of a resource, often only temporarily. For example, a severe hailstorm may reduce the supply of wheat, thus affecting the supply of bread in the economy. This type of supply shock does not reduce the economy's output permanently, since wheat production can return to normal levels the next year.

Appendix: The Market for Resources

The appendix presents a brief discussion of resource markets by focusing on the market for labor. The demand curve for labor slopes down because of the *law of diminishing returns*, and the supply curve for labor tends to slope upward because workers value leisure time and must be compensated more for giving up more leisure. Workers are interested in the real wage and make decisions concerning how much time to work based on the expected real wage. If the actual price level equals the expected price level, then the same amount of labor is both demanded and supplied. This will be the equilibrium amount of labor as long as expectations are met and there are no changes in factors that affect resource demand or resource supply, such as an increase in the size of the labor force. If expected prices rise, the demand for labor will shift to the right and the supply of labor will shift to the left so that the nominal wage rises but the equilibrium quantity of labor remains unchanged. Similar adjustments take place in all resource markets. Consequently, potential output is associated with equilibrium in each resource market. That is, when the economy is operating at potential output, the quantity supplied equals the quantity demanded in each resource market and the expected price level equals the actual price level.

IV. LAGNIAPPE

Contracts and Price Stickiness

The existence of a contract, even a long-term contract, does not imply that prices are fixed for the length of the contract. Often prices are not stated in long-term contracts; instead, formulas based on inflation and other relevant conditions are used to determine prices at future dates. It is not uncommon for the parties to a contract to renegotiate the terms of the contract before it has expired. Examples of this are fairly common in professional sports, especially when a rookie turns out to be a star. The owners of the team often increase the player's salary even though they are under no contractual obligation to do so. Even so, prices determined by contracts are not as flexible in the short run as prices determined in spot markets. As long as the firm hires resources and pays resource prices that differ in their flexibility, the firm's costs will not change at the same rate as the price level changes.

Question to Think About: Why would firms want long-term contracts for some resources but not for others?

Downward Stickiness of Price

You may wonder why wages would be stickier downward than upward. Presumably, if workers were interested in their real wage and they knew that prices had fallen, they would accept a lower nominal wage to keep working. However, workers may not realize that the price level has fallen. If they agreed to lower nominal wages when the price level was lower, firms might try to fool workers and fake a curtailment in production to induce workers to accept lower nominal wages. Workers would probably be skeptical of the need to accept a lower wage given this type of opportunistic behavior on the part of employers. Further, if a contract were involved, the workers might not have to accept a lower wage; in addition, workers would be free to go elsewhere if higher wages were offered by other firms. In such cases, wages would be more flexible in an upward direction than in a downward direction.

Question to Think About: How would you determine whether the firm you worked for was doing poorly because of mismanagement or because of a weak economy?

V. KEY TERMS

Nominal wage
Real wage
Potential output
Natural rate of unemployment
Efficiency wage theory
Short-run aggregate supply curve (*SRAS*)
Short run
Expansionary gap
Long run
Contractionary gap
Long-run aggregate supply curve (*LRAS*)
Supply shocks
Beneficial supply shocks
Adverse supply shocks
Stagflation
Hysteresis
Law of diminishing marginal returns

VI. QUESTIONS

A. Completion

1. The supply of resources to producers is held constant along a(n) ____________________ supply curve.

2. The ____________________ wage is measured in terms of current dollars.

3. The nominal wage is difficult to change during the short run because relationships between resource owners and firms are governed by ____________________ contracts and ____________________ contracts.

4. The economy's ____________________ is the level of output that would prevail if the price expectations of all economic agents were met.

5. The unemployment rate that prevails when the economy is producing its potential output is the ____________________ rate of unemployment.

6. In the ____________________, expectations about the price level may differ from the actual price level.

7. When the actual price level rises above the expected price level in the short run, __________________ increase at a lower rate than the price level, and profits increase if output expands.

8. If the actual output exceeds the economy's potential output in the short run there is a(n) __________________.

9. The __________________ argues that employers keep wages above the market-clearing wage to make workers compete to keep their jobs.

10. Layoffs often occur when there is a(n) __________________ gap.

11. The _______________ aggregate supply curve slopes upward, and the _______________ aggregate supply curve is vertical.

12. __________________ affect the short-run aggregate supply curve but do not affect the long-run aggregate supply curve.

13. The combination of reduced output and a higher price level is known as _______________.

14. The idea that the natural rate of unemployment depends on its recent history is known as __________________.

*15. As more labor is hired, the marginal value added by each additional worker declines because of __________________.

B. *True/False*

______ 1. The short-run aggregate supply curve slopes up for the same reasons that the supply curves for individual goods slope up.

______ 2. The nominal wage is determined by factors from the past, and the real wage is based on expectations about the future.

______ 3. Explicit contracts determine real wages; implicit contracts determine nominal wages.

______ 4. The potential output of the economy is its maximum sustainable output level, given the supply of resources and the level of technology.

______ 5. When the economy is producing its potential output, all resources in the economy are employed.

______ 6. The natural rate of unemployment is higher today than it was in the 1960s.

______ 7. If actual prices are greater than expected prices reflected in long-term contracts, firms find it profitable to expand production beyond the economy's potential output.

______ 8. Production costs tend to rise when actual output exceeds potential output.

______ 9. When actual prices are lower than expected prices reflected in long-term contracts, the unemployment rate tends to rise above the natural rate of unemployment.

______ 10. The short run is the period during which some resource prices are set by agreement.

______ 11. The short-run aggregate supply curve is drawn for a contract period reflecting a given expected price level.

______ 12. Actual output cannot exceed potential output in the long run.

______ 13. The long-run aggregate supply curve slopes upward.

______ 14. The economy's potential output is consistent with any actual price level.

______ 15. Technological change can lead to a higher level of potential output.

______ 16. Supply shocks can lead to temporary changes in the price level.

______ 17. Adverse supply shocks cause only the short-run aggregate supply curve to shift; beneficial supply shocks cause only the long-run aggregate supply curve to shift.

______ 18. Unemployment rates increased throughout the 1980s in Europe and in the United States.

______ *19. The quantity of labor supplied tends to increase as the nominal wage rate increases, other things constant.

______ *20. An increase in the expected price level causes both the supply curve of labor and the demand curve for labor to shift to the right.

C. *Multiple Choice*

1. If all prices increase by 10 percent, then in the long run
   a. nominal wages increase by 10 percent and real wages are constant.
   b. nominal wages are constant and real wages increase by 10 percent.
   c. nominal wages are constant and real wages decrease by 10 percent.
   d. nominal wages and real wages are equal.
   e. none of the above

2. If the price level is higher than expected, firms tend to increase production in the short run because
   a. real wages are also increasing.
   b. the costs of producing a unit of a good are falling.
   c. the extra revenue from an additional unit of output rises relative to the extra cost of producing an additional unit.
   d. the real wage rises relative to the nominal wage.
   e. all of the above

3. Nominal wages tend to be relatively constant in the short run
   a. for workers with explicit contracts but not for those with implicit contracts.
   b. because of the existence of explicit and implicit contracts.
   c. because real wages tend to be constant in the short run.
   d. except when actual prices differ from expected prices.
   e. none of the above

4. Potential output is
   a. the maximum level of output that is sustainable.
   b. the level of output when actual prices equal expected prices.
   c. the level of output that exists when there are no surprises about the price level.
   d. all of the above
   e. b and c

5. The natural rate of unemployment
   a. is zero.
   b. depends on the price level.
   c. occurs when the economy is producing its potential output.
   d. exists when there is no frictional unemployment.
   e. is always lower than the actual rate of unemployment.

6. If the actual price level equals the expected price level reflected in long-term contracts,
   a. potential output will exceed actual output.
   b. unemployment will be less than the natural rate of unemployment.
   c. firms will reduce production in order to lower nominal wages.
   d. firms will increase production in order to lower real wages.
   e. none of the above

7. When the actual price level exceeds the expected price level reflected in long-term contracts,
   a. firms find it profitable to expand production beyond the economy's potential output.
   b. firms cut back production because the higher prices make extra production too costly.
   c. firms cut back production because they believe that prices will be even higher in the future and profits will be greater in the future.
   d. firms cut back production because costs rise relative to the price of the product.
   e. none of the above

8. Which of the following is true when actual output exceeds potential output?
   a. In the short run, the costs of production stay constant because of explicit and implicit costs.
   b. Labor costs tend to increase even though there are contracts because of overtime or the hiring of those who had been structurally unemployed.
   c. Labor costs increase because workers tend to break their labor contracts and refuse to work unless they get paid more.
   d. Overall production costs tend to remain constant. Labor costs tend to rise but the costs of other resources tend to fall, and the two effects offset each other.
   e. Overall production costs tend to remain constant and the economy quickly returns to its potential output.

9. The short-run aggregate supply curve
   a. slopes upward.
   b. is drawn for a contract period reflecting a given expected price level.
   c. intersects the long-run aggregate supply curve at the potential output.
   d. reflects the relationship between the actual price level and the quantity of aggregate output producers are willing and able to supply.
   e. all of the above

10. If short-run actual output exceeds potential output,
   a. there is pressure to increase productive capacity so that potential output can increase.
   b. there is a contractionary gap that closes as actual output and potential output become equal.
   c. there is an expansionary gap that is reduced as potential output increases.
   d. there is upward pressure on the actual price level.
   e. none of the above

11. Actual output can exceed potential output because
   a. the natural rate of unemployment can be reduced.
   b. resources can work harder than usual for a short period of time.
   c. technological change can increase actual output.
   d. people work more for a higher real wage.
   e. none of the above. Actual output cannot exceed potential output.

12. The efficiency wage theory argues that firms attract a sufficient number of highly qualified workers by
   a. advertising heavily.
   b. offering wages equal to the equilibrium level of wages.
   c. offering wages higher than the wages necessary to attract enough workers.
   d. offering payment as a function of output instead of a wage rate.
   e. none of the above

13. At long-run equilibrium,
   a. the actual price level equals the expected price level reflected in long-term contracts.
   b. short-run aggregate output equals long-run aggregate output.
   c. the quantity of aggregate output demanded equals the quantity of aggregate output supplied.
   d. the quantity demanded of any resource equals the quantity supplied of the resource.
   e. all of the above

14. A vertical long-run aggregate supply curve is
   a. consistent with classical economists' views of the economy.
   b. consistent with Keynes's view of the economy.
   c. feasible only if there are no explicit labor contracts.
   d. impossible because potential output varies with the price level.
   e. a, b, and c

15. Which of the following will be observed if nominal wages are stickier downward than upward?
    a. The long-run aggregate supply curve will slope upward instead of being vertical.
    b. Real wages will increase over time as the economy moves closer to its potential output.
    c. The short-run aggregate supply curve will become more vertical.
    d. The economy will return rapidly to its potential output from a period of high unemployment.
    e. An unemployment rate that is higher than the natural rate of unemployment will persist longer than a rate that is lower than the natural rate of unemployment.

16. Wages could be sticky downward because of
    a. minimum wage laws.
    b. the efficiency wage theory.
    c. long-term contracts.
    d. the presence of powerful labor unions.
    e. all of the above.

17. Which of the following would cause the potential output level to decrease?
    a. a winter that is more severe than usual
    b. an increase in the amount of unskilled labor
    c. technological change that destroys an industry
    d. a decline in the labor force
    e. a decline in the actual unemployment rate

18. Potential output will increase if
    a. aggregate demand increases.
    b. inflation is reduced.
    c. supply shocks are avoided.
    d. immigration increases.
    e. all of the above

*19. An increase in the nominal wage along a given supply curve of labor implies that
    a. expected real wages are falling.
    b. expected real wages are rising.
    c. expected real wages are constant.
    d. the law of diminishing returns does not hold.
    e. none of the above

*20. If the expected price level rises, then
    a. the nominal wage will fall.
    b. the labor supply curve will shift upward.
    c. the labor supply curve will shift downward.
    d. the labor demand curve will shift downward.
    e. b and d

D. *Discussion Questions*

1. What can cause aggregate supply to increase?

2. What is the difference between the nominal wage and the real wage? What happens to the real wage when the actual price level is below the expected price level reflected in long-term contracts?

3. What is the potential output of the economy? How is the potential output determined? How are the potential output and the natural rate of unemployment related?

4. Suppose that a firm is making zero profits and that labor prices, which are set by a contract, account for 25 percent of the firm's costs. Now suppose average prices increase by 10 percent. What happens to the firm's profits?

5. Given the information in question 4, explain what will happen to the firm's profits in the long run.

6. Why do firms tend to expand output when the actual price level exceeds the expected price level reflected in long-term contracts?

7. Why do production costs rise when actual output exceeds potential output?

8. Why are workers willing to work the same number of hours when their real wage falls because of inflation?

9. Explain the derivation of a short-run aggregate supply curve.

10. What determines the slope of the short-run aggregate supply curve?

11. Suppose the actual price level is below the expected price level reflected in long-term contracts. Using a graph, illustrate the short-run and long-run adjustments that would occur.

12. What is the shape of the long-run aggregate supply curve? Why does it have this shape?

13. If the labor force grows over time, what happens to real GDP? Explain. What happens to the price level? Explain.

14. What are supply shocks? How do they affect the short-run aggregate supply curve? the long-run aggregate supply curve?

*15. Why does the demand curve for labor slope down? Why does the supply curve for labor slope up?

VII. ANSWERS

A. *Completion*

1. aggregate
2. nominal
3. explicit; implicit
4. potential output
5. natural
6. short run
7. costs
8. expansionary gap
9. efficiency wage theory
10. contractionary
11. short-run; long-run
12. Temporary supply shocks
13. stagflation
14. hysteresis
15. the law of diminishing returns

B. *True/False*

1. False
2. False
3. False
4. True
5. False
6. True
7. True
8. True
9. True
10. True
11. True
12. True
13. False
14. True
15. True
16. True
17. False
18. False
19. True
20. False

C. *Multiple Choice*

1. a
2. c
3. b
4. d
5. c
6. e
7. a
8. b
9. e
10. d
11. b
12. c
13. e
14. a
15. e
16. e
17. d
18. d
19. b
20. b

D. *Discussion Questions*

1. Aggregate supply would increase if the supply of resources increased, technology improved, or the economic institutions provided better incentives to produce more. (Remember, an increase in the price level causes an increase in the quantity of aggregate supply in the short run.)

2. The nominal wage is the wage measured in dollars; the real wage is measured in terms of the goods and services it will buy. The real wage increases as the actual price level falls below the expected price level, since the prices of some goods and services fall, allowing consumers to buy more with the same nominal wage.

3. The potential output of an economy is the maximum output that can be sustained for a long period of time. It will be produced if economic agents experience no surprises. This situation occurs when the actual price level equals the expected price level reflected in long-term contracts, so nobody makes incorrect decisions and all resource markets are cleared. The potential output is defined for a given level of technology and supply of resources. The natural rate of unemployment is the unemployment rate that prevails if the economy is producing its potential output.

4. If prices increase by 10 percent, total revenues increase by 10 percent, assuming the rate of sales stays constant. Total costs increase by less than 10 percent because the price of labor is fixed. Hence, profits increase, and the firm is willing to increase its rate of output.

5. In the long run, wages will increase by 10 percent and the firm's profits will return to zero.

6. The answer to question 4 illustrates what happens when the actual price level is greater than expected. Some costs are stable in the short run, so production costs rise less than the actual price level. Hence, the extra revenue from an additional unit of output rises above the extra cost of producing an additional unit, and expanding output generates higher profits. The firm expands output to obtain the higher profits.

7. Costs increase when output exceeds potential output because the increased demand for resources drives up any resource prices that are not set by contract. Furthermore, the firm must offer higher nominal wages to get new workers to come to work or pay overtime wages to get current workers to work more hours.

8. They may be merely fulfilling their contractual obligations, or they may have been receiving an above-market wage rate. The latter would be true if the firm paid higher wages in order to attract a large pool of good workers.

9. A short-run aggregate supply curve is drawn for a given expected price level in a given contract period. If the actual price level equals the expected price level, actual output equals the potential output. If actual prices exceed expected prices, firms expand production. The higher prices do not mean all prices increase. Some resource prices are fixed for a while by contract. Consequently, revenues increase more than costs increase, and it is profitable to expand production. The opposite occurs when prices fall, so the short-run aggregate supply curve slopes upward.

10. The slope of the short-run aggregate supply curve depends on how quickly the cost of additional production rises as aggregate output increases. The faster the costs rise, the steeper the short-run aggregate supply curve.

11. If actual prices are below expected prices, there is a contractionary gap. In the following graph, potential output is $5.0 trillion and the expected price level is 120, but the actual price level is 112. Therefore, the short-run equilibrium is at *e*, where $SRAS_{120}$ intersects the aggregate demand curve. The contractionary gap is \$5.0 - 4.2 = \$0.8 trillion. The contractionary gap exists because some resource prices are locked in by contract and product prices are lower than expected, which implies that profits are lower than the firm expected. The firm responds by reducing output, so aggregate output is less than potential output. In time the explicit and implicit contracts come to an end, and labor and management

renegotiate the nominal wage in light of lower actual prices. Nominal wages fall, or at least rise more slowly than the price level. The real wage falls to the level consistent with potential output, firms return production to normal levels, and the short-run aggregate supply curve shifts out. The new equilibrium is achieved when the new short-run aggregate supply curve, $SRAS_{100}$, intersects the aggregate demand curve at e'. The economy is now producing its potential output, and the expected price level and the actual price level both equal 100.

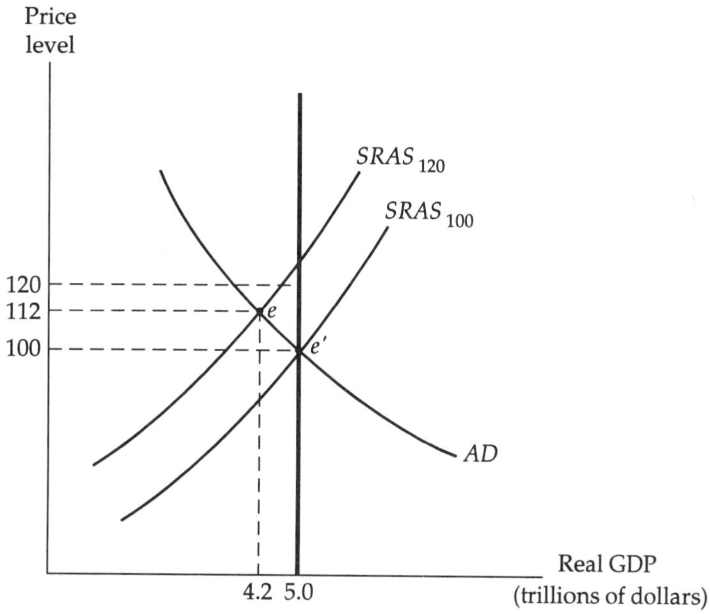

12. The long-run aggregate supply curve is vertical at the level of potential output. The potential output is determined by the level of technology and the amounts of resources available for production. Resource owners determine how much to supply to the market on the basis of expected real resource prices. Regardless of the overall price level, these expected real resource prices will be attained once all markets clear. Consequently, the potential output does not depend on the actual price level; that is, in the long run, the economy will produce its potential output, so the long-run aggregate supply curve is vertical.

13. Real GDP will increase over time as the labor force increases because potential output increases. We cannot be certain about what will happen to the price level, since an increase in the labor force is likely to be associated with an increase in aggregate demand. For a given aggregate demand curve, the price level would fall.

14. Supply shocks are unexpected events that (often temporarily) affect aggregate supply. A temporary shock, such as a drought, causes the short-run aggregate supply curve to shift to the left but does not affect the long-run aggregate supply curve. Temporary supply shocks do not affect the economy's potential output. Supply shocks with more permanent effects, such as a prolonged drop in oil prices or a technological breakthrough, also generate changes in the long-run aggregate supply curve and in potential output.

15. The demand curve for labor slopes down because of the law of diminishing marginal returns, which states that the additional output produced eventually declines as additional units of labor are employed, holding the quantity of other resources constant. The hiring of additional labor causes the marginal value added by each worker to fall. Firms will not pay more than the marginal value of labor for a worker, so the maximum wage a firm would pay for a worker falls as more workers are hired. The supply curve of labor slopes up because the opportunity cost of leisure increases as the wage rate increases. If people consume less leisure, they work more hours.

CHAPTER 12

Fiscal Policy

I. INTRODUCTION

This chapter examines how the government sector affects the output of the economy. The government affects output through government purchases, taxes, and transfer payments. An appendix derives the various multipliers discussed in this chapter. In the next few chapters we will examine the use and effects of money on the economy.

II. OUTLINE

1. Theory of Fiscal Policy. The government affects the circular flow of income by collecting taxes, purchasing goods and services, and making transfer payments. Fiscal policy involves the use of government purchases, transfer payments, and taxes to influence aggregate output, employment, and the price level.

   1.1 Changes in Government Purchases
   - a. An increase in government purchases, other things constant, increases equilibrium real GDP directly and by means of the multiplier.
   - b. The multiplier for any change in autonomous government purchases (with taxes held constant) is the same as that for a change in investment spending: 1/(1 - MPC).

   1.2 Changes in Net Taxes
   - a. A change in net taxes also affects the equilibrium quantity of real GDP demanded but in a less direct manner than does a change in government purchases.
   - b. A reduction in net taxes increases disposable income, which generates an increase in consumption spending.
   - c. A reduction in net taxes causes the consumption function to shift up by the same amount.
   - d. The effect of a change in autonomous net taxes on equilibrium quantity of real GDP demanded is the shift in the consumption function times the autonomous spending multiplier. That is, the change in Y = change in net taxes x [–MPC/(1 - MPC)].

   1.3 Changes in Net Taxes and Government Purchases Combined
   - a. The total effect of changes in government purchases and autonomous taxes equals the sum of their individual effects.
   - b. The absolute value of the multiplier is greater for a given change in government purchases than for an equal change in autonomous net taxes because the change in government purchases affects aggregate spending directly whereas changes in autonomous net taxes do not.
   - c. The balanced budget multiplier indicates that if autonomous net taxes and government purchases change by the same amount, other things constant, the equilibrium quantity of aggregate output demanded also changes by that amount.

2. Including Aggregate Supply

2.1 Fiscal Policy with a Contractionary Gap

a. Expansionary fiscal policy can be used to stimulate aggregate demand to move the economy to its potential GDP.
b. An increase in government purchases or transfer payments or a reduction in taxes shifts the aggregate expenditure function.
c. The increased output generally is accompanied by rising prices.

2.2 Fiscal Policy with an Expansionary Gap

a. Fiscal policy can be used to reduce aggregate demand when there is an expansionary gap.
b. The chosen policy may be to increase taxes, to reduce government expenditures, to reduce transfer payments, or to use some combination of the three.
c. With just the right reduction in aggregate demand, output falls to the potential output level and the price level drops to the expected price level.

2.3 The Multiplier and the Time Horizon

a. The short-run aggregate supply curve slopes upward, so changes in the price level reduce the effect on output of any shift in aggregate demand. The short-run multiplier therefore is smaller than the multiplier when the price level is constant.
b. If the economy is at its potential output, the long-run spending multiplier is zero.

3. Fiscal Policy in Practice

3.1 The Great Depression and World War II

a. The Great Depression led some economists to doubt the self-correcting power of the economy.
b. The positive effects on output and employment of increased government spending during World War II provided evidence of the possible effectiveness of fiscal policy.
c. The passage of the Employment Act of 1946 gave the federal government responsibility for full employment and price stability.
d. After the Great Depression and World War II, policymakers gave up trying to achieve the goal of annual balanced budgets.

3.2 Automatic Stabilizers

a. *Automatic stabilizers* smooth fluctuations in disposable income over the business cycle, maintaining aggregate expenditure in recessionary periods and restraining aggregate expenditure in expansionary periods.
b. Examples of automatic stabilizers include the progressive income tax, unemployment insurance, and welfare benefits.
c. *Discretionary fiscal policy* is the conscious manipulation of taxes and government spending to achieve macroeconomic stability.

3.3 From the Golden Age to Stagflation

a. President Kennedy expanded the scope of fiscal policy to promote long-term economic growth during the 1960s.
b. The stagflation of the 1970s created concerns that demand-management policies were insufficient to keep the economy at potential output with stable prices.

3.4 Fiscal Policy and the Natural Rate of Unemployment
   a. Fiscal policy cannot reduce the rate of unemployment below its natural level in the long run.
   b. Demand-management attempts to increase real GDP beyond potential output in the long run only lead to inflation.

3.5 Lags in Fiscal Policy
   a. It takes time to implement fiscal policy; this may hamper its effectiveness.
   b. Sometimes a change in fiscal policy actually causes harm because time lags cause the policy change to take effect after economic conditions have already changed—when the policy change is no longer appropriate.

3.6 Discretionary Policy and Permanent Income
   a. *Permanent income* is the income households expect to receive on average over the long term.
   b. To the extent that households base consumption decisions on permanent income, short-term manipulation of tax rates will have little effect if people believe the changes are temporary.

3.7 Feedback Effects of Fiscal Policy on Aggregate Supply. Fiscal policy may adversely affect individual work incentives, thus reducing aggregate supply.

3.8 Giant U.S. Budget Deficits of the 1980s and 1990s
   a. In the early 1980s, a large tax cut, designed to stimulate aggregate supply, and a major increase in military spending provided a sizable fiscal stimulus to the economy.
   b. Despite improvements in labor productivity, real GDP did not grow enough to offset the budget impact of lower tax rates and increased government purchases.
   c. The size of the federal budget deficits increased substantially, reducing the government's ability to use discretionary fiscal policy as a tool for economic stabilization.

3.9 *Case Study:* The Supply-Side Experiment

3.10 *Case Study:* Discretionary Policy and Presidential Elections

4. Appendix: The Algebra of Demand-Side Fiscal Policy

4.1 Net-Tax Multiplier
   a. The consumption function when autonomous net taxes are included is $C = a + b(Y - NT)$.
   b. When the consumption function is substituted into the aggregate expenditure function, we get $Y = a + b(Y - NT) + I + G + (X - M)$.
   c. The autonomous net tax multiplier is $-b/(1 - b)$.

4.2 The Multiplier When Both G and NT Change. When autonomous net taxes and government purchases increase by the same amount, the multiplier is 1.

4.3 The Multiplier with a Proportional Income Tax
   a. If the tax rate is t, disposable income is $Y - Yt = Y(1 - t)$.
   b. The multiplier is $1/[1 - b(1 - t)]$.

4.4 Including Variable Net Exports

a. The spending multiplier for a model with a proportional income tax and a foreign sector (MPM equals m) is $1/[(1 - b + m) + t(b - m)]$.

b. The multiplier decreases with a lower marginal propensity to consume, a higher marginal propensity to import, or a higher income tax rate.

III. DISCUSSION

Theory of Fiscal Policy

Government affects national income in several ways. By taxing households, government reduces their disposable income. This in turn reduces the consumption component of aggregate expenditure. Some of the taxes are used to finance transfer payments, which partially offset the effect of the taxes on disposable income. Government purchases of goods and services are an injection into the circular flow, which directly raises aggregate expenditure. *Fiscal policy* refers to the ways government can affect income through changes in purchases, transfer payments, and/or taxes.

The equilibrium quantity of GDP demanded occurs when total spending consumption (C) plus investment (I) plus net exports ($x - m$) plus government purchases (G) equals GDP. A change in government purchases financed through borrowing has the same effects as a change in investment spending and has the same multiplier: 1/(1 – MPC). Like an increase in investment, an increase in government purchases increases the incomes of those from whom the purchases are made, which causes them to increase their spending by an amount equal to the change in income times the MPC. The increased spending in the first round leads to higher incomes for some in the second round, inducing additional spending, and so forth.

Government spending need not be financed through borrowing. Taxes are another important source of financing for government spending. Further, government transfer payments affect disposable income. *Net taxes* are taxes minus transfer payments and are assumed to be autonomous. The effect on national income of autonomous net taxes is similar, but not identical, to the effect of a decrease in government purchases or a decrease in investment spending. For a given increase in autonomous net taxes, autonomous consumption falls by an amount equal to the tax increase times the marginal propensity to consume.

If consumption spending had been $10,000 and the MPC is 0.8, a tax increase of $2,000 reduces autonomous consumption by $2,000 x 0.80 = $1,600. That is, consumption spending falls to $8,400. The total effect of the tax increase is even greater, however. The reduction in autonomous consumption spending generates multiplier effects as the reduced spending reduces incomes. The reduction in equilibrium GDP demanded equals the change in autonomous consumption times 1/(1 – MPC), or $1,600 x 1/0.2 = $8,000. Putting the two effects together, we find that the multiplier for a change in autonomous net taxes is –MPC/(1 – MPC). In our example this equals –0.8/0.2 = –4. In other words, a $2,000 increase in autonomous net taxes generates an $8,000 reduction in equilibrium quantity of GDP demanded.

Since the multiplier for a change in autonomous net taxes differs from the multiplier for government purchases, a neutral fiscal policy change (in which an increase in purchases is financed by an equal increase in autonomous net taxes) will generate a change in equilibrium GDP demanded. Suppose government purchases increase by $1,000 and autonomous net taxes increase by $1,000. Note that an increase in government purchases of $1,000 causes aggregate expenditure to increase in the first round by $1,000, whereas an increase in taxes of $1,000 causes consumption spending, and thus aggregate expenditure, to fall in the first round by less than $1,000. This is because some of the taxes come out of saving. Thus, the overall impact on aggregate expenditure of the increase in government purchases is greater than the impact of the tax. The total change in equilibrium output demanded equals $1,000 x 1/(1 – MPC), which is the effect of the change in government purchases, plus $1,000 x –MPC/(1 – MPC), which is the effect of the change in taxes. Using an MPC of 0.8, we obtain the total change of $1,000(1/0.2) – $1,000(0.8/0.2) = $5,000 – $4,000 = $1,000. That is, equilibrium real GDP demanded increases by the amount of the increase in government purchases when the purchases are financed by an equal increase in autonomous net taxes.

Including Aggregate Supply

The use of fiscal policy to correct a contractionary gap is illustrated in Exhibit 1. Potential output is $5 trillion but actual income is $4.5 trillion, determined by the intersection of *AD* and $SRAS_{110}$. The question is, how can the contractionary gap between $4.5 trillion and $5.0 trillion be removed? A glance at Exhibit 1 suggests two possibilities: an increase in short-run aggregate supply (a shift to *SRAS´*) through natural adjustments in resource markets or an increase in aggregate demand (a shift to *AD´*) through government intervention. (The first approach was discussed in the last chapter.) It may take a long time to accomplish an increase in aggregate supply since it depends on a drop in wages and other resource prices. As we have seen in previous chapters, prices tend to be sticky in the downward direction. Aggregate demand will increase if consumption spending increases, investment spending increases, net exports increase, or government purchases increase. With the tools discussed so far, the government can increase government purchases or it can increase consumption spending by reducing net taxes (that is, by reducing taxes or increasing transfer payments). Thus, the government can remove the contractionary gap by employing fiscal policy.

Exhibit 1

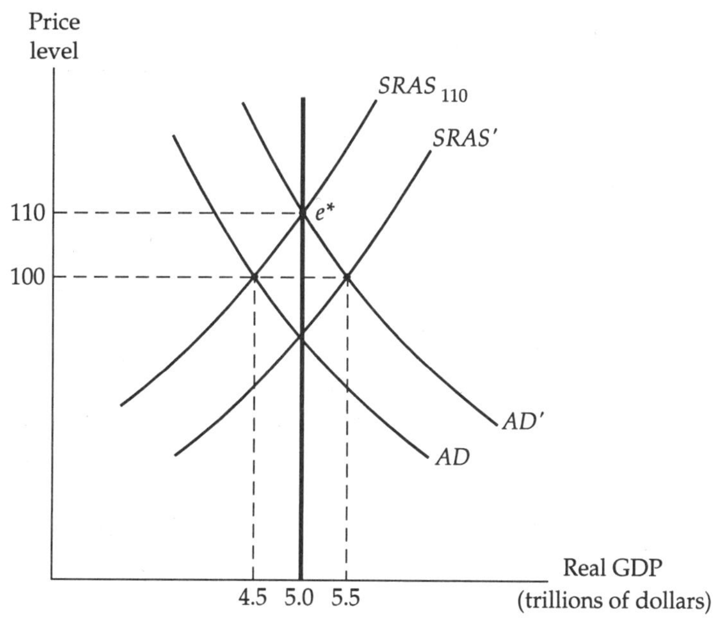

If the government increases spending to remove the contractionary gap, aggregate demand shifts out to *AD´*. At the current price level of 100, the quantity of GDP demanded increases to $5.5 trillion, which exceeds potential output. There is an excess quantity demanded, and prices increase, which generates a shift along *AD´* until the equilibrium is reached at *e**. The fiscal policy has been accompanied by a price increase, but it has eliminated the contractionary gap. (A review of Exhibit 4 in your textbook will help you understand fiscal policy and expansionary gaps.)

It is important to note that the effects of fiscal policy may differ in the long run and the short run. Since the short-run aggregate supply curve slopes upward, shifts of aggregate demand caused by changes in fiscal policy cause both output and price changes. That is, a stimulating fiscal policy increases output but also increases the price level, which reduces the quantity of output demanded. Consequently, the multiplier in the short run is smaller than the multiplier calculated when the price level was assumed constant. Further, the potential output of the economy is determined by real forces such as technology and the supply of resources, and fiscal policy cannot be used to stimulate the economy into a sustained level of output that exceeds potential output.

Fiscal Policy in Practice

Prior to the Great Depression, the government did not make use of *discretionary fiscal policy*, which involves conscious decisions to change government spending or taxation to affect the macroeconomy. Instead, the government sought to balance the budget each year. From the publication of Keynes's *General Theory* until the early 1970s, many economists believed that discretionary fiscal policy could be used to fine-tune the economy so as to maintain economic growth and relatively stable prices. The rising inflation rate that began in the late 1960s proved difficult to control with fiscal policy, however, and some problems associated with lags in implementing fiscal policy came to be more widely recognized. It became clear that fiscal policy often has less impact even in the short run because people make decisions on the basis of their *permanent incomes* and not their current incomes alone. Further, it came to be recognized that fiscal policy may affect aggregate supply by affecting the incentives people have to work.

Appendix: The Algebra of Demand-Side Fiscal Policy

The appendix to this chapter provides formal algebraic derivations of the multipliers. The equilibrium condition is expressed by the equation

$$Y = C + I + G + (x - m)$$

I, $(x - m)$, and G are not functions of income; they are autonomous. Consumption is a function of disposable income, so

$$C = a + b(Y - NT)$$

where a equals autonomous consumption spending, b equals the marginal propensity to consume, and NT equals net taxes.

The effects of changes in autonomous net taxes can be calculated. The total change in equilibrium GDP demanded caused by a change in autonomous net taxes is

$$Y' - Y = [(a - bNT' + I + G + (x - m))/(1 - b)] - [(a - bNT + I + G + (x - m))/(1 - b)] = [-b/(1 - b)](NT' - NT)$$

Thus, the autonomous net tax multiplier is $-b/(1 - b)$, or $-\text{MPC}/(1 - \text{MPC})$. We can combine the effects of a change in government purchases and a change in autonomous net taxes. If government purchases increase by G'' and autonomous net taxes increase by NT'', then the total effect is

$$Y' - Y = [1/(1 - b)]G'' + [-b/(1 - b)]NT'' = (G'' - bNT'')/(1 - b)$$

If $G'' = NT''$, the expression simplifies to $(1 - b)/(1 - b) = 1$. In other words, the *balanced budget multiplier* is 1.

If the government taxes income at rate t, income (Y) must be replaced in the consumption function by disposable income (DI). $\text{DI} = Y(1 - t)$, so $C = a + bY(1 - t)$. Equilibrium GDP demanded is then

$$Y = a + bY(1 - t) + I + G + (x - m)$$
$$Y - bY(1 - t) = a + I + G + (x - m)$$
$$Y[1 - b(1 - t)] = a + I + G + (x - m)$$
$$Y = (a + I + G + (x - m))/1 - b(1 - t)]$$

A \$1 change in a, I, $(x - m)$, or G would cause Y to change by

$$\$1/[1 - b(1 - t)]$$

which is the autonomous spending multiplier with a proportional income tax.

Next, variable net exports are included. Exports (X) are autonomous, but imports depend on income, so $M = mY$, where m is the marginal propensity to import. Equilibrium output demanded now equals

$$Y = a + bY(1 - t) + I + G + X - mY(1 - t) = (a + I + G + X)/[1 - b + m + t(b - m)]$$

The introduction of m makes the denominator larger, so the multiplier is smaller.

IV. LAGNIAPPE

Fine-Tuning

Policymakers in the early 1960s were highly optimistic about the government's ability to fine-tune the economy to maintain full employment and stable prices. Some even believed that the government could effect frequent minor adjustments to government spending or tax rates in order to keep the economy on the full-employment path. Several factors make it unlikely that fine-tuning will be effective. First, there is a time lag between when a change occurs in the economy and when that change is observed. For example, a recession is defined as a decline in real GDP for two consecutive quarters. That means that at least six months must pass before the problem is recognized. Second, it takes time to initiate fiscal policy, since both tax changes and expenditure changes must be approved by Congress. This often takes a year or two. Third, Congress is also susceptible to pressure from interest groups that want specific changes in either taxes or spending. Fourth, it takes time for a change in fiscal policy to take effect. When all the time lags are combined, it is likely that by the time a specific change in fiscal policy occurs, the problem it was designed to control will have disappeared and new problems will have developed.

Question to Think About: Can you think of any way to reduce some of these lags?

Spillover Effects of Fiscal Policy

An important assumption in President Reagan's economic policy was that government spending and taxing activities affect incentives to work, invest, and save. The text discussed a proportional income tax, but in fact the U.S. income tax system has been progressive. Reagan and his supporters argued that high marginal tax rates discourage work and investing. If so, aggregate supply is affected by the government policies on taxes. Hence, the president pushed for reductions in the tax rates and in the extent of their progressivity. In its 1987 Annual Report, the president's Council of Economic Advisers stated, "An efficient tax system entails low and unvarying marginal tax rates that have minimal effects on private investment and consumption choices." High marginal tax rates encourage tax avoidance activities that generally do not enhance the productivity of the economy.

Question to Think About: What taxes (other than the personal income tax) might affect investment and consumption choices?

V. KEY TERMS

Fiscal policy
Autonomous government purchases
Net taxes
Autonomous net taxes
Balanced budget multiplier
Automatic stabilizers
Discretionary fiscal policy
Permanent income
Political business cycles
Proportional income tax

VI. QUESTIONS

A. *Completion*

1. ________________ involves the various ways government can influence GDP through changes in purchases, taxes, and transfer payments.

2. ________________ government purchases do not vary with the level of real GDP.

3. Autonomous net taxes are taxes minus ________________.

4. An increase in government purchases ________________ through the economy, raising real GDP.

5. Government ________________ affect aggregate demand directly; ________________ and ________________ affect aggregate demand indirectly.

6. The government purchases multiplier is ________________ than the multiplier associated with changes in transfer payments.

7. An increase in autonomous net taxes causes the ________________ function to shift down.

8. The value of the ________________ multiplier is one.

9. To close a contractionary gap, the government can increase ________________.

10. An increase in taxes may be an appropriate policy response in the face of a(n) ________________ gap.

11. The long-run multiplier when the economy is producing its potential output is ________________.

12. ________________ are changes in government purchases, transfer payments, or taxes that do not require discretionary actions on the part of the government.

13. Deliberate efforts to promote full employment through changes in government purchases, transfer payments, or taxes involve ________________.

14. The ________________ associated with implementing fiscal policy often hamper the policy's effectiveness.

15. People tend to be less responsive to changes in ________________ income than to changes in ________________ income.

B. *True/False*

______ 1. Fiscal policy involves ways the government can influence the economy's income through changes in the banking system.

______ 2. Net taxes must always be greater than or equal to zero.

______ 3. An increase in autonomous net taxes, other things constant, reduces the equilibrium level of real GDP demanded.

______ 4. Transfer payments affect the equilibrium level of real GDP demanded indirectly, whereas taxes affect it directly.

______ 5. The multiplier for a change in autonomous government purchases is the same as the multiplier for a change in autonomous investment spending.

______ 6. If the multiplier for a change in autonomous government purchases is 4, the multiplier for a change in autonomous net taxes is 3.

______ 7. An increase in autonomous net taxes of $1 million will cause both consumption spending and the equilibrium level of real GDP demanded to fall by $1 million.

______ 8. The balanced-budget multiplier equals the multiplier for autonomous government purchases minus the multiplier for autonomous net taxes.

______ 9. An increase in government purchases of $1 billion has a bigger effect on real GDP than an increase in transfer payments of $1 billion.

______ 10. If the aggregate supply curve slopes upward, an increase in autonomous spending will generate a smaller increase in aggregate expenditure than is implied by the autonomous spending multiplier.

______ 11. The government can increase aggregate expenditure without a price increase by using fiscal policy.

______ 12. If society is producing its potential GDP, the spending multiplier in the long run is zero.

______ 13. Discretionary fiscal policy is implemented only after government officials make a conscious choice to change government spending or taxes.

______ 14. Lags reduce the effectiveness of fiscal policy as a tool of economic stabilization.

______ 15. Fiscal policy is used by policymakers to influence aggregate supply.

______ 16. The huge federal deficits of the 1980s crowded out private investment spending.

______ 17. Political business cycle theory argues that the business cycle is the same length as the term of office of the president of the United States.

______ *18. The higher the proportional tax rate, the less households have to spend and the lower the equilibrium level of real GDP demanded.

______ *19. A proportional income tax increases the autonomous spending multiplier.

______ *20. A decrease in the marginal propensity to import will cause the spending multiplier to increase.

C. *Multiple Choice*

1. Which of the following is expected to increase equilibrium GDP demanded?
   a. increases in government purchases of goods
   b. a reduction in taxes
   c. increases in net exports
   d. increases in transfer payments
   e. all of the above

2. Which of the following is assumed to be autonomous?
   a. consumption spending
   b. saving
   c. government spending
   d. all of the above
   e. b and c only

3. Taxes and transfer payments affect aggregate spending
   a. directly.
   b. by changing disposable income.
   c. by affecting interest rates because the government has to borrow whenever taxes do not equal transfer payments.
   d. all of the above
   e. none of the above. They do not affect aggregate spending.

4. Which of the following has the same effects on equilibrium GDP demanded as a $1,000 increase in government purchases?
   a. a $1,000 increase in transfer payments
   b. a $1,000 decrease in autonomous net taxes
   c. a $1,000 increase in exports
   d. a $1,000 decrease in investment spending
   e. all of the above

5. Suppose that government purchases increase by $1 million and that business investment spending falls at the same time by $1 million. If the MPC is 0.8, the change in aggregate expenditure will be
   a. -$1 million.
   b. zero.
   c. $1 million.
   d. $4 million.
   e. $5 million.

6. An increase in autonomous net taxes causes
   a. the slope of the consumption function to change.
   b. government spending to increase.
   c. the aggregate expenditure curve to shift down.
   d. equilibrium real GDP demanded to increase.
   e. none of the above.

7. If the MPC is 0.9, the absolute value of the autonomous net taxes multiplier is
   a. 0.
   b. 1.
   c. 1.11.
   d. 9.
   e. 10.

8. If the marginal propensity to consume is 0.75, the level of autonomous consumption spending is $1 billion, and net taxes are zero, the balanced budget multiplier is
   a. 0.
   b. 1.
   c. 3.
   d. 4.
   e. 5.

9. If the MPC = 0.8, which of the following would cause the biggest change in real GDP?
   a. a $200 million increase in government purchases
   b. a $250 million increase in transfer payments
   c. a $1 billion increase in government purchases and a $1 billion increase in net taxes
   d. all of the above
   e. a and b only

10. If the economy is experiencing a contractionary gap, it might be appropriate for the government to use fiscal policy to
   a. stimulate aggregate supply.
   b. stimulate aggregate demand.
   c. reduce aggregate supply.
   d. reduce aggregate demand.
   e. a and b

11. Because the aggregate supply curve slopes upward, expansionary fiscal policy tends to be accompanied by
    a. falling prices.
    b. rising prices.
    c. stable prices.
    d. any of the above.
    e. increased investment spending.

12. The economy is producing its potential output and the government increases transfer payments. As a result,
    a. unemployment falls in the short run and in the long run.
    b. prices increase in the short run and in the long run, but output remains constant.
    c. output increases in the short run, but falls back to its original level in the long run.
    d. there are no effects, since changes in transfer payments do not affect the macroeconomy.
    e. none of the above

13. Prior to the Great Depression, the goal of fiscal policy was
    a. to maintain full employment.
    b. to maintain stable prices.
    c. to encourage economic growth.
    d. to balance the budget.
    e. all of the above.

14. Which of the following is not an example of an automatic stabilizer?
    a. a temporary increase in the income tax rate
    b. an unemployment compensation program
    c. a progressive income tax
    d. a proportional income tax
    e. welfare programs

15. One result of automatic stabilizers is that
    a. disposable income varies less during economic fluctuations than does GDP.
    b. disposable income grows faster over time.
    c. tax receipts increase during recessions and decrease during expansions.
    d. net taxes vary inversely with real GDP.
    e. none of the above

16. Which of the following makes discretionary fiscal policy less effective?
    a. lags in fiscal policy
    b. the fact that individuals make decisions based on permanent income instead of current income
    c. the fact that fiscal policy may affect aggregate supply as well as aggregate demand
    d. the fact that the aggregate supply curve slopes upward
    e. all of the above

17. If people base decisions on their permanent income,
    a. spending multipliers are larger.
    b. the multiplier associated with changes in autonomous net taxes is larger.
    c. consumption is less responsive to temporary changes in income than to permanent changes.
    d. all of the above
    e. a and b only

18. According to the theory of political business cycles,
    a. presidents use contractionary discretionary policies to hold down inflation during an election year.
    b. presidents use expansionary discretionary policies to stimulate the economy during an election year.
    c. Republican presidents try to hold down inflation whereas Democratic presidents try to stimulate the economy during election years.
    d. the only goal of an incumbent president is to be reelected.
    e. both c and d

*19. Which of the following will make the autonomous spending multiplier smaller?
    a. a decrease in autonomous net taxes
    b. a decrease in the income tax rate
    c. an increase in the marginal propensity to consume
    d. an increase in autonomous net taxes
    e. an increase in the income tax rate

*20. If the current equilibrium GDP demanded is $100 billion, the MPC is 0.8, the marginal propensity to import is 0.1, the income tax rate is 0.2, and there is a $10 billion increase in government purchases, what is the change in equilibrium GDP demanded?
    a. $17.9 billion
    b. $35.7 billion
    c. $10.0 billion
    d. $22.7 billion
    e. $33.3 billion

D. *Discussion Questions*

1. In discussion question 1 in the chapter titled *Aggregate Expenditure and Demand-Side Equilibrium*, equilibrium output demanded was $8,000. Suppose government spending amounts to $1,000. Using the information from that chapter, calculate the new equilibrium level of output demanded. Are planned saving and planned investment still equal? Why or why not?

2. Using the information from the chapter titled *Aggregate Expenditure and Demand-Side Equilibrium*, calculate what the level of equilibrium output demanded would be if the government purchases were financed by autonomous net taxes of $1,000. Explain.

3. Explain why the balanced budget multiplier is equal to one.

4. Why is an increase in output that is generated by stimulative fiscal policy accompanied by rising prices? Use a graph to illustrate your answer.

5. How does aggregate supply affect the multiplier?

6. Can fiscal policy be used to increase potential output? Explain.

7. How do automatic stabilizers differ from discretionary fiscal policy tools?

8. In what ways can fiscal policy affect aggregate supply?

9. Explain the factors that make it difficult for the government to fine-tune the economy by using fiscal policy.

*10. How does a proportional income tax affect the spending multiplier?

*11. The slope of the consumption function without an income tax is b. What is the slope of the consumption function if the proportional tax rate is t?

*12. If I = \$1,500, G = \$2,500, $(x - m)$ = –\$500, b = 0.7, a = \$500, and t = 0.25, what is the equilibrium quantity of real GDP demanded?

*13. In question 12, suppose the income tax rate falls to 20 percent but autonomous net taxes increase by \$500. What is the new equilibrium quantity of real GDP demanded?

*14. In question 12, if the MPI is 0.1 and exports are \$2,000, what is the new equilibrium quantity of real GDP demanded?

VII. ANSWERS

A. *Completion*

1. Fiscal policy
2. Autonomous
3. transfer payments
4. multiplies
5. purchases; taxes; transfer payments
6. greater
7. consumption
8. balanced budget
9. governmental purchases (or transfer payments)
10. expansionary
11. zero
12. Automatic stabilizers
13. discretionary fiscal policy
14. lags
15. current; permanent

B. *True/False*

1. False
2. False
3. True
4. False
5. True
6. True
7. False
8. True
9. True
10. True
11. False
12. True
13. True
14. True
15. False
16. False
17. False
18. True
19. False
20. True

C. *Multiple Choice*

1. e
2. c
3. b
4. c
5. b
6. c
7. d
8. b
9. d
10. b
11. b
12. c
13. d
14. a
15. a
16. e
17. c
18. b
19. e
20. d

D. Discussion Questions

1. In discussion question 1 in the chapter titled *Aggregate Expenditure and Demand-Side Equilibrium*, the MPC was 0.7, so the government purchases multiplier is 3.33. The change in equilibrium output demanded that is due to government purchases is $1,000 x 3.33 = $3,333, which raises equilibrium output demanded to $11,333. Consumption spending increases by $2,333 ($3,333 x 0.7), and saving increases by $1,000 ($3,333 x 0.3). Planned saving is now $2,000 and no longer equals planned investment of $1,000. Instead, saving now equals planned investment plus government purchases. Since $Y = C + I + G$ and $Y = C + S4$, it must be true that $S = I + G$.

2. The equilibrium before the government purchases and changes in autonomous net taxes was $8,000, of which $7,000 was consumption spending and $1,000 was investment spending. Government purchases are $1,000, but disposable income falls by $1,000 because of the increase in autonomous net taxes. Therefore consumption spending falls to $6,300 and saving falls to $700. Real GDP equals $8,000, but aggregate expenditure equals $8,300 (*C*= $6,300, planned investment = $1,000, and *G* = $1,000). Inventories are being drawn down because actual investment is less than planned investment, so production increases. When real GDP equals $9,000, disposable income equals $8,000, *C* equals $7,000, *I* = $1,000, *G* = $1,000, and *S* = $1,000. Hence, aggregate expenditure equals real GDP, and $9,000 is the new equilibrium real GDP demanded.

3. The balanced budget multiplier applies to an increase in government purchases that is financed by an increase of equal size in autonomous net taxes. An increase in government purchases alters aggregate expenditure directly in the first round by an amount equal to the change in government purchases. In the second round, consumer spending increases by the increase in government purchases (which has generated an equal increase in income) times the MPC. The extra consumer spending results in more income and then more spending equal to the MPC times the extra consumer spending, and so forth. Equilibrium output demanded changes by the initial spending change times the autonomous spending multiplier, or by the increase in government purchases times 1/(1 – MPC). An increase in autonomous net taxes affects aggregate expenditure only indirectly, by reducing disposable income by the amount of the change in autonomous net taxes. Consumer spending is then reduced by an amount equal to the tax increase times the MPC. Equilibrium output demanded changes by this initial consumer spending change times the autonomous spending multiplier, or by the tax increase times –MPC/(1 – MPC). The overall effect of the change in government purchases and the change in taxes is found by combining their individual effects. Note that the total change in spending due to the tax increase exactly offsets the changes in spending that result *after* the first round from increased government purchases. The overall effect then is equal to the effect in the first round of increased government purchases. Hence, the overall change in equilibrium output demanded equals the increase in government purchases, which equals the increase in autonomous net taxes: the multiplier is equal to 1.

4. The short-run aggregate supply curve slopes upward and is drawn for a given expected price level. Fiscal policy can eliminate a contractionary gap by shifting the aggregate demand curve to the right. Because the short-run aggregate supply curve slopes upward, there is an excess quantity demanded at the current price level after aggregate demand shifts. The excess quantity demanded causes prices to increase. See Exhibit 1 in the discussion section of this chapter for the graphical analysis.

5. A positively sloped aggregate supply curve reduces the multiplier because some of the changes in spending and income cause prices to change; this dampens the multiplier effects.

6. Potential output is determined by the level of technology and the supply of resources. Fiscal policy does not tend to affect these determinants, so fiscal policy cannot be used to increase potential output.

7. Automatic stabilizers are government programs already in place that smooth fluctuations in disposable income over the business cycle so that consumption spending does not vary as much as GDP. In this way, the effects of changes in GDP are reduced. In contrast, discretionary fiscal policy involves intentional manipulation of government spending and taxes. It requires that legislation be passed, which often is a time-consuming process.

8. Since fiscal policy involves government spending and taxes, fiscal policy may affect the incentives people have to work and invest. An increase in the tax rate decreases the cost of leisure activity, which may induce people to work less and consume more leisure. An increase in transfer payments raises the opportunity cost of work, which suggests that some will work less. In either case, aggregate supply is affected.

9. Time lags associated with observing that a disequilibrium exists and with passing legislation to implement policies hamper the effectiveness of fiscal policy. Further, changes in fiscal policy may affect the incentives of economic actors, which may affect aggregate supply. To the extent that households base consumption decisions on permanent income, changes in current income have little impact on spending.

10. An income tax reduces disposable income; changes in consumption and saving are related to changes in disposable income. The change in disposable income equals the change in income times $(1 - t)$, where t is the tax rate. The change in consumption spending equals the change in disposable income times the MPC. Putting the two effects together yields the change in consumption spending, which equals the change in income times $(1 - t)$ times the MPC. The multiplier without an income tax is $1/(1 - \text{MPC})$; with an income tax it is equal to $1/[1 - \text{MPC}(1 - t)]$. That is, the value of the multiplier with an income tax is less than the value of the multiplier without an income tax.

11. A proportional income tax means that income (Y) must be replaced by disposable income (DI) in the consumption function. $\text{DI} = (1 - t)Y$, so the consumption function becomes $C = a + b(1 - t)Y$, and the slope is $b(1 - t)$. Since t is less than one, the slope with an income tax is less than the slope without an income tax.

12. $Y = [a + I + (x - m) + G]/[1 - b(1 - t)]$
$= [\$500 + \$1{,}500 - \$500 + \$2{,}500]/[1 - 0.7(1 - 0.25)]$
$= \$4{,}000/0.475 = \$8{,}421$

13. $Y = [\$500 - 0.7(\$500) + \$1{,}500 - \$500 + \$2{,}500]/[1 - 0.7(1 - 0.2)]$
$= \$3{,}650/0.44 = \$8{,}295.45$

14. $Y = (\$500 + \$1{,}000 + \$2{,}500 + \$2{,}000)/[1 - 0.7 + 0.1 + 0.25(0.7 - 0.1)]$
$= \$6{,}000/0.55 = \$10{,}909$

CHAPTER 13

Money and the Financial System

I. INTRODUCTION

The subject of this chapter is money. The chapter defines many new terms and presents a historical overview of the development of money and a description of the U.S. monetary system. The chapter also describes how the U.S. monetary system works and how money is created. The role of monetary policy will be discussed in the following chapter.

II. OUTLINE

1. The Evolution of Money

1.1 Barter and the Double Coincidence of Wants

a. *Barter* involves the trading of one commodity directly for another.

b. Barter requires a *double coincidence of wants*, which occurs when one trader is willing to exchange a product for what another trader is selling.

c. The more specialized the economy, the more difficult it is to rely on barter.

1.2 Earliest Money and Its Functions

a. Money serves four important functions:

(1) Medium of exchange. Whatever serves as money must be generally accepted in return for goods and services.

(2) Unit of account. Prices of all goods are defined in terms of the commodity that serves as money.

(3) Store of value. Money retains its purchasing power over time.

(4) Standard of deferred payment. Money is a yardstick for future payments and receipts.

b. Any commodity that is widely accepted in payment for goods and services is *money*.

1.3 Problems with Commodity Money

a. The quality of the commodity that serves as money may be difficult to maintain.

b. Commodity money tends to be bulky.

c. *Gresham's Law* states that "bad money drives out good money"—that is, people trade away inferior commodity money and hoard better commodity money. The quality of the commodity money in circulation therefore declines, reducing its acceptability.

d. The value of the commodity depends on supply and demand of the commodity, which may vary unpredictably.

1.4 Coins

a. Both the quality and quantity of precious metals are difficult to determine.

b. Coinage developed to control the quantity and quality of silver and gold used as money.

c. The power to coin money came to be associated with sovereigns.

d. When the face value of a coin is greater than the cost of the coinage, the minting of coins can generate government revenue, which is referred to as *seigniorage*.

1.5 Money and Banking
   a. People began to leave their gold in the safes of local goldsmiths.
   b. Depositors began writing instructions to goldsmiths to pay people instead of getting their gold from the goldsmiths and paying their debts themselves. This process led to the first checking accounts.
   c. The goldsmiths began making loans by creating accounts against which borrowers could write checks, thereby creating money.
   d. This system was a type of fractional reserve banking system because the claims against the bank, or total deposits, exceeded the bank's gold and other reserves.

1.6 Paper Money
   a. *Bank notes* were pieces of paper promising that the bearer would receive a specific amount of gold when the paper was presented to the bank.
   b. *Fiduciary money* is notes backed by gold or other valuable commodities.
   c. *Fiat money* does not have any commodity backing it. It is declared legal tender by the government, so creditors must accept it in payment for debts.

1.7 The Value of Money
   a. The value of money is reflected in its purchasing power.
   b. The value of a dollar (relative to a base year) is found by dividing 100 by the price index for the year.

1.8 When Money Performs Poorly
   a. A well-balanced money system can increase an economy's performance.
   b. Too much money in the economy generates inflation, which makes it more difficult to use money as a store of wealth, a medium of exchange, or a standard of value. If the currency becomes so inflated that it is no longer accepted as payment, people resort to barter.
   c. If the official currency is scarce or fails to serve as a medium of exchange, some other form of money may evolve to facilitate exchange.

1.9 *Case Study:* When the Monetary System Breaks Down

2. Financial Institutions in the United States

2.1 Commercial Banks and Thrifts
   a. Financial institutions serve as intermediaries between savers and borrowers.
   b. Depository institutions obtain funds primarily by accepting deposits from the public.
      (1) Commercial banks were established to make loans primarily to businesses.
      (2) Thrift institutions were established to make loans to households.
   c. Other financial intermediaries obtain funds by collecting premiums or by borrowing.

2.2 Development of the Dual Banking System. The United States has a system consisting of both state banks and national banks.

2.3 Birth of the Federal Reserve System
   a. Because of a series of bank failures, the government established the Federal Reserve System in 1914 as the U.S. central bank and monetary authority.
   b. All national banks were required to become members of the Fed.

2.4 Powers of the Federal Reserve System

a. The authority to issue bank notes was taken away from national banks and turned over to the Federal Reserve System.

b. The Federal Reserve can also buy and sell government securities, extend loans to member banks, clear checks, and establish levels of required reserves equal to some percentage of member banks' deposits.

2.5 Banking During the Great Depression

a. Many banks failed because the Fed failed to perform properly.

b. The Fed should have extended more loans to banks experiencing short-term shortages of funds.

c. The Fed contributed to the deterioration of the economy by failing to stabilize the banking system.

2.6 Roosevelt's Reforms

a. The Federal Reserve Board became the Board of Governors, with newly centralized authority to set monetary policy.

b. The Federal Open Market Committee, consisting of the seven members of the Board of Governors plus the presidents of five reserve banks, was established to consolidate decisions about the purchase and sale of government securities by the Fed.

c. The Board of Governors could control the money supply by its power to vary the percentage of deposits member banks were required to hold as reserves and to set discount rates.

d. The Federal Deposit Insurance Corporation (FDIC) and the Federal Savings and Loan Insurance Corporation (FSLIC) were established to insure deposits held in member banks and savings and loans.

e. Commercial banks were forbidden to buy and sell corporate stocks and bonds.

2.7 Branch Banking Restrictions

a. Each state controls the type and number of branches that a bank may open.

b. Federal laws prevent interstate branching.

c. Two developments have allowed banks to get around the restrictions on branches.

(1) *Bank holding companies* are corporations that may own several different banks; many states have allowed holding companies to cross state lines.

(2) Automatic teller machines may be shared by several banks.

2.8 The Quiet Life of Depository Institutions

a. For decades banks and thrifts were highly regulated and insulated from competitive pressures.

b. The inflation of the 1970s increased market interest rates and changed the banking environment considerably.

3. Recent Problems with Depository Institutions

3.1 Depository Institutions Were Losing Deposits

a. Depositors left depository institutions as interest rates offered by other financial institutions rose above the rates the Fed permitted depository institutions to pay depositors.

b. Depository institutions often had to support outstanding loans by borrowing at higher interest rates than they earned on their loans.

3.2 Bank Deregulation
   a. Banks and thrifts were given greater control over their operations, and interest rate ceilings were eventually eliminated.
   b. Many states reduced regulation of state-chartered savings and loan associations.
   c. The thrifts were able to make high-risk loans, knowing that the FSLIC protected depositors.
   d. Many thrifts failed in the 1980s.

3.3 Bailing Out the Thrifts
   a. The collapse of so many thrifts prompted Congress in August of 1989 to approve a huge financial bailout for the industry.
   b. Under the new law, the FSLIC was abolished, thrift deposits were insured by the FDIC, and thrifts were put under the supervision of the U.S. Treasury. New regulations were established to dictate the types of investments thrifts could make.

3.4 *CASE STUDY:* Easy Money, Empty Buildings

3.5 Commercial Banks Were Also Failing. Commercial banks experienced difficulties similar to those of the thrifts in the late 1980s and early 1990s.

III. DISCUSSION

Since this chapter focuses on the historical development of the U.S. monetary system and introduces many new terms, this discussion section will review the terms introduced in the chapter.

Barter is trading one commodity directly for another. A major problem with barter is that it requires a *double coincidence of wants* on the part of the traders. That is, each party in the exchange must be willing to exchange his or her product for what the other is willing to sell. Barter becomes more difficult as the number of goods increases and as the economy becomes more complex and specialized.

Money makes exchange easier. If one good becomes generally accepted in return for all other goods, it begins to function as money. To be considered money, a good must serve four functions: (1) it must act as a *medium of exchange*—it must be generally accepted in exchange for other goods and services; (2) it must serve as a *unit of account*—prices of all other goods must be defined in terms of money; (3) it must be a *store of value*—it must hold its value over time; and (4) it must act as a *standard of deferred payment*—it must act as a yardstick both today and in the future. Whatever good serves these four functions is money.

Commodity money is a good or commodity, such as corn or gold, that also serves as money. There are problems with using most commodities as money: many commodities deteriorate over time; in addition, they tend to be bulky, to vary in quality, and to change value with changes in supply and demand. According to *Gresham's Law*, when commodities differ in quality, bad money drives out good. That is, people tend to trade away the inferior money and hoard the best, so the quality of the commodity in circulation declines; this reduces its usefulness as a medium of exchange.

Over time, metals came to be used instead of other commodities for money. But precious metals could be debased with cheaper metals, so people had to determine both the quantity and the quality of the precious metals. Coinage was developed to handle the problem of quality control. Governments took over coinage, often earning *seigniorage*: revenues arising from the difference between the face value of a coin and the cost of coinage. Coins whose value exceeded their metallic value were called *token money*.

The 17th century saw the development of a *fractional reserve banking system*, in which a bank kept reserves to back up only a fraction of the deposits placed in the bank. Banks created money by making loans through the creation of new deposits on which borrowers could write checks, even though the reserves were not there to back up the deposits. *Bank notes* are pieces of paper that promise that the bearer will receive a specific amount of gold when the paper is presented to the bank. Such notes are a type of *fiduciary money*. *Fiat money* is notes that are not redeemable in gold or other valuable metals. Fiat money is declared to be *legal tender* by the government that issues it, which means that it must be accepted for payment of debts. Most paper money throughout the world, including U.S. currency, is fiat money.

People accept fiat money because they have confidence in its value or in the government that issued it. If people lose confidence in fiat money, other commodities are used for money on the black market, or barter is used. When this happens, the economy is working inefficiently. A smoothly functioning monetary system is essential to a modern industrial society.

Financial intermediaries are institutions that link savers and borrowers by accepting funds from savers and lending these funds to borrowers. *Commercial banks* and *thrift institutions* are two examples of *depository institutions*: financial intermediaries that acquire funds by accepting deposits from the public. A *demand deposit* is an account that a depositor can draw from at any time by writing a check. In this country, banks have been chartered both by states and by the national government, which means that the United States has a dual banking system.

Today the Board of Governors of the *Federal Reserve System* is responsible for controlling the U.S. money supply. The Fed requires banks to hold a certain percentage of their deposits in the form of reserves. The Fed also influences the money supply by *open market operations*—the buying and selling of government securities. It also lends money to member banks and charges an interest rate called the *discount rate*. For a long time, the Fed set maximum interest rates banks could pay on deposits. The deregulation of depository institutions in the 1980s was a response to their insolvency problems, which had been caused by the inflation of the 1970s. Regulation of thrifts has resumed, however, as a result of the failure of many thrifts in the 1980s and the financial bailout approved by Congress.

IV. LAGNIAPPE

When Money Loses Its Value

There have been instances in history when a country's money supply increased so fast that the inflation rate became astronomical. One of the best examples was the hyperinflation in Germany after World War I. The inflation rate was so great that workers demanded to be paid several times a day and would give their pay to family members so that they could buy products before the prices increased again. Prior to World War I, the value of all home mortgages in Germany was 40 million marks. During the height of the hyperinflation in the early 1920s, 40 million marks could buy a postcard.

Question to Think About: How could relative prices be determined in such a situation?

The Gold Standard

Some politicians today are advocating a return to the gold standard. Under a gold standard, the dollar and other currencies are convertible into gold at a fixed price. For many years the official price of gold in the United States was $35 an ounce. That is, if you had an ounce of gold you could get $35 for it from the government, or you could buy an ounce of gold from the government for $35. When a currency is fully backed by gold, the money supply is determined by the amount of gold the government has.

In the past, the United States was not on a true gold standard because the government did not have enough gold to back all the dollars that had been printed. Instead, the government kept enough gold to back a fraction of the money supply. In this way, the money supply was still related to the gold stock but not on a one-for-one basis. The United States officially abandoned the gold standard in 1973.

Question to Think About: What price would be set for gold if the United States returned to the gold standard?

V. KEY TERMS

Double coincidence of wants
Money
Medium of exchange
Commodity money
Unit of account
Store of value
Standard of deferred payment
Gresham's Law
Seigniorage
Token money
Fractional reserve banking system
Bank notes
Fiat money
Legal tender
Financial intermediaries
Depository institutions
Commercial banks
Demand deposits
Thrift institutions (thrifts)
Federal Reserve System
Reserves
Discount rate
Federal Open Market Committee
Bank holding company
Money market mutual fund

VI. QUESTIONS

A. *Completion*

1. Barter requires a ________________.
2. Anything that people generally accept in payment for goods and services is ________________.
3. If prices of all goods are expressed in terms of a commodity used as money, then the commodity becomes a ________________.
4. Money serves as a ________________ when it retains purchasing power over time.
5. The expression "bad money drives out good" is known as ________________.
6. Coins whose face value exceeds their metallic value are ________________ money.
7. Revenue earned from coinage is known as ________________.

8. Reserves as a proportion of total claims against total deposits is the ________________.

9. ________________ money is not backed by anything of intrinsic value.

10. The rate at which money is exchanged for goods and services is the ________________ of money.

11. ________________ were developed to make loans primarily to businesses rather than to households.

12. When member banks borrow from a Federal Reserve bank, they pay the ______________.

13. The Fed engages in ________________ operations when it buys and sells U.S. government securities.

14. The United States has more banks than other countries because of government restrictions on ________________.

15. The nation's major banks are all owned by ________________.

B. *True/False*

______ 1. Increased specialization made the barter system more costly.

______ 2. There is no common measure of value in a barter economy.

______ 3. Money allows the sale of one good to be separate from the purchase of another.

______ 4. To serve as money, a good must be durable.

______ 5. Gresham's Law says that good money drives out bad money.

______ 6. Before coinage was fully developed, one problem with metallic money was that the quality of the metal had to be determined at each exchange.

______ 7. Seigniorage is earned when the face value of a coin exceeds the cost of minting the coin.

______ 8. U.S. coins now in circulation are examples of token money.

______ 9. The total claims against a bank cannot exceed the bank's reserves under a fractional reserve banking system.

______ 10. Bank notes are a type of fiduciary money.

______ 11. Fiat money is money backed by gold.

______ 12. Federal Reserve notes are backed by gold.

______ 13. The value of money is measured by its purchasing power.

______ 14. An insurance company is an example of a depository institution.

______ 15. The United States no longer has a dual banking system.

______ 16. The Fed is empowered to set reserve requirements for banks.

______ 17. Federal Reserve banks can fail if they do not have enough reserves.

______ 18. Bank holding companies are used to circumvent federal laws against interstate branch banking.

______ 19. During the inflation of the 1970s, ceilings on interest rates resulted in depositors' withdrawing deposits from commercial banks and thrifts.

______ 20. Federal deposit insurance encourages managers of thrifts and banks to engage in risky loans.

C. *Multiple Choice*

1. Which of the following is a problem of barter?
   a. negotiating numerous exchange rates among commodities
   b. achieving a double coincidence of wants
   c. seigniorage
   d. a and b
   e. none of the above

2. Money is
   a. anything that is generally accepted as payment for goods and services.
   b. something that the government of a nation has always made and controlled.
   c. gold and other precious metals.
   d. something that is backed by a commodity that has intrinsic value.
   e. all of the above.

3. Which of the following is not a function of money?
   a. medium of exchange
   b. creator of seigniorage
   c. store of value
   d. standard of deferred payment
   e. b and c

4. Which of the following commodities would work best as a store of value?
   a. pebbles
   b. milk
   c. gold
   d. corn
   e. cattle

5. For a commodity to serve as money and be a store of value, it must
   a. be easily divided up.
   b. have value as a commodity.
   c. maintain its purchasing power.
   d. be easily reproduced.
   e. be declared legal tender by the government.

6. One problem with using commodity money is
   a. the commodity's homogeneity.
   b. the value of the commodity depends on its supply and demand.
   c. good money drives out bad money.
   d. the commodity tends to lack intrinsic value.
   e. the difficulty of achieving a double coincidence of wants.

7. Which of the following was not a means of maintaining the value and quality of gold or silver coins?
   a. stamping the coins
   b. making sure the metal in the coin was worth more than its face value
   c. putting borders on the coins
   d. making counterfeiting illegal
   e. none of the above

8. Debasement of a currency could be accomplished by
   a. printing more paper money.
   b. adding base metals to coins.
   c. shaving small amounts of metal off a coin.
   d. clipping small amounts of metal off the edges of the coin.
   e. all of the above.

9. Early banks created money by
   a. loaning out reserves to people.
   b. coining money.
   c. creating fiduciary money.
   d. creating deposits against which borrowers could write checks.
   e. issuing commodity money.

10. Bank notes differ from checks in that
    a. checks are written against thrifts and bank notes against banks.
    b. checks are backed by gold and notes are not.
    c. checks are created by banks and notes by the government.
    d. checks can be redeemed only by the individual to whom they are directed whereas notes can be redeemed by anyone who holds them.
    e. checks are legal tender and notes are not.

11. Fiat money derives its status as money from
    a. the gold that backs it.
    b. the power of the government.
    c. its intrinsic value.
    d. being redeemable for commodity money.
    e. all of the above are possible.

12. The value of money falls when
   a. the price level rises.
   b. the price level falls.
   c. it can be exchanged for more goods.
   d. interest rates fall.
   e. none of the above. The value of money is constant.

13. When there is too little money in an economy, people often resort to
   a. strict price controls.
   b. barter.
   c. demanding more frequent payment for labor.
   d. frequent price changes.
   e. all of the above.

14. The dual banking system refers to
   a. a time when states owned some banks and citizens owned other banks.
   b. a time when banks and thrifts competed for deposits.
   c. the current deregulated system, in which banks compete with other financial intermediaries such as brokerage houses and insurance companies.
   d. a system that only existed prior to the formation of the Fed, in which some banks were chartered by states and some by the federal government.
   e. a system that still is in existence, in which some banks are chartered by states and others are chartered by the federal government.

15. The Federal Reserve System has the power to
   a. issue bank notes.
   b. buy and sell government securities.
   c. extend loans to member banks.
   d. set reserve requirements of member banks.
   e. all of the above

16. The interest rate the Fed charges on loans made to member banks is the
   a. reserve ratio.
   b. reserve rate.
   c. discount rate.
   d. bank rate.
   e. prime rate.

17. During the Great Depression, the Fed
   a. prevented the depression from being worse by solving the banking crisis.
   b. extended too many loans to member banks, which got them into further trouble.
   c. initiated discretionary fiscal policy that made the depression worse.
   d. failed to act as a lender of last resort to member banks, causing many of them to fail.
   e. purchased securities in order to prevent a collapse of the securities markets.

18. As a result of legislation passed during the Great Depression,
   a. the Fed set reserve requirements of 100 percent.
   b. commercial banks were forbidden to buy and sell corporate securities.
   c. interest rate ceilings were set.
   d. all of the above
   e. b and c

19. Commercial banks and thrifts faced difficult times in the 1970s because of
    a. deflation.
    b. high interest rates on borrowed funds relative to interest rates on mortgages.
    c. excessive competition between banks and thrifts.
    d. deregulation of financial markets.
    e. a, b, and c.

20. The financial bailout of the thrift industry passed by Congress in 1989
    a. deregulated the thrift industry too.
    b. established the FSLIC to insure deposits in thrifts.
    c. required that thrifts hold at least 70 percent of their assets in mortgages.
    d. required that thrifts hold at least 40 percent of their assets in junk bonds.
    e. made it more difficult for commercial banks to acquire thrifts.

D. *Discussion Questions*

1. a. Suppose there are two goods, A and B, and the price of A in terms of B is 1A = 2B. What is the price of B in terms of A? How many different relative prices are there?
   b. A third good, C, is added, and 1A = 4C. What is the price of B in terms of C? How many different price ratios are there, and what are they?
   c. A fourth good, D, is added, and 1A = 8D. What is the price of D in terms of C? How many different price ratios are there?

2. Discuss the advantages of money over barter.

3. What are the four functions of money, and why are they important?

4. State whether each of the following would be a good or bad commodity to use as money and discuss why.
   a. beads
   b. tobacco
   c. cattle
   d. boulders
   e. cigarettes

5. How did coinage help solve the quality control problems associated with using precious metals as money?

6. Are coins that are currently minted in the United States milled around the edges to prevent "clipping"? Why or why not?

7. Describe a fractional reserve banking system.

8. Are all forms of paper money fiat money? Explain.

9. Why do people accept fiat money? What might cause people to stop accepting fiat money?

10. What determines the value of fiat money?

11. What happens if there is too much money in the economy? What happens if there is not enough money in the economy?

12. Wars are often associated with inflation. Based on what you have learned so far, offer an explanation for this observation.

13. Why was the Federal Reserve System created? What are its powers under current banking law?

14. Explain why the text describes banking prior to the 1970s as a "quiet life."

15. Discuss the factors that led to deregulation of U.S. financial markets in the 1980s.

VII. ANSWERS

A. *Completion*

1. double coincidence of wants
2. money
3. unit of account
4. store of value
5. Gresham's Law
6. token
7. seigniorage
8. reserve ratio
9. Fiat
10. purchasing power
11. Commercial banks
12. discount rate
13. open-market
14. branches
15. bank holding companies

B. *True/False*

1. True
2. True
3. True
4. True; otherwise money would not serve as a store of value.
5. False
6. True
7. True
8. True
9. False
10. False
11. False
12. False
13. True
14. False
15. False
16. True
17. False
18. True
19. True
20. True

C. *Multiple Choice*

1. d
2. a
3. b
4. c
5. c
6. b
7. b
8. e
9. d
10. d
11. b
12. a
13. b
14. e
15. e
16. c
17. d
18. e
19. b
20. c

D. *Discussion Questions*

1. a. 1B = 0.5A; there is one relative price.
   b. Since 1B = 0.5A and 0.5A = 2C, 1B = 2C; there are three price ratios: P_A/P_B is one ratio; P_A/P_C is a second; and P_B/P_C is a third. (The reciprocals are not different price ratios.)
   c. Since 1A = 4C and 1A = 8D, 8D = 4C, or 1D = 0.5C; there are ten price ratios.

2. Barter requires a double coincidence of wants, which is difficult to achieve in highly specialized economies. The more goods there are, the more difficult it is to obtain a double coincidence of wants and the more exchange rates there are to negotiate. Money permits the separation of the decision to sell one good from the decision to buy another and permits more efficient exchange.

3. Money functions as a medium of exchange, a unit of account, a store of value, and a standard of deferred payment. As a medium of exchange, money facilitates exchange by separating the purchase of one commodity from the sale of another commodity. As a unit of account, money eliminates the need to establish exchange rates between all possible pairs of commodities. As a store of value, money permits people to hold their wealth in a convenient form. As a standard of deferred payment, money provides a yardstick for future payments and receipts.

4. None of the items would be very good choices for money. The values of beads, tobacco, cattle, and cigarettes can vary widely, as they are determined by the interaction of the supply and demand for each. Boulders would not be divisible, so paying for small items would be difficult. All the items listed have been used for money at some time in history, however.

5. The quality of precious metals is hard to determine because of the possibility of adding cheaper metals. The government took over coinage to control the quality. There were still problems, however, because people scraped small amounts of the metal off coins to make extra money. The milling of the edges and the stamping of coins helped to reduce this problem.

6. No. The value of the metal in the coins is too low to make clipping profitable. The coins are fiat money and not commodity money.

7. A fractional reserve system is one in which banks do not keep enough reserves on hand to cover all possible withdrawals. Deposits and withdrawals tend to balance out, so a steady pool of funds remains available for lending. Banks make loans by creating demand deposits for borrowers and use their reserves to cover the relatively small portion of the demand deposits that is withdrawn. Bankers know that not all deposits will be withdrawn at any given time, so they can make the loans safely.

8. No. Fiat money is money because the government says it is money. Paper money could be backed by commodities such as gold, in which case it would not be fiat money.

9. Fiat money is accepted because the government declares it to be legal tender and because other people readily accept it. People would stop accepting fiat money if the value of the money fell substantially because of inflation or if they lost confidence in the government backing the money.

10. The value of money is determined by its purchasing power—the rate at which it can be exchanged for goods and services. This rate is determined by the quantity of money that has been placed in circulation relative to the quantity of goods and services produced. When more money is created and the goods and services produced by the economy have not increased, the prices of the goods and services increase, which means that the value of money falls.

11. Too much money is associated with inflation, which makes it more costly to use markets. In this situation, it is difficult to determine whether a price change results from inflation or is only a relative price change. Under these conditions money fails to serve as a standard of value or a store of wealth. Economic actors expend resources trying to determine the source of a change in a price and to protect themselves from the effects of inflation. The economy becomes less productive. When there is too little money, people have a hard time making transactions that require money. Hence, they will either find an alternative to money, such as the money of another country or some commodity that serves as money, or they will engage in barter more frequently.

12. During wars, governments purchase many more goods and services than they do during peacetime. Because of the additional revenues required for the war effort, governments often use their power to coin and to print money to increase the amount of money in the economy; this leads to inflation.

13. The Federal Reserve System was created to stabilize the country's financial system. For many years the banking system experienced bank failures during recessions. The Fed is empowered to control the money supply by buying and selling government securities, by setting reserve requirements for member banks, and by being a lender of last resort to member banks.

14. Prior to the 1970s, banks were strictly regulated; they had little freedom and experienced little competition. Interest rate ceilings prevented depository institutions from competing for deposits by offering higher interest rates. Depository institutions also could not buy or sell corporate securities, and commercial banks generally did not compete for borrowers with thrifts.

15. Inflation and higher interest rates at other financial institutions caused depository institutions to lose deposits in the 1970s. As banks and thrifts lost deposits, they had to support their outstanding low-interest loans by borrowing at higher market interest rates. Thrifts were hardest hit because of the long-term nature of their loans. Further, new saving instruments such as money market funds were created and provided competition for deposits. Deregulation helped commercial banks and thrifts compete on a more equal footing with other financial institutions.

CHAPTER 14

Banking and the Money Supply

I. INTRODUCTION

In this chapter we examine how the Federal Reserve System controls the nation's money supply. The chapter covers the role of depository institutions as well as the types of deposits they hold. The next chapter examines the effect of money on the economy.

II. OUTLINE

1. Banks, Their Deposits, and the Money Supply

   1.1 Banks Are Financial Intermediaries
   a. Banks serve as financial intermediaries by bringing borrowers and savers together.
   b. The market for loans is characterized by asymmetric information—borrowers know their credit history better than the lenders.
   c. Banks specialize in assessing information about prospective borrowers.
   d. Banks minimize risk to each individual saver through diversification.

   1.2 Money and Liquidity
   a. A deposit is a *liability* to the bank because the bank must promise to repay the depositor.
   b. When the bank lends funds to borrowers, the borrowers' promises to repay are *assets* to the institution.
   c. *Checkable deposits* are deposits against which checks can be written. They include demand deposits, NOW accounts, credit union share draft accounts, and the like.
   d. The narrowest definition of the money supply is *M1*, which consists of currency held by the nonbank public, checkable deposits, and travelers checks.
   e. Checks are not legal tender, but they are so widely accepted as a medium of exchange that checkable deposits are considered part of the money supply.
   f. Federal Reserve notes are liabilities of the Federal Reserve banks and provide the primary currency in the economy. The other component of currency is coins.
   g. *Liquidity* is the ease with which any asset can be converted into the medium of exchange without a significant loss of value. Currency is the most liquid asset.

   1.3 Other Deposits
   a. Some other assets perform the standard-of-value and store-of-wealth functions of money.
   b. The most important of these assets are
      (1) *Savings deposits* (or *passbook savings accounts*): deposits that earn interest but do not have a specific maturity
      (2) *Time deposits*: deposits that earn a fixed amount of interest if held for a specified period of time

(3) *Money market mutual fund accounts*: shares representing claims on a portfolio of short-term interest-earning assets

c. The definition of money is often broadened to include some of these assets.

d. Monetary aggregates are measures of money used by the Federal Reserve.

(1) *M2* is M1 plus savings deposits, small-denomination time deposits, and money market mutual funds.

(2) *M3* is M2 plus large-denomination time deposits.

2. How the Banking System Works

2.1 Starting a Bank

a. To start a bank, the founders must have a charter from the U.S. Comptroller of the Currency in the case of a national bank or the state banking authority in the case of a state bank.

b. The founders must invest funds in the bank in exchange for shares of stock in the bank. The stock is the *owners' equity*, or net worth of the bank.

c. *Assets* are physical property and financial claims owned by the bank.

d. Assets must equal liabilities plus net worth.

e. *Liabilities* are claims on the bank by nonowners (for example, checkable deposits).

2.2 Reserve Accounts

a. *Reserves* are cash held in the bank's vault or deposits held at the Fed. They do not earn interest.

b. The *required reserve ratio* is set by the Fed and determines what proportion of deposits must be held as reserves.

c. *Required reserves* are the dollar amount the Fed requires banks to hold in reserve. Reserves must equal total deposits times the required reserve ratio.

d. *Excess reserves* are reserves in excess of required reserves and can be used to make loans or purchase interest-bearing assets.

2.3 Liquidity Versus Profitability

a. A bank must be prepared to satisfy depositors' demands for funds.

b. A bank loses reserves whenever a depositor demands cash or writes a check that is deposited in another bank.

c. A bank wants to maintain sufficient liquidity to meet unexpected demands on its reserves or to make loans to valued customers.

d. A bank also wants to make profits, which are generated by earning interest on loans and other assets.

e. Since the assets earning the highest interest rates tend to be the least liquid, the two objectives of liquidity and profitability are often at odds.

f. Banks can borrow in the federal funds market to meet temporary reserve deficiencies.

2.4 The Fed's Balance Sheet

a. The Fed's assets include government securities and discount loans extended by the Fed to depository institutions.

b. The Fed's liabilities include Federal Reserve notes and deposits from depository institutions.

c. The Fed clears checks for, extends loans to, and holds deposits of depository institutions.

d. The Fed earns income because its primary assets earn interest and its primary liabilities do not pay interest.

e. The Fed is also active in foreign exchange markets.

2.5 *Case Study:* Tracking the Supernote

3. How Banks Create Money

3.1 Creating Money Through Excess Reserves

a. The Fed can create excess reserves by buying government securities on the open market, lending reserves to depository institutions through the discount window, or lowering the required reserve ratio.

b. Banks create money by loaning out excess reserves.

c. A bank makes a loan by creating a checkable deposit, which is money.

d. When the borrower writes a check that is deposited in another bank, the excess reserves of that bank are increased. That bank can lend the excess reserves out, creating more money.

e. An individual bank cannot lend out more than its excess reserves because borrowers usually spend the amount borrowed.

f. When a bank lends its excess reserves, the reserves do not leave the banking system. Thus the system can expand checkable deposits by a multiple of the initial increase in excess reserves.

3.2 Summary of Rounds

a. The banking system increases the money supply by a multiple of new reserves.

b. When a check clears, the reserves of one bank fall, but the drop in reserves is offset by an increase in the reserves of another bank.

c. Deposit expansion stops when the increase in required reserves resulting from the new deposits matches the initial increase in excess reserves.

3.3 *Case Study:* Banking on the Net

3.4 Another Possibility

a. The Fed could buy securities from a dealer instead of a bank, but the dealer would deposit the check into a bank and excess reserves would be created.

b. The Fed is not constrained by reserve requirements.

3.5 Excess Reserves, Reserve Requirements, and Money Expansion

a. Money creation requires the injection of excess reserves into the banking system.

b. Once additional excess reserves enter the system, the total possible expansion of the money supply equals the new excess reserves times the money multiplier.

c. The simple money multiplier equals $1/r$, where r is the required reserve ratio. It indicates the maximum possible expansion of the money supply from a given injection of excess reserves.

3.6 Limitations on Money Expansion

a. The money multiplier is reduced when people take cash out of the system or when banks hold excess reserves.

b. The Fed can make excess reserves available to banks, but cannot make banks extend loans or make people borrow.

3.7 Multiple Contraction of Money. A sale of government securities by the Fed has the opposite effect from a purchase of government securities by the Fed.

3.8 Change in the Discount Rate
   a. The discount rate is another tool of monetary policy.
   b. A lower discount rate encourages more loans and expands the money supply.
   c. A higher discount rate tends to decrease the money supply.

4. Conclusion. The Fed has three ways to pursue an expansionary monetary policy: (1) purchasing government securities from the public or from depository institutions; (2) lowering the discount rate; and (3) reducing the reserve requirement. The Fed has three ways to pursue a tight monetary policy: (1) selling government securities; (2) raising the discount rate; (3) increasing the reserve requirement. The Fed relies primarily on open-market operations to control the money supply.

III. DISCUSSION

Banks, Their Deposits, and the Money Supply

Savers and borrowers are not the same people. Most people who save want access to their funds. Thus, they do not want to lend their money directly to other people or firms. Instead, savers place their deposits in banks and other depository institutions; these institutions lend the funds out to borrowers and retain reserves to meet the withdrawal demands of their depositors. Banks serve as financial intermediaries, and the matching of savers and borrowers is called *intermediation.* This matching is an important function of banks. Banks specialize in making loans, so they develop expertise in evaluating loan applicants and monitoring contracts. This expertise makes it possible for banks to economize on the transaction and enforcement costs associated with loan agreements. Further, they are able to reduce the risk to individual savers by diversifying their loan portfolios.

From a macroeconomic standpoint, the importance of banks stems from their role in the creation of money. Deposits are *liabilities* to banks because they represent a promise to repay the depositor. Loans issued by the banks are *assets* because they represent the borrower's promise to repay funds to the bank. *Checkable deposits* are deposits against which checks can be written; the bank must be prepared to honor these liabilities. Checkable deposits are considered part of the money supply because checks are widely accepted as a medium of exchange. There are other assets that are very liquid, so they serve all the functions of money except that of a medium of exchange. The narrowest definition of the money supply, M1, encompasses currency held by the nonbank public, checkable deposits, and travelers checks. Broader definitions also include these other assets.

How the Banking System Works

Banks are businesses, and their stockholders expect banks to earn profits like other businesses. Although banks earn income by charging fees for checking and savings accounts, check cashing services, safe deposit boxes, and travelers checks, the biggest source of bank profits is the interest earned on loans and other assets. As stated earlier, banks bring together savers and borrowers. This suggests that we can examine banks from the perspective of their sources of funds and their uses of funds.

In general terms, banks have three sources of funds: deposits, borrowing, and owners' equity. Deposits include checkable deposits, savings deposits, and time deposits. Borrowing includes borrowing from the Fed or in the *federal funds market*. Owners' equity, or *net worth*, refers initially to the investment by the founders of the bank. Over time, it is measured as the difference between the assets of the bank and the liabilities of the bank. Deposits and borrowings are liabilities of the bank.

Bankers use double-entry bookkeeping. In this type of system, the sum of assets must be equal in value to the sum of liabilities and owners' equity. Assets tend to be created or purchased as the bank uses the funds it has raised. A bank has numerous uses for its funds; these uses include purchasing buildings and furnishings, making loans, purchasing government securities, purchasing stock in the Fed if the bank is a member bank, making deposits with the Fed, and maintaining cash on hand.

This discussion of bank assets and liabilities illustrates the fact that one person's assets are another's liabilities. Checkable deposits are assets to the depositor but liabilities to the bank; the bank's deposits at the Fed are assets to the bank and liabilities to the Fed. Further, loans made by the bank are assets to the bank and liabilities to the borrowers.

Exhibit 1 shows a *balance sheet* for a new bank that has not yet accepted deposits or extended loans. The right-hand side lists liabilities and net worth, which at this stage includes the amount of $2,000,000 raised by the initial investors. The assets side includes $1,400,000 for buildings and furnishings; $500,000 in stock in the Federal Reserve bank; and $100,000 in cash. At this point the bank has nothing to generate a profit and has only $100,000 to work with. It can use the $100,000 in cash to buy government securities and earn a return, but the investors could have done this directly. To generate profits, the bank must attract deposits and create loans that generate returns greater than those the investors could earn in the capital markets.

Exhibit 1

Assets		*Liabilities and Net Worth*	
Buildings and furnishings	$1,400,000	Net worth	$2,000,000
Stock in Fed	500,000		
Cash	100,000		
Total	$2,000,000	Total	$2,000,000

The fundamental tradeoff between *liquidity* and profitability is illustrated in Exhibit 2. The bank has received checkable deposits of $3,000,000. The bank has placed $300,000 of the funds on deposit with the Fed and has kept $2,700,000 in cash. The bank must always be ready to convert checkable deposits to cash whenever depositors write checks against their checkable deposits. Since the bank knows that not all deposits will be demanded at once, it does not need to keep cash on hand to cover the entire $3,000,000 in checkable deposits. Neither the cash on hand nor the deposits in the Fed earn interest, so the bank must find other uses for at least some of these funds in order to make a profit. The more funds that are used in profit-making activities, the fewer funds the bank has available to cover checks written against the checkable deposits. On one hand, the bank wants to keep funds available in the event that checks are written against checkable deposits; on the other hand, the bank wants to use the funds in profit-making activities. The more the bank leans toward making profits, the less liquid it is; the more liquid the bank, the lower its profitability.

Exhibit 2

Assets		*Liabilities and Net Worth*	
Buildings and furnishings	$1,400,000	Checkable deposits	$3,000,000
Stock in Fed	500,000	Net worth	2,000,000
Deposits in Fed	300,000		
Cash	$2,800,000		
Total	$5,000,000	Total	$5,000,000

The bank generates profits by using its funds to make loans and investments. Loans vary in duration, risk, and size, and the interest earned will depend on these factors. Interest rates tend to be greater the longer the loan period and the riskier the borrower. Hence, to enhance profitability, the bank may want to generate many long-term loans to risky individuals and firms. The bank still must be concerned about liquidity, however, and a portfolio of loans that are all long term will reduce the bank's liquidity considerably. Further, high-risk loans will have a higher default rate, which the bank will not want either. Thus, the bank will attempt to structure its assets to generate profitability but in ways that do not decrease liquidity or increase risk beyond acceptable levels. Keep in mind, too, that the bank can borrow from the Fed or in the federal funds market if it runs short of cash to cover checks written against checkable deposits.

The Federal Reserve requires banks to keep a portion of their deposits as reserves. The balance sheet in Exhibit 2 shows that the bank has $3,100,000 in reserves, since reserves include cash held in the bank's vault ($2,800,000) and the bank's deposits with the Fed ($300,000). If the *required reserve ratio* is 20 percent, then the *required reserves* are $600,000 ($3,000,000 x 0.2) and *excess reserves* are $2,500,000. The bank can lend up to $2,500,000 to individuals or businesses. If actual reserves fall below $600,000, the bank will have to call in some loans or borrow from either the Fed or the federal funds market.

Checkable deposits are part of the money supply, but what about the cash held in the bank's vault? It is not part of the money supply, and neither are the deposits the bank holds at the Fed. The money supply as measured by *M1* (a *monetary aggregate*) includes currency in the hands of the nonbank public, deposits in checkable accounts, and travelers checks. Money is not created when depositors deposit currency in their checking accounts. When this happens, money in the form of currency is merely converted into money in the form of checkable deposits. The same is true when a depositor removes cash from a checkable deposit: money in the form of a checkable deposit is converted into currency. But banks can create money because they are able to lend money.

How Banks Create Money

In our discussion of Exhibit 2, we noted that the bank can use $2,500,000 to make investments or to extend loans. Suppose it loans $1,000,000 to a business. The loan creates an asset for the bank—the business's promissory note—and creates a new liability—the business's checkable deposits of $1,000,000. Exhibit 3 shows the bank's balance sheet after it makes the loan to the business. Total checkable deposits are now $4,000,000, so required reserves equal $800,000 and excess reserves are $2,300,000.

Exhibit 3

Assets		*Liabilities and Net Worth*	
Buildings and furnishings	$1,400,000	Checkable deposits	$4,000,000
Stock in Fed	500,000	Net worth	2,000,000
Deposits in Fed	300,000		
Cash	$2,800,000		
Loan	1,000,000		
Total	$6,000,000	Total	$6,000,000

What has happened to the money supply as a result of the loan? The newly created checkable deposits are part of the money supply, so the money supply has increased by $1,000,000. By creating checkable deposits for the business that borrowed funds, the bank created an additional amount of money equal to the amount of the loan. The bank did not merely alter the form of the money; it actually increased the quantity of money in the economy. The business can spend the $1,000,000 just as it could if it had created the checkable deposit by depositing its own $1,000,000 in cash in the bank.

Suppose the business spends the loan on equipment. It pays for the equipment by writing a check for $1,000,000, and the supplier deposits the check in another bank. Once the check has cleared, the first bank's checkable deposits fall back to $3,000,000, its required reserves fall to $600,000, its total reserves fall to $2,100,000, and its excess reserves fall to $1,500,000. Now the maximum loan the bank can make is $1,500,000. Exhibit 4 shows changes in the balance sheet of the bank that received the $1,000,000 deposit. Its checkable deposits have increased by $1,000,000, and its deposits at the Fed have increased by $1,000,000. If the bank had zero excess reserves before, it now has $800,000 in excess reserves and $200,000 in additional required reserves. This means that the bank can loan up to $800,000. If it does so, checkable deposits and therefore the money supply will increase by $800,000. If the $800,000 ends up in a third bank, then that bank can extend additional loans up to $640,000. This process can continue as long as deposits in a bank generate excess reserves for the bank.

Exhibit 4

Assets		*Liabilities and Net Worth*	
Deposits in Fed	+$1,000,000	Checkable deposits	+$1,000,000

The money-creating ability of banks is limited by the quantity of excess reserves in the banking system. If the banking system receives an increase in excess reserves of $1,000,000, the money supply can increase by $1,000,000 times the *money multiplier*. The *simple money multiplier* is $1/r$, where r is the required reserve ratio; that is, the simple money multiplier is the reciprocal of the required reserve ratio. In our example, the money multiplier is $1/0.20 = 5$. That is, the money supply can increase by $5,000,000 when the banking system receives an injection of $1,000,000 in excess reserves.

The Fed controls the nation's money supply through its ability to control the quantity of excess reserves. The Fed can increase excess reserves by lowering the reserve requirement or by purchasing government securities from banks or the public. It can also encourage additional bank lending by lowering the discount rate; this allows banks to hold fewer excess reserves and borrow from the Fed at more favorable terms when they experience temporary shortages of required reserves. The Fed relies primarily on the buying and selling of government securities to control the money supply.

IV. LAGNIAPPE

Liability Management and the Profitability-Liquidity Tradeoff

In the past, banks operated very conservatively and worked hard at maintaining liquidity. Liquidity was achieved by stocking up on such liquid assets as short-term government securities. Beginning in the 1960s, banks altered their behavior and began relying increasingly on liabilities to maintain liquidity rather than on assets. Banks would take on short-term liabilities, such as loans in the federal funds market or repurchase agreements, to maintain liquidity, which allowed them to earn higher interest on their reserves by using them to extend longer-term loans. As inflation and interest rates increased, banks did not want to be holding only short-term government securities—the opportunity costs of doing so were too great. Instead, they extended loans that generated higher interest payments and handled short-term liquidity problems by borrowing in the federal funds market or by entering the negotiable CD market.

Question to Think About: Does the change in banking behavior imply that deposits in banks are not as safe today as they were thirty years ago?

Cash, Excess Reserves, and Money Creation

Banks generally cannot create money to the extent implied by the simple money multiplier, for two reasons. First, people usually carry some money in the form of currency. When a bank makes a loan and creates checkable deposits for a borrower and the borrower writes a check against the checkable deposits, the recipient of the check may not deposit the entire amount in his or her checking account. Instead, the recipient may hold some of the amount in cash and deposit the rest. Consequently, the deposit in the second bank is less than the check written against the checkable deposits in the first bank, and there has been a loss of reserves to the banking system. Second, banks generally do not loan out all of their excess reserves. Instead, they often hold a fraction of their excess reserves to protect against an unexpected demand for reserves.

Question to Think About: What factors are likely to affect a bank's decision concerning the amount of excess reserves to maintain?

V. KEY TERMS

Asymmetric information
Liability
Asset
Checkable deposits
Monetary aggregates
M1
Liquidity
Time deposits
Savings deposits
Money market mutual fund account
M2
M3
Net worth
Balance sheet
Required reserve ratio
Required reserves
Excess reserves
Federal funds market
Federal funds rate
Money multiplier
Simple money multiplier

VI. QUESTIONS

A. *Completion*

1. The market for loanable funds is characterized by ________________ because lenders do not know the reliability of borrowers as well as borrowers know themselves.

2. Banks serve as financial ________________ when they bring savers and borrowers together.

3. A customer's deposit is a ________________ to a depository institution.

4. Money consists primarily of ________________.

5. ________________ measures the ease with which any asset can be converted into the medium of exchange without a significant loss of value.

6. M1 is made up of ________________, ________________, and ________________.

7. Time deposits are not considered money because they do not function as a ________________.

8. The two sides of a bank's ledger must always be in ________________.

9. The proportion of deposits that must be held in reserve by banks is called the ________________.

10. The two conflicting objectives of a bank are ________________ and ________________.

11. A bank can borrow the excess reserves of another bank in the ________________ market.

12. A depository institution's deposits at the Fed are ________________ to the Fed and ________________ to the depository institution.

13. The maximum amount that an individual depository institution can loan out equals the amount of its ________________.

14. The ________________ equals the reciprocal of the required reserve ratio.

15. Borrowing from the Fed is cheaper when the Fed lowers the ________________ rate.

B. *True/False*

______ 1. Banks specialize in information so they know more about the reliability of a potential borrower than the borrower knows.

______ 2. Finance companies get part of their funds from depositors.

______ 3. Banks reduce the risk to each individual saver by choosing a diversified portfolio of assets.

______ 4. Checkable deposits are liabilities and time deposits are assets to depository institutions.

______ 5. Both checks and currency are legal tender.

______ 6. The most liquid asset is currency.

______ 7. Money market mutual fund accounts are part of M2.

______ 8. The two sides of the balance sheet must always be equal.

______ 9. A deposit by a customer increases the bank's assets and net worth.

______ 10. A bank can only loan out its required reserves.

______ 11. The greater the required reserve ratio, other things constant, the greater the excess reserves.

______ 12. Banks can meet an unexpected demand for reserves by selling some short-term assets.

______ 13. Generally speaking, the more liquid the bank, the more profitable the bank.

______ 14. The Fed puts reserves into the banking system when it sells government securities.

______ 15. Banks create money by converting IOUs into checkable deposits.

______ 16. A flow of excess reserves into the banking system can generate an increase in the money supply of no more than the increase in excess reserves.

______ 17. When a check clears, the reserves of the entire banking system are reduced.

______ 18. The smaller the required reserve ratio, other things constant, the larger the simple money multiplier.

______ 19. The actual money multiplier tends to be larger than the simple money multiplier.

______ 20. The Fed often buys and sells securities issued by foreign governments.

C. *Multiple Choice*

1. Which of the following would lead to a problem of asymmetric information?
   a. A borrower will have a difficult time repaying a loan if she loses her job.
   b. A borrower defaulted on a loan two years ago.
   c. A borrower does not know which bank is offering the lowest interest rates.
   d. A borrower knows he will soon be out of work and does not tell the bank.
   e. all of the above

2. Which of the following are important functions of depository institutions?
   a. serving as intermediaries
   b. eeducing risk to individual savers by holding diversified portfolios of assets
   c. specializing in making loans so that the costs of evaluating alternative loan applicants are reduced
   d. all of the above
   e. a and b

3. According to the narrowest definition, money includes
   a. legal tender only.
   b. currency and coins held by the nonbank public only.
   c. currency and coins held by the nonbank public, checkable deposits, and credit card balances.
   d. currency and coins held by the nonbank public, checkable deposits, and travelers checks.
   e. checkable deposits only.

4. Federal Reserve notes are IOUs from the Fed and can be exchanged for
   a. gold.
   b. government securities.
   c. other Federal Reserve notes.
   d. silver.
   e. none of the above.

5. Which of the following assets is the most liquid?
   a. time deposits
   b. checkable deposits
   c. nonnegotiable certificates of deposit
   d. land
   e. savings accounts

6. The amount of money in the economy (as defined by M1) increases when
   a. an individual cashes a check written by a business.
   b. an individual purchases clothes with a credit card.
   c. an individual switches funds from a savings account to a checking account.
   d. a bank buys a piece of furniture by writing a check.
   e. all of the above

7. Which of the following is not included in M2?
   a. large-denomination time deposits
   b. money market mutual funds
   c. checking accounts
   d. currency held by the nonbank public
   e. a and b

8. Among a bank's liabilities is
   a. its net worth.
   b. the cash held in the bank.
   c. checkable deposits.
   d. its stock in the Fed.
   e. its deposits in the Fed.

9. Legal reserves include
   a. a bank's deposits in the Fed.
   b. a bank's government securities.
   c. stock in the Fed.
   d. business loans.
   e. a, b, and c.

10. A bank's required reserves will increase and its excess reserves fall when
    a. the required reserve ratio is increased.
    b. a customer makes a deposit in a checking account.
    c. a customer repays a loan.
    d. the bank sells a government security to the Fed.
    e. a borrower defaults on a loan.

11. A bank manager can increase the bank's liquidity by
   a. increasing its reserves.
   b. buying short-term government securities with the funds provided when a mortgage is paid off.
   c. borrowing from the federal funds market.
   d. buying a new computer system.
   e. a, b, and c.

12. Among the liabilities of the Federal Reserve System are
   a. Federal Reserve notes.
   b. deposits of the U.S. Treasury.
   c. deposits of banks.
   d. deposits of thrifts.
   e. all of the above.

13. The Fed can decrease bank reserves by
   a. lowering the discount rate.
   b. lowering the required reserve ratio.
   c. selling government securities.
   d. destroying old Federal Reserve notes.
   e. none of the above.

14. The supernote is
   a. the largest denomination for American currency.
   b. a reference to the Fed's ability to produce money.
   c. a $100 bill made by the Fed but used in Europe.
   d. a counterfeit $100 bill of high quality.
   e. none of the above.

15. When a person deposits a check drawn on another bank into a checking account,
   a. the reserves in the entire banking system increase.
   b. the reserves in the bank where the deposit is made are unchanged.
   c. the money supply decreases.
   d. the reserves in the entire banking system are unchanged, but the reserves in the bank in which the deposit is made increase and reserves in the other bank decrease.
   e. the money supply increases.

16. The money-creating ability of the banking system will be less than indicated by the simple money multiplier when
   a. interest rates are high.
   b. banks decide to hold excess reserves.
   c. people hold a portion of their money in the form of currency.
   d. all of the above
   e. b and c

17. The maximum that an individual bank can loan out is
   a. the value of its excess reserves times the money multiplier.
   b. the sum of its excess reserves and its vault cash.
   c. the value of its excess reserves times the reserve ratio.
   d. the sum of the checkable deposits and time deposits held in the bank.
   e. the value of its excess reserves.

18. The reserves of the entire banking system will fall when
    a. an individual pulls cash out of a checking account.
    b. an individual deposits a check drawn on another bank.
    c. the Fed burns old, worn-out Federal Reserve notes.
    d. the Fed increases the required reserve ratio.
    e. all of the above

19. A bank can replenish reserves by
    a. extending more loans at a higher rate of interest.
    b. recalling outstanding loans.
    c. increasing its vault cash by drawing down its deposits at the Fed.
    d. repaying loans to the Fed.
    e. none of the above.

20. The Fed can pursue a tight monetary policy by
    a. selling government securities.
    b. raising the discount rate.
    c. raising the reserve requirement.
    d. all of the above.
    e. none of the above.

D. *Discussion Questions*

1. Explain how banks are financial intermediaries.

2. Explain why "d" is the correct answer to multiple choice question 1 and why choices "a" through "c" are incorrect.

3. Explain how a checkable deposit can be both an asset and a liability.

4. What is the difference between money and other assets that are similar to money?

5. What are the differences among the various monetary aggregates?

6. Discuss the competing objectives of a bank: liquidity and profitability.

7. The text states that the Fed is both literally and figuratively a money machine. Explain why this is true.

8. Suppose three banks have zero excess reserves. Show how each bank's balance sheet changes as a result of the following transactions. (Assume that the banks always carry zero excess reserves and that the reserve ratio is 0.2.)
    a. Mr. Smith deposits $1,000 in his checking account in Bank A. Mrs. Jones then borrows all she can from the bank.
    b. Mrs. Jones uses her loan to buy furniture from the Acme Furniture Co., which deposits the check from Mrs. Jones into Bank B.
    c. Ms. Anderson borrows all she can from Bank B and buys a used car from the Fly-by-Night Auto Co., which deposits the check from Ms. Anderson in Bank C.
    d. Bank C buys a government security from the Fed with all of its excess reserves.

9. By how much does the money supply change as a result of the transactions described in question 8? If Bank C had also made a loan instead of buying the government security and the process had continued, what is the maximum amount of money the banking system could have created?

10. What are reserves? What are excess reserves? Explain how the Fed can affect the quantity of excess reserves in the banking system.

11. Explain why an individual bank can increase the money supply by the amount of its excess reserves, whereas the banking system as a whole can increase the money supply by a multiple of its excess reserves.

12. Explain how the money multiplier can actually be less than the reciprocal of the reserve ratio.

13. Explain why the Fed can be more confident of its ability to contract the money supply than of its ability to expand the money supply through credit expansion.

14. How can the Fed affect the money supply by using the discount rate?

VII. ANSWERS

A. *Completion*

1. asymmetric information
2. intermediaries
3. liability
4. checkable deposits
5. Liquidity
6. checkable deposits; currency held by the nonbank public; travelers checks
7. medium of exchange
8. balance
9. required reserve ratio
10. liquidity; profitability
11. federal funds
12. liabilities; assets
13. excess reserves
14. simple money multiplier
15. discount

B. *True/False*

1. False
2. False
3. True
4. False
5. False
6. True
7. True
8. True
9. False
10. False
11. False
12. True
13. False
14. False. Reserves fall when the Fed sells government securities.
15. True
16. False
17. False
18. True
19. False
20. True

C. *Multiple Choice*

1. d	6. c	11. e	16. e
2. d	7. a	12. e	17. e
3. d	8. c	13. c	18. a
4. c	9. a	14. d	19. b
5. b	10. a	15. d	20. d

D. *Discussion Questions*

1. Banks bring together two sides of the market—those who want to save and those who want to borrow. Then they act as a go-between, or a financial intermediary.

2. The idea of asymmetric information is that information held by one party to a transaction is not held by the other party. Answer d describes a situation in which the borrower knows something the bank cannot know unless the borrower provides the information. Answers a and b describe situations in which information is known by both parties, or can be known with a normal credit check. The situation in answer c does not involve asymmetric information since the borrower can obtain the information by contacting a number of banks.

3. A checkable deposit is a liability to the bank because the bank must pay out the funds if a check is drawn on the account. It is an asset to the depositor because he or she can draw on the account at any time.

4. Some financial assets have some, but not all, of the characteristics of money. In particular, they are like money except that they do not serve as a medium of exchange. These assets are less liquid than currency and checkable deposits.

5. M1 includes checkable deposits, currency held by the nonbank public, and travelers checks. The other monetary aggregates include other financial assets. M2 includes M1 plus savings deposits, small denomination time deposits, and money market mutual funds. M3 includes M2 plus large-denomination time deposits.

6. A bank is a business designed to make profits. To make profits, banks must use reserves in profit-making ways, such as purchasing securities or other assets and extending loans that earn interest. Loans and assets that earn high interest tend not to be very liquid, however. Banks must also be prepared to satisfy depositors' requests for funds. If a bank does not do so, it could fail. The more the bank tries to be liquid, the lower its profits. The more the bank strives for profits, the less liquid it is and the greater the possibility of bank failure.

7. The Fed provides the economy with Federal Reserve notes, which are part of the money supply; that is, it literally creates paper money. The Fed also earns interest with its assets but pays no interest on its liabilities, so the Fed makes a profit, which is turned over to the U.S. Treasury. This creates money in the figurative sense.

8. a. Bank A:

Assets		*Liabilities and Net Worth*	
Deposits in Fed	+$1,000	Checkable Deposits	+$1,800
Loan	+ 800		
	$1,800		

b. Bank A:

Assets		Liabilities and Net Worth	
Deposits in Fed	$ 200	Checkable Deposits	$1,000
Loan	800		
	$1,000		

Bank B:

Assets		Liabilities and Net Worth	
Deposits in Fed	+$800	Checkable Deposits	+$800

c. Bank B:

Assets		Liabilities and Net Worth	
Deposits in Fed	$160	Checkable Deposits	$800
Loan	+ 640		
	$800		

Bank C:

Assets		Liabilities and Net Worth	
Deposits in Fed	+ $640	Checkable Deposits	+ $640

d. Bank C:

Assets		Liabilities and Net Worth	
Deposits in Fed	+$128	Checkable Deposits	$640
Loan	+ 512		
	$640		

9. The money supply increased by $800 in part a of question 8 and by $640 in part c of question 8, a total increase of $1,440. The maximum amount of money that could have been created is the product of the initial increase in excess reserves and the simple money multiplier, or

$$\$800 \times (1/r) = \$800 \times (1/0.02) = \$800 \times 5 = \$4{,}000.$$

10. Reserves are made up of the cash a bank holds in its vault and the bank's deposits in the Fed. Excess reserves are reserves in excess of the quantity required by the Fed. The Fed can affect the quantity of excess reserves by buying or selling government securities. If it sells government securities to banks, for example, the banks pay for them with reserves, so they have fewer reserves. The Fed can also change the required reserve ratio, which directly affects required reserves and excess reserves. It can also change the discount rate. The lower the discount rate, the cheaper it is for banks to borrow reserves in case they find themselves with no excess reserves and the more likely they are to lend a greater proportion of the reserves they have on hand.

11. An individual bank can increase the money supply only by the amount of its excess reserves because it can make loans only with its excess reserves. The bank must operate on the assumption that a borrower will spend a loan and the check will be deposited in another bank, in which case the first bank has no more excess reserves to use in creating money. On the other hand, a check written on one bank and deposited in another stays within the banking system as a whole. That is, the excess reserves of the entire banking system can support a greater expansion of money because the reserves are never lost to the banking system.

12. The money multiplier is less than $1/r$ when people hold some of their loans in the form of currency and when banks decide to hold more reserves than required by the Fed.

13. The Fed can be certain that it can successfully restrict credit by pursuing a tighter credit policy since banks must hold required reserves in the amount dictated by the Fed. The Fed cannot force banks to lend out excess reserves, however, so when the Fed wishes to pursue an expansionary policy it cannot be certain that the banks will lend the excess reserves to borrowers.

14. Banks can borrow from the Fed if their excess reserves are depleted, and they pay the Fed an interest rate equal to the discount rate. If the discount rate is low, banks can loan more of their excess reserves because they can borrow cheaply if their reserves fall below the required level. Higher discount rates increase the cost of allowing reserves to fall below the required level. Therefore, banks are more likely to lend more of their excess reserves when the discount rate is low than when the discount rate is high.

CHAPTER 15

Monetary Theory and Policy

I. INTRODUCTION

In the last two chapters, we examined the functions of money, how the banking system creates money, and how the Fed controls the money supply. In this chapter, we turn to a discussion of monetary theory and monetary policy. We examine the effects of changes in the money supply on the economy and then discuss the possible policies the government can pursue in trying to achieve full employment and stable prices. Other macroeconomic policy issues are addressed in the next two chapters.

II. OUTLINE

1. Money and the Economy: The Indirect Channel. Money and income are not the same thing. Money is a stock variable and is measured at a particular point in time. Income is a flow variable and is measured over a period of time. The demand for money is a demand for cash balances in the form of checking accounts, currency, or travelers checks to carry out transactions. The demand for money is a demand for a stock—a desire to hold some amount of money. The phrase "demand for money" does *not* refer to a desire for more income or wealth.

1.1 The Demand for Money

a. The *transactions demand for money* is the money demanded to support exchange.
b. Two factors determine the transactions demand for money:
   (1) The number of transactions to be financed over a given period
   (2) The average selling price of each unit of output
c. People hold money to finance both anticipated and unanticipated exchanges.
d. Money is also a store of wealth, and people demand money in order to store purchasing power for future expenditures.
e. People can store their purchasing power in the form of money or in the form of some other financial asset.
f. Money's advantage as a store of wealth derives from its liquidity.
g. The opportunity cost of holding money is the interest that is forgone when money is not placed in assets with higher interest.

1.2 Money Demand and Interest Rates

a. The lower the interest rate, the lower the opportunity cost of holding money, so the larger the fraction of wealth people hold as money.
b. The demand for money varies inversely with the real interest rate, other things constant.
c. The money demand curve shows the quantity of money demanded at alternative interest rates.
d. The price level and the level of real GDP are held constant along a money demand curve. An increase in the level of prices or real GDP shifts the money demand curve to the right.

1.3 Supply of Money and the Equilibrium Interest Rate

a. For the most part, the Fed determines the supply of money.
b. The money supply curve is vertical if we make the simplifying assumption that the quantity supplied is independent of the interest rate.
c. The intersection of the money demand curve and the money supply curve determines the equilibrium interest rate.
d. When demand for money is held constant, increases in the money supply lower interest rates and decreases in the money supply raise interest rates.

2. Money and Aggregate Demand

2.1 Interest Rates and Planned Investment

a. Investment spending is the component of aggregate demand that is most affected by changes in interest rates.
b. Monetary policy affects the interest rate, which affects the level of planned investment.
c. An increase in the money supply lowers interest rates, which induces increased investment spending and increased aggregate demand.
d. As long as investment is sensitive to changes in the interest rate and the interest rate is sensitive to changes in the money supply, then changes in the money supply alter planned investment.

2.2 Money and the Slope of the Aggregate Demand Curve

a. The quantity of aggregate output demanded is inversely related to the price level, other things constant.
b. The aggregate demand curve is drawn for a given supply of money in the economy.
c. Higher prices cause the demand for money to increase; this generates higher interest rates and reduces investment spending, thus leading to a lower quantity of real GDP demanded.
d. The aggregate demand curve also slopes down because higher prices (1) reduce the real value of household wealth, causing consumption to fall, and (2) increase the cost of domestic products relative to foreign products, causing net exports to fall.

2.3 Adding Aggregate Supply

a. An increase in the money supply causes aggregate demand to increase.
b. Because the aggregate supply curve slopes upward, an increase in the money supply that leads to an increase in aggregate demand also generates a higher price level.
c. The steeper the aggregate supply curve for a given shift in aggregate demand, the smaller the increase in real GDP and the larger the increase in the price level.
d. The Fed can attempt to close a contractionary gap with an expansionary monetary policy.

2.4 Fiscal Policy with Money

a. In the short run, an increase in government spending leads to an increase in both the level of real output and the price level.
b. An increase in either real output or the price level leads to an increase in the demand for money.
c. An increase in the demand for money, when the supply of money is held constant, leads to higher real interest rates, which cause a reduction in investment spending and dampen the effect of fiscal policy on real output.
d. Consequently, the simple spending multiplier overstates the increase in real output generated by any given fiscal stimulus.

3. Money and the Economy: The Direct Channel.
   a. In the direct channel, money is seen as an asset that can be a store of value and can be similar to other financial real assets.
   b. An increase in the money supply makes the quantity supplied exceed the quantity demanded at the initial interest rate, so people try to reduce their holdings of money.
   c. When people attempt to reduce their monetary holdings, they increase their demand for all types of assets, real and financial, which directly increases aggregate demand.

3.1 The Equation of Exchange
   a. The *equation of exchange* is $M \times V = P \times Y$, where M is the money supply, V is the velocity of money, P is the price level, and Y is real GDP.
   b. The *velocity of money* is the average number of times per year each dollar is used to purchase final goods and services.
   c. The equation of exchange is an identity, not a theory.

3.2 The Quantity Theory of Money
   a. Monetarists argue that the velocity of money changes very little in the short run, and any changes that do occur are predictable. Thus, the equation of exchange can be used to predict the effects of changes in the money supply on nominal income, $P \times Y$.
   b. If the velocity of money is stable, then changes in the money supply must lead to proportional changes in nominal income.
   c. Whether a change in the money supply leads to a change in real output or a change in the price level depends on the shape of the aggregate supply curve.
   d. In the long run, changes in the money supply lead to changes in the price level only. The economy's potential output is not influenced by changes in the money supply.
   e. Monetarists caution that there are time lags of variable and uncertain length in the process. Consequently, monetary policy is a poor tool for changing nominal income.

3.3 *Case Study:* The Money Supply and Inflation

3.4 What Determines the Velocity of Money?
   a. Customs and conventions of commerce, such as the use of credit cards.
   b. The frequency with which people get paid.
   c. The effectiveness of money as a store of wealth.

3.5 How Stable Is Velocity?
   a. From 1915 to 1947, velocity of M1 fluctuated greatly, with a downward trend.
   b. Velocity of M1 was more stable from 1947 to 1979, but with an upward trend.
   c. Since 1979, velocity of M1 has been more erratic, making the equation of exchange a less reliable predictor of the effects of a change in M1 on nominal GDP.
   d. The velocity of M2 has been more stable than the velocity of M1.

4. Money Supply Versus Interest Rate Targets. According to the indirect channel, monetary policy affects the economy via its effect on interest rates. The monetarist view is that monetary policy has a direct effect on aggregate demand. Thus, there is much debate over whether monetary authorities should target interest rates or the stock of money.

4.1 Contrasting Policies
   a. If there is a change in the demand for money, monetary authorities can either do nothing, thereby keeping the money stock constant and letting the interest rate change, or they can try to keep the interest rate constant by changing the money supply.

b. Monetary authorities cannot keep both the money stock and the interest rate constant.

c. Interest rate fluctuations can be undesirable if they create similar fluctuations in investment. However, changes in the money supply designed to stabilize interest rates tend to reinforce fluctuations in economic activity, adding instability to the economy.

4.2 Targets Until 1982

a. Between the end of World War II and October of 1979, the Fed tried to stabilize interest rates.

b. In October 1979, the Fed announced it would de-emphasize targeting interest rates and focus more on targets for monetary growth.

c. In October 1982, the Fed announced it would pay attention to both interest rates and money growth.

4.3 Targets After 1982

a. The rapid pace of financial innovations and deregulation make it difficult to measure the money supply.

b. In recent years, the Fed has used short-term interest rates as the instrument of monetary policy.

4.4 *Case Study:* International Finance

5. Conclusion. The model that focuses on the indirect channel sees money supply changes as primarily affecting aggregate demand through changes in interest rates. Monetarists see changes in the money supply as more directly affecting prices and output.

III. DISCUSSION

Monetary theory is concerned with the effects of the quantity of money on the economy's price level and the level of real output. There is considerable debate among economists concerning what these effects are. One difficulty in determining the effects is that *monetary policy* changes and fiscal policy changes often occur at the same time, so it is difficult to sort out the effects of one from those of the other. This chapter describes two views of how money affects the economy: an indirect channel and a direct channel.

Money and the Economy: The Indirect Channel

A person's demand for money is not the same as the person's desire for a greater income. When economists speak of a demand for money, they are referring to the desire to hold a particular amount of money, either in checking accounts or as cash. That is, the *demand for money* is a demand to hold a stock of money at a particular time.

The concept of the *transactions demand for money* is straightforward and intuitive. Since money is used to facilitate exchange of goods and services and people engage in exchange on a regular basis, people hold money balances. The demand for money is greater the greater the number of transactions (as measured by real GDP) and the higher the average price at which each good is sold, that is, the greater nominal GDP.

Money also competes with other financial assets as a store of wealth. Compared with other financial assets, money has one major advantage and one major disadvantage. Money's advantage is its liquidity—it can be directly exchanged for goods and services. Its disadvantage is that it earns either no interest or substantially less interest than other financial assets. The opportunity cost of holding money is the additional interest that could have been earned by using the money to buy alternative interest-bearing financial assets. Consequently, the cost of holding money increases with the real interest rate, and we expect the demand for money to vary inversely with the real interest rate, other things constant. That is, the demand curve for money slopes downward when real interest rates are on the vertical axis.

The supply of money in the economy is determined primarily by the Fed, so we make the simplifying assumption that the quantity of money supplied is constant no matter what the interest rate is. Hence, the supply curve for money is a vertical line at whatever quantity of money the Fed has determined. Exhibit 1 illustrates the money market. The demand for money slopes down, as mentioned, and the supply curve for money is perfectly inelastic. Suppose that the supply of money is indicated initially by supply curve *S*. The intersection of the two curves determines the equilibrium interest rate, 10 percent. An increase in the supply of money shifts the supply curve to *S´* and generates a lower equilibrium interest rate, 6 percent; an increase in the demand for money generates a higher interest rate.

Exhibit 1

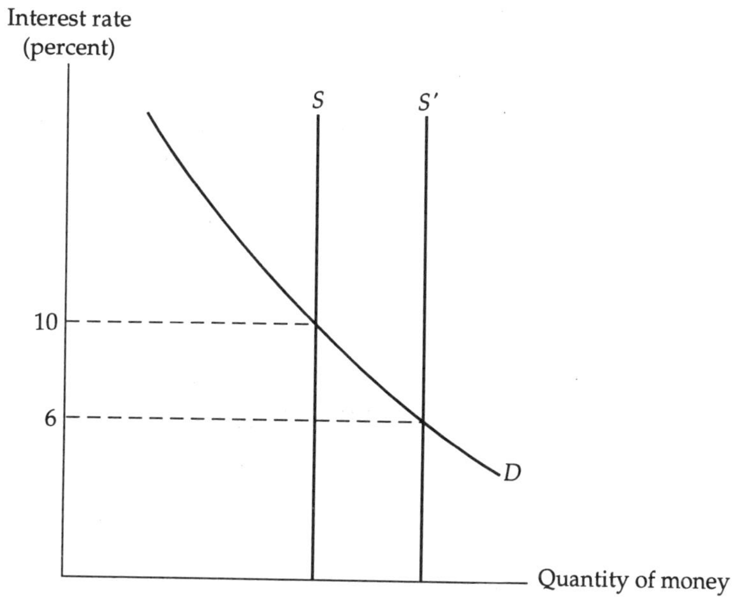

Money and Aggregate Demand

If money is to affect aggregate demand, it must do so by affecting one of several things: consumption spending, investment spending, government spending, or net exports. As we have just seen, changes in the supply of money cause changes in interest rates. In the model that uses the indirect channel, then, monetary policy affects aggregate demand indirectly by influencing the market rate of interest, which affects the level of planned investment.

Suppose the Fed wants to pursue a tight monetary policy and reduce the supply of money. The Fed can reduce the money supply by raising the discount rate, selling government securities, or raising the required reserve ratio. Regardless of which method is used, the money supply curve shifts to the left and the market rate increases. In Exhibit 2, the higher interest rate causes a movement along the demand curve for investment and the level of investment falls. The top half of Exhibit 3 shows how in this situation the $C + I + G + NX$ curve (where NX refers to net exports) shifts down to $C + I' + G + NX$, generating a lower level of real GDP demanded. As a result, aggregate demand shifts to the left, as shown in the lower half of Exhibit 3.

Exhibit 2

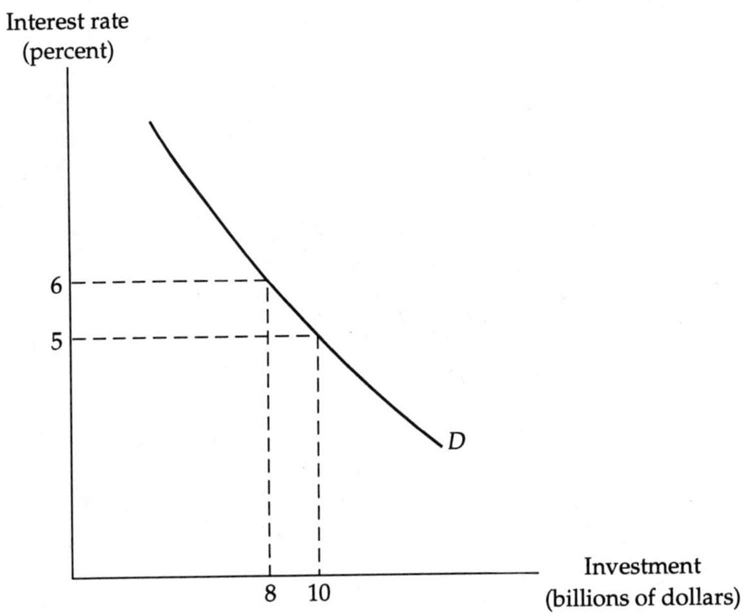

Exhibit 3

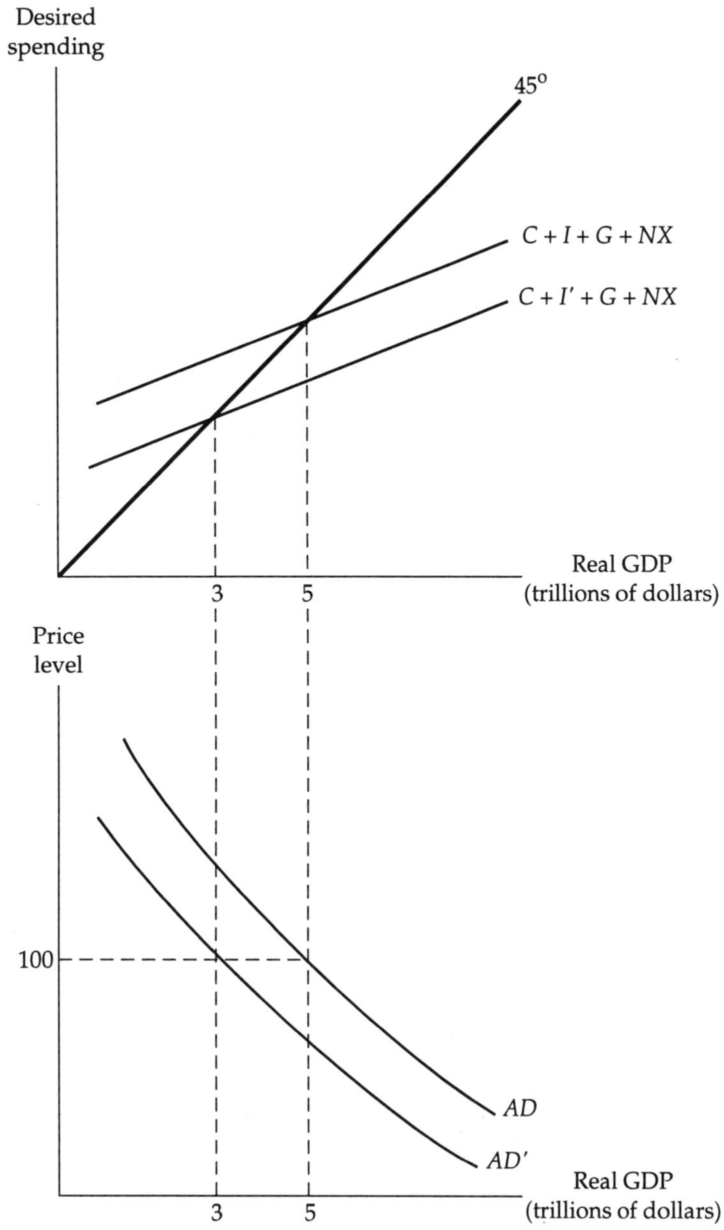
Desired spending
45°
C + I + G + NX
C + I′ + G + NX
Real GDP (trillions of dollars)
3
5
Price level
100
AD
AD′
Real GDP (trillions of dollars)
3
5

The shifts in the curves in Exhibit 3 are not the end of the story. The aggregate supply curve slopes upward, so the ultimate effects of a change in the money supply are partially determined by the shape of the aggregate supply curve. Exhibit 4 shows the bottom part of Exhibit 3 with a short-run aggregate supply curve added. At the original price level, 100, there is an excess supply after the aggregate demand curve shifts from *AD* to *AD´*. The excess supply causes prices to fall until equilibrium is reached at price level 90 and real GDP of $4 trillion. Thus, the reduction of the money supply has generated a reduced level of GDP and a lower price level.

Exhibit 4

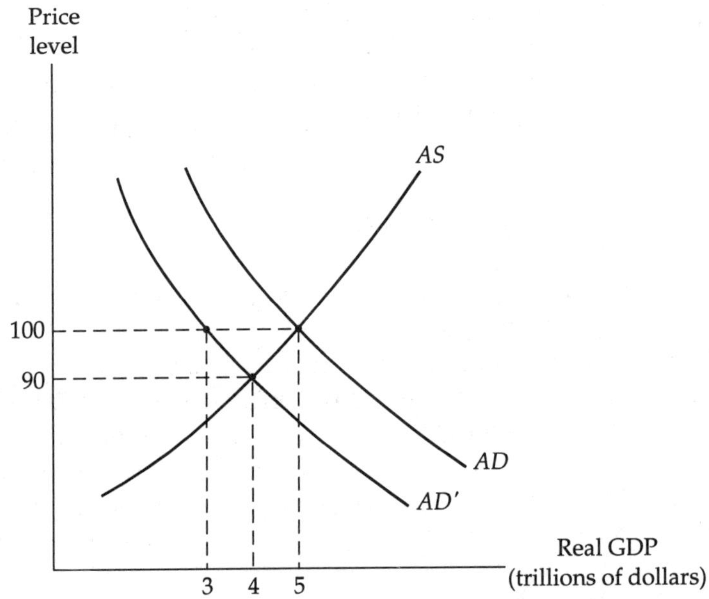

With the tools developed in this chapter, we can offer another explanation for the shape of the aggregate demand curve. A change in the price level leads to a change in the demand for money. In particular, an increase in the price level leads to an increase in the demand for money because the average dollar cost of each transaction has increased. If the money supply does not change, an increase in the demand for money leads to higher interest rates. Higher interest rates cause investment spending to fall, which means that the quantity of aggregate output demanded falls as well.

Money and the Economy: The Direct Channel

Monetarists believe money affects aggregate demand directly as well as indirectly. They use the *equation of exchange* to analyze the effects of changes in the money supply. Monetarists argue that an increase in the money supply leaves individuals with larger money balances than they desire. Individuals reduce their money balances by increasing their spending on all goods, not just other financial assets. The increased spending on all goods has a direct effect on aggregate demand.

The equation of exchange is a tautology—that is, it is true by definition. Nominal income equals real output, Y, times the price level, P. Since money is used in exchange, nominal income must be equal to the quantity of money in the economy, M, multiplied by the average number of times per year money changes hands to purchase final goods and services, V. Hence, $M \times V = P \times Y$. The average number of times money changes hands in a year, V, is called the *velocity of money*. The *quantity theory of money* states that velocity is predictable and stable. Consequently $M = (P \times Y)/V$, and changes in the money supply cause predictable changes in nominal income. Whether the change in nominal income is due to changes in the price level or to changes in real output depends on the shape of the aggregate supply curve. In the short run, the aggregate supply curve slopes upward, so an increase in aggregate demand induced by an increase in the supply of money leads to increased real output and higher prices. In the long run, the aggregate supply curve is vertical, and an increase in aggregate demand leads only to an increase in the price level.

Those who focus on the indirect channel do not accept the monetarist belief that velocity is stable. Instead, they believe that velocity varies with the interest rate. According to this view, an increase in the interest rate increases the opportunity cost of holding money, so the quantity of money held falls and the velocity of money rises. To the extent that a change in interest rates affects velocity, changes in the money supply are offset by changes in velocity.

Money Supply Versus Interest Rate Targets

Given the differences in their views of the effects of money on the economy, it should not be surprising that the policy prescriptions of those who focus on the indirect channel differ from the prescriptions of those who focus on the direct channel. Those who believe that monetary policy affects the economy by affecting interest rates argue that monetary policy should focus on interest rates. Monetarists believe that money has a more direct effect on nominal income, so they argue that monetary authorities should focus more on money supply targets. For most of the postwar period, monetary authorities have focused on interest-rate targets rather than on monetary growth-rate targets. In recent years there have been large movements of funds into and out of the United States in response to interest-rate differentials between the United States and other countries. These flows affect the exchange rate and the level of imports and exports. Consequently, the Fed has been forced to give greater consideration to the international effects of its monetary policy decisions.

IV. LAGNIAPPE

Money and Inflation

Suppose you wake up tomorrow and have twice as much money as you have today. Are you wealthier? It depends. Suppose that everyone else has twice as much money as before. Then you, along with everyone else, try to spend most of your new funds on goods and services. But the fact that the money supply has doubled does not mean that the amount of goods and services available has doubled. As everyone tries to increase spending on goods and services, prices of the goods and services will be driven up. Ultimately prices will double, total spending will double, and money balances held by individuals will double. Real GDP will not change, however, and neither will the real value of the money held by the individuals. Consequently, the doubling of the money stock will lead to a doubling of prices and no change in real output. That is, increases in the money supply tend to lead only to increases in the price level.

Question to Think About: Is this relationship between money and the price level likely to be a long-run or a short-run relationship?

The Money Supply, Interest Rates, and Inflation

Monetarists argue that the Fed should not make nominal interest rates the targets of its monetary policy. The initial effect of an expansionary monetary policy is to lower interest rates. This occurs because the Fed generally expands the money supply by buying government bonds. The increased demand for bonds leads to higher prices for bonds, which implies lower interest rates on the government bonds. Suppose that the Fed has been pursuing an expansionary monetary policy that has generated inflation. Investors are interested in their real return, so the nominal interest rate must increase to cover the inflation rate plus the desired real rate of interest. If the Fed is targeting interest rates, the higher nominal interest rates cause the Fed to increase the money supply further to bring interest rates back down. The Fed can be successful in this attempt only in the short run. Over time the increased money supply causes additional inflation, which in turn raises nominal interest rates and generates another round of bond sales to bring nominal interest rates back down. Hence, the Fed may be prone to pursue inflationary policies if it targets nominal interest rates.

Question to Think About: What would happen if the Fed tried to target real interest rates?

V. KEY TERMS

Monetary policy
Monetary theory
Transactions demand for money
Equation of exchange
Velocity of money
Quantity theory of money

VI. QUESTIONS

A. *Completion*

1. Monetary __________________ is concerned with the effect of the quantity of money on the economy's price level and on the level of real output.

2. The __________________ is a desire to hold a particular amount of money.

3. Money's role as a medium of exchange leads to the __________________ demand for money.

4. The advantage of money as a store of wealth is its __________________.

5. The demand for money varies inversely with the __________________, other things constant.

6. A vertical supply curve of money indicates that the quantity of money supplied is __________________ of the market rate of interest.

7. According to the indirect channel view, monetary policy affects aggregate demand indirectly through its effect on __________________.

8. An increase in the money supply increases aggregate expenditures by increasing __________________ spending.

9. For a given shift in the aggregate demand curve, the steeper the short-run aggregate supply curve, the ________________ the increases in the price level.

10. An increase in government purchases increases money demand, which causes ________________ to increase and the quantity of investment spending to fall.

11. The ________________ of money measures the average number of times per year each dollar is used to purchase final goods and services.

12. One aspect of ________________ is the view that changes in the money supply directly affect aggregate demand.

13. According to the ________________ of money, the velocity of money is stable or at least predictable.

14. $M \times V = P \times Y$ is the ________________.

15. Monetary policy can focus on keeping either ________________ or interest rates stable.

B. *True/False*

______ 1. People demand money because more money is the same as more income.

______ 2. Most people demand all the money they can get their hands on.

______ 3. The transactions demand for money is greater if the volume of exchange is greater.

______ 4. The desire to carry cash in case of car trouble is an example of the transactions demand for money.

______ 5. The demand for money varies directly with the interest rate, other things constant.

______ 6. The supply curve of money is horizontal at the market rate of interest.

______ 7. Decreases in the supply of money raise the interest rate.

______ 8. A drop in the rate of interest tends to increase investment spending.

______ 9. According to those who focus on the indirect channel of money, an increase in the money supply does not have a direct effect on aggregate demand.

______ 10. The flatter the aggregate supply curve, the greater the effect on real GDP of an increase in the money supply.

______ 11. Any fiscal policy designed to reduce aggregate demand will be tempered by monetary effects.

______ 12. According to monetarists, an increase in the supply of money leads to an increase in the demand for financial assets but not to a direct increase in the demand for goods and services.

______ 13. The equation of exchange holds only when velocity is a constant.

______ 14. Monetarists claim that the velocity of money changes little in the short run.

______ 15. Monetarists claim that changes in the money supply cause changes in real GDP in the long run.

______ 16. The velocity of money is greater the more often people get paid.

______ 17. In the indirect channel framework, changes in velocity offset changes in the money stock.

______ 18. Monetarists argue that the Fed should set monetary policy to maintain interest rates at a certain level.

______ 19. Through most of the postwar era, the Fed has used money supply targets rather than interest rate targets.

______ 20. The Fed can use monetary policy to stabilize the money supply and interest rates simultaneously.

C. *Multiple Choice*

1. An important distinction between money and income is that
   a. money is only one component of income.
   b. money is a measure of wealth whereas income is a source of wealth.
   c. money is a flow variable whereas income is a stock variable.
   d. money is a stock variable whereas income is a flow variable.
   e. there is no important distinction.

2. People demand money
   a. by selling their labor to get money.
   b. by holding money despite the opportunity cost of doing so.
   c. because money increases their wealth.
   d. all of the above
   e. a and b

3. Other things constant, the quantity of money demanded is greater
   a. the lower the interest rate.
   b. the higher the interest rate.
   c. the greater the opportunity cost of money.
   d. the lower the price level.
   e. during a recession.

4. Like other assets, money is demanded for the flow of services it provides. Its most important service is
   a. protection against inflation.
   b. the interest income it provides.
   c. insurance against theft.
   d. its liquidity.
   e. none of the above.

5. The demand for money
   a. varies directly with the interest rate.
   b. varies inversely with the interest rate.
   c. is constant no matter what the interest rate is.
   d. is indicated by a vertical line.
   e. none of the above

6. The supply of money
   a. is inversely related to the interest rate.
   b. is directly related to the interest rate.
   c. varies with the demand for money.
   d. is determined primarily by commercial banks.
   e. is determined primarily by the Fed and can be assumed to be constant no matter what the interest rate is.

7. An increase in the money supply
   a. generates an increase in the quantity of money demanded.
   b. generates a lower interest rate.
   c. increases the level of planned investment.
   d. leads to a higher level of nominal GDP.
   e. all of the above

8. According to the indirect channel, a decrease in the supply of money would
   a. increase aggregate demand.
   b. reduce aggregate demand because the quantity of money demanded would fall.
   c. generate a reduction in government spending, which would cause aggregate demand to fall.
   d. reduce aggregate demand because interest rates would increase and planned investment would fall.
   e. cause a reduction in aggregate supply.

9. One reason the aggregate demand curve slopes downward is that decreases in the price level generate
   a. decreases in the money supply.
   b. increases in the transactions demand for money.
   c. increases in the money supply.
   d. decreases in the transactions demand for money.
   e. decreases in investment spending.

10. The behavior of money demand in the economy causes the effects of fiscal policy to be
   a. enhanced.
   b. completely neutralized.
   c. diminished.
   d. uncertain.
   e. none of the above. Money demand makes no difference.

11. One reason the aggregate demand curve slopes down is
   a. the inverse relationship between the demand for money and the price level.
   b. the volatility of velocity.
   c. that higher price levels lead to an increase in the money supply.
   d. that higher price levels lead to higher interest rates, which result in less planned investment.
   e. that higher price levels lead to increases in the supply of loanable funds.

12. According to monetarists, a decrease in the money supply
   a. decreases interest rates.
   b. has no effect on interest rates but causes aggregate demand to fall.
   c. has a direct impact on aggregate demand and an indirect impact caused by rising interest rates and falling investment.
   d. has effects on aggregate demand that are opposite those predicted by those who focus on the indirect channel.
   e. none of the above

13. According to monetarists, an increase in the money supply
   a. increases the interest rate.
   b. decreases aggregate demand.
   c. increases aggregate demand directly.
   d. increases aggregate demand only indirectly.
   e. has no effect on aggregate demand or on the interest rate.

14. The equation of exchange is expressed as
   a. $M \times Y = P \times V$.
   b. $M \times V = P \times Y$.
   c. $R \times P = V \times V$.
   d. $M = V/P \times Y$.
   e. none of the above.

15. Which of the following is not an identity?
   a. MPG = miles driven/gallons of gasoline
   b. $Y = C + I + G + NX$
   c. $M = P \times Y/V$, where $V =$ a constant
   d. $M \times V = P \times Y$
   e. All are identities.

16. The quantity theory of money states that
   a. the equation of exchange is true.
   b. the money supply is directly related to the interest rate.
   c. the velocity of money is stable or at least predictable.
   d. the aggregate supply curve slopes upward.
   e. all of the above

17. The velocity of money is
    a. lower the better money serves as a store of wealth.
    b. highly variable, according to monetarists.
    c. lower the more often people get paid.
    d. constant over long periods of time.
    e. greater the greater the quantity of money balances held by the public.

18. According to those who focus on the indirect channel, the velocity of money is
    a. lower the greater the interest rate.
    b. constant over long periods of time.
    c. very predictable.
    d. greater the greater the interest rate.
    e. b and c.

19. Suppose $M = \$1,000$, $V = 5$, and $P \times Y = \$5,000$ initially. If the money supply doubled, then nominal income would be _____________, according to the monetarist view.
    a. \$5,000
    b. \$7,000
    c. \$7,500
    d. \$10,000
    e. \$15,000

20. Monetary authorities can
    a. keep the money supply constant.
    b. keep interest rates constant.
    c. do either a or b but not both simultaneously.
    d. do both a and b simultaneously.
    e. none of the above

D. *Discussion Questions*

1. "If people want to be rich they will demand all the money they can." Is this statement true or false? Briefly explain.

2. What is meant by the demand for money? Which way does the demand curve for money slope? Why?

3. Money serves as both a medium of exchange and a store of value. What competes with money in these roles?

4. What can cause the demand curve for money to shift to the left? What can cause a movement along the demand curve for money?

5. What can cause the supply curve for money to shift to the right?

6. Use an indirect channel perspective to explain how monetary policy affects aggregate demand.

7. Why does the aggregate demand curve slope downward?

8. Suppose the economy is in long-run equilibrium. What would be the short-run and the long-run effects of an increase in the money supply?

9. What would be the short-run and long-run effects of a decrease in government purchases?

10. How do monetarists differ from those who focus on the indirect channel in their views of how a change in the money supply affects aggregate demand?

11. If nominal GDP is $10 billion and the velocity of money is 4, what is the quantity of money in the economy?

12. How do monetarists turn the equation of exchange from an identity into a theory?

13. Since the equation of exchange is an identity, why do those who focus on the indirect channel of money *not* agree with monetarists that increases in the money supply directly affect aggregate demand?

14. The velocity of M1 is less stable than the velocity of M2. Can you offer an explanation?

15. Explain why the Fed can attempt to target either changes in the money supply or changes in interest rates, but not both.

VII. ANSWERS

A. *Completion*

1. theory
2. demand for money
3. transactions
4. liquidity
5. interest rate
6. independent
7. interest rates
8. investment
9. greater
10. the interest rate
11. velocity
12. monetarism
13. quantity theory
14. equation of exchange
15. the money stock

B. *True/False*

1. False
2. False
3. True
4. True
5. False
6. False
7. True
8. True
9. True
10. True
11. True
12. False
13. False. The equation of exchange always holds.
14. True
15. False
16. True
17. True
18. False
19. False
20. False

C. *Multiple Choice*

1. d	6. e	11. d	16. c
2. b	7. e	12. c	17. a
3. a	8. d	13. c	18. d
4. d	9. d	14. b	19. d
5. b	10. c	15. c	20. c

D. *Discussion Questions*

1. False. The demand for money refers to the demand to hold onto money balances in order to make transactions. It is not a demand for wealth. Since most forms of money do not provide an income, people do not want all of their wealth tied up in money. Instead, they want assets that will provide a return.

2. The demand for money refers to people's desire to hold money balances at a given time. The opportunity cost of holding money is the additional interest one could have earned if the money had been used to purchase alternative interest-bearing financial assets. The demand curve for money shows the quantity of money demanded at various interest rates, other things constant. It slopes down because at lower interest rates people forgo less interest if they hold their wealth in the form of money. Therefore they hold more money and buy fewer alternative interest-bearing financial assets.

3. Nothing competes with money as a medium of exchange, since a medium of exchange is money. Other financial assets compete with money as a store of value and usually also provide a return, in the form of interest.

4. The demand curve for money will shift to the left if the price level falls or if the level of real GDP falls. A change in interest rates causes a movement along the demand curve for money.

5. The supply curve of money will shift to the right if the Fed increases the money supply by buying government bonds, lowering the required reserve ratio, or lowering the discount rate.

6. Since the demand curve for money slopes down, a change in the money supply causes the interest rate to change. The change in the interest rate causes investment spending to change, and investment spending is one component of aggregate expenditure. The equilibrium quantity of real GDP demanded at the prevailing price level changes by the change in investment times the spending multiplier, causing a corresponding shift in aggregate demand.

7. The aggregate demand curve slopes down for three reasons. First, an increase in the price level lowers the real value of dollar-denominated assets, which in turn lowers individuals' wealth and consumption spending and the quantity of aggregate output they demand. Second, as the price level increases, domestic products become more costly relative to foreign products, so exports decrease and imports increase. The drop in net exports causes a reduction in the quantity of aggregate output demanded. Third, money is demanded to finance transactions. An increase in the price level increases the average dollar cost of each transaction. More money is needed to finance transactions, so the demand for money increases, which drives the interest rates higher. The higher interest rates cause investment spending to fall, which means the quantity of aggregate output demanded decreases.

8. You can see the effects of an increase in the money supply by referring to the graph. Point *e* is the original equilibrium. The increase in the money supply causes the aggregate demand curve to shift to the right as falling interest rates stimulate investment spending. The new short-run equilibrium is at *e´*, and there is an increase in both real output and the price level. The rate of output exceeds the potential output of the economy, however, and the actual price level is greater than the expected price level. Once people learn the new situation, the short-run aggregate supply curve shifts to *SRAS*(105), and the new long-run equilibrium is at *e**.

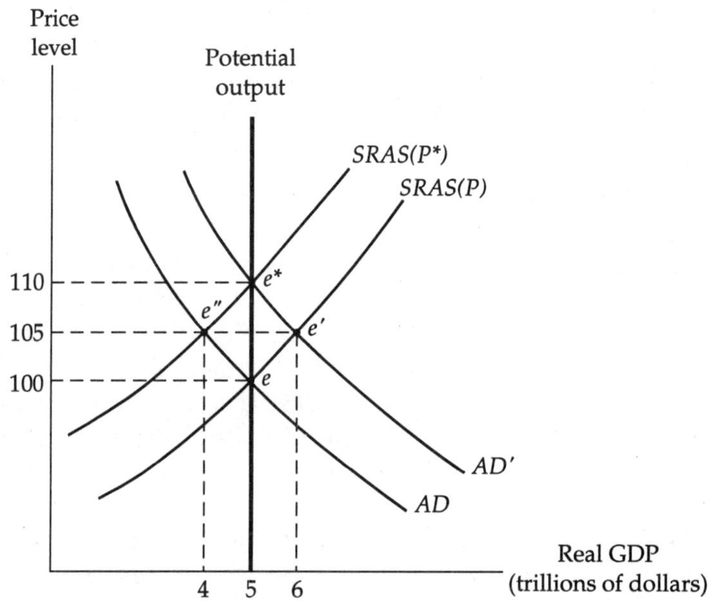

9. Refer again to the graph, starting at *e**. A reduction in government purchases shifts the aggregate demand curve from *AD´* to *AD*, and the new short-run equilibrium is at *e˝*. Unemployment increases, real output falls below the economy's potential output, and the actual price level is less than the expected price level. Once people realize the new situation, the short-run aggregate supply curve shifts to *SRAS*(100), and *e* is again the long-run equilibrium.

10. Those who focus on an indirect channel believe that a change in the money supply affects aggregate demand only indirectly, by affecting interest rates, which affect investment spending. Monetarists believe that when people try to change the amount of money they hold, they change their purchases of all assets and not just their purchases of financial assets. Hence, according to this view, a change in the supply of money also has a direct effect on aggregate demand.

11. $M \times V = P \times Y$. If $P \times Y =$ \$10 billion and $V = 4$, then $M = (P \times Y)/V =$ \$10 billion/4 = \$2.5 billion.

12. Monetarists assume that velocity is constant or at least very predictable, so the equation of exchange becomes the quantity theory of money. This theory states that increases in the money supply lead to predictable increases in nominal GDP.

13. Monetarists convert the equation of exchange from an identity to a theory by assuming that velocity is constant or at least predictable. Those who focus on the indirect channel believe that changes in the money supply will be offset by changes in velocity. If they are correct, then changes in the money supply will not directly affect aggregate demand.

14. Changes in government regulations and innovations in financial markets may be responsible for the differences in velocity. What were formerly near moneys may now be more like money and may need to be included in our definition of money.

15. The demand curve for money slopes down; the supply curve for money is vertical. A shift in the demand curve for money will cause interest rates to change. The only way the Fed can keep interest rates stable is to change the money supply. That is, it cannot keep both the money supply and interest rates stable in the face of a shift in demand for money.

CHAPTER 16

The Policy Debate: Active or Passive?

I. INTRODUCTION

In the previous chapters, we examined how fiscal policy and monetary policy affect the level of output and the inflation rate. The effectiveness of either policy in stabilizing the economy is a topic that is hotly debated among economists. This chapter discusses the views of both those who advocate active government intervention in the economy and those who advocate that the government adopt a passive role. The role of expectations in neutralizing government stabilization policies is also discussed.

II. OUTLINE

1. Active Policy Versus Passive Policy. The passive approach states the private economy is basically self-correcting; the active approach does not.

    1.1 Closing a Contractionary Gap
    - a. The passive approach is to allow natural market forces to shift the short-run aggregate supply curve outward and bring the economy to its potential output.
    - b. According to the passive approach, wages and prices are flexible enough to correct short-run surpluses or shortages fairly quickly; the active approach stresses that wages and prices are less flexible, especially in the downward direction.
    - c. The longer it takes for the economy to move naturally to its potential output, the more costly the passive approach.
    - d. The activist approach is to speed the return to potential output by increasing aggregate demand through changes in fiscal policy, monetary policy, or a combination of the two.
    - e. One cost of an activist approach is an increase in the price level.

    1.2 Closing an Expansionary Gap
    - a. According to the passive approach, natural market forces will prompt firms and workers to renegotiate higher nominal wage agreements, increasing production costs and shifting the short-run aggregate supply curve until the expansionary gap is eliminated. The price level will rise.
    - b. According to the active approach, the economy can return to its potential output without inflation if aggregate demand is reduced.

    1.3 Problems with Active Policy
    - a. It is difficult to identify the economy's potential output.
    - b. In order to pursue an active policy, policymakers must
        - (1) be able to predict what would happen if they did nothing.
        - (2) have access to the tools necessary to achieve the desired result in a timely manner.
        - (3) be able to forecast the effects of their policy on the economy's key performance measures.

(4) obtain cooperation of the separate government bodies that implement fiscal policy and monetary policy.
(5) implement the appropriate policy.
(6) deal with a variety of lags.

1.4 The Problem of Lags

a. Recognition lag: it takes time to recognize that the economy is not at its potential output.
b. Decision-making lag: it takes time for policymakers to decide on the correct actions to take.
c. Implementation lag: it takes time to carry out a change in policy, especially when it is a fiscal policy.
d. Effectiveness lag: it takes time for the policy to have an impact on the economy.

1.5 Review of Policy Perspectives

a. An active approach emphasizes that there is a high cost associated with a noninterventionist policy, particularly when unemployment is high. Prolonged unemployment may cause potential GDP to fall.
b. A passive approach emphasizes that the uncertainties in the economy and the lags associated with policy changes often cause harm, so nonactivists want to allow the natural forces in the economy to work.

1.6 *CASE STUDY:* Presidential Economies

2. Role of Expectations. People's expectations influence the short-run aggregate supply curve and therefore the effects of a particular policy. The *rational expectations* school of thought argues that people form expectations on the basis of all relevant information, including information about the likely future actions of policymakers.

2.1 Monetary Policy and Expectations

a. A greater-than-expected increase in the money supply can cause a short-run increase in output and employment if economic actors are surprised by the monetary authorities' policies.
b. The long-run effect of unanticipated changes in monetary policy is an increase in the price level with no change in output.
c. The time inconsistency problem arises when policymakers have an incentive to announce one policy, hoping to affect expectations, but then pursue another policy after expectations have been formed.

2.2 Anticipating Monetary Policy

a. When people have been caught by surprise by policymakers in the past, they are less likely to believe them in the future.
b. If people do not believe policymakers and policymakers pursue their stated policies, then the result may be a relatively large short-run gap between actual and potential GDP.
c. People form expectations on the basis of what they believe policymakers will do and not on the basis of what policymakers say they will do.
d. The rational expectations school believes that government discretionary policies have no short-run or long-run effect on output or employment if the policies are fully and correctly anticipated.

2.3 Policy Credibility

a. If policymakers think of their reputations as valuable resources, they are less likely to seek short-term reductions in unemployment that generate greater inflation in the long run.

b. Policy is more likely to be stable over time if policymakers take a long-run view of their duties.

2.4 *Case Study:* Central Bank Independence and Price Stability

3. The Phillips Curve. The Phillips curve represents a tradeoff faced by policymakers between unemployment and inflation. According to the Phillips curve, lower employment comes at the cost of higher inflation. The stagflation of the 1970s caused economists to reexamine the concept that policymakers face a stable, long-run tradeoff between inflation and employment.

3.1 Short-Run Phillips Curve

a. The short-run aggregate supply curve reflects an inverse relationship between the inflation rate and the level of unemployment.

b. If the inflation rate, and therefore the price level, is lower than expected, unemployment tends to be greater than the natural rate of unemployment.

c. If the inflation rate, and therefore the price level, is higher than expected, unemployment tends to be lower than the natural rate of unemployment.

d. The intersections of alternative aggregate demand curves with a given short-run aggregate supply curve determine inflation-unemployment combinations along a short-run Phillips curve. The short-run aggregate supply curve, and therefore the short-run Phillips curve, is based on a given expected inflation rate.

3.2 Long-Run Phillips Curve

a. Monetary or fiscal policy that is unexpected affects only the price level in the long run.

b. The long-run Phillips curve is a vertical line at the natural rate of unemployment; policymakers only choose from among alternative inflation rates.

3.3 The Natural Rate Hypothesis

a. The *natural rate hypothesis* contends that the economy tends toward the natural rate of unemployment in the long run.

b. The *weak version of the natural rate hypothesis* is that policymakers can influence the tradeoff between unemployment and inflation only in the short run. Unemployment can be maintained below the natural rate only at the cost of ever-increasing inflation.

c. The *strong version of the natural rate hypothesis* is that policymakers' abilities to influence the tradeoff in the short run diminishes over time as the public learns to predict the behavior of the policymakers.

3.4 Evidence of the Phillips Curve

a. Evidence from the 1960s tends to be consistent with the Phillips curve.

b. A tradeoff was less apparent in the 1970s.

4. Policy Rules Versus Discretion

4.1 Rationale for Rules

a. Monetarists believe that stability in the money supply growth rate is better for the economy than any discretionary monetary policy.

b. Monetarists often advocate the use of monetary rules, which are rules that specify the relationship between a policy instrument and policy objectives.
c. Monetarists argue that in the long run, excessive monetary growth generates inflation.

4.2 Rules and Rational Expectations
a. Followers of the rational expectations school advocate rules because they believe the public on average predicts the behavior of policymakers with reasonable accuracy.
b. Discretionary policy tends to be ineffective when anticipated correctly by the public. It affects only the price level.
c. Economists in this school advocate a fixed rule because it makes it easier for economic actors to predict the future state of the economy, thus reducing departures from potential output.

4.3 Theory of Real Business Cycles
a. *Real business cycle theory* holds that fluctuations in real GDP are caused by real shocks to the economy, such as changes in technology.
b. Wages are thought to be very flexible and the aggregate supply curve is vertical.
c. Monetary policy would have no effect on real GDP but would affect the price level.

III. DISCUSSION

Active Policy Versus Passive Policy

The federal government is very concerned with economic policy questions. The Employment Act of 1946 makes the federal government responsible for maintaining full employment. Even without such a law, politicians would be interested in economic policy. Incumbents find it easier to be reelected when the economy is functioning well than when inflation is high and rising or unemployment rates are high. Thus, the question of interest is which policy is the best policy. Unfortunately for policymakers, the answer to the question remains unclear, and the topic is hotly debated among economists.

Some economists advocate an *active* role for the federal government. An active policy is one in which policymakers make use of discretionary stabilization policies to keep the economy running at or near potential output while maintaining relatively stable prices. Discretionary fiscal and monetary policies tend to focus on shifting the aggregate demand curve to achieve full employment. An expansionary monetary policy is used to stimulate spending when real GDP is below potential, and a restrictive monetary policy is used to reduce spending when the economy is overheated. Fiscal policy can also be used to stimulate or reduce aggregate demand. Advocates of an active policy tend to argue that the private economy is basically unstable and private spending cannot be counted upon to maintain aggregate demand at the full employment level. According to this view, by implementing the correct discretionary policies the government can stabilize the economy around potential output.

Other economists disagree and advocate a *passive* role for the government. They believe the private economy is inherently stable and self-correcting. Deviations from potential GDP tend to be short-lived because self-correcting market forces push the economy toward its potential output. Since the economy is basically stable, there is no need for discretionary stabilization policy. In fact, according to this view, government stabilization policies are inherently destabilizing because there are various time lags between the recognition of a problem, the selection and implementation of a policy to correct it, and the impact of a policy change on the economy. During the time lags, the economy's self-correcting mechanisms return the economy to its full employment level. Consequently, when the discretionary policy takes effect, it may generate a new problem, since the problem it was designed to alleviate has already corrected itself.

Role of Expectations

Individuals make economic decisions on the basis of their experiences; the information they have about prices, inflation, and the like; and their expectations, which are based on information about future economic conditions. This information comes from many sources. For example, a possible change in government tax policy is discussed and debated in public for a considerable time before it is implemented. Money supply figures are published regularly, as are unemployment rates and numerous other measures of economic activity.

By affecting short-run aggregate supply, the expectations of economic actors play a crucial role in determining whether a particular discretionary policy will be effective. The *rational expectations* school of thought holds that people form expectations on the basis of all relevant information, including information about how government stabilization policy operates and is implemented. Consequently, if policymakers attempt to stimulate the economy by increasing the rate of growth of the money supply and people correctly anticipate that the Fed is going to do this, then the monetary growth will not have any short-run effect on output. Instead, the only effect will be a long-run increase in the inflation rate.

Exhibit 1

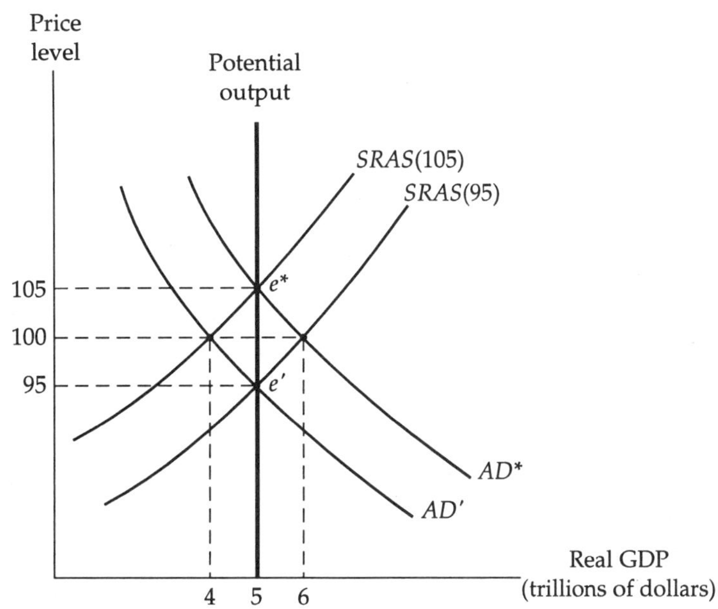

Exhibit 1 illustrates the views of the rational expectations school. Potential output is $5 trillion, and the current equilibrium is at *e**. Suppose the Fed announces a restrictive monetary policy in an effort to reduce the price level to 95, and it initially pursues the restrictive monetary policy. Aggregate demand shifts to *AD*′, real GDP falls to $4 trillion, and the price level falls to 100. Once the public perceives the new conditions and they adjust their decisions about supplying resources in the light of their new information, the short-run aggregate supply curve shifts to *SRAS*(95), and the new long-run equilibrium is at *e*′. Suppose, however, that the Fed abandons its restrictive monetary policy before the public adjusts its price expectations to 95. If the public is unaware of this change, aggregate demand returns to *AD** at the same time that the short-run aggregate supply curve shifts to *SRAS*(95), and real GDP increases to $6 trillion. The public gets caught by surprise. Eventually, people will realize the true state of the economy, and the short-run aggregate supply will shift back to *SRAS*(105).

By failing to implement its announced policy, the Fed loses its credibility with the public. If the Fed now announces a restrictive monetary policy to combat inflation, the public will be less likely to believe the announcement. Consequently, people will not change their price expectations, and the short-run aggregate supply curve will not shift. The Fed would have to pursue its restrictive monetary policy for a longer period of time to convince the public that it was serious. During this time, however, real GDP would be below potential output, and unemployment would be above the natural rate of unemployment.

The Phillips Curve

The *Phillips curve* is a graphical representation of a tradeoff between inflation and unemployment. The tradeoff shown by a Phillips curve is between low unemployment rates and low inflation rates; it is not possible to have both. That is, if the government wants to lower the unemployment rate, it must be willing to accept a higher inflation rate. Exhibit 2 illustrates two possible Phillips curves. During the 1960s, policymakers acted on the belief that there was a stable, long-run tradeoff between inflation and unemployment for the economy. As inflation became a greater problem in the late 1960s and early 1970s, however, this view became suspect. Critics of an active policy argued that the tradeoff is a short-run, not a long-run, phenomenon. According to this view, the government may be able to trade greater inflation for lower unemployment in the short run. Once the public realizes the true state of the economy, however, unemployment will return to its natural rate. In Exhibit 2, the natural rate of unemployment is 6 percent. Suppose the economy is at point *a*. The government can temporarily reduce unemployment by creating inflation; in that case, the economy moves to point *b*. Once the public perceives the new economic situation, people adjust their expectations, and the economy returns to the natural rate of unemployment (point *c*). Now the natural rate of unemployment is associated with a higher inflation rate, and there is a new short-run Phillips curve. The long-run Phillips curve is vertical at the natural rate of unemployment.

Policy Rules Versus Discretion

Since advocates of a passive policy believe the government's use of discretionary policy tends to destabilize the economy, they advocate the use of monetary policy rules. A monetary policy rule specifies the relationship between a policy instrument and a policy objective. Monetarists tend to support rules on the grounds that the government cannot effectively control the economy because it is so complex and the lags involved in discretionary policies are too long and variable. Those who favor this rational expectations approach advocate rules because they believe the public is sophisticated enough in forming its expectations that discretionary policy tends to affect only the level of prices. By making policy on the basis of a rule, the Fed makes it possible for the public to formulate expectations about the future with greater certainty and permits the economy to achieve the natural rate of output.

Real business cycle theory holds that fluctuations in both real GDP and employment are caused by real shocks to the economy. A *real shock* is something that affects real variables and not financial variables. For example, a freeze that destroys crops is a real shock. Real business cycle theory says that monetary policy cannot affect real variables such as real GDP. The Fed should concentrate on keeping inflation low.

Exhibit 2

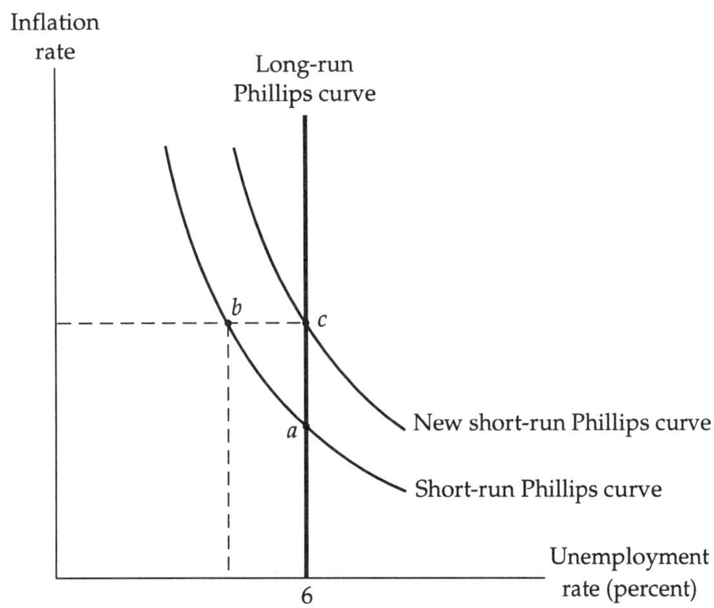

IV. LAGNIAPPE

Leading Economic Indicators and Stabilization Policy

An important lag mentioned in the text is the *recognition lag*, which is the time needed to determine that a problem has developed in the economy. Economists have developed a number of leading economic indicators to try to identify turning points in economic activity. If we knew that a recession was coming in the near future, it might be possible to take corrective actions that would reduce the severity of the recession. Unfortunately, the leading indicators are not accurate enough to form the basis of monetary and fiscal policy. Although the leading indicators often predict turning points in the economy, they err on too many occasions. That is, leading indicators sometimes fail to reveal turning points and sometimes predict turning points that do not materialize.

Question to Think About: What degree of accuracy would you require of leading economic indicators before allowing them to be used in setting stabilization policy?

Is the Market Self-Correcting?

As we have seen in this and several other chapters, there is considerable debate among economists about whether the market is self-correcting. Those who believe it is not self-correcting often use the Great Depression of the 1930s as evidence. Those who believe the market is self-correcting argue that the severity of the depression was increased by government attempts to stabilize the economy. They also argue that the economy has proven to be basically self-correcting throughout most of the postwar period.

A possible synthesis of the two views has been suggested by Axel Leijonhufvud. He argues that the economy is self-correcting most of the time. People and firms use buffers to protect against unexpected layoffs or business downturns. Buffers include savings, inventories, and insurance. If a shock to the economy is much greater than usual, however, then the buffers may get used up. When this happens, the economy's ability to correct itself is weakened considerably, and the recessionary state can persist for a long time—as it did during the Great Depression when the Fed cut the money stock by a third. (See articles in Axel Leijonhufvud, *Information and Coordination: Essays in Macroeconomic Theory*. New York: Oxford University Press, 1981.)

Question to Think About: Were the oil shocks of the 1970s enough to cause people to use up the kinds of buffers discussed by Leijonhufvud?

V. KEY TERMS

Active approach
Passive approach
Recognition lag
Decision-making lag
Implementation lag
Effectiveness lag
Rational expectations
Time inconsistency problem
Cold turkey
Monetary rule
Phillips curve
Short-run Phillips curve
Long-run Phillips curve
Natural rate hypothesis
Weak version of the natural rate hypothesis
Strong version of the natural rate hypothesis
Real business cycle theory

VI. QUESTIONS

A. *Completion*

1. A(n) __________________ approach emphasizes the vigorous use of discretionary policies.

2. According to the active approach, economic fluctuations are due to instabilities in the __________________ sector.

3. Those who advocate a(n) __________________ approach consider the private sector to be relatively stable.

4. The __________________ approach to a contractionary gap or an expansionary gap is to allow natural market forces to close the gap.

5. Since it takes time to identify a problem, policymakers face a __________________ lag.

6. The time needed to carry out a change in policy is called the __________________ lag.

7. The time needed for a policy to have an impact on the economy is called the __________________ lag.

8. The school of thought that argues that people form expectations on the basis of all relevant information is known as __________________.

9. The __________________ problem occurs when policymakers have an incentive to announce one policy but then pursue another policy.

10. The Fed will be more __________________ if it consistently pursues the policies it says it will pursue.

11. A __________________ specifies the relation that ties monetary policy instruments to policy objectives.

12. Many monetarists advocate that the Fed follow a __________________ monetary policy.

13. A __________________ illustrates a tradeoff between unemployment and inflation.

14. The long-run Phillips curve is __________________.

15. The __________________ rate of unemployment is the unemployment rate consistent with the economy's potential level of output.

B. *True/False*

______ 1. According to the active approach, wage reductions take a long time to work through the economy.

______ 2. An active approach emphasizes the use of monetary policy; a passive approach emphasizes the use of fiscal policy.

______ 3. In order to pursue an appropriate active policy, policymakers must be able to forecast what aggregate demand would be without government intervention.

______ 4. The implementation lag associated with fiscal policy tends to be longer than the implementation lag associated with monetary policy.

______ 5. According to those who advocate a passive approach, the lags associated with discretionary policies cause such policies to destabilize the economy.

______ 6. According to the rational expectations school of thought, short-run aggregate supply is affected by the macroeconomic course policymakers are expected to pursue.

______ 7. Members of the rational expectations school tend to favor active discretionary policy on the part of the government.

______ 8. According to the rational expectations school, the best policy for government policymakers is to keep the public surprised continually.

______ 9. The rational expectations school believes that an expansionary monetary policy has no effect on output or employment if the policy is fully and correctly anticipated.

______ 10. One solution to the time inconsistency problem is to allow policymakers no discretion.

______ 11. One cost to the Fed of implementing unanticipated changes in monetary policy is a loss of credibility.

______ 12. A monetary rule always represents a passive form of monetary policy.

______ 13. Milton Friedman argues that the precise rate of growth decided upon is more important than the fact that a rate of growth of the money supply is established.

______ 14. Monetarists advocate the use of rules because of ignorance on the part of policymakers.

______ 15. A rule that links money supply growth to interest rates is an active rule.

______ 16. Followers of the rational expectations school believe that the public's behavior neutralizes discretionary policy.

______ 17. A high unemployment rate will be associated with a high inflation rate, according to the short-run Phillips curve.

______ 18. Countries with high rates of growth of money supply also have high inflation rates.

______ 19. The long-run Phillips curve is a vertical line that corresponds to the economy's potential GDP.

______ 20. The natural rate of unemployment is determined by the short-run Phillips curve.

C. *Multiple Choice*

1. According to the active approach,
   a. prices and wages are not very flexible, especially downward.
   b. wage reductions in the face of unemployment tend to take a long time.
   c. the private economy is inherently unstable.
   d. discretionary policy can make the economy more stable.
   e. all of the above

2. A comparison of an active approach and a passive approach toward stabilization policy reveals that
   a. the cost of the passive approach is greater.
   b. the active approach is more concerned with problems of inflation than is the passive approach.
   c. the active approach relies on monetary policy whereas the passive approach relies on fiscal policy.
   d. the passive approach is more concerned with the inflexibility of wages and prices than is the active approach.
   e. the passive approach relies on the self-correcting tendencies of the economy more than the active approach does.

3. On December 7, 1992, then President-elect Clinton convened an economic summit in Little Rock, Arkansas. This activity was a signal that the Clinton administration would pursue a(n)
   a. monetarist policy.
   b. rational expectations approach to policy.
   c. active policy.
   d. passive policy.
   e. inflationary policy.

4. Increasing government spending to stimulate the economy is an example of
   a. a passive policy.
   b. an attempt to increase potential output.
   c. an active policy.
   d. a policy consistent with the rational expectations school.
   e. none of the above.

5. To pursue an active policy, policymakers must
   a. be able to forecast what aggregate demand and aggregate supply would be without government action.
   b. have automatic stabilizers in place.
   c. control fiscal policy but allow the Fed to do whatever it wants.
   d. be concerned primarily with getting the president reelected.
   e. none of the above

6. The lag in the time it takes to identify a problem in the macroeconomy is known as the
   a. recognition lag.
   b. decision-making lag.
   c. implementation lag.
   d. effectiveness lag.
   e. registration lag.

7. Those who advocate a passive policy argue that lags imply that an active approach should not be used because
   a. policymakers do not know what should be done to correct the existing problem.
   b. the active policy will delay the moment when the economy begins moving back to potential output.
   c. the active policy imposes additional fluctuations in the price level and the output level.
   d. the potential output level of the economy shifts frequently.
   e. all of the above

8. The effect of stabilization policy depends on what the public expects the government to do because
   a. the public tends to be irrational.
   b. the short-run aggregate supply curve is based on price expectations.
   c. the long-run aggregate supply curve is vertical.
   d. the public knows that the government will select the correct stabilization policy.
   e. the government employs such a large portion of the labor force.

9. Followers of the rational expectations school believe that
   a. the government does not have enough information to pursue a reasonable stabilization policy.
   b. the public anticipates the policies the government will implement and the effects of the policies on output and prices.
   c. the government establishes a stabilization policy by anticipating how the public will react to the policy and the effects of the public's actions on the implementation of the policy.
   d. b and c
   e. none of the above

10. Which of the following represents the time inconsistency problem?
   a. The lags associated with discretionary policy sometimes cause the discretionary policy to take effect after market forces have adjusted and eliminated the original problem.
   b. Leading economic indicators do not perfectly predict upturns or downturns in the economy.
   c. Policies that have certain effects in the short run may be ineffective in the long run.
   d. Elected officials may announce a policy to reduce inflation but not stick with the policy out of fear of losing the next election.
   e. Discretionary policy is ineffective in altering the natural rate of unemployment.

11. The Fed will have a difficult time getting its policy to be effective if
   a. the economy is in a recession.
   b. it is pursuing a contractionary policy.
   c. policymakers take a long-run view of their duties.
   d. monetary policymakers have lost credibility.
   e. all of the above

12. If the public forms expectations rationally, then any correctly anticipated discretionary policy will
   a. affect short-run output and prices but have no long-run effect.
   b. affect output in the short run but have no effect on short-run prices.
   c. affect prices in the short run but not in the long run.
   d. be effective more quickly than if the public formed no expectations.
   e. have no effects on output or employment.

13. Many monetarists advocate
   a. that the Fed pursue an active stabilization policy.
   b. fine-tuning the economy.
   c. a monetary rule that fixes the rate of growth of the money supply.
   d. a monetary rule that pegs interest rates to a certain nominal rate.
   e. a monetary rule that pegs interest rates to a certain real rate.

14. If monetary policy is fully anticipated by workers and firms,
   a. it will be effective more quickly.
   b. it will have no effect on output.
   c. it will have no effect on the price level.
   d. the economy moves along the short-run Phillips curve.
   e. none of the above

Exhibit 3

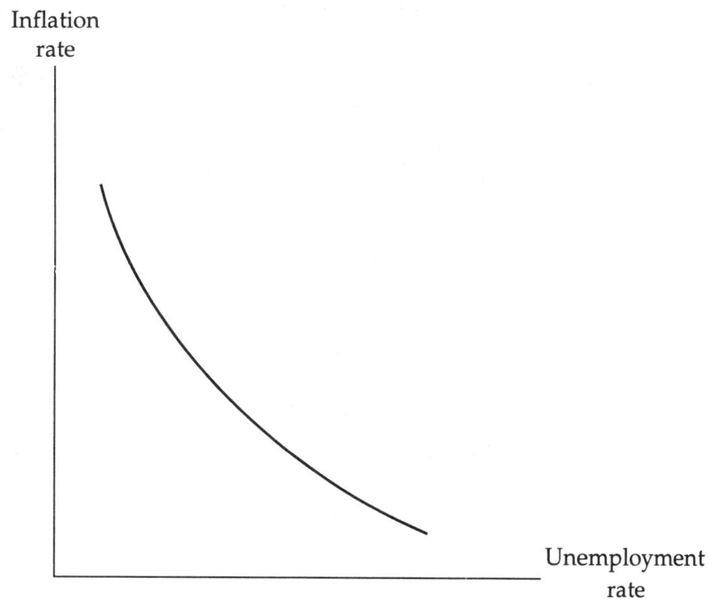

15. What is the name of the relationship shown in Exhibit 3?
    a. the natural rate hypothesis
    b. the Phillips curve
    c. monetarism
    d. rational expectations
    e. the aggregate demand curve

16. The relationship illustrated in Exhibit 3 shows that
    a. lower inflation brings about lower employment.
    b. lower inflation brings about higher unemployment.
    c. inflation and unemployment are directly related.
    d. inflation and unemployment have the same causes.
    e. inflation is a short-run phenomenon.

17. The short-run Phillips curve can be derived if
    a. the short-run aggregate supply curve slopes upward.
    b. the short-run aggregate supply curve is vertical.
    c. the short-run aggregate demand curve is horizontal.
    d. we are discussing the long run.
    e. none of the above

18. According to the natural rate hypothesis,
    a. the long-run Phillips curve is vertical at the natural rate of unemployment.
    b. the long-run Phillips curve is vertical at the natural rate of inflation.
    c. the natural rate of unemployment is 4 percent.
    d. the unemployment rate is inversely related to the inflation rate.
    e. c and d

19. The tradeoff between inflation and unemployment expressed by a short-run Phillips curve is more likely to exist when
    a. shifts in aggregate supply are large.
    b. shifts in aggregate supply dominate shifts in aggregate demand.
    c. shifts in aggregate demand dominate shifts in aggregate supply.
    d. neither aggregate demand nor aggregate supply is shifting.
    e. monetary policy is used instead of fiscal policy.

20. According to the theory of real business cycles,
    a. the long-run aggregate supply curve is steeper than the short-run aggregate supply curve.
    b. the short-run aggregate supply curve is steeper than the long-run aggregate supply curve.
    c. the long-run and the short-run aggregate supply curves are both vertical.
    d. there is no aggregate supply curve.
    e. monetary policy is more effective than fiscal policy.

D. *Discussion Questions*

1. Explain how an active policy differs from a passive policy.

2. Suppose the economy is operating at a real GDP greater than its potential output and the price level is greater than the expected price level. What would an active policy to correct the problem be?

3. What would happen if a passive approach were taken to address the situation described in question 2?

4. Explain the lags associated with discretionary policy and the problems they cause.

5. What problems are caused by following a passive approach if the economy is not self-correcting? What problems are caused by following an active approach if a passive approach is needed?

6. Explain the rational expectations theory. Does the theory imply that the public never makes mistakes? Explain.

7. What is the time inconsistency problem? What factors contribute to the problem?

8. The text discusses the role of expectations in the context of monetary policy. Discuss the relationship between expectations and fiscal policy. Assume that the government's stated goal is to reduce the deficit.

9. Explain why credibility is hard to develop but easy to undermine and how credibility is relevant to stabilization policy.

10. What is a policy rule and what is the purpose of such a rule?

11. Suppose the relationship between unemployment and inflation actually is as depicted by a downward-sloping Phillips curve. What implications does this have for the conduct of stabilization policy?

12. What is the natural rate hypothesis?

13. How do the weak version and the strong version of the natural rate hypothesis differ?

14. Explain how the short-run Phillips curve, the long-run Phillips curve, the short-run aggregate supply curve, the long-run aggregate supply curve, and the natural rate hypothesis are all related. How do active and passive views of these concepts differ?

15. What is real business cycle theory, and what are the policy implications of it?

VII. ANSWERS

A. *Completion*

1. active
2. private
3. passive
4. passive
5. recognition
6. implementation
7. effectiveness
8. the school of rational expectations
9. time inconsistency
10. credible
11. monetary rule
12. fixed-growth-rate
13. short-run Phillips curve
14. vertical
15. natural

B. *True/False*

1. True
2. False
3. True
4. True
5. True
6. True
7. False
8. False
9. True
10. True
11. True
12. False. Some monetary rules may be relatively active.
13. False
14. True
15. True
16. True
17. False
18. True
19. True
20. False

C. *Multiple Choice*

1. e
2. e
3. c
4. c
5. a
6. a
7. c
8. b
9. b
10. d
11. d
12. e
13. c
14. b
15. b
16. b
17. a
18. a
19. c
20. c

D. *Discussion Questions*

1. According to the passive policy approach, the private economy is relatively stable, and natural market forces will rapidly correct any deviations from potential output. An active approach states that the private economy is basically unstable and that wages and prices are inflexible enough that deviations from potential output can persist for long periods of time. Consequently, the latter claims that it is important for the government to implement discretionary monetary and fiscal policy in order to maintain economic stability.

2. An active policy would reduce aggregate demand by using either fiscal policy, monetary policy, or both. The use of fiscal policy could involve a reduction in government spending or a tax increase. The goal of monetary policy would be to reduce the money supply and increase interest rates, which would reduce investment spending.

3. Firms and workers would negotiate higher wage agreements, which would increase production costs and shift the short-run aggregate supply curve to the left. Output would fall to the potential output and prices would be higher.

4. There are four lags associated with discretionary policy. The recognition lag is the time it takes to recognize that an economic problem exists. The decision-making lag is the time it takes to decide what policy to use. The implementation lag is the time it takes to put the selected policy into action. The effectiveness lag is the time it takes for the policy to affect the economy once it is implemented. The problem created by these lags is that natural market forces may already be in operation by the time a discretionary policy takes effect. Consequently, the problem the discretionary policy was created to solve may no longer exist, and the discretionary policy may generate new problems.

5. If the economy is not self-correcting and a passive approach is adopted, then the economy will persist in disequilibrium indefinitely. With a contractionary gap, the cost will be lost output and higher unemployment in each period. With an expansionary gap, the cost is ongoing inflation. On the other hand, if an active policy is pursued when a passive policy is called for, then the economy is likely to experience wider swings in the expansion–contraction cycle. For example, if the economy is in a recession and the government pursues expansionary policies, there is a lag before they take effect. If the economy is already moving out of the recession when the expansionary policies take effect, then the economy may overheat, causing greater inflationary pressures than would have occurred normally.

6. Rational expectations theory assumes that people learn from observation how the economy functions and how government policymakers respond to various economic problems. People then take actions based on their expectations about the future state of the economy and the likely policy responses. The theory does not imply that the public never makes a mistake. It does imply that the public will not continually be surprised by policymakers.

7. The time inconsistency problem refers to the situation when policymakers have an incentive to announce one policy in the hope that people will adjust their expectations in a certain way, and then pursue a different policy. The various lags associated with discretionary policy and the desire of politicians to get reelected contribute to the problem.

8. In the graph, the economy is initially at point *e*. If the government decides that it is going to reduce the deficit, it must either reduce government spending or increase taxes, either of

which reduces consumption spending. In either case, aggregate demand falls to *AD*′. For *AD*′ to be consistent with potential output of $5 trillion, the price level must fall to 95. For this to happen, the public must expect lower prices and cause the short-run aggregate supply curve to shift to *SRAS*(95). The new equilibrium would be *e*′.

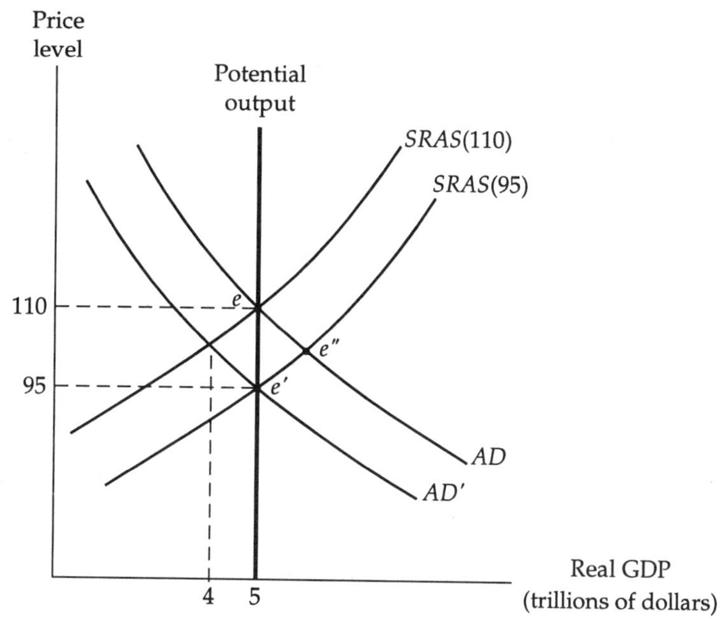

If the public believes the government policy will take effect but the government fails to implement its policy, the economy moves to *e*″. Eventually, the public adjusts to the actual economic conditions; the short-run aggregate supply curve returns to its original position, and the economy is in equilibrium at *e*. The next time the government announces a policy of deficit reduction, the public is less likely to believe that it will actually be implemented. Consequently, the short-run aggregate supply curve does not shift. If the aggregate demand curve does shift to *AD*′, output is reduced to $4 trillion and unemployment rises. To return the economy to potential output, the government must maintain its policy for a long time until natural forces adjust or allow deficit spending to increase again.

9. If previous policymakers have often failed to follow through on their stated policies, the public is unlikely to believe the policy statements of future policymakers. Consequently, the new policymakers must be persistent in their selected policies. It will take time for the public to believe and trust them. Further, it will take only a few cases of inconsistent behavior for the policymakers to lose their credibility. The success of stabilization policy depends on the public's view of policymakers' credibility because the public's expectations determine the behavior of the short-run aggregate supply curve.

10. A policy rule is the opposite of discretionary behavior. It establishes a specified policy response to specific economic conditions, or even fixes policy on a permanent basis. The purpose of such rules is to reduce discretionary behavior on the part of policymakers on the assumption that such discretionary policies are actually destabilizing.

11. If the relationship depicted by the Phillips curve does exist, then policymakers can choose the combination of unemployment and inflation that they think is optimal for the economy and use an active discretionary policy to achieve that combination.

12. The natural rate hypothesis states that in the long run the economy tends toward the rate of unemployment that is consistent with the economy's potential output. Hence, attempts to reduce the unemployment rate below the natural rate through increases in aggregate demand must fail in the long run.

13. Both versions of the natural rate hypothesis argue that there is not a long-run tradeoff between inflation and unemployment. The weak version admits there is a tradeoff in the short run, whereas the strong version argues that the short-run reductions in unemployment from a given increase in inflation get smaller over time as people learn what policymakers are doing.

14. The intersections of various aggregate demand curves with a given short-run aggregate supply curve can generate a short-run Phillips curve; movement along a long-run aggregate supply curve generates different inflation–unemployment combinations along a long-run Phillips curve. The short-run aggregate supply curve slopes upward, whereas the long-run aggregate supply curve is vertical at the economy's potential output. The shapes of both the short-run aggregate supply curve and the short-run Phillips curve result from the public's being misinformed about the true inflation rate. The natural rate hypothesis states that in the long run the economy moves to the natural rate of unemployment, which is the rate of unemployment that would prevail if the economy operated at its potential output. Hence, the long-run Phillips curve is vertical at the natural rate of unemployment.

    Advocates of a passive approach believe that the transition from the short run to the long run occurs fairly quickly; advocates of an active approach believe that it takes a long time for the market to achieve potential output on its own. Hence, advocates of an active approach urge the use of discretionary policy to maintain the economy at its potential output.

15. Real business cycle theory holds that fluctuations in real GDP are caused by real shocks to the economy. Wages are assumed to be very flexible so that unemployment is always at its natural rate. The aggregate supply curve is vertical. This theory does not advocate an active policy.

CHAPTER 17

Budgets, Deficits, and Public Policy

I. INTRODUCTION

The federal budget deficit has been an important topic of public policy debates in recent years. In this chapter, we examine the government budget process and how the deficits have grown in recent years. The chapter also discusses the effects of the national debt and examines some of the policy prescriptions that have been offered to control the deficit.

II. OUTLINE

1. The Federal Budget Process. The government budget is a plan for government expenditures and revenues for a specified period. The U.S. federal government's fiscal year runs from October 1 to September 30. About one-third of the federal budget is spent directly on goods and services.

    1.1 The Presidential Role in the Budget Process
    - a. The president was not involved in the federal budget process prior to 1921.
    - b. The Budget and Accounting Act of 1921 changed the budget procedure to include the president.
    - c. The act created the Office of Management and Budget (OMB) to help the president develop budget proposals.
    - d. The Employment Act of 1946 created the Council of Economic Advisers to assist the president in formulating fiscal policy.
    - e. Now the president presents a budget proposal to Congress in January of each year.

    1.2 The Congressional Role in the Budget Process
    - a. Expenditure decisions often are made in two stages: authorization and appropriations.
    - b. Congress passes a budget resolution, which presents an overall strategy that is supposed to establish the framework within which committees make spending and revenue decisions.
    - c. The difference between expenditures and revenues is one measure of the budget's fiscal impact, since a rising deficit is expected to stimulate aggregate demand and a rising surplus is expected to dampen aggregate demand.

    1.3 Problems with the Budget Process
    - a. Congress passes continuing resolutions instead of making budget decisions.
    - b. Overlapping committee authority: several committees have authority over most budget sections.
    - c. The lengthy budget process hampers fiscal policy: budget preparations begin more than a year and a half before the budget goes into effect.
    - d. Much of the budget is difficult to control; about three-fourths of the budget is in categories determined by existing law.

e. The minute detail in the budget reduces the executive branch's ability to respond to changing economic conditions.

1.4 Suggested Budget Reforms
- a. Convert the annual budget into a biennial budget.
- b. Consolidate authorization and appropriation.
- c. Simplify the budget by concentrating on major groupings and eliminating line items.

2. Federal Budget Deficits

2.1 Rationale for Deficits
- a. Some outlays are for investments that should be financed over time. However, a capital budget is not part of the federal budget process.
- b. Before the Great Depression, only wars generated federal budget deficits.
- c. Keynes developed a rationale for deficits to stimulate the economy in recessions.

2.2 Budget Philosophies and Deficits
- a. Annually balanced budget
  - (1) The budget should be balanced every year.
  - (2) This view prevailed prior to World War II.
- b. Cyclically balanced budget
  - (1) The government should run deficits during recessions and surpluses during expansions.
  - (2) The budget should be balanced over the business cycle.
- c. Functional finance
  - (1) Use the budget to ensure that the economy produces at its potential output and do not worry about balancing the budget.
  - (2) It appears that this approach has been used in the United States since World War II.
- d. The structural deficit is an estimate of what the deficit would be if the economy were producing its potential output. The larger the structural deficit, the more stimulative the fiscal policy.

2.3 Deficits in the 1980s
- a. U.S. federal budget deficits increased substantially in the 1980s.
- b. The government cut taxes but did not cut spending.
- c. The recession in the early 1980s also created larger deficits.

2.4 Deficit Reduction Measures
- a. The 1990 Budget Enforcement Act (BEA) was a package of spending cuts and tax measures designed to reduce the deficit.
- b. A tax increase on high income earners was passed in 1993.

2.5 *Case Study:* The 1996 Federal Budget Deadlock

2.6 Why Deficits? Why Now?
- a. Public choice theory suggests that politicians seeking reelection have a tendency to pass expenditure bills but not tax bills.
- b. Some argue that prior to the Great Depression it was considered immoral to run deficits. Keynes provided an economic justification for deficits.

2.7 The Relationship between Deficits and Other Aggregate Variables
   a. There is no necessary relationship between deficits and various measures of economic performance such as the price level, interest rates, or real output.
   b. A deficit resulting from automatic stabilizers is associated with lower levels of prices and real output, which reduce the demand for money. The effect on the interest rate will depend on the size of the decrease in the demand for money relative to the increase in the supply of government securities sold to finance the deficit.
   c. A deficit resulting from discretionary fiscal policy is associated with higher levels of prices, real output, and interest rates.

2.8 Crowding Out and Crowding In
   a. Crowding out occurs when government borrowing causes interest rates to increase so that private business investment declines.
   b. The extent of crowding out is a matter of debate.
   c. In some situations, government borrowing could stimulate investment, which is called "crowding in."

2.9 The Twin Deficits
   a. In part as a result of relatively high U.S. interest rates, the U.S. balance of trade has been in deficit throughout the 1980s; this means foreigners have accumulated dollars.
   b. Foreigners have purchased U.S. assets, including government securities; this process helped fund the federal budget deficit.

2.10 Deficits in Other Countries. In terms of deficit as a share of GDP, the United States is about in the middle of all industrial countries.

3. The Ballooning National Debt. Whereas the federal deficit is a flow variable, the national debt is a stock variable that measures the net accumulation of past deficits. The total debt includes U.S. Treasury securities purchased by various federal agencies, which is debt the federal government owes to itself. Generally, debt figures exclude debt held by government agencies and focus on debt held by the public.

3.1 The National Debt since World War II
   a. In nominal terms, the U.S. national debt increased slowly from the end of World War II until 1974 and then increased very rapidly.
   b. In real terms, the U.S. national debt decreased from the end of World War II until 1974 and then increased.

3.2 Debt Relative to GDP
   a. National debt expressed as a percentage of GDP measures debt compared to the economy's production and income.
   b. U.S. national debt as a percentage of GDP decreased from the end of World War II until 1980 and then increased.

3.3 An International Perspective on National Debt. In terms of the level of its debt as a percentage of GDP, the United States is about in the middle of all industrial countries.

3.4 Interest Payments on the Debt
   a. Gross interest payments are determined by the size of the national debt and the interest rate on the debt.
   b. Interest on public debt in 1990 represented about 15 percent of the U.S. federal budget.

3.5 Interest Payments and Seigniorage
  a. Net interest payments are lower by amounts returned to the U.S. Treasury by the Fed.
  b. Most of the interest earned by the Fed is turned over to the Treasury.

3.6 Who Bears the Burden of the Debt?
  a. Foreign Ownership of Debt
    (1) The inflow of credit from abroad keeps interest rates lower than they would be otherwise.
    (2) The increased reliance on foreigners increases the burden of the debt to future generations because future debt service payments no longer stay in the United States.
  b. Crowding Out and Capital Formation
    (1) Crowding out leads to reduced domestic investment and net exports because of higher interest rates and appreciation of the dollar.
    (2) The long-run effect of crowding out is to reduce total investment as well as the portion of investment funded by domestic residents.
    (3) The opportunity cost of crowding out depends on the use to which the government puts the funds it invests.
    (4) If the government uses the funds to make capital investments that are productive, then there may be no harmful effects on the economy's capital formation from crowding out.

3.7 *Case Study:* An Intergenerational View of Deficits and Debt

4. Reducing the Deficit. Some believe that taxes must be increased to reduce the deficit. Others argue that an outside force is needed to control the budget process and reduce deficit spending.

4.1 Line-Item Veto. One proposal to control spending is the line-item veto, suggested on the grounds that the president is less susceptible to special-interest pressure than senators and members of Congress.

4.2 Balanced Budget Amendment
  a. Some argue for a constitutional amendment that requires a balanced budget.
  b. Some are afraid that such an amendment would reduce the government's ability to deal with problems in the economy.
  c. Others argue that the amendment would be ineffective and that Congress would find ways around its restrictions.

III. DISCUSSION

The Federal Budget Process

Until this century, Congress handled the federal budget process, and the president was not involved. However, a number of measures have increased the president's role in the budget process, which has become very complex. In recent years, many have come to believe that it is out of control. As evidence these observers cite the increasing tendency of Congress to pass continuing resolutions instead of making specific budget decisions.

There are numerous problems with the current budget process. Several congressional committees have jurisdiction over the same budget items, so decisions require extensive committee deliberations. The budget process is very lengthy, and this makes fiscal policy less effective as a discretionary tool. Also, as noted, Congress has often relied on continuing resolutions that keep the government functioning but do not address the existing budget problems. The budget is very detailed and gives the executive branch little leeway in specifics while burdening the Congress with the detail. Finally, much of the budget is difficult to control because the expenditures are set by previous legislation.

Critics of the current budget process have offered suggestions for its reform. So that Congress spends less time on the budget, some have suggested adopting two-year budgets instead of annual budgets. However, this would limit the budget's usefulness as a tool of fiscal policy. Another suggestion is to combine the authorization and appropriation stages of the budget process. A third reform is to simplify the budget document by having Congress consider only major budget headings and leave specifics to the relevant government agencies.

Federal Budget Deficits

U.S. federal budget deficits, which have increased dramatically in recent years, have become a hotly debated topic. For much of the time since the publication of Keynes's *General Theory*, the U.S. government has attempted to use fiscal policy as a counter-cyclical discretionary tool. Prior to Keynes, the government attempted to balance the budget annually. Those who advocate a cyclically balanced budget would use fiscal policy to counter recessions and temper expansions. Such an approach allows deficit spending during recessions and has the government accumulate a surplus in expansions. The goal is to balance the budget over the business cycle instead of every single year. It appears the U.S. government has actually followed a philosophy of functional finance, in which fiscal policy is used to keep the economy at or close to its potential output. Since the actual budget fluctuates automatically as the economy moves through the business cycle, the *structural deficit* is a better measure of the stimulative role of fiscal policy.

Some critics of the recent budget deficits argue that deficits are associated with inflation or rising interest rates. Neither economic theory nor empirical evidence supports a consistent link between government deficits and other aggregate variables, however. The relationship varies depending on whether a rising deficit is due to automatic stabilizers or discretionary fiscal policy.

The Ballooning National Debt

A federal budget deficit adds to the national debt. In nominal terms, the U.S. national debt grew slowly between 1946 and 1974, after which it grew at a more accelerated rate. When national debt figures are deflated to account for inflation or taken as a percentage of GDP, a different picture emerges. The national debt in real terms and as a percentage of GDP declined from the end of World War II to 1974 and has increased since 1974. The national debt is not something that is necessarily worrisome. Families undertake debt for many reasons. A family that borrows to buy a house or to finance a college education is not considered foolish or spendthrift; a family that borrows extensively for dinners out and vacations is. Similarly, government borrowing may be worthwhile if the funds are spent on assets that enhance the productivity of the economy over many years, such as roads and education.

The national debt creates current expenditures for the government: interest payments. The importance of interest payments in the budget increased when inflation drove interest rates to record levels in the 1970s. But the interest payments actually paid to people overstate their importance in the budget. Since interest payments are income to the recipients, income taxes are paid on the payments. Seigniorage also makes net interest payments less than gross interest payments.

Deficits occur when current government expenditures exceed current tax receipts. As a result, the national debt increases, generating interest payments in future years. Thus, the national debt imposes burdens on future generations. Is this a problem? Again, there is debate concerning the answer. If government borrowing is used to finance the purchase of government investment goods, then the future productivity of the economy is enhanced, and the debt does not impose a burden on future generations. This is true even when government borrowing *crowds out* private investment, as long as the productivity of the government investment equals or exceeds the productivity of the private investment.

The U.S. federal deficit has been financed, in part, by the purchase of government securities by foreigners. As a result, U.S. interest rates have not increased as much as they would have otherwise. Increased foreign participation may increase the burden of the debt on future generations, however, since the future debt service payments will be paid to foreigners.

Reducing the Deficit

Several proposals for reducing the federal deficit have been offered in recent years. Recent administrations have lobbied for a line-item veto that would allow presidents to veto specific items on the budget without having to veto the entire budget. Some economists argue for the passage of a constitutional amendment that would require the federal government to maintain a balanced budget. They argue that such an amendment would provide the discipline necessary for Congress to refuse the requests of special-interest groups.

IV. LAGNIAPPE

Crowding Out and Foreign Capital

Crowding out of private investment occurs when government borrowing increases interest rates, thereby reducing private sector borrowing for investment spending. Have the huge U.S. deficits in recent years caused a lot of such crowding out? Probably not. World financial markets are very interrelated. A slight rise in the interest rate in the United States, other things constant, generally leads to an increase in foreign purchases of U.S. government securities. That is, the deficit has not been crowding out investment as much as it has increased the amount of the national debt held by foreigners.

Question to Think About: What problems might be associated with foreigners' owning so many government securities?

Deficits and Inflation

Exhibit 1 presents figures on the size of the U.S. federal budget deficit and U.S. inflation rates from 1960 through 1992. Through the 1960s and 1970s, there was some evidence of a positive relationship between deficits and inflation. In the 1980s, however, deficits rose to record levels and inflation fell from record levels. As the text points out, deficits are not systematically related to other aggregate variables.

Exhibit 1
Federal Deficits and Inflation Rates

Fiscal Year	Federal Surplus (+) or Deficit (-) ($ billions)	Federal Deficit/GDP (percent)	Inflation Rate (percent)
1960	+0.3	n/a	1.5
1961	-3.3	0.6	0.7
1962	-7.1	1.2	1.2
1963	-4.8	0.8	1.6
1964	-5.9	0.9	1.2
1965	-1.4	0.2	1.9
1966	-3.7	0.5	3.4
1967	-8.6	1.1	3.0
1968	-25.2	2.8	4.7
1969	+3.2	n/a	6.1
1970	-2.8	0.3	5.5
1971	-23.0	2.1	3.4
1972	-23.4	1.9	3.4
1973	-14.9	1.1	8.8
1974	-6.1	0.4	12.2
1975	-53.2	3.4	7.0
1976	-73.7	4.2	4.8
1977	-53.7	2.7	6.8
1978	-59.2	2.7	9.0
1979	-40.2	1.6	13.3
1980	-73.8	2.7	12.4
1981	-79.0	2.6	8.9
1982	-128.0	4.1	3.8
1983	-207.8	6.3	3.8
1984	-185.4	5.0	3.9
1985	-212.3	5.4	3.8
1986	-221.2	5.3	1.1
1987	-149.8	3.4	4.4
1988	-155.2	3.2	4.4
1989	-152.5	2.9	4.6
1990	-221.4	4.0	6.1
1991	-269.5	4.7	3.1
1992	-290.2	4.9	2.9

Source: *Economic Report of the President*, February 1993.

Question to Think About: Are the deficits likely to lead to higher inflation rates in the future?

V. KEY TERMS

Government budget
Fiscal year
Budget resolution
Continuing resolutions
Entitlement programs
Budget deficit
Biennial budget
Annually balanced budget
Cyclically balanced budget
Functional finance
Crowding out
Crowding in
National debt
Budget Enforcement Act
Line-item veto
Balanced budget amendment

VI. QUESTIONS

A. *Completion*

1. The government __________________ is a plan for government expenditures and revenues for a specified period, usually a year.

2. The Budget and Accounting Act of 1921 created the __________________ to help the president develop budget proposals.

3. The Council of Economic Advisers was created by the __________________ of 1946.

4. A __________________ resolution sets the framework that guides spending and revenue decisions for the new budget.

5. A rising __________________ is expected to stimulate aggregate demand.

6. In recent years, Congress has passed __________________ resolutions when budget decisions have not been made by the start of a new fiscal year.

7. The budget philosophy called __________________ does not attempt to balance the budget over any specific period of time.

8. A __________________ budget calls for budget deficits during recessions and budget surpluses during expansions.

9. The view before the Great Depression was that budget deficits were __________________.

10. __________________ occurs when government borrowing replaces private borrowing for investment.

11. The ability of government deficits to stimulate private investments is called __________________.

12. The __________________ is the net accumulation of past federal budget deficits.

13. Unlike the budgets of private firms, the U.S. federal budget does not include a __________________ budget.

14. A ________________ would allow the president to reject particular portions of the budget.

15. One proposed solution to continuing U.S. federal deficits is a ________________ amendment to the U.S. Constitution.

B. *True/False*

______ 1. During the nineteenth century and the early part of the twentieth century, the president had little power over the U.S. federal budget.

______ 2. In January of each year, Congress presents a budget proposal to the president for approval.

______ 3. Today authorization and appropriations are handled at the same time in the U.S. federal budget process.

______ 4. The current U.S. federal budget process is a lengthy one that hampers fiscal policy.

______ 5. The heads of U.S. government agencies have a lot of discretion in the allocation of funds within their departments.

______ 6. The U.S. federal budget treats capital expenditures differently from current expenditures.

______ 7. An annually balanced budget calls for spending reductions in recessions and spending increases during expansions.

______ 8. U.S. federal budget deficits increased with the tax cuts in the early 1980s even though federal spending fell sharply.

______ 9. Federal budget deficits have a consistently positive relation to inflation.

______ 10. Crowding out occurs when government borrowing raises interest rates, thereby reducing private investment spending or net exports.

______ 11. Crowding in refers to the situation when foreigners buy many of the bonds sold by the government to finance the deficit.

______ 12. The federal deficit is a flow variable, and the national debt is a stock variable.

______ 13. Although the U.S. national debt has grown larger in recent years, it has actually grown smaller as a percentage of GDP.

______ 14. The United States has a higher deficit-to-GDP ratio and a higher debt-to-GDP ratio than any other country except Italy.

______ 15. GDP must grow in real terms for the national debt as a percentage of GDP to decline.

______ 16. Some of the interest payments made by the U.S. federal government on its debt actually return to the U.S. Treasury.

______ 17. If crowding out occurs, then deficit spending must reduce the economy's long-run productive capacity.

______ 18. Increased borrowing by the federal government that leads to higher interest rates usually also leads to a reduction in net exports.

______ 19. Current law allows the president to make use of a line-item veto.

______ 20. A balanced budget amendment would make discretionary fiscal policy less useful as a tool for stabilizing the economy.

C. *Multiple Choice*

1. The portion of the federal budget that is spent directly on goods and services is approximately
   a. one-fifth.
   b. one-fourth.
   c. one-third.
   d. one-half.
   e. two-thirds.

2. The president's role in the U.S. federal budget process is to
   a. authorize the budget expenditures.
   b. appropriate the money for the budget expenditures.
   c. alter taxes to bring the budget into balance.
   d. develop the budget resolution to cover the budget process.
   e. none of the above

3. The budget has a congressional gestation period of approximately
   a. six weeks.
   b. three months.
   c. six months.
   d. nine months.
   e. one year.

4. Which of the following is a problem with the U.S. federal budget process?
   a. Congressional committees have overlapping authority.
   b. The budget process is a lengthy procedure.
   c. The budget is too detailed.
   d. The budget timetable tends to be ignored by Congress.
   e. all of the above

5. An advantage of a biennial budget is that
   a. it makes discretionary fiscal policy more effective.
   b. it would force Congress to quit using continuing resolutions.
   c. it would reduce the proportion of time spent by Congress on budgetary considerations.
   d. it would prevent the use of better long-range economic forecasts.
   e. none of the above

6. Prior to the Great Depression, budget deficits were usually associated with
   a. recessions.
   b. depressions.
   c. war.
   d. all of the above.
   e. none of the above.

7. The U.S. federal budget deficits of the 1980s were caused by
   a. the Reagan administration's efforts to stimulate the economy by using deficit financing.
   b. increases in military spending.
   c. tax cuts.
   d. b and c.
   e. none of the above.

8. A budget philosophy that advocates a deficit during recessions and a surplus during expansionary periods is known as
   a. an annually balanced budget.
   b. a cyclically balanced budget.
   c. functional finance.
   d. a structural budget.
   e. a biennial budget.

9. The relationships between deficits and inflation and deficits and unemployment are best described as
   a. positive.
   b. negative.
   c. positive for inflation and negative for unemployment.
   d. inconsistent.
   e. positive for inflation and nonexistent for unemployment.

10. Crowding out of private investment is more likely
    a. the more elastic the savings curve.
    b. the more foreigners are willing to buy U.S. securities.
    c. the greater the increase in the interest rate due to government borrowing.
    d. the deeper the economy is in a recession.
    e. all of the above

11. The impact on U.S. interest rates of the increasing size of the U.S. federal deficits in the 1980s was dampened by
    a. expansionary monetary policy.
    b. falling inflation.
    c. increased foreign purchases of U.S. government securities.
    d. rising military expenditures.
    e. income tax cuts.

12. The country with the biggest budget deficit relative to GDP in 1992 was
    a. the United States.
    b. Japan.
    c. Germany.
    d. France.
    e. Italy.

13. If the budget were balanced next year, the national debt would
    a. stay the same.
    b. increase.
    c. decrease.
    d. drop to zero.
    e. either stay the same or increase, but more information is needed to determine which.

14. If the federal government used conventional accounting practices, the deficit would
    a. be larger.
    b. be the same size.
    c. be smaller.
    d. be larger, but the net debt would be smaller.
    e. Any of the above is possible.

15. Net interest payments are smaller than gross interest payments because
    a. interest payments are tax deductible.
    b. the Fed pays a higher interest rate than the Treasury.
    c. the primary purpose of the Fed is to reduce the burden of the national debt.
    d. those who receive interest payments must pay taxes on them.
    e. b and d

16. The potential long-run effect of crowding out is
    a. a reduction in the spending multiplier.
    b. a reduction in the growth rate of the capital stock.
    c. to harm the economy's long-run productive capability.
    d. a reduction in the real interest rate.
    e. b and c.

17. U.S. government deficits can lead to reductions in U.S. net exports because
    a. the deficit is created by the government's buying goods that would otherwise be sold to foreigners.
    b. the borrowing increases interest rates, which causes the dollar to appreciate.
    c. the borrowing increases interest rates, which causes the dollar to depreciate.
    d. the borrowing increases interest rates, which causes investment spending to fall, causing net exports to fall.
    e. none of the above. The deficit has no effect on net exports.

18. Which of the following would reduce national debt as conventionally measured?
    a. selling Yellowstone National Park to private investors and using the proceeds to pay off government bonds
    b. canceling government job training programs and making employers pay for the programs
    c. reducing spending on highways
    d. all of the above
    e. none of the above

19. Which of the following are suggested methods of reducing U.S. federal deficits?
    a. selling off national parks
    b. line-item veto for the president
    c. an expansionary monetary policy
    d. biennial budgets
    e. all of the above

20. Critics of the balanced budget amendment to the U.S. Constitution assert that
    a. it would hamper autonomous fiscal policy.
    b. it would hamper discretionary fiscal policy.
    c. it would be too easy to bypass the intent of the amendment.
    d. the government would substitute direct regulation for government spending.
    e. all of the above

D. *Discussion Questions*

1. Describe the current U.S. federal budget process.

2. What problems are associated with the U.S. federal budget process? What solutions have been offered to these problems?

3. Which of the following government expenditures would likely enhance future productivity and why?
    a. spending to expand the interstate highway system
    b. an increase in farm subsidies
    c. an increase in government loans for education
    d. payments to construct a new missile system
    e. payments to dredge the Mississippi River

4. How does a cyclically balanced budget differ from functional finance?

5. What factors contributed to the large U.S. federal deficit in the 1980s?

6. What budget deficit reduction laws have been enacted recently? Have they been successful?

7. Why does the United States tend to have budget deficits? Why didn't the country often have deficits before World War II?

8. Is it accurate to state that deficits are a cause of inflation? Why or why not?

9. How are automatic stabilizers related to deficits?

10. Distinguish between crowding out and crowding in.

11. Describe what has happened to the U.S. national debt since the end of World War II.

12. Could the federal government reduce the deficit and save on future taxes by selling off some federal assets, such as national parks? Explain.

13. Why are net interest payments lower than gross interest payments on the U.S. national debt?

14. Why is crowding out not necessarily harmful to the economy's long-run productive capability?

15. Discuss some suggested methods of reducing the U.S. federal budget deficit.

VII. ANSWERS

A. *Completion*

1. budget
2. Office of Management and Budget
3. Employment Act
4. budget
5. deficit
6. continuing
7. functional finance
8. cyclical balance
9. immoral
10. Crowding out
11. crowding in
12. national debt
13. capital
14. line-item veto
15. balanced budget

B. *True/False*

1. True
2. False
3. False
4. True
5. False
6. False
7. True
8. False
9. False
10. True
11. False
12. True
13. False. The national debt has grown as a percentage of GDP since 1980.
14. False
15. False. Nominal GDP must grow faster than nominal debt.
16. True
17. False
18. True
19. False
20. True

C. *Multiple Choice*

1. c
2. e
3. d
4. e
5. c
6. c
7. d
8. b
9. d
10. c
11. c
12. e
13. a
14. c
15. d
16. e
17. b
18. d
19. b
20. e

D. *Discussion Questions*

1. The president initiates the budget process by submitting a budget to Congress in January. The budget reflects the president's spending proposals for the coming fiscal year. Congress then develops an overall budget strategy, which is expressed in a budget resolution, and establishes a timetable for making budget decisions. Various congressional committees and subcommittees assess the budget and recommend authorization of the budget items that come under their jurisdictions. Congress approves the entire budget. Once the president has accepted the budget, Congress then has to pass appropriations bills in order for spending to actually take place. If the budget process is not complete by October 1, Congress passes continuing resolutions to allow agencies to spend at the rate of the previous year's budget until a new budget is approved.

2. The overlapping authority of congressional committees makes it difficult to arrive at final budget figures. Further, the process takes so much time that it is difficult to use fiscal policy for stabilization purposes. Often the budget process breaks down, and Congress relies on continuing resolutions instead of making budget decisions by the October 1 deadline. Many believe the budget is too detailed. Finally, many of the items in the budget, such as entitlement programs, are beyond Congress's control. Suggested reforms include using a biennial budget instead of an annual budget, combining the authorization and appropriations stages of the process, and having Congress consider a broad budget plan, leaving it to the relevant government departments to work out budget details.

3. Expansion of the interstate highway system would probably enhance future productivity because the system is important to the country's transportation system. Similarly, increasing loans to college students and dredging the Mississippi would likely enhance future productivity—the former by increasing the productivity of the recipients of the loans and the latter by enhancing the Mississippi as a route for shipping. Increasing farm subsidies would not increase future productivity, as it would encourage current consumption. The impact of a new missile system is more complex. The missiles would not have the same effect on future productivity as the roads or loans but would be part of the national defense system, for which the federal government is responsible. Note that there is no guarantee that any of these items would in fact enhance future productivity. If the funds used would have been more productive in the private sector, the future productivity of the economy could be harmed rather than enhanced.

4. A cyclically balanced budget would allow deficits during recessions and surpluses during expansions, such that the budget would be balanced over the length of the business cycle. Functional finance strives to operate the economy at its potential output rather than to balance the federal budget.

5. The deficit grew as a result of tax cuts, increased government spending, and a recession.

6. The Budget Enforcement Act of 1990 was passed as a deficit reduction act, and a tax increase was enacted in 1993. In recent years, the deficit has fallen but is expected to increase again by the end of the decade.

7. The public choice model suggests that deficits occur because politicians seeking reelection have a greater incentive to pass expenditure bills than tax bills. Some believe that prior to the Great Depression, deficits were considered immoral, so the government did not generate

deficits. According to this view, Keynes's work showed that deficits could be useful in stabilizing the economy, so the national aversion to deficit spending faded.

8. Deficits do not cause inflation; they can be associated with rising inflation, disinflation, or falling prices. Deficits often rise automatically when aggregate demand falls and moves the economy into recession, which is usually a time when prices are falling or disinflation occurs. Alternatively, discretionary fiscal policy to increase aggregate demand leads to higher prices as the deficit is rising.

9. Automatic stabilizers are programs that increase the deficit during recessions and decrease the deficit during expansions. For example, during a recession unemployment increases, decreasing tax revenues and increasing government spending on unemployment benefits. During an expansion, the opposite occurs.

10. Crowding out occurs when government borrowing drives up interest rates and reduces private investment. Crowding in occurs when government borrowing stimulates the economy, which encourages private investment.

11. The national debt has increased since the end of World War II, especially since 1974. When measured in constant dollars, however, the national debt as a percentage of GDP declined between 1945 and 1974 and increased after 1974.

12. No. The durable assets of the federal government are part of the financial strength of the government. Selling them might reduce the deficit and the national debt as currently measured but would not generate savings to the government.

13. Interest payments received by individuals are treated as income and are subject to taxation. Thus, a portion of the interest payments made by the government will return to the government as taxes. Further, some of the interest payments are paid to the Fed, which returns the bulk of the interest it receives to the U.S. Treasury.

14. It is true that the private investment that is crowded out by government borrowing would have increased the future productive capability of the economy. Federal government spending may also increase the future productive capability of the economy, however. Only if the private investment crowded out would have been more productive than the investment made by the government will crowding out be harmful to the future productive capability of the economy.

15. The line-item veto and the balanced budget amendment have been proposed as methods of reducing the deficit. The line-item veto would permit the president to veto portions of the budget without having to veto the entire budget. Advocates believe that the president would be less susceptible to pressure by special-interest groups than are members of Congress. A balanced budget amendment would require a balanced budget. Some believe that this would hamper the government's ability to stabilize the economy; others believe it would be ineffective. Proponents argue that it is necessary to counter the pressure that special-interest groups put on Congress.

CHAPTER 18

International Trade

I. INTRODUCTION

This chapter examines trade among nations. Given the growing importance of international trade, you should understand the forces that determine patterns of trade.

II. OUTLINE

1. The Gains from Trade

   1.1 A Profile of Imports and Exports
   a. Countries' levels of involvement in international trade differ.
   b. U.S. exports are about 12 percent of GDP.
   c. The main exports of the United States are high-technology manufactured products and agricultural products.
   d. The main imports of the United States are manufactured goods, petroleum products, and agricultural products.

   1.2 Production Possibilities without Trade
   a. In the absence of trade, a country's consumption possibilities are determined by its production possibilities.
   b. A country's possible production combinations can be portrayed graphically.

   1.3 Consumption Possibilities Based on Comparative Advantage
   a. Each country specializes in the product for which its opportunity cost is lowest relative to other countries.
   b. Two countries can each consume more by trading than they could before trading when the terms of trade are based on the two countries' opportunity costs.
   c. Total world production of each good increases if each country specializes in producing the good for which it has a comparative advantage.
   d. The exchange of goods between two countries yields a surplus to both consumers and producers.

   1.4 Reasons for International Specialization
   a. People expect to benefit when they engage in trade.
   b. Exchange can benefit those involved when
      (1) there are differences in resource endowments
      (2) there are differences in tastes
      (3) there are economies of scale

2. Trading on the World Market

2.1 What If World Price Is above Domestic Equilibrium Price?

a. If the world price of steel rises above the domestic equilibrium price, then domestic production increases and consumption decreases.
b. The difference between production and consumption is exported to other countries.

2.2 What If World Price Is Below the Domestic Equilibrium Price?

a. If the world price is below the domestic equilibrium price, the quantity of steel demanded in the United States is greater than the quantity supplied.
b. The difference between consumption and production is imported from other countries.

2.3 The Rest of the World. Imports and exports of other countries also vary with price.

2.4 Determining the World Price

a. The world price of steel is determined by international supply and demand.
b. *World price* is established at the level where total exports of the good equal total imports.

2.5 Consumer and Producer Surplus

a. Market exchange usually yields a surplus, or a bonus, to both producers and consumers.
b. Consumer surplus and producer surplus are affected by international trade.

2.6 The Net Effect of Trade on Social Welfare

a. The net change in social welfare is determined by summing the changes in consumer and producer surpluses.
b. The gain in consumer surplus resulting from the lower price in the importing country more than offsets the reduction in producer surplus generated by the lower price.
c. In the exporting country, the gain in producer surplus resulting from a higher price more than offsets the reduction in consumer surplus generated by the higher price.

3. Trade Restrictions

3.1 Tariffs

a. A *tariff* is a tax on imports or exports.
    (1) A *specific tariff* is a lump-sum tariff per unit of a good.
    (2) An *ad valorem tariff* is a percentage of the cost of the imports at the port of entry.
b. Tariffs generate higher prices for domestic producers of goods that compete with imports.
c. Consumers are harmed by tariffs; domestic producers whose products compete with imports benefit from tariffs.
d. The loss in consumer surplus from tariffs is greater than the increase in producer surplus and government revenue from tariffs.
e. Tariffs redistribute income from consumers to producers and government.

3.2 Import Quotas

a. An *import quota* is a legal limit on the quantity of a particular commodity that can be imported per year.
b. Tariffs and effective quotas have similar effects.
c. An effective quota limits imports and raises domestic price.

d. If a tariff and an effective quota have the same effect on price, then they result in the same quantity demanded, the same loss in consumer surplus, and the same increase in producer surplus for domestic firms.
e. The difference between a quota and a tariff is that the government obtains revenue with tariffs, whereas those with the right to export gain revenues with quotas.

3.3 Other Trade Restrictions
a. Free trade is restricted by government subsidies to export firms and low-interest loans to foreign buyers.
b. Other rules and regulations, such as domestic content requirements, can be used to discriminate against foreign producers.

3.4 Freer Trade by Multilateral Agreement
a. The General Agreement on Tariffs and Trade (GATT) is an international treaty to reduce trade barriers.
b. Tariffs have fallen sharply since World War II due to GATT.

3.5 *Case Study:* The World Trade Organization

3.6 Common Markets. Some countries join together into common markets in order to take advantage of free trade with other countries.

4. Arguments for Trade Restrictions

4.1 National Defense Argument
a. Certain industries are essential in wartime so they must be kept viable.
b. Many industries try to use this argument even though their military application is often nebulous.
c. Government subsidies to domestic producers would be more efficient than import restrictions.

4.2 Infant Industry Argument
a. Emerging domestic industries need temporary protection so they can compete with mature industries in other countries until they can exploit economies of scale.
b. Among the problems with this rationale are the fact that it is difficult to identify industries with the potential to become competitive and the fact that it is possible that protection itself will foster inefficiencies so that protected industries will not mature.

4.3 Antidumping Argument
a. *Dumping* is the sale of a commodity abroad for less than its domestic price.
b. Predatory dumping by foreign firms may deter domestic firms from entering an industry.

4.4 Jobs and Income Argument
a. Some foreign countries are able to compete because of low wages.
b. The high wages in the United States reflect the greater productivity of U.S. labor.

4.5 Declining Industries Argument
a. Tariffs can be used to ease the transition of domestic industries that are in decline.
b. If tariffs are imposed for this reason, care must be taken to ensure that the protection is not so great as to encourage new investment in the industry.
c. Wage subsidies or special tax breaks can be used instead of import restrictions.

4.6 Problems with Protection
   a. Protecting one industry often leads to protecting other industries because of the need to counteract the effects of higher prices in the protected industry on the other industries.
   b. Costs of rent seeking also are associated with protection.
   c. Policing protective arrangements can be costly.

4.7 *Case Study:* Enforcing Trade Restrictions

5. Conclusion. Losers from trade restrictions include consumers, exporting industries, and businesses that use the same resources as the protected industries. Winners from trade restrictions include the domestic producers of goods that compete with imports and, in the case of quotas, those who have secured rights to import a good.

III. DISCUSSION

The Gains from Trade

People exchange goods with those in other nations for the same reasons they exchange goods with other people in their own nation—because they believe they will be better off as a result. Individuals gain by specializing in the production of one thing, selling their output for money, and using the money to buy the goods and services they want. Similarly, nations specialize in production and sell the goods they specialize in for goods in which they do not specialize. There is one difference between individuals who specialize and nations that specialize. Individuals often specialize completely and produce none of the goods they buy; nations often produce some of almost all goods but not enough to satisfy domestic demand for some goods.

Suppose a worker in the United States can produce either 10 units of wheat or 5 units of cloth per day, and a worker in Britain can produce either 5 units of wheat or 3 units of cloth per day. The U.S. worker is more productive than the British worker in either case, so the United States has an absolute advantage in producing both commodities. However, trade is based on comparative, not absolute, advantage. The opportunity cost of a unit of wheat in the United States is 1/2 unit of cloth, and the opportunity cost of a unit of cloth is 2 units of wheat. In Britain, the opportunity cost of a unit of wheat is 3/5 unit of cloth, and the opportunity cost of a unit of cloth is 5/3 units of wheat. Hence, the opportunity cost of wheat is lower in the United States than in Britain ($1/2 < 3/5$), and the opportunity cost of cloth is lower in Britain than in the United States ($5/3 < 2$). The United States has a comparative advantage in wheat and Britain has a comparative advantage in cloth.

The different opportunity costs in the two countries mean that world production of wheat and cloth can increase if each country specializes in the commodity that it can produce more cheaply. If the United States produces 1 less unit of cloth, it can produce 2 additional units of wheat. If Britain produces 1 less unit of wheat, it can produce 5/3 additional units of cloth. So the United States produces 1 less unit of cloth, Britain produces an additional 5/3 units of cloth, and, on net, there is 2/3 unit of cloth more than before. Similarly, Britain produces 1 less unit of wheat, but the United States has produced 2 additional units of wheat. On net, the world now has 1 additional unit of wheat and 2/3 additional unit of cloth.

Since world production is greater when each country specializes, it is possible for residents of each country to consume more with trade than without. Suppose each country has 100 workers (and consumers). Exhibit 1 presents the production possibilities schedule for each country, and Exhibit 2 illustrates the production possibilities frontier (PPF) of each. The PPF for the United States is line *AB*, with a slope equal to the opportunity cost of cloth in the United States, and the PPF for Britain is line *CD*, with a slope equal to the opportunity cost of cloth in Britain. The price of a unit of cloth in the United States is 2 units of wheat, but the price of cloth in England is 5/3 units of wheat. Trade is beneficial to both as long as they trade cloth at a price that is between the domestic prices without trade. That is, both can benefit if wheat can be exchanged for cloth at a rate that is more than 1. 67 (5/3) but less than 2.

Exhibit 1

Production Possibilities Schedules

			United States			
Wheat	1,000	800	600	400	200	0
Cloth	0	100	200	300	400	500
			Britain			
Wheat	500	400	300	200	100	0
Cloth	0	60	120	180	240	300

Exhibit 2

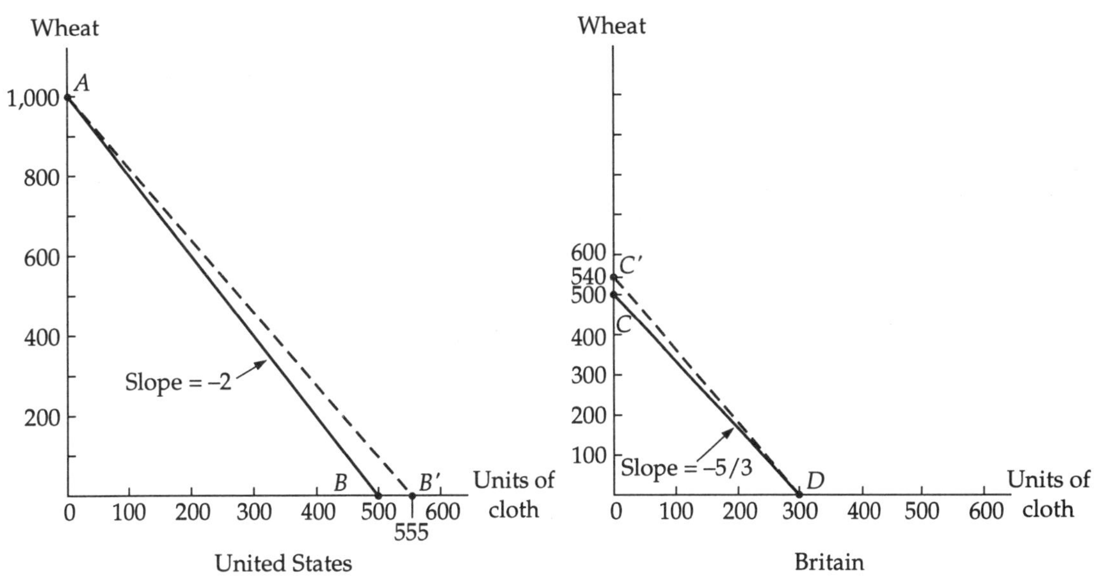

Suppose the exchange ratio, or *terms of trade*, is 1.8 units of wheat per unit of cloth. Without trade, in the United States 2 units of wheat had to be given up to get a unit of cloth. Now the United States can completely specialize and produce 1,000 units of wheat, and exchange wheat for cloth at a rate of 1.8 instead of 2. Exhibit 3 presents the consumption possibilities schedules when the rate of exchange is 1.8 units of wheat for 1 unit of cloth and the United States produces wheat while Britain produces cloth. Exhibit 2 also shows the consumption possibilities frontiers: *AB′* in the United States and *C′D* in Britain. Each country is able to consume more of both commodities than it could when it did not trade.

Exhibit 3

Consumption Possibilities Schedules
(Terms of trade = 1.8 units of wheat for 1 unit of cloth)

			United States				
Wheat	1,000	800	600	400	200	0	
Cloth	0	111	222	333	444	555	
			Britain				
Wheat	540	450	360	270	180	90	0
Cloth	0	50	100	150	200	250	300

Exchange among nations can be beneficial when the nations involved differ in resource endowments. Resources are not equally distributed among countries. Some countries have more oil than others; other countries have more skilled labor. Countries with a relatively large supply of skilled labor have a comparative advantage in producing goods that require skilled labor. Exchange can also be beneficial if there are differences in tastes among nations. Further, exchange can occur if there are economies of scale so that specialization generates lower production costs.

Trading on the World Market

The world demand and supply of a product determine the *world price* of the product. For example, Exhibits 4 and 5 in the text illustrate how domestic supply and demand for steel in two countries are related to world supply and demand and to the quantities imported and exported. Without trade, the equilibrium price for steel in Japan would be $100 per ton and the equilibrium price in the United States would be $150 per ton. At a price of $150 per ton, the quantity supplied in Japan exceeds the quantity demanded; at a price of $100 per ton in the United States, the quantity demanded exceeds the quantity supplied. Any price below $150 per ton causes the United States to import steel. Any price greater than $100 per ton causes Japan to export steel. Hence, the world price for steel will fall between $100 and $150 per ton, and Japan will export steel to the United States.

Exhibit 4 shows how the world price of wheat is determined. Panel (a) shows the U.S. supply and demand curves for wheat; panel (c) shows the British supply and demand curves for wheat. The domestic equilibrium price in the United States is $2.00, indicated by point *j*. Panel (b) shows the import and export curves of each country. At a price of $2.00, the United States does not import or export any wheat, so point *k* is equivalent to equilibrium point *j* in panel (a). Similarly, point *n* in panel (b) is at the British domestic equilibrium price and is equivalent to point *m* in panel (c). At a price of $3.00, the quantity of wheat supplied in the United States exceeds the quantity demanded by the distance *ab*. Hence, the United States is willing to export this amount of wheat, which is represented in panel (b) by the distance *cd*. At this price, Britain is willing to import wheat in the quantity given by distance *ef* in panel (c), which also equals distance *cd* in panel (b). The world price is $3.00, and the United States exports wheat to England.

Exhibit 4

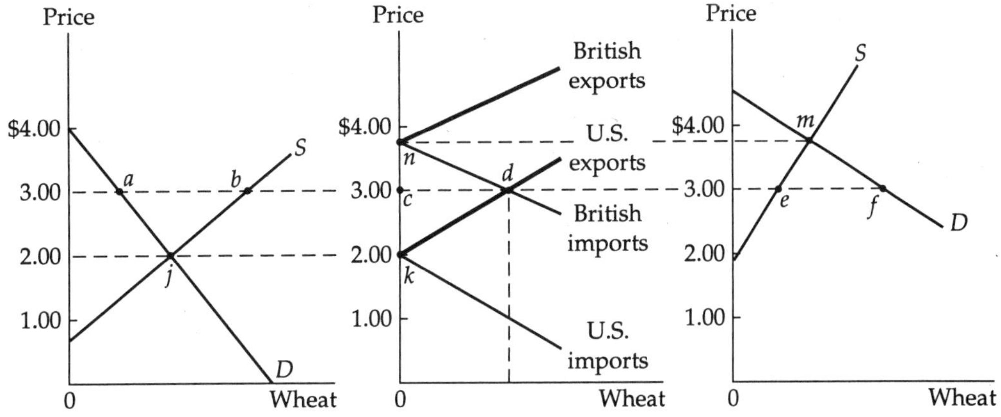

(a) U.S. supply and demand (b) Imports and exports (c) British supply and demand

Each country gains as a result of the trade. In the United States, the gain to producers from the higher U.S. price exceeds the loss to consumers by the area indicated by triangle *ajb*. The gain to British consumers from the lower price in Britain exceeds the loss to British wheat producers by the area indicated by triangle *emf*.

Trade Restrictions

Even though the gains from trade exceed the losses from trade, restrictions on trade are ubiquitous. The two major types of trade restrictions are import *tariffs* and import *quotas*. Both have the effect of raising price in the domestic economy above the world price. A tariff raises price directly, since an import tariff is a tax on imports. Import quotas raise prices indirectly by restricting the quantity of imports. Their effects are almost identical to those of a tariff.

Exhibit 5 illustrates the effects on imports of tariffs and effective quotas. Domestic demand and supply of cloth are represented by *D* and *S*, respectively. The world price, $5.00, is below the domestic equilibrium price, so in the absence of trade restrictions the relevant supply curve is mnS_w. It intersects the demand curve at point *v*, so domestic quantity demanded is 6,000 units, and 2,000 units is the quantity supplied by U.S. cloth producers. The United States imports 4,0,00 units of cloth. A specific tariff adds $1.00 to the world price, so the new domestic price is $6.00, and the new supply curve is $mn'S'_w$. Quantity demanded falls to 5,000 units, the amount of cloth produced by domestic firms increases to 3,000 units, and imports fall to 2,000 units. Instead of a tariff, the government could have imposed a quota and achieved the same result. A quota equal to 2,000 units of cloth causes the supply curve to shift to $mnrS'$. In other words, the supply curve shifts out by the quota limit at the world price of $5.00. It intersects domestic demand at *f*, which implies a price of $6.00. Domestic production increases from 2,000 to 3,000 units, and domestic consumption falls from 6,000 to 5,000 units.

Exhibit 5

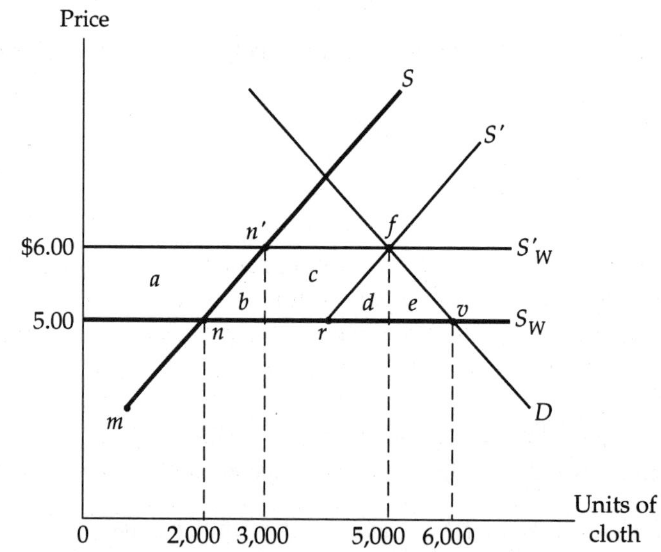

The increase in price due to the tariff (or quota) makes consumers worse off. Consumer surplus falls by areas *a*, *b*, *c*, *d*, and *e*. Some of the loss to consumers is transferred to other members of society, but the rest of the loss to consumers represents a deadweight loss to society. In Exhibit 5, area *a* represents a transfer of surplus from consumers to domestic producers and areas *c* and *d* represent revenue received by the government as the result of a tariff. (In the case of a quota, areas *c* and *d* represent a transfer from domestic consumers to those who obtain the right to import cloth.) The remaining areas, *b* and *e*, represent deadweight losses to society of the tariff (or quota). Clearly, the losses from the trade restrictions exceed the gains from the restrictions.

Arguments for Trade Restrictions

Arguments for trade restrictions are generally expressed in terms of national welfare. Proponents of trade restrictions justify them by using national defense, infant industry, and antidumping arguments. In recent years, proponents in the United States have argued that restrictions are needed to protect U.S. labor from cheap foreign labor. Wages in the United States are considerably higher than wages in many less developed nations, and those in favor of trade restrictions fear that U.S. labor cannot compete with the foreign labor. However, this argument ignores the reason for the higher U.S. wages: labor in the United States is more productive than labor in less developed nations. Thus, many goods can still be produced at lower cost in the United States.

IV. LAGNIAPPE

The Cost of Automobile Quotas

Robert Crandall attempted to estimate the cost to U.S. consumers of import quotas on Japanese autos. He calculated the difference between the average price of autos with the quotas and the average price without the quotas. He found that the quotas added approximately $235 to the price of a car in 1981 and 1982, and $829 in 1983. He also estimated the number of jobs saved in the U.S. auto industry because of quotas and concluded that the cost to consumers per job saved was nearly $160,000 per year.

(See Robert W. Crandall, "Import Quotas and the Automobile Industry: The Costs of Protection," *The Brookings Review*, Summer 1984: 8-16.)

Question to Think About: Can you think of ways to help auto workers that might be less expensive than using import quotas?

Economists, Tariffs, and Influence

George Stigler, a winner of the Nobel Prize in economics, has argued that the continued use of tariffs is proof that economists have no influence on policy. Since virtually all economists believe that free trade is preferable to protection, and since all countries decide to protect a large portion of their economies, politicians must not be paying attention to economists.

Given that tariffs and quotas do more harm than good, why do they continue to be used? Free trade does not benefit all members of society. In particular, it harms those who work in industries that compete with lower-priced foreign goods. The owners and workers in the industries that face considerable competition from abroad lobby their representatives for help. Those who are harmed tend to be harmed a great deal, even though the number of people harmed may not be large relative to the total population. Consumers are major beneficiaries of free trade. However, each individual consumer receives relatively small benefits from free trade in any particular industry. Consumers are unlikely to lobby their representatives concerning tariff legislation. Consequently, the industry groups lobby harder than consumers, and the tariff legislation passes.

Question to Think About: Are there groups that might lobby effectively against tariffs?

V. KEY TERMS

Consumption possibilities schedule
Autarky
Comparative advantage
Terms of trade
World price
Tariff
Import quota
GATT
Most-favored-nation clause
Common markets
Dumping
Rent seeking
World Trade Organization (WTO)

VI. QUESTIONS

A. *Completion*

1. The two main types of exports from the United States are ________________ and ________________.

2. In the absence of trade, a country's production possibilities schedule is also its ________________ possibilities schedule.

3. National self-sufficiency is called ________________.

4. Trade is based on ________________ advantage rather than on ________________ advantage because gains can be made from specialization and trade whenever relative production costs of two goods in two countries differ.

5. The ________________ must lie between the no-trade equilibrium prices in two countries.

6. The only constraint on trade is that, for each good, total world ________________ must equal total world ________________.

7. ________________ is the difference between the actual sum producers receive for the quantity traded and the minimum sum they would accept for the quantity traded.

8. Countries can benefit from trade when there are differences in ________________ or differences in tastes.

9. Countries can gain from trade if production is subject to ________________ so that the per-unit cost of production falls as a country specializes in a good.

10. The ________________ shows the quantity exported by a country at prices above the no-trade equilibrium price.

11. A tariff on oil of $10 a barrel is a(n) ________________ tariff.

12. A(n) ________________ is a legal limit on the quantity of a commodity that can be imported into a country.

13. Tariff reductions granted to one country must be granted to all other trading members of GATT under the ________________ clause.

14. Domestic firms may not find entry into an industry attractive if foreign producers are ________________.

15. The cost of protection includes the deadweight loss arising from the higher domestic prices and the cost of ________________.

B. *True/False*

______ 1. Foreign trade is more important to the United States than to most of the countries in western Europe.

______ 2. The majority of U.S. imports are manufactured consumer goods.

______ 3. Under autarky, each country can concentrate on producing those goods and services that involve the least opportunity costs.

______ 4. A country can have a comparative advantage in all goods.

______ 5. If wheat and cloth are the only goods under consideration and the production costs of wheat in terms of cloth are less in the United States than in mythical Izodia, then the production costs of cloth are less in Izodia than in the United States.

______ 6. All countries can benefit if countries specialize in producing the goods for which they are the least-cost producers.

______ 7. Market exchange usually benefits one country at the expense of the other country.

______ 8. Differences in resource endowments generate differences in costs of production, which lead to trade.

______ 9. A country will import a good for which the world price is above the domestic equilibrium price.

______ 10. An excess demand for a commodity at the world price indicates that a country has a comparative advantage in producing that commodity.

______ 11. The gains from trade to an importing nation tend just to offset the losses from trade to an exporting nation, so the world is neither better nor worse off.

______ 12. A tariff raises the price of the good to consumers, but a quota does not.

______ 13. Tariff revenue represents a net loss to a society.

______ 14. Each member of GATT has agreed to treat all other member nations equally with respect to trade.

______ 15. The effect of an import quota is to redistribute income from consumers to producers and to impose losses on consumers that are not transferred to anyone.

______ 16. Consumers who are also taxpayers do better if government imposes a tariff than if it imposes an equivalent quota.

______ 17. Regional trading blocs like NAFTA and the EC are permitted by the rules of GATT.

______ 18. The infant industry argument for tariffs is an argument for temporary tariffs.

______ 19. The Trade Agreement Act of 1979 prohibits only predatory dumping.

______ 20. Using tariffs to protect domestic jobs often reduces trade and the gains from trade.

C. *Multiple Choice*

1. The largest trading partner of the United States is
   a. Japan.
   b. Germany.
   c. Canada.
   d. Mexico.
   e. Great Britain.

Consider the following information in answering questions 2 through 7. A worker in the United States can produce either 8 computers or 6 motorcycles in a day; a worker in Japan can produce either 12 computers or 9 motorcycles in a day.

2. If there are 100 million workers in the United States, then the autarkic equilibrium will be
   a. 800 million computers and 600 million motorcycles produced and consumed.
   b. 400 million computers and 300 million motorcycles produced and consumed.
   c. 400 million computers and 600 million motorcycles produced and consumed.
   d. 800 million computers and 300 million motorcycles produced and consumed.
   e. The question cannot be answered without more information.

3. Which of the following is true?
   a. Japan has an absolute advantage in both goods and a comparative advantage in computers.
   b. Japan has an absolute advantage in both goods and a comparative advantage in neither good.
   c. Japan has an absolute advantage in both goods and a comparative advantage in motorcycles.
   d. Japan has an absolute and a comparative advantage in both goods.
   e. The United States has an absolute advantage in computers and a comparative advantage in motorcycles.

4. Which of the following is true?
   a. Japan will specialize in motorcycles because its opportunity cost of producing motorcycles is less than the opportunity cost of producing motorcycles in the United States.
   b. Japan will specialize in computers because its opportunity cost of computers is less than the opportunity cost of computers in the United States.
   c. The opportunity cost of computers is the same in both countries, so there will be no specialization in trade.
   d. Japan will specialize in both computers and motorcycles because the cost of each is less in Japan than in the United States.
   e. none of the above

5. Suppose the conditions change so that a worker in Japan can now produce 15 motorcycles in a day. Under these conditions,
   a. Japan has a comparative advantage in computers.
   b. the opportunity cost of motorcycles in Japan is less than the opportunity cost of motorcycles in the United States.
   c. the United States has a comparative advantage in motorcycles.
   d. the cost of a motorcycle in Japan is 1.25 computers.
   e. a, c, and d

6. Given the change described in question 5,
   a. Japan has an absolute advantage in motorcycles but a comparative advantage in computers.
   b. Japan will export motorcycles and import computers.
   c. Japan will export computers and import motorcycles.
   d. there will be no trade.
   e. The question cannot be answered without more information.

7. Given the information in question 5, suppose the terms of trade are 1 computer in exchange for 0.8 motorcycle. We know that
   a. Japan's consumption possibilities frontier shifts farther out from its production possibilities frontier than does that of the United States.
   b. The United States' consumption possibilities frontier shifts farther out from its production possibilities frontier than does that of Japan.
   c. the consumption possibilities frontiers shift out by the same amount in both countries.
   d. both countries share equally in the gains from trade.
   e. both c and d

8. If all countries had an equal endowment of all resources,
   a. there would be no trade.
   b. trade would arise only from differences in taste or economies of scale.
   c. trade would depend on absolute advantage rather than comparative advantage.
   d. trade flows would be larger than they currently are.
   e. none of the above

9. Moving from autarky to free trade will generate
   a. increases in consumer surplus for consumers of the imported good.
   b. decreases in consumer surplus for consumers of the exported good.
   c. increases in producer surplus for the producers of the exported good.
   d. decreases in producer surplus for the producers of the imported good.
   e. all of the above.

10. If the domestic equilibrium price of wheat in the United States is $4.00 a bushel, then
   a. the United States will export wheat at any world price below $4.00.
   b. the United States will export wheat at any world price above $4.00.
   c. there will be an excess demand for wheat at any world price above $4.00, and this excess demand will be met by imports.
   d. a and c
   e. none of the above. More information is necessary to answer the question.

Exhibit 6

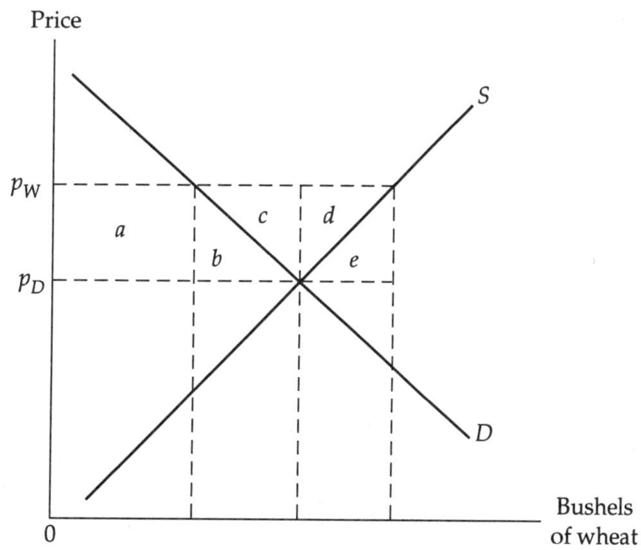

11. The world price for wheat in Exhibit 6 is p_W and the price in the United States is p_D. The loss to domestic consumers if trade occurs in the wheat market is represented by area(s)
   a. *a*.
   b. *a* and *b*.
   c. *b*.
   d. *b* and *c*.
   e. *a*, *b*, and *c*.

12. The gain to domestic producers from trade is represented in Exhibit 6 by area(s)
   a. *c*.
   b. *d*.
   c. *c* and *d*.
   d. *a*, *b*, *c*, and *d*.
   e. *e*.

13. In Exhibit 6, if the United States imposes a tariff equal to $p_W - p_D$,
   a. trade will stop.
   b. domestic producers will be harmed and domestic consumers will benefit.
   c. domestic consumers will be harmed and domestic producers will benefit.
   d. a and b
   e. none of the above. The tariff will have no effect since the United States is exporting wheat.

14. In Exhibit 6, if the trading partner imposed a prohibitive tariff on wheat from the United States,
   a. the gain to U.S. consumers of wheat would be greater than the loss to U.S. producers of wheat.
   b. the gain to U.S. consumers of wheat would be less than the loss to U.S. producers of wheat.
   c. the gain to U.S. consumers of wheat would exactly offset the losses to U.S. producers of wheat.
   d. the gain to U.S. consumers of wheat would exactly offset the loss to U.S. consumers of whatever good had been imported from the trading partner.
   e. The question cannot be answered without more information.

15. The net social loss of a tariff is greater,
   a. the steeper the domestic supply curve.
   b. the flatter the domestic demand curve.
   c. the steeper the domestic demand curve.
   d. the larger the tariff revenue the government receives.
   e. all of the above except c

16. An import quota differs from a tariff in that
   a. a quota does not affect the domestic price of a commodity.
   b. a quota does not harm consumers the way a tariff does.
   c. a quota encourages increased domestic production more than a tariff does.
   d. a tariff generates revenue to the government but a quota does not.
   e. a tariff harms all consumers of the commodity; a quota harms only those who cannot obtain as much of the commodity as they would like.

17. Japanese auto producers would prefer
    a. a tariff on their cars rather than a quota because tariffs tend to be removed before quotas.
    b. a tariff on their cars rather than a quota because tariffs do not cost the exporter as much.
    c. a quota on their cars rather than a tariff because quotas generate extra profits for the exporter.
    d. a quota on their cars rather than a tariff because quotas tend to be reversed faster.
    e. none of the above.

18. Suppose it costs a U.S. steel company $20 a ton to produce steel, it costs a Japanese firm $15 a ton, the domestic price of steel in Japan is $18, and the domestic price in the United States is $22. Japanese firms would be dumping if they charged U.S. firms
    a. any price below $22.
    b. any price below $20.
    c. any price below $18.
    d. any price below $15.
    e. none of the above.

19. Low wages in developing countries indicate that
    a. U.S. workers cannot compete with workers in developing countries.
    b. the United States cannot have a comparative advantage in any product produced by developing countries.
    c. the standard of living of U.S. workers must fall in order for them to compete with workers from developing countries.
    d. all of the above
    e. none of the above

20. One problem with trade restrictions is that
    a. policing and enforcing restrictions is costly.
    b. they do not last long enough to have the beneficial effects they are designed to provide.
    c. they tend to be imposed in inefficient ways, i.e., tariffs tend to be used instead of more efficient quotas.
    d. the national defense argument is not used for some industries vital to the defense of the country.
    e. all of the above

D. *Discussion Questions*

1. What additional information is needed to answer multiple choice question 2?

2. How can two countries both be better off as a result of trade?

3. Suppose that a worker in Brazil can produce 10 units of coffee and 6 units of cloth per day, and a worker in the United States can produce 5 units of coffee and 5 units of cloth. Brazil has 500 workers; the United States has 1,000 workers.
    a. What is the opportunity cost of cloth in Brazil? in the United States?
    b. What is the opportunity cost of coffee in Brazil? in the United States?

c. Which country has a comparative advantage in producing coffee? in producing cloth?
d. Draw production possibilities frontiers for both Brazil and the United States, with cloth on the horizontal axis. What is the slope of Brazil's production possibilities frontier? What is the slope of the production possibilities frontier for the United States?
e. If the United States and Brazil trade, which country will export coffee and which will export cloth? At what rate will trade take place?
f. Show on your graph the gains from trade for both countries for one set of prices that would lead to trade.

4. If the terms of trade in question 3 are 1.01 units of coffee for 1 unit of cloth, which country receives a larger share of the gains from trade? How do you know?

Exhibit 7

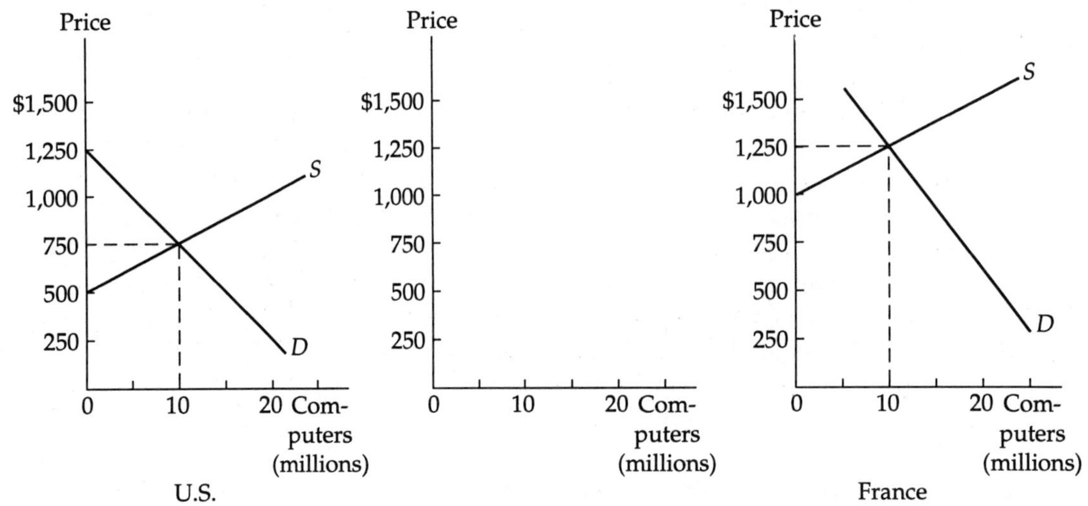

5. Exhibit 7 shows supply curves and demand curves for computers in the United States and France.
   a. Draw the export and import curves for each country on the graph in the center.
   b. At what price will trade occur?
   c. Which country imports computers and which exports computers? What is the volume of trade?
   d. Label the area that represents the net social gain from trade in each country.

6. (Use the information in question 5.) At the world price for computers, U.S. consumers of computers face higher prices and a loss of consumer surplus when compared to autarky. How can we say that the United States is better off as a result of the trade?

7. Why do differences in resource endowments lead to trade?

8. How does an ad valorem tariff differ from a specific tariff?

9. Suppose a $10 shirt is subject to a $1 specific tariff and a $10 blouse is subject to a 10-percent ad valorem tariff. If the prices of both goods double, what happens to the tariff on each good?

10. What is an import tariff? What are the effects of a tariff? Use a graph to illustrate your answers.

11. What is an import quota? What are the effects of an effective quota? Use the same graph you used for question 10 to illustrate your answers to this question.

12. How can tariffs protect U.S. jobs? Do tariffs lead to a net increase in jobs? Explain.

13. Explain why true/false question 17 is false.

14. What are some of the problems associated with trade restrictions?

15. Who are the winners and losers from trade restrictions? Given that trade restrictions impose losses on an economy, why are trade restrictions so common?

III. ANSWERS

A. *Completion*

1. high-technology manufactured goods; agricultural products
2. consumption
3. autarky
4. comparative; absolute
5. terms of trade
6. production; consumption
7. Producer surplus
8. resource endowments
9. economies of scale
10. export line
11. specific
12. import quota
13. most-favored-nation
14. dumping
15. rent seeking

B. *True/False*

1. False. Trade as a percent of GDP is less for the United States than for the western European countries.
2. True
3. False
4. False
5. True
6. True
7. False
8. True
9. False. The country will export goods whose world price exceeds the domestic equilibrium price.
10. False
11. False
12. False
13. False
14. True
15. True
16. True
17. False
18. True
19. False
20. True

C. *Multiple Choice*

1. c
2. e
3. b
4. c
5. b
6. b
7. a
8. b
9. e
10. b
11. b
12. d
13. e
14. b
15. b
16. d
17. c
18. c
19. e
20. a

D. *Discussion Questions*

1. Information concerning the tastes of the citizens is needed in order to determine which part of the production possibilities frontier the autarkic equilibrium will lie on.

2. Two countries can be better off as a result of trade if their opportunity costs of producing the goods being traded differ. Different opportunity costs imply that relative prices in the two countries are different, which means that each country can gain if it produces the good for which its opportunity cost is lowest and buys the other good from the other country.

3. a. 10/6, or $1^2/_3$, units of coffee; 1 unit of coffee
   b. 0. 6 unit of cloth; 1 unit of cloth
   c. Brazil has a comparative advantage in producing coffee and the United States in producing cloth. That is, the opportunity cost of coffee is lower in Brazil than it is in the United States, and the opportunity cost of cloth is lower in the United States than it is in Brazil.
   d. The slope of Brazil's PPF is –10/6 (or $^5/_3$) and the slope of the United States' PPF is –1. (See the exhibit.)

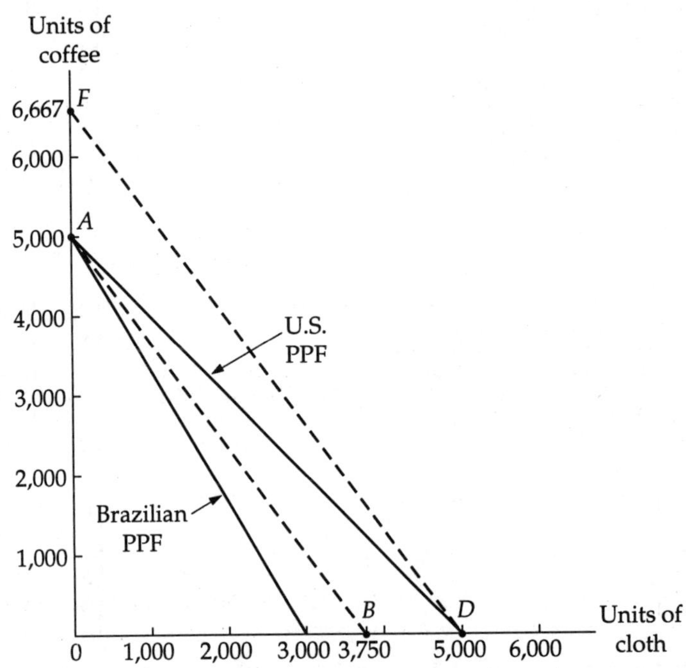

   e. Brazil will export coffee and the United States will export cloth. The rate at which trade will take place lies between 1 and 10/6 units of coffee for 1 unit of cloth.
   f. Refer again to the graph. At a rate of exchange of 4 units of coffee for 3 units of cloth, each country's consumption possibilities frontier is farther from the origin than its PPF. (Brazil's consumption possibilities curve is line *AB* and the United States' is line *DF*, assuming Brazil specializes in the production of coffee and the United States specializes in the production of cloth.)

4. Brazil will receive larger gains from trade. The terms of trade imply a very large shift of Brazil's consumption possibilities frontier, whereas the consumption possibilities frontier for the United States lies very close to its production possibilities frontier.

5. a.

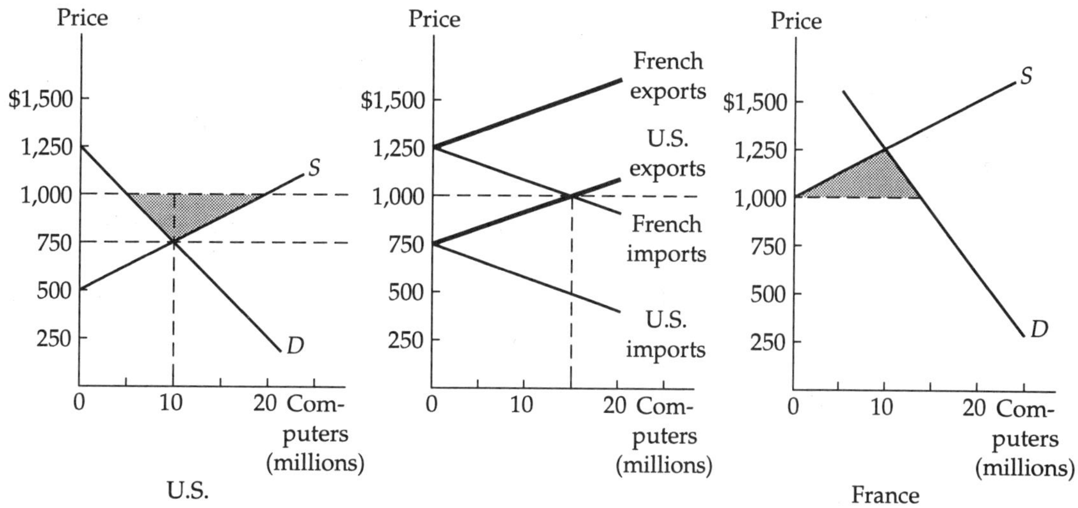

b. $1,000 per unit

c. The United States exports computers and France imports them. The volume of trade is 15 million computers.

d. The areas on the graphs that represent the net social gain from trade are shaded in.

6. The lost consumer surplus is transferred to producers and becomes a part of producer surplus. The United States gains as a whole because producer surplus increases more than consumer surplus falls.

7. Differences in endowments of resources lead to differences in opportunity costs of production, which lead to trade.

8. A specific tariff is an amount per unit of the good; an ad valorem tariff is a percent of the price.

9. At the initial prices, the tariffs are equivalent. If prices double, the ad valorem tariff doubles because it is based on the price of the good. The specific tariff remains $1, so the price of the shirt is now $21, whereas the price of the blouse is $22.

10. A tariff is a tax on imports. A tariff raises the domestic price of an imported good. The graph shows that 245 units of a good are purchased when the world price is p_w; of these, 30 are produced domestically. Hence, imports are 215 units. A tariff of T per unit raises the domestic price to $p_w + T$. At this price, quantity demanded drops to 200 units, domestic producers supply 85 of them, and imports fall to 115 units (200 – 85). Area a represents a transfer of surplus from consumers to producers, areas c plus d represent the revenue raised by the tariff, and areas b and e represent net social losses from the tariff.

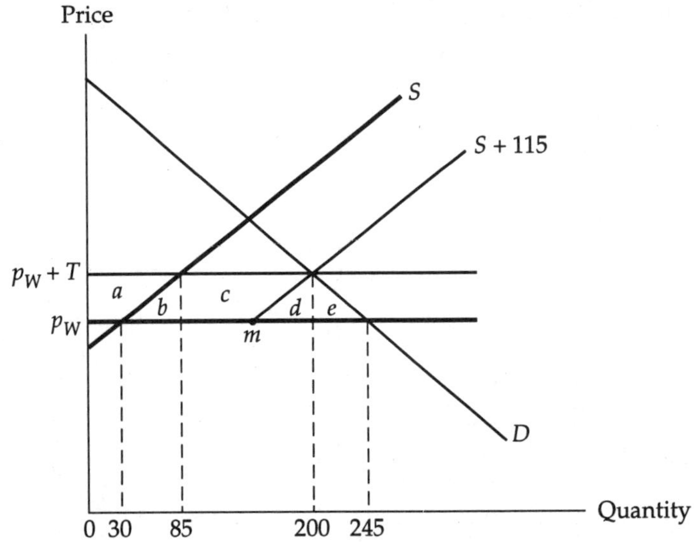

11. An import quota is a limit on the number of units of a good that can enter a country. A quota of 115 units generates the same results as the tariff of T. The relevant supply curve is $S + 115$ (see the graph in answer 10). With a quota, price increases from p_W to $p_W + T$, and imports are at 115 units. The revenue shown by areas c plus d no longer flows to the government but instead is a transfer from consumers to firms that obtain the right to import the good.

12. In the graph in answer 10, the tariff was shown to increase domestic production of the good from 30 to 85 units. This increase in production creates jobs for people in the industry. However, the tariff does not necessarily create a net increase in jobs. If we buy fewer imports we usually sell fewer exports, so some people may lose their jobs in the export industries.

13. Trading blocs violate the GATT provision that requires all members of the GATT agreement to treat all the other members equally with respect to trade. Trade blocs require an exemption from the GATT rules.

14. Protecting one industry often requires protecting other industries. For example, protecting the steel industry raises the price of steel for the auto industry, which may in turn require protection because of its higher costs. Since protection creates higher profits for domestic firms, firms may lobby for protection; the resources expended on lobbying are also lost to the economy. Further, it is often difficult to police and enforce trade restrictions.

15. The winners are the domestic producers of goods that compete with imports (and their employees), who receive higher prices as a result of trade restrictions. With an import quota, those to whom the quota is allocated are also winners. The losers are consumers, domestic producers who use imported intermediate goods, and producers (and their employees) in export industries, especially if other countries respond to tariffs by instituting tariffs of their own. Firms facing stiff competition from trade are obviously harmed a great deal by the competition, so they have a strong incentive to lobby Congress for protection. Consumers are harmed by protection, but no single consumer is harmed enough to make it worth his or her while to lobby against a tariff bill. Hence, Congress is likely to pass a given trade restriction bill.

CHAPTER 19

International Finance

I. INTRODUCTION

Exchange between people in different countries usually requires at least one of the traders to use the currency of the other country. International finance deals with the markets for the currencies of countries and the arrangements involving international payments. This chapter examines the payment mechanism that is currently in use as well as some mechanisms that were used in the past. We will also discuss the balance of payments accounts.

II. OUTLINE

1. Balance of Payments. A *balance of payments* is a summary statement reflecting all economic transactions that occur during a year between residents of one country and residents of all other countries.

   1.1 International Economic Transactions
      a. The *balance of payments* measures the volume of transactions that occur during a particular period of time; it is a flow measure.
      b. Some transactions do not involve payments of money but are still included in the balance of payments.
      c. Balance of payments accounts are maintained according to the principles of double-entry bookkeeping.

   1.2 Merchandise Trade Balance
      a. The *merchandise trade balance* measures the difference in the value of a country's exports of merchandise and its imports of merchandise.
      b. The United States had a merchandise trade deficit throughout the 1980s and early 1990s.
      c. When the economy expands, spending on all goods, including imports, increases.

   1.3 Balance on Goods and Services
      a. *Services* are intangible goods, such as banking, insurance services, and tourism.
      b. The *balance on goods and services* measures the difference in the value of a country's exports of goods and services and its imports of goods and services.

   1.4 Unilateral Transfers
      a. Transfers and gifts to foreigners from domestic residents or from the government are called *unilateral transfers*.
      b. The *balance on current account* equals net unilateral transfers plus exports of goods and services minus imports of goods and services.

1.5 Capital Account

a. The *capital account* records transactions involving the purchase or sale of financial assets.
b. U.S. capital inflows reflect foreign purchases of U.S. assets, and U.S. capital outflows reflect purchases of foreign assets by Americans.
c. The U.S. capital account is in surplus if U.S. residents sell more assets to foreigners than they buy from foreigners.
d. The United States was a net capital exporter in the past but is now a net capital importer.
e. The *official reserve transactions* account shows the net amount of international reserves that must be shifted among central banks to settle international transactions.

1.6 Statistical Discrepancy

a. Some international transactions go unreported, so the total of debits often does not equal the total of credits.
b. The account called the *statistical discrepancy* is used to equalize the total of debits and the total of credits.

1.7 Deficits and Surpluses

a. A deficit in a country's current account means that its foreign exchange earnings from its exports are less than the foreign exchange it needs to pay for its imports plus net unilateral transfers.
b. Any surplus or deficit in the current account must be offset by other changes in the balance of payments account.
c. In 1989, for example, U.S. deficits in the current account and in the official reserve transactions account were offset by surpluses in the capital account and a credit entry in the statistical discrepancy.
d. When all transactions are considered, the balance of payments must balance.

2. Foreign Exchange Rates and Markets

2.1 Foreign Exchange

a. The *exchange rate* is the price of one country's currency in terms of another country's currency.
b. *Foreign exchange* is the currency of another country needed to carry out international transactions.
c. The foreign exchange incorporates all the arrangements used to buy and sell foreign exchange. It is always open since some trading center is always open somewhere in the world.
d. An increase in the number of dollars needed to purchase a unit of currency of another country indicates a depreciation of the dollar, and a decrease in the number of dollars needed indicates an appreciation of the dollar.

2.2 Demand for Foreign Exchange

a. People must have foreign currency to buy goods or services from foreign countries, to purchase foreign assets, and the like.
b. The demand for foreign exchange is related to the demand for foreign goods and services.
c. The demand curve for foreign exchange slopes down, as a decrease in the exchange rate decreases the price of foreign goods for domestic residents, so they increase the quantity of foreign goods demanded.

2.3 Supply of Foreign Exchange
   a. The supply of foreign exchange to the market defined in terms of dollars is generated by the desire of foreign residents to buy dollars.
   b. An increase in the dollar-per-foreign-currency exchange rate makes U.S. products cheaper to foreigners, so the foreigners increase the quantity demanded of U.S. goods and services.
   c. The increased demand for U.S. goods and services usually means an increase in the quantity supplied of foreign exchange, so the supply curve for foreign exchange slopes up.

2.4 Determining the Exchange Rate
   a. The exchange rate is determined at the intersection of the demand curve for foreign exchange and the supply curve for foreign exchange.
   b. In an international monetary system based on flexible exchange rates, the exchange rate will vary with changes in domestic or foreign income levels, expected inflation rates, price levels, interest rates, and consumer preferences.

2.5 Arbitrageurs and Speculators
   a. An *arbitrageur* buys a currency in markets where the price is low and immediately sells it in markets where the price is higher.
   b. Arbitrage assures that any discrepancies between exchange rates across markets will be eliminated quickly.
   c. *Speculators* buy and sell foreign exchange at the current exchange rate in hopes of profiting by buying or selling it at a different exchange rate later.

2.6 Purchasing Power Parity
   a. The *purchasing power parity theory* predicts that under free trade and floating exchange rates, exchange rates between two nations will adjust to reflect differences in the price levels of the two nations.
   b. The purchasing power parity theory is a theory of the long-run relationship between the price level and the exchange rate.

2.7 *CASE STUDY:* The Big Mac Index

2.8 Flexible Exchange Rates
   a. *Flexible*, or *floating*, *exchange rates* adjust to the forces that affect the foreign exchange market.
   b. Wild swings in exchange rates have forced policymakers to consider alternatives.

2.9 Fixed Exchange Rates
   a. *Fixed exchange rates* are rates that are set at some specific level by government.
   b. Government central banks must intervene in foreign exchange markets to maintain the fixed exchange rate.

2.10 Enforcing a Rate Ceiling
   a. Under fixed exchange rates, an increase in demand for foreign goods and services causes an excess demand for foreign exchange.
   b. To keep the exchange rate constant, monetary authorities must sell the foreign currency in the markets at the fixed exchange rate.

2.11 Enforcing a Rate Floor

a. A decrease in demand for foreign exchange causes an excess supply of foreign exchange.

b. Monetary authorities must be willing to buy the excess foreign exchange at the fixed rate of exchange in order to maintain the fixed rate.

c. If the equilibrium exchange rate continually remains above the pegged rate on a long-term basis, the central bank is likely to deplete its reserves of foreign exchange. There are several methods of dealing with this situation.

(1) The central bank can increase the pegged exchange rate—a devaluation of the domestic currency.

(2) The government can restrict imports or capital outflows to directly reduce the demand for foreign exchange.

(3) The government can adopt contractionary fiscal or monetary policies to decrease demand for foreign exchange indirectly.

(4) The central bank can ration the available foreign currency using exchange controls.

2.12 *Case Study:* Mexico's Peso Problems

3. History and Development of the International Monetary System. The gold standard prevailed from 1879 to 1914. The gold standard provided a stable exchange rate but generated inflation or deflation whenever gold production varied substantially.

3.1 The Bretton Woods Agreement

a. The Bretton Woods Agreement established a system of fixed exchange rates that lasted from 1945 to 1971.

b. The U.S. dollar was the key reserve currency, and all other exchange rates were fixed in terms of the dollar.

c. The United States was ready to convert dollars to gold or gold to dollars at a fixed rate.

d. The Bretton Woods Agreement created the International Monetary Fund and the World Bank.

e. The IMF issues Special Drawing Rights (SDR) to function in place of gold in international transfers among central banks.

3.2 Demise of the Bretton Woods System

a. In the late 1960s, the dollar was overvalued, and foreigners were demanding gold from the United States.

b. In 1971, the United States refused to exchange gold for dollars, and the dollar was devalued. The Bretton Woods system ended in 1973 when West Germany stopped defending the dollar.

3.3 The Current System: Managed Float

a. The current system involves floating exchange rates among the world's major currencies but allows substantial intervention by the central banks of many countries.

b. Some countries try to tie their currencies together. Many smaller countries continue to peg their exchange rates.

c. Criticisms of flexible exchange rates:

(1) They are inflationary.

(2) They are often very volatile.

III. DISCUSSION

Balance of Payments

A country's *balance of payments* is a summary statement that reflects all economic transactions between residents of that country and residents of the rest of the world. Balance of payments accounts use double-entry bookkeeping, which means that one side of the ledger reflects assets and the other liabilities. Further, the total of all liabilities must equal the total of all assets. Thus, the balance of payments is always in balance. An outflow of payments is entered as a debit, and an inflow of payments is entered as a credit.

Exhibit 1 provides balance of payments data for the United States for 1994. Total debits equal total credits, so the overall balance is zero. However, the total of debits at any point above the "bottom line" may exceed or be less than the total of credits. That is, it is likely that segments of the balance of payments will be in deficit and other segments in surplus. In 1994, the *merchandise trade balance* was in deficit, but the service account was in surplus. The *balance on goods and services* ran a deficit of

Exhibit 1

U.S. Balance of Payments, 1994
(billions of dollars)

Item	*Debits*	*Credits*	*Balance*
Current Account			
Merchandise exports		502.7	
Merchandise imports	-669.1		
Merchandise trade balance			-166.4
Investment income		134.9	
Investment payments	-109.9		25.0
Travel and transportation services (net)		21.1	
Other services (net)	-1.3		
Balance on goods and services			-121.6
Unilateral transfers	-34.1		
Current account balance			-155.7
Capital Account	-131.0		
Outflows of U.S. capital		275.7	
Inflows of U.S. capital			
Capital account balance			144.7
Official Reserve Transaction Balance		44.2	
Statistical discrepancy	-33.2		
TOTAL	-978.6	978.6	0.0

Source: *Economic Report of the President,* February 1993.

$121.6 billion. The *balance on current account* was also in deficit. Given the nature of double-entry bookkeeping, a deficit in the current account plus a debit entry in the statistical discrepancy implies that private and government capital inflows must exceed private and government capital outflows. In 1994, this was the case because foreign purchases of U.S. assets exceeded U.S. purchases of foreign assets by almost $140 billion.

Foreign Exchange Rates and Markets

Foreign exchange is the currency of another country needed to carry out international transactions. Foreign exchange can be bought in foreign exchange markets. The price is called the *exchange rate* and can be expressed in two ways. First, the exchange rate can be expressed as the domestic currency price for a unit of the foreign currency. Second, the exchange rate can be expressed as the foreign currency price for a unit of the domestic currency. The two exchange rates are reciprocals. That is, if the U.S. dollar price of one French franc is $1.50, then the French franc price of a dollar is 1/1.50, or 0.67 franc.

The foreign exchange market includes the whole world. It consists of a network of telephone and other communication systems that connect large banks in all the major cities. If the exchange rate between the dollar and the franc in Tokyo differs from the exchange rate between the two currencies in New York, then *arbitrageurs* will buy the currency that is relatively cheap in Tokyo and sell it in New York. Because of arbitrage, exchange rates tend to be the same all over the world.

Consider the market for German marks in terms of U.S. dollars. Americans do not desire marks, or other foreign exchange, for the currencies themselves. Instead, they demand foreign exchange because they wish to buy goods or services from foreign countries. Residents of a foreign country want to be paid in their own currency rather than in dollars. Thus, Americans wishing to buy products from Germany must obtain German marks, and Germans who wish to buy U.S. products must obtain dollars. An increase in demand for foreign goods and services causes a greater demand for foreign exchange. The demand curve for foreign exchange slopes down because at lower exchange rates, other things constant, the dollar price of foreign goods and services falls, Americans buy more goods and services from foreigners, and the quantity of foreign exchange demanded rises. When Americans are demanding foreign exchange, they are also supplying dollars to foreign exchange markets. Hence, in general, the supply of foreign exchange is determined by foreigners wishing to buy dollars. The quantity of foreign exchange supplied to foreign exchange markets usually increases as the exchange rate (defined in dollars) increases. The exchange rate is determined by the intersection of the demand curve for foreign exchange and the supply curve of foreign exchange. The curves are drawn holding other things constant, including domestic and foreign income levels, price levels, interest rates, and expected inflation rates.

Exchange rates are flexible when the exchange rate is determined by supply and demand in the marketplace. Exchange rates are fixed when they are set by the government, and central banks intervene in markets to keep rates fixed. Central banks must have a supply of other currencies, especially reserve currencies, to sell in order to keep the exchange rate fixed when the quantity demanded of the foreign currency exceeds the quantity supplied at the fixed rate.

History and Development of the International Monetary System

The international monetary system operated on a *gold standard* from 1879 to 1914. The currencies of all countries were defined in terms of gold, and each country agreed to buy or sell gold at fixed rates.

The gold system meant that exchange rates were fixed, but each country's money supply was determined by the flow of gold between countries. World War I and the Great Depression brought about the end of the gold standard.

After World War II, the international monetary system operated under the Bretton Woods Agreement. The U.S. dollar was defined in terms of gold, and all other currencies were defined in terms of the dollar. The United States agreed to buy or sell gold at the predetermined rate; countries in the rest of the world used dollars as their reserve currency. For example, under the Bretton Woods system, the French central bank could send British pounds to the Bank of England and receive dollars. In the late 1960s, the dollar became overvalued, and many countries were turning dollars in for gold. The United States stopped converting dollars to gold in 1971. The Bretton Woods system collapsed in 1973, and major world economies moved to a managed float system, which allows for occasional central bank intervention to moderate fluctuations in floating exchange rates.

IV. LAGNIAPPE

Exchange Rate Changes and Prices

Suppose the U.S. dollar price of a German mark is 50 cents and that a German car costs 50,000 marks. The dollar price of the car is thus $25,000. Now, if the dollar depreciates against the mark so that the dollar price of a mark is 55 cents, the price of the car rises to $27,500. On the other hand, if the dollar appreciates and the mark moves to 45 cents, the price of the car is $22,500. A 10-percent change in the exchange rate, other things constant, leads to a 10-percent change in the dollar price of German goods. When the price of the mark falls, German goods are cheaper, but when the price of a mark increases, German goods are more expensive.

Question to Think About: What happens to the price of U.S. goods in Germany when the price of a mark rises or falls?

The Gold Standard

The gold standard is appealing to some people because it gives politicians no discretionary authority in determining monetary policy. Advocates of a gold standard argue that the current system tends to be inflationary. For a gold standard to be effective, all major nations must use the system and define their currencies in terms of gold. Suppose the United States defines $1 to be equal to 1/35th of an ounce of gold, and Germany defines the mark as 1/70th of an ounce of gold. Then an ounce of gold costs either $35 or 70 marks, which means that $1 equals 2 marks. If Americans increase their purchases of German goods, dollars go to Germany. The Germans can then turn the dollars in to the Federal Reserve Board in exchange for gold. Since the U.S. money stock is tied to the quantity of gold held by the Fed, the money stock falls. In the long run, the lower money stock implies lower prices. If U.S. prices fall relative to German prices, U.S. products should be relatively more attractive. The gold standard provides an automatic adjustment mechanism.

Question to Think About: If we return to the gold standard, what should the price of gold be in dollars?

V. KEY TERMS

Balance of payments
Merchandise trade balance
Balance on goods and services
Net unilateral transfers
Balance on current account
Capital account
Official reserve transactions account
Statistical discrepancy
Deficit
Surplus
Exchange rate
Foreign exchange
Currency depreciation
Currency appreciation
Arbitrageur
Speculator
Purchasing power parity theory
Flexible exchange rates
Fixed exchange rates
Currency devaluation
Currency revaluation
Gold standard
Bretton Woods Agreement
International Monetary Fund
Special Drawing Rights (SDR)
Managed float system

VI. QUESTIONS

A. *Completion*

1. Because the balance of payments measures the volume of transactions over a particular time period, it measures a __________________.
2. Balance of payments accounts utilize the principles of __________________ bookkeeping.
3. The __________________ trade balance involves trade in tangible products.
4. A trade __________________ exists when the value of merchandise exports exceeds the value of merchandise imports.
5. The demand for imports usually __________________ when the economy is expanding.
6. A gift to a friend abroad is a(n) __________________.
7. A nation has a __________________ when its outflow of payments exceeds its inflow of receipts for transactions in currently produced goods and services plus net unilateral transfers.
8. An initial debit entry in a country's current account will generate some sort of offsetting __________________ entry in the balance of payments.
9. International investments and borrowing are __________________ transfers.
10. The currency of another country needed to carry out international transactions is known as __________________.
11. A currency undergoes __________________ when more units of the currency are needed to buy foreign exchange.

12. Exchange rates are almost always equal at different places around the country because of __________________.

13. __________________ are people who buy and sell foreign exchange in hopes of profiting from fluctuations over time in exchange rates.

14. The International Monetary Fund was created by the __________________.

15. The current international monetary system is known as a __________________.

B. *True/False*

______ 1. In balance of payments terminology, "residents" refers to individuals and families only.

______ 2. To be included in balance of payments accounts, a payment must be made in money.

______ 3. Balance of payments accounting requires that the total of debits equal the total of credits.

______ 4. The trade deficit tends to increase when the economy expands.

______ 5. The merchandise trade balance includes unilateral transfers.

______ 6. The hotel bill of an English tourist in San Francisco is listed as a credit in the U.S. balance of payments and a debit in the United Kingdom's balance of payments.

______ 7. The capital account records transactions involving purchases or sales of assets.

______ 8. A trade deficit indicates that the value of merchandise imports exceeds the value of merchandise exports.

______ 9. The United States is the world's largest debtor nation.

______ 10. The rate of exchange between the U.S. dollar and the German mark can be expressed as either the number of dollars per mark or the number of marks per dollar.

______ 11. The foreign exchange market is located in New York City.

______ 12. Appreciation of the dollar occurs when fewer dollars are needed to buy foreign exchange.

______ 13. Exchange rates tend to change in all markets by the same amount simultaneously.

______ 14. An appreciation of the dollar can cause the quantity demanded of foreign exchange to increase.

______ 15. The supply of foreign exchange in the United States is generated by the desire of foreign residents to buy dollars.

______ 16. An increase in the demand by U.S. residents for foreign exchange leads to a depreciation of the dollar, other things constant.

______ 17. In the long run, economic theory predicts that exchange rates between two national currencies will reflect the price level differences in the two countries.

______ 18. Monetary authorities maintain fixed exchange rates by fixing the supply of money.

______ 19. Under the Bretton Woods Agreement, the U.S. dollar was the key reserve currency in the international monetary system.

______ 20. Central banks do not intervene in foreign exchange markets today.

C. *Multiple Choice*

1. Which of the following represent international economic transactions that must be included in the balance of payments?
   a. A family that recently immigrated sends money to other family members in its home country.
   b. A corporate executive flies to London on a French airline.
   c. The U.S. government gives wheat to India.
   d. all of the above
   e. a and b only.

2. The balance of payments accounts use double-entry bookkeeping, which implies that
   a. a country cannot run a perpetual deficit in its balance of merchandise trade.
   b. balance of payments figures cannot be used to tell anything about the economic strength of a nation.
   c. each account must be in balance every year.
   d. changes in exchange rates cannot affect balance of payments accounts.
   e. the total must always be in balance, but different accounts can be in deficit or surplus.

3. Which of the following transactions would not be included in the merchandise trade balance?
   a. IBM sells $10 million worth of computers to Mexico.
   b. GM buys spark plugs from a Canadian firm.
   c. The CEO of a German firm flies on an American airline to New York.
   d. An American subscribes to the German magazine *Die Zeit*.
   e. All would be included in the merchandise trade balance.

4. Which of the following would generate a credit in the U.S. balance of payments?
   a. An American tourist in London buys a cup of coffee.
   b. A Mexican citizen working in Texas sends money to her family in Mexico.
   c. An American buys a Toyota.
   d. all of the above
   e. none of the above

5. A U.S. capital outflow results when
   a. Americans purchase foreign assets.
   b. Americans sell foreign assets.
   c. Americans sell capital goods to foreigners.
   d. foreigners buy U.S. assets.
   e. none of the above

6. Which of the following is not part of official reserves?
   a. gold
   b. dollars
   c. yen
   d. special drawing rights
   e. none of the above. All are part of official reserves.

7. If the United States is running a current account deficit, it can acquire additional reserves by
   a. Americans' buying foreign bonds.
   b. Americans' buying foreign stocks.
   c. borrowing from foreigners.
   d. all of the above.
   e. a and b only.

8. In the U.S. balance of payments in recent years,
   a. the net outflow of capital has offset the deficit in the current account.
   b. the current account has had a smaller deficit than the capital account.
   c. there is evidence that the United States has been a less attractive place to invest than many other countries.
   d. the net inflow of capital has offset the deficit in the current account.
   e. the net inflow of capital has increased the deficit in the balance of goods and services.

9. In order to reduce foreign claims on U.S. assets, it is necessary to
   a. increase the sale of U.S. assets to foreigners.
   b. increase imports of foreign goods and services.
   c. increase net exports of goods and services.
   d. increase the gold stock held by the Fed.
   e. none of the above

10. If the price of one British pound is $3, the price of one dollar is
    a. 3 pounds.
    b. 2 pounds.
    c. 0.5 pound.
    d. 0.33 pound.
    e. The question cannot be answered without more information.

11. Which of the following might demand foreign exchange?
    a. consumers
    b. investors
    c. speculators
    d. arbitrageurs
    e. all of the above

12. The demand for British pounds would decrease when
    a. the pound depreciated.
    b. the pound appreciated.
    c. the demand for imports increased in Britain.
    d. the foreign demand for British goods decreased.
    e. the supply of pounds increased.

13. The supply of U.S. dollars in the foreign exchange market comes from
    a. foreigners who want gold.
    b. foreigners who want to purchase U.S. goods.
    c. foreigners who want dollars.
    d. Americans who demand foreign exchange.
    e. none of the above.

14. Under flexible exchange rates, an increase in the demand for marks by Americans will
    a. also cause an increase in the supply of dollars.
    b. cause the price of marks to increase.
    c. cause the mark price of the dollar to fall.
    d. cause the mark to appreciate.
    e. all of the above

15. Under fixed exchange rates, an increase in the demand for marks by Americans will
    a. cause the Fed to buy marks.
    b. cause the German central bank to buy marks.
    c. cause the dollar to appreciate.
    d. cause the Fed to buy dollars.
    e. b and d

16. If the price of one pound is $3 in New York and $3.10 in London, arbitrageurs will
    a. buy dollars in New York and sell them in London.
    b. buy pounds in New York and sell them in London.
    c. simultaneously buy pounds in both New York and London.
    d. not do anything, since the difference is only 10 cents.
    e. speculate by buying pounds and holding them.

17. If the German mark and the French franc are in long-run equilibrium at DM = 1 Fr and then French domestic prices increase by 50 percent while German prices remain constant, the new long-run equilibrium exchange rate will be
    a. 1 DM = 1 Fr.
    b. 1 DM = 2 Fr.
    c. 1 DM = 0.5 Fr.
    d. 1 Fr = 0.2 DM.
    e. both b and d.

18. Under a gold standard, a balance of payments deficit in a given country would ultimately lead to
    a. a change in the price of gold in the country.
    b. an inflow of gold.
    c. a fall in the price level in the country.
    d. a deficit in the country's capital account.
    e. none of the above.

19. Special Drawing Rights are a substitute for
    a. gold.
    b. dollars.
    c. pounds.
    d. yen.
    e. long-term bonds.

20. The current international monetary system is characterized by
    a. fixed exchange rates.
    b. freely fluctuating exchange rates.
    c. a gold exchange standard.
    d. both floating and managed exchange rates.
    e. a commodity standard.

D. *Discussion Questions*

1. If merchandise exports equal $50, merchandise imports equal $50, net unilateral transfers equal –$10, and both the capital account and the statistical discrepancy are zero, what is the balance on goods and services?

2. If the balance on goods and services is –$40, net unilateral transfers are –$5, official reserve transactions are zero, and the statistical discrepancy is zero, what is the current account balance and what is the capital account balance?

3. Why can't all the balance of payments accounts be in surplus?

4. Would relatively high interest rates in the United States cause a U.S. capital inflow or a U.S. capital outflow? Why?

5. Suppose the exchange rate between the British pound and the U.S. dollar is $1.64 per pound and the exchange rate between the dollar and the German mark is $0.55.
    a. What would be the dollar price of a German camera that sells for 650 marks?
    b. What would be the price in pounds of a U.S.-made personal computer that sells for $2,200?
    c. What would be the pound price of the German camera?

6. Suppose the exchange rate between the U.S. dollar and the mark is $0.55 in New York and $0.57 in Frankfurt. How would arbitrageurs profit by this difference?

7. What factors determine the demand for marks in foreign exchange markets?

8. What determines the supply of marks in foreign exchange markets?

9. How are exchange rates determined under a flexible exchange rate system?

10. What does the purchasing power parity theory predict about equilibrium exchange rates?

11. Suppose a fixed exchange rate system is in effect, and the exchange rate between the dollar and the mark is $0.55, with a 2-cent margin on either side permitted. What actions will authorities take to maintain the exchange rate if the demand for marks increases? if the demand for dollars increases?

12. Suppose a fixed exchange rate is in effect. What problem is likely to develop if the equilibrium exchange rate continually remains above the pegged rate? How can the government eliminate the disequilibrium at the pegged rate?

13. How did the Bretton Woods system operate? What caused its collapse?

14. The fixed exchange rate system under the Bretton Woods Agreement had an asymmetry that forced deficit countries to respond to a disequilibrium faster than surplus countries. Can you explain why this was so? (Hint: What is used to pay for a deficit?)

15. Explain why the correct answer to multiple choice question 18 is c.

VII. ANSWERS

A. *Completion*

1. flow
2. double-entry
3. merchandise
4. surplus
5. increases
6. unilateral transfer
7. current account deficit
8. credit
9. capital
10. foreign exchange
11. depreciation
12. arbitrage
13. Speculators
14. Bretton Woods Agreement
15. managed float system

B. *True/False*

1. False
2. False
3. True
4. True
5. False. Unilateral transfers are included in the current account.
6. True
7. True
8. True
9. True
10. True
11. False
12. True
13. True
14. True
15. True
16. True
17. True
18. False
19. True
20. False

C. *Multiple Choice*

1.	d	6.	e	11.	e	16.	b
2.	e	7.	c	12.	d	17.	b
3.	c	8.	d	13.	d	18.	c
4.	e	9.	c	14.	e	19.	a
5.	a	10.	d	15.	d	20.	d

D. *Discussion Questions*

1. The merchandise trade balance, the current account, and the capital account are all in balance. Since the net unilateral transfers equal –$10, imports of services must be $10 less than exports of services, so the balance of goods and services has a $10 surplus.

2. The current account balance equals the balance on goods and services plus net unilateral transfers; thus, the current account balance is –$45. The capital account balance must offset the current account balance, so it must equal $45.

3. If all accounts were in surplus, the total would have to be in surplus, too. This cannot happen under a double-entry bookkeeping system.

4. High interest rates in the United States would cause a capital inflow. Foreign investors would seek the high return in the United States and buy U.S. financial instruments. (This assumes the high interest rates are not due to expected higher inflation rates in the United States.)

5. a. 650 marks x $0.55/mark = $357.50
   b. $2,200/1.64 = 1,341.46 pounds
   c. $357.50 x 0.61 pound/dollar = 218.08 pounds

6. An arbitrageur could use $1,000 to buy 1,818.18 marks in New York and then immediately sell the 1,818.18 marks in Frankfurt and receive $1,036.36, making a profit of $36.36 for every $1,000. These actions would help equalize the exchange rates in the two cities.

7. The demand for marks is determined by the foreign demand for German products by producers and consumers (including Americans who travel to Germany), the foreign demand for German assets, cash gifts from foreign residents to German residents, and the like. Demand is also determined by speculators who hope to profit by exchange-rate changes in the future and arbitrageurs who hope to profit from differences in exchange rates across markets.

8. The supply of marks is determined by the demand for foreign exchange, such as dollars, in Germany. That is, it is determined by the German demand for foreign goods and services, foreign assets, and the like.

9. Exchange rates are determined by the interaction of supply and demand for foreign exchange. The demand for foreign exchange depends on the demand for imports and the demand for financial securities denominated in other currencies. The supply of foreign exchange depends on the demand of foreigners for U.S. export goods and services.

10. According to the purchasing power parity theory, as long as trade across borders is unrestricted and exchange rates are allowed to adjust freely, exchange rates between two currencies should adjust in the long run to reflect the price level differences in the two countries. For example, if a given basket of traded commodities costs $1,000 in the United States and 2,000 marks in Germany, the long-run equilibrium exchange rate between the United States and Germany should be $0.50 per mark.

11. An increase in the demand for marks will cause the exchange rate to increase. If the equilibrium rate now exceeds its upper limit of $0.57, the Fed will have to sell marks at the rate of $0.57 to maintain the exchange rate. An increase in the demand for dollars will cause the exchange rate to decrease. If the equilibrium rate falls below its lower limit of $0.53, the German central bank will have to sell dollars at the $0.53 rate to maintain the exchange rate.

12. If the equilibrium exchange rate continually remains above the pegged rate, the central bank is likely to run out of foreign exchange reserves to sell in order to maintain the pegged rate. There are several ways to eliminate the disequilibrium at the pegged rate: (1) the pegged exchange rate can be increased (a devaluation of the domestic currency); (2) the government can impose restrictions on imports or capital outflows in order to reduce demand for foreign exchange directly; or (3) the government can adopt contractionary fiscal or monetary policies in order to reduce domestic income, interest rates, or inflation and indirectly reduce the demand for foreign exchange.

13. The Bretton Woods Agreement established a reserve currency standard by which the U.S. dollar was defined in terms of gold, and all other currencies were defined in terms of the dollar. Exchange rates were fixed, and both gold and dollars served as international reserves. Central banks of other countries could turn in dollars to the United States in exchange for gold. Inflation in the United States in the 1960s induced other countries to try to turn more dollars in for gold. The dollar became overvalued and, as confidence in the dollar fell, so did the exchange rate system.

14. Deficit countries had to meet the deficit with official reserves. Eventually, the reserves would run out. Surplus countries were receiving reserves and could do so forever.

15. The deficit would be financed by gold. The country's money supply is determined by the supply of gold in the country, so an outflow of gold would mean the money supply would decrease, which would cause the price level to fall.

CHAPTER 20

Developing and Transitional Economies

I. INTRODUCTION

This chapter discusses the economic situation of the majority of the world's population. The majority of people are poor and live in less-developed countries. The chapter contrasts the characteristics of developing and developed countries and discusses some causes of the problems of the developing countries. In the last section, the transitions currently going on in countries that used central planning to organize production is discussed. The material in this chapter is more descriptive than analytical.

II. OUTLINE

1. Worlds Apart. *First-world countries* are the advanced capitalist nations. *Second-world countries* are the economically advanced socialist countries. *Third-world countries* are the developing countries of Africa, Asia, and Latin America.

   1.1 Developing Countries
   a. *Developing countries* are those with high rates of illiteracy, unemployment, and population growth, and exports consisting of agricultural products and raw materials.
   b. Developing countries tend to be rural and the people tend to be very poor.

   1.2 Classifications of Economies. Although intercountry comparisons of GDP are tricky, per-capita GDP is the most common criterion for classifying countries.
   a. The World Bank divides countries that report income data into three major groups: low-income economies, middle-income economies, and high-income economies.
   b. Another group of countries does not provide data to the World Bank. Most of these are the socialist countries such as Cuba and North Korea.

   1.3 Health and Nutrition
   a. Life expectancy is lower in developing countries.
   b. Infant mortality rates are much higher in the developing countries than in the developed countries.
   c. People in the poorest countries tend to have insufficient food to maintain good health; they consume half the calories of those in high-income countries.
   d. The population per physician is about twelve times greater in low-income nations than in high-income nations.

   1.4 High Birth Rates
   a. Birth rates are much greater in developing countries than in developed countries.
   b. Aid from developed nations has often come in the form of medical assistance, which has increased life expectancy and added to the growing populations.

   1.5 Women in Developing Countries. Poverty is greater among women than among men.

2. Productivity: Key to Development

2.1 Low Labor Productivity
a. Labor productivity is lower in developing countries because there is less physical and human capital to combine with labor.
b. Capital formation requires saving, but savings tend to be low because people are so poor.

2.2 Technology and Education
a. Education tends to be linked to economic growth.
b. Literacy rates remain low in most developing countries, and only one percent of those aged twenty to twenty-four are enrolled in post-secondary education in low-income countries.

2.3 Inefficient Use of Labor
a. Unemployment, especially in urban areas, tends to be high in developing countries. Underemployment tends to be high in rural areas.
b. Agricultural productivity is low because of the large number of farmers relative to the amount of land farmed and a lack of other inputs such as capital and fertilizer.
c. Low productivity results in low incomes, but low incomes also result in lower productivity.

2.4 Natural Resources. Some developing countries are hampered by a lack of natural resources.

2.5 Financial Institutions. A good financial system is needed as a source of investment funds for development. Banks in many developing countries do not function well as financial intermediaries.

2.6 Capital Infrastructure. Many developing countries have severe deficiencies in their infrastructure of transportation and communication networks.

2.7 Entrepreneurial Ability. A country needs entrepreneurs to bring together the resources and take the risks of starting new enterprises. The colonial system offered local populations little opportunity to develop entrepreneurial skills.

2.8 Government Monopolies. Government monopolies often hinder development.

3. International Trade and Development. Developing countries need to trade with developed countries in order to obtain capital and technology. Developing countries export mainly primary products.

3.1 Import Substitution Versus Export Promotion
a. An *import substitution* policy protects domestic industries by restricting imports.
b. *Export promotion* is a strategy that concentrates on developing export markets.
c. Export promotion has been a more successful strategy than import substitution.

3.2 Migration and the Brain Drain
a. Migration can provide a safety valve on population growth.
b. Often the ones who migrate are the educated and skilled.

3.3 Trade Liberalization and Special Interests
a. Free trade harms some special interests in developing countries.

b. Governments that cater to special interests tend to generate low rates of economic growth.

4. Foreign Aid and Economic Development

4.1 Foreign Aid

a. *Foreign aid* is an international transfer on concessional terms made for the purpose of promoting economic development.

b. Several international agencies exist to provide multilateral assistance to developing countries.

4.2 Does Foreign Aid Promote Economic Development?

a. It is unclear whether foreign aid supplements or substitutes for domestic saving.

b. A donor's motives may often be geopolitical or commercial rather than humanitarian.

4.3 *Case Study:* Privatizing Foreign Aid

5. Transitional Economies

5.1 Types of Economic Systems

a. Economic systems can be classified based on the ownership of resources, the way resources are allocated and the incentive structure.

b. In capitalist systems, resources are owned by individuals and allocated through markets

c. In socialist economies, resources (except labor) are owned by the state.

5.2 Enterprises and Soft Budget Constraints

a. Enterprises that earned a "profit" had the profit taken by the state; those that experienced losses received a subsidy to cover the loss.

b. Shortages in many products developed because the planning system was often inefficient.

5.3 *Case Study:* Ownership and Resources Use

5.4 Markets and Institutions

a. Institutions are the incentives and constraints that structure political, economic, and social interaction.

b. A reliable system of property rights and enforceable contracts are necessary for creating incentives that support a healthy market economy.

5.5 Institutions and Economic Development

a. Political decisions can change the formal rules of society, but the informal constraints are more difficult to change.

b. Centrally planned economies often experience widespread corruption.

c. The exchange relation is impersonal in market economies but more personal in centrally planned economies.

5.6 The "Big Bang" Versus Gradualism

a. Some economists advocate a gradual approach to the transformation to a market economy.

b. A "big bang" approach depends on a very short transition.

c. China is experimenting with gradualism in transforming parts of its economy.

5.7 Privatization

a. *Privatization* is the turning of public enterprises into private enterprises.

b. Privatization requires the development of modern accounting and other information systems.

III. DISCUSSION

Worlds Apart

Standards of living vary widely across countries. The industrialized nations that are characterized as market economies are called First World nations. The Second World is made up of economically advanced socialist countries, although many countries in eastern Europe are being converted to market economies. Third World countries are the remaining nations, which tend to be less-developed or developing countries. The World Bank divides countries into three major groups that range from low-income developing countries to the industrial market economies.

The text discusses several societal characteristics that reflect differences in development among countries. These include health and nutrition, birth rates, and the role of women. The distribution of income is shown to be more skewed in most developing countries than in the developed economies.

Productivity: Key to Development

One reason that standards of living tend to be low in developing countries is that labor productivity tends to be low as a result of the lack of physical and human capital for labor to work with. Developing countries are also characterized by low levels of education, poor use of labor, a lack of well-developed financial markets and infrastructure, low savings rates, and other obstacles to development. Make sure you are familiar with the factors that contribute to the level of productivity in developing countries.

International Trade and Development

Developing countries need to trade with developed countries in order to acquire capital goods and technology. Developing countries trade mainly primary products. Prices of primary products tend to fluctuate, and developing countries have a hard time generating foreign exchange to buy capital goods. Special interests in developing counties are often able to get protection from foreign competition; this makes the country worse off as a whole.

Foreign Aid and Economic Development

Developing countries often must rely on foreign capital to finance the investment needed to encourage economic growth. Several international agencies and institutions exist to provide the capital. The World Bank provides loans to support activities that are viewed as prerequisites for development. Some countries do not qualify for loans from the World Bank because they are perceived as poor credit risks. The International Development Association was formed to provide financing for poor credit risks. The International Finance Corporation makes loans directly to private enterprises in developing nations instead of to governments. It is unclear whether foreign aid fosters development. A stable political climate with well-defined property rights and a good system of education appear to be the important prerequisites for development.

Transitional Economies

Capitalism refers to the private ownership of all resources, *socialism* to the state ownership of all resources except labor, and *communism* to state ownership of all resources. The former Soviet Union and other countries that were referred to as "communist" were actually socialist.

All societies must find ways to coordinate the economic activities of their members. Under capitalism, coordination is achieved by individuals' responding to market forces and trying to maximize utility or profits. Under planned socialism, coordination is achieved by bureaucratic control. Central planners determine what is to be produced, and other planners determine how it is to be produced. To some extent, the distribution of the output is determined by individual choice.

Enterprises had soft budget constraints. An enterprise that generated a residual ("profit") found that the central government took it. Enterprises that generated losses received subsidies. Under such a system, plant managers had little incentive to be efficient.

Societies develop institutions that support their political and economic arrangements. A market economy requires property rights, contract law, and other institutions that are often taken for granted in capitalist countries. Political decisions can introduce some of these formal institutions, but many informal constraints still exist that may be incompatible with a market economy. No unified and generally accepted theory of the formation of institutions has been developed, so it is difficult for anyone to advise the Russian government with confidence. Some advocate a rapid transition to a market economy; others argue for a policy of gradualism.

IV. LAGNIAPPE

The Economics of Being Poor

Theodore W. Schultz, in his Nobel lecture, discussed the general results of research on economic development he and others conducted over the course of forty years. He concluded that the poor are just as concerned about improving their position as other people are, but that wealthier people have a difficult time understanding the choices the poor make. Schultz argues that economists have made two errors in their approach to the problems of economic development. The first error is to assume that standard economic analysis does not apply to poor countries. The second error, Schultz argues, is that economists tend to neglect economic history. Since all developed nations were developing nations at one time, an understanding of the way developed nations actually developed can help our understanding of the problems faced by developing nations today.

Schultz also argued that land is often overrated and the quality of human beings is underrated in assessing the prospects of poor nations. Japan has poor land and yet is highly developed, whereas India has good land and is poor. Schultz pointed out that labor productivity can increase when the population becomes healthier and better educated. Further, he argued that the policies of many developing nations encourage industrialization, which encourages migration to urban areas and neglects the agricultural sector. The result is reduced agricultural production, which makes it more difficult to feed the population.

He urged an approach that does not distort the incentives that farmers have to grow more food. (See Theodore W. Schultz, "The Economics of Being Poor," *Journal of Political Economy* 88, August 1979: 639–651.)

Question to Think About: What effect would longer life expectancies have on decisions concerning the number of years spent in obtaining an education?

What Is the Optimal Speed of Adjustment?

There is a great deal of uncertainty about the optimal speed of adjustment to a market economy. Alfred Kahn was head of the U.S. Civil Aeronautics Board when the government deregulated the airlines. Initially, Kahn favored a policy of gradualism, but later he changed his views and advocated a very short transition. The main reason for his change in views was that the long transition created some perverse incentives that made the adjustment more difficult. Does this imply that Russia and other formerly socialist countries should aim for a rapid transition? Not necessarily. There are many important differences between deregulating one industry and deregulating an entire economy. One important difference is that the institutions associated with capitalism were in place in the United States, and the deregulation only involved one segment of the economy. Just because a rapid transition involving one industry in the United States is optimal does not imply that a rapid transition to a market economy is optimal for an entire economy.

Question to Think About: Would a gradual transition to a market economy likely create perverse incentives that would make the transition more difficult?

V. KEY TERMS

Developing countries
Industrial market countries
Import substitution
Export promotion
Foreign aid
Soft budget constraint
Privatization

VI. QUESTIONS

A. Completion

1. France is an example of a __________________ nation, and Peru is an example of a __________________ nation.

2. __________________ are countries with high rates of illiteracy, rapid population growth, and primarily agricultural production.

3. The __________________ is an economic development institution affiliated with the United Nations.

4. Countries with low life expectancies usually also have high __________________ rates.

5. __________________ is a primary or contributing factor in the majority of deaths among children under the age of five in low-income countries.

6. The number of __________________ in a country is used as a measure of the availability of health care.

7. __________________ are lower when women have better employment opportunities.

8. Poor nutrition may generate low labor __________________, resulting in low income.

9. Other resources may be used inefficiently if __________________ is insufficient.

10. Constraints that structure economic interactions such as property rights are __________________.

11. The imposition of tariffs to insulate domestic industries is part of a policy of __________________.

12. An international transfer made on concessional terms to promote economic development is called __________________.

13. Under market coordination, transactions occur because each party expects to benefit, so exchange is __________________.

14. In centrally planned economies, the exchange relation is usually __________________.

15. The process of turning public enterprises into private enterprises is called ______________.

B. *True/False*

______ 1. Differences in the level of economic development are greater among developing countries than among developed industrial countries.

______ 2. The gross domestic product of the United States is greater than the combined gross domestic products of all developing countries.

______ 3. Per-capita GDP figures for developing countries tend to overstate the quantity of goods and services consumed by citizens in the country.

______ 4. More than half the population of most developing countries is employed in agriculture.

______ 5. Countries with high life expectancy rates tend to have low infant mortality rates.

______ 6. Developing countries have significantly higher birth rates than developed countries.

______ 7. Poverty is greater among men than women in most developing countries.

______ 8. In developing countries, income is low, so saving tends to be low and thus investment is low.

______ 9. Low income and low productivity reinforce each other.

______ 10. Some development economists believe that the single most important ingredient in economic development is the political organization of a country and the administrative competence of its government.

______ 11. A country's institutions can be an obstacle to development.

______ 12. Primary products make up the bulk of developing countries' imports.

______ 13. Import substitution helps a country by capitalizing on comparative advantage.

______ 14. An export promotion strategy forces firms in developing countries to be more efficient because they are in competition with firms in other countries.

______ 15. Many developing countries have a shortage of entrepreneurs.

______ 16. The prices of the primary goods produced by developing nations tend to fluctuate more than the prices of the manufactured goods produced by the industrialized nations.

______ 17. The law of demand does not apply in a centrally planned economy.

______ 18. The soft budget constraint faced by enterprises permitted directors to be inefficient, since a state subsidy would always be available to bail them out of trouble.

______ 19. People in the Soviet Union tended to treat public property with more care than Americans do.

______ 20. The accounting systems of socialist firms are valueless in a market economy.

C. *Multiple Choice*

1. Which of these developed countries were developing countries at one time?
   a. Japan
   b. Germany
   c. United States
   d. Canada
   e. all of the above

2. Developing countries tend to be characterized by all of the following except
   a. low unemployment.
   b. high rates of illiteracy.
   c. rapid population growth.
   d. exports consisting mainly of agricultural and primary products.
   e. low farm productivity.

3. Which of the following is a new industrialized country?
   a. Canada
   b. France
   c. South Korea
   d. India
   e. All of the above

4. Infant mortality rates are
   a. slightly higher in the less-developed countries than in the industrial countries.
   b. significantly higher in the developing countries than in the industrial countries.
   c. higher in the industrial countries than in the developing countries, because of pollution.
   d. lower in countries with lower life expectancies.
   e. none of the above.

5. Families tend to be larger in developing countries because
   a. government policies are designed to encourage high birth rates.
   b. international aid has made medical care a low priority.
   c. infant mortality rates are low.
   d. children are a source of labor on farms.
   e. a and b

6. Fertility rates decline when
   a. infant mortality rates increase.
   b. health care availability increases.
   c. employment opportunities for women get better.
   d. income falls.
   e. none of the above

7. Which of the following is a true statement about developing countries?
   a. Poverty is greater among women even though women are better educated.
   b. Women have fewer opportunities for employment than men in rural areas but not in urban areas.
   c. Poverty is greater among women, and women have fewer educational opportunities.
   d. Women are not covered by minimum wage laws whereas men are.
   e. b, c, and d only

8. Women in developing countries tend to
   a. work more outside of the home than women in developed countries.
   b. be better educated relative to men than women in developed countries.
   c. head up fewer households than women in developed countries.
   d. have more employment opportunities than men.
   e. none of the above

9. Labor productivity tends to be lower in developing countries because
   a. there is less capital for labor to work with than in industrial nations.
   b. technological breakthroughs tend to occur in developed nations.
   c. education levels are lower than in developed countries.
   d. all of the above
   e. a and c

10. More educational achievement benefits developing countries by
    a. increasing the productivity of labor.
    b. increasing the productivity of other resources.
    c. making people more receptive to new ideas and technology.
    d. increasing productivity of farmers in the economy.
    e. all of the above.

11. Poverty can result in
    a. less saving.
    b. less capital formation.
    c. malnutrition.
    d. low productivity.
    e. all of the above.

12. To have a sound market economy, a country needs
    a. a reliable system of property rights.
    b. a highly educated labor force.
    c. extensive government involvement in the economy.
    d. protection from foreign competition.
    e. all of the above.

13. Developing countries need foreign exchange to import capital and technology, and the foreign exchange is obtained by
    a. producing exports.
    b. receiving foreign aid.
    c. soliciting private investment from abroad.
    d. all of the above.
    e. a and b only.

14. One advantage to a developing country of an import substitution policy is that
    a. it reduces competition faced by domestic firms.
    b. it requires less bureaucratic intrusion.
    c. demand already exists for the products protected by the tariffs.
    d. all of the above.
    e. a and b only

15. Which of the following countries has relied primarily on an export promotion strategy?
    a. Argentina
    b. Peru
    c. India
    d. Hong Kong
    e. Somalia

16. The governments of developing countries often hinder development by
    a. failing to obtain foreign aid.
    b. creating state enterprises and granting them monopoly status.
    c. relying too much on private entrepreneurs to develop new industry.
    d. keeping taxes too low.
    e. all of the above.

17. Which of the following is an example of foreign aid?
    a. a grant that never has to be repaid
    b. a loan at market interest rates
    c. a shipment of wheat
    d. concessional loans
    e. all of the above except b

18. A problem with foreign aid is that
    a. it comes from international agencies rather than the United States.
    b. loans are not made to countries that are credit risks.
    c. it focuses too much on education and agriculture and not enough on manufacturing.
    d. there is no attempt to promote self-sufficiency.
    e. it sometimes distorts domestic prices and discourages domestic agriculture.

19. Under planned socialism, the three economic questions are answered by
    a. bureaucratic coordination.
    b. economic incentives and the profit motive.
    c. making choices that lead to an equal distribution of income.
    d. referring to the dictum, "from each according to his ability, to each according to his need."
    e. none of the above.

20. State ownership of property tends to
    a. promote greater cooperation among people.
    b. promote greater concern for the upkeep and care of the property.
    c. promote waste and inefficient use of the property.
    d. decrease the use of black markets and illegal markets.
    e. a and b

21. One problem facing Russia in its attempt at privatization is that
    a. people prefer enterprises that are publicly owned.
    b. many of the enterprises have been so inefficient no one wants to buy them.
    c. falling prices make investing in the firms unattractive.
    d. the government is unwilling to sell the most important enterprises.
    e. all of the above

22. Russia's move to a market economy has been hampered by
    a. the lack of some institutions needed in a capitalist economy.
    b. a constitution that prevents privatization in key industries.
    c. a refusal by Russian leaders to follow well-known paths of institutional development.
    d. all of the above.
    e. a and c only.

D. *Discussion Questions*

1. What are some characteristics of developing countries?

2. What problems arise when trying to compare per-capita GDP figures across countries?

3. The text describes several characteristics of developing countries. Discuss how these characteristics are interrelated.

4. What factors can reduce fertility rates?

5. The text says that improved health does little to avert poverty. Why not?

6. What factors contribute to low labor productivity in the developing countries?

7. How are education and development related?

8. How are institutions and development related?

9. How can international trade help a developing country?

10. What obstacles may prevent international trade from being a source of economic growth?

11. Why do economists tend to favor export promotion policies rather than import substitution policies?

12. The text cited a number of factors that contribute to the productivity and growth of a developing country. Which of these factors can be enhanced by foreign aid? What are some of the reasons that foreign aid might not foster development?

13. How are resources allocated under planned socialism? How does this differ from the way resources are allocated under capitalism?

14. Why might you expect market coordination to be more efficient than bureaucratic coordination?

15. Why might the Soviet people take better care of their personal property than people in capitalist countries?

16. What is privatization? How effective has privatization been in Russia?

17. Discuss the role of institutions in a market system. Should Russia pursue a fast transition or should it pursue gradualism?

VII. ANSWERS

A. *Completion*

1. First World (or industrial market); Third World (or developing)
2. Developing countries
3. World Bank
4. infant mortality (birth rates is also an answer here)
5. Malnutrition
6. physicians
7. Fertility (or birth) rates
8. productivity
9. knowledge
10. institutions
11. import substitution
12. foreign aid
13. voluntary
14. personal
15. privatization

B. *True/False*

1. True
2. True
3. False. Per-capita GDP figures tend to understate consumption.
4. True
5. True
6. True
7. False
8. True
9. True
10. True
11. True
12. False
13. False
14. True
15. True
16. True
17. False
18. True
19. False
20. True

C. *Multiple Choice*

1. e
2. a
3. c
4. b
5. d
6. c
7. c
8. e
9. d
10. e
11. e
12. a
13. d
14. c
15. d
16. b
17. e
18. e
19. a
20. c
21. b
22. a

D. *Discussion Questions*

1. Developing countries are characterized by high illiteracy rates, high unemployment, high infant mortality rates, poor nutrition, short life expectancy, few physicians per capita, high birth rates, and a heavy reliance on agriculture.

2. Countries use different national income accounting procedures, exchange rates are often inappropriate, and the proportion of output sold on markets varies across countries.

3. Several of the characteristics of developing countries are interrelated. The high infant mortality rates and the short life expectancy rates are obviously related. Malnutrition is related to both, since it makes people more susceptible to disease. All of these also lower the productivity of labor in a country, which contributes to low income and thus to low savings and investment.

4. Fertility rates tend to fall as incomes rise, as education levels of women increase, and as employment opportunities for women increase.

5. Better health generates longer life spans, which increase the size of the population and the stress on resources. There is usually a lag before it also reduces fertility rates.

6. Productivity is low because labor does not have much capital to work with and the quality of the existing capital is poor. Education levels tend to be low, which makes it difficult for industry to take advantage of technological change. The labor force tends to be underutilized, which also reduces productivity.

7. Increased education levels in a country improve the efficiency with which all resources, including labor, are used. Education also makes people more receptive to new ideas and technology, which helps stimulate economic growth.

8. Institutions affect the incentives people have to invest and to produce. A reliable system of property rights can aid development. Some institutions may hinder development. For example, restrictions on the activities women can participate in may reduce output.

9. Trade can help a country develop by providing foreign exchange to purchase capital, a market for products produced by the country, an opportunity for technology transfer that will increase labor productivity, and competition to force greater efficiencies in the economy.

10. It is possible that international trade will not be a source of economic growth. First, developing countries tend to export primary products, whose prices fluctuate more widely than the prices of manufactured goods. Therefore, exports may not provide a stable source of foreign exchange. Second, many industrial countries impose trade restrictions that hinder trade in primary products. Finally, government policies within the developing countries themselves sometimes obstruct exports.

11. Import substitution policies tend to reduce welfare, retard efficiency, and prevent gains from trade. Export promotion policies do not close markets to trade and rely on the discipline of markets to encourage firms to be efficient. Firms are more likely to adopt new technology when they face competition from other firms. Finally, the evidence suggests that export promotion has been more effective in encouraging development than has import substitution.

12. Foreign aid can help a developing country develop its natural resources. It also can help provide technological know-how and the capital necessary to build the infrastructure that will contribute to growth. Foreign aid will not foster development if it simply substitutes for domestic saving, thus increasing consumption rather than investment. Further, much foreign aid is motivated by geopolitical and commercial concerns or is ill-conceived, so it leads to a misallocation of the country's resources. Finally, development aid often insulates the country's leaders from the consequences of the country's problems, thus reducing incentives to implement appropriate government policies.

13. Resources are directed by central planning under planned socialism. Bureaucrats set up plans and direct those lower in the hierarchy in implementing those plans. Capitalism relies on market forces to allocate resources; individual consumer responses to changes in prices create incentives to make profits.

14. Market coordination relies on voluntary exchange, in which all participants are seeking their own best deal. Consequently, they have the incentive to produce efficiently. Under bureaucratic control, the people making the decisions often do not have all the information they need and also lack the incentive to act in an efficient way.

15. Since durable goods were hard to obtain and expensive, and since repair parts were also hard to obtain, the Soviet people had incentives to take very good care of the durable goods they did buy.

16. Privatization is the transfer of enterprises owned by the government to private owners. So far, the efforts at privatization in Russia have met with limited success. Many of the formerly publicly owned plants had been very inefficient, which did not make them desirable purchases by private citizens. The overall state of the economy has also hampered the transition to a privately owned system.

17. A market economy requires certain institutions to be able to function. For example, a legal system that recognizes and enforces contracts and a system of private property rights are usually associated with market economies. The planned socialism that existed for decades in the Soviet Union did not rely on these institutions, so they did not exist when the government changed and the policies changed. The transition has been a difficult one. Whether you believe the transition should be rapid or not is up to you, but you should be able to support your point of view by reference to the issues raised in the latter portions of the chapter.